Close Encounters: Sea- and Riverborne Trade, Ports and Hinterlands, Ship Construction and Navigation in Antiquity, the Middle Ages and in Modern Time

Edited by

Marinella Pasquinucci
Timm Weski

BAR International Series 1283
2004

Published in 2016 by
BAR Publishing, Oxford

BAR International Series 1283

Close Encounters: Sea- and Riverborne Trade, Ports and Hinterlands, Ship Construction and Navigation in Antiquity, the Middle Ages and in Modern Time

ISBN 978 1 84171 636 7

BAR Publishing is the trading name of British Archaeological Reports (Oxford) Ltd. British Archaeological Reports was first incorporated in 1974 to publish the BAR Series, International and British. In 1992 Hadrian Books Ltd became part of the BAR group. This volume was originally published by Archaeopress in conjunction with British Archaeological Reports (Oxford) Ltd / Hadrian Books Ltd, the Series principal publisher, in 2004. This present volume is published by BAR Publishing, 2016.

Printed in England

BAR
PUBLISHING

BAR titles are available from:

BAR Publishing
122 Banbury Rd, Oxford, OX2 7BP, UK
EMAIL info@barpublishing.com
PHONE +44 (0)1865 310431
FAX +44 (0)1865 316916
www.barpublishing.com

Contents

List of Contributors

D. E. Atkinson. University of St. Andrews, School of History, Fife KY16 9AL. Scotland United Kingdom.

Sergio Bargagliotti. Via Bonamici 42, 57125 Livorno. Italy. Email: sergio.bargagliotti@tin.it

Rodolfo Bargnesi. Dipartimento di Scienze dell'Antichità, Università di Pavia, Strada Nuova 65, 27100 Pavia. Italy. Email: rodolfobargnesi@hotmail.com

Mike Beach. University of St. Andrews, School of History, Fife KY16 9AL. Scotland
United Kingdom.

Ronald Bockius. Museum für Antike Schiffart, Neutorstrasse 2b, D-55116 Mainz. Email: rzentral@mainz-online.de

Josep Burriel Alberich. SIAM, Ajuntament de Valencia, 46018 Valencia. Spain.

Giulio Ciampoltrini. Soprintendenza per i Beni Archeologici della Toscana, via della Pergola 65, 50121 Firenze. Italy. Email: giuliociampoltrini@libero.it

Franca Cibecchini. Dipartimento di Scienze Storiche del Mondo Antico, University of Pisa, via Galvani 1, 56126 Pisa. Italy. Email: f.cibecchini@tin.it

Antonella Del Rio. Dipartimento di Scienze Storiche del Mondo Antico, University of Pisa, via Galvani 1, 56126 Pisa. Italy. Email: antdelr@libero.it

Luisa Ferrer Dias. Av. João XXI, 11-2° Dt°, 1000-298 Lisboa. Portugal.

Pamela Gambogi. Soprintendenza per i Beni Archeologici della Toscana, via della Pergola 65, 50121 Firenze. Italy. Email: pamelagambogi@katamail.com

Ana Catarina Garcia. Centro Nacional de Arqueologia Nàutica e Subaquàtica, Department of the Azores.

Alexis Gorgues. Casa de Velasquez, Ciudad Universitaria, c/ Pal Guinard, 3 E 28040 Madrid (Spain)

Brad Loewen. Département d'anthropologie, Université de Montréal, C.P. 6128, Succursale Centre-Ville, Montréal. Québec. Email: Brad.Loewen@UMontreal.ca.

Luc Long. DRASSM, Fort Saint-Jean, 13235 Marseille, Cedex 02. Email: luc.long@culture.fr

Piera Melli. Soprintendenza per i Beni Archeologici della Liguria, via Balbi 10, 16126 Genova. Italy. Email: piera.melli@tin.it

Simonetta Menchelli. Dipartimento di Scienze Storiche del Mondo Antico, University of Pisa, via Galvani 1, 56126 Pisa. Italy. Email: s.menchelli@sta.unipi.it

John Naylor. Dept. of Archaeology, South Road, Durham, DHI 326, UK.
Email: J.D.Naylor@durham.ac.uk

Guillermo Pascual Berlanga. Departament de Prehistoria i Arqueologia, Facultat de Geografia i Historia, B. Ibanez 28, 46010 Valencia. España.

Marinella Pasquinucci. Dipartimento di Scienze Storiche del Mondo Antico, University of Pisa, via Galvani 1, 56126 Pisa. Italy.
Email: pasquinucci@sta.unipi.it

José Pérez Ballester. Departament de Prehistoria i Arqueologia, Facultat de Geografia i Historia, B. Ibanez 28, 46010 Valencia. España.
Email: Jose.Perez-Ballester@uv.es

Peter E. Pope. University of Newfoundland, Archaeology Unit, St. John's, NF, Canada A1C 5S7. Email: ppope@mun.ca.

Maria Cecilia Profumo. Soprintendenza per i Beni Archeologici delle Marche, via Birarelli 18, 60121 Ancona. Italy. Email: mcpancona@katamail.com

Paola Rendini. Soprintendenza per i Beni Archeologici della Toscana, via della Pergola 65, 50121 Firenze. Italy. Email: giuliociampoltrini@libero.it

Albert Ribera i Lacomba. SIAM, Ajuntament de Valencia, 46018 Valencia. Spain.
Email: aribera@digitel.es.

Christian Rico. Unité Toulousaine d'Archéologie et d'Histoire, UMR 5 608, Maison de la Recherche, Université Toulouse le Mirail, 5, Allées Machado, Toulouse, Cedex. Email: chrico@club-internet.fr.

Marisa Serrano Marco. SIAM, Ajuntament de Valencia, 46018 Valencia. Spain.

Carlo Tronchetti. Soprintendenza per i Beni Archeologici della Sardegna, Piazza Indipendenza 7, 09100 Cagliari. Email: ctronchetti@hotmail.com

Inês Vaz Pinto. Departamento de História, Universidade Lusiada, Rua da Junqueira 188-198, 1349-001 Lisboa. Portugal. Email: invpinto@mail.telepac.pt

Catarina Viegas. Faculdade de Letras, Universidade de Lisboa, UNIARCH, Alameda da Universidade, 1600-124 Lisboa. Portugal. Email: c.viegas@mail.doc.fl.ul.pt

Close Encounters:
Sea- and Riverborne Trade, Ports and Hinterlands, Ship Construction and Navigation in Antiquity, Middle Ages and Modern Time

Since the origins of navigation, harbours and calls are encounter areas between sea- and/ or river routes and hinterlands peopled by settlements of various typology and characterised by agricultural, pastoral ,woodland and manufacturing activities.

The aim of this volume is to study the links between trade and local production and between sea routes, shipbuilding and navigation techniques in a diachronic perspective from Antiquity to the Middle Ages and Modern times, in areas of the Ancient and of the New World, through historical sources including urban and settlement archaeology, landscape and underwater archaeology.

The European expansion overseas led to a great change in the maritime world which concerned vessel size, navigation methods, sails, charted coasts, etc. There were not only exchange of goods and people with the new colonies, but also new peculiar economic activities . All this had influence on the European homelands.

Topics of specific interest are the mechanisms and organization of trade (local and medium or long-distance exchange) including means of transport, relations between state and free market, links between productive areas and commercial flows, the peculiar role of single areas, harbours, sites etc.

Core of the volume are several papers presented in 2000 in Lisbon at the 6th Annual Meeting of the European Association of Archaeology.

Marinella Pasquinucci, Timm Weski

The role of Genoa in the Mediterranean trade in Antiquity

Piera Melli

Abstract
This paper is focussed on Genoa (Italy), its hinterland and trades from the end of the 6th century BC up to the 7th century AD.

Since 1950, urban archaeology investigations have been carried out in Genoa, especially during the last fifteen years (Melli 1996b). This fact makes it possible to record the city's urban and cultural evolution, although with many gaps, showing the range of Genoa's Mediterranean links up to 7th century AD and, later, the rise and development of the medieval town, its economy and its extraordinary harbour growth.

One of the prime reasons for siting Genoa in the centre of the homonymous gulf was to take advantage of one of the most favourable landing places in the Ligurian sea, at a crucial junction of the route network reaching the Po valley and the Tyrrhenian trade route to the coast of Southern Gaul. Genoa had a partially sandy coastline where it was easy to beach the boats and to draw fresh-water.

Even under Augustus, the Ligurian coastline was described as "not only exposed to the wind but also harbourless, except for shallow mooring-places and anchorages" (Strabo 4. 6.2). The route from *Genua* through the Polcevera valley is the most direct for reaching the Padane plain (Pasquinucci 1998), explaining why links with the Trans-Apennine lands seem to have always been maintained.

From the pre-Roman settlement to the modern town, the long-term survival of the location is one of organic development renewed over time, every step in its progress being strictly connected with harbour activity. As for antiquity, Genoa seems to have played an important role over three main periods (the second Iron Age, the late Republic, and late antiquity).

Other contributory factors, including wise alliances, allowed the city to profit from its strategic location: in several periods of its history the town was chosen as a naval and military base (Mennella 1996, 29-30), while steadily increasing its trading activities.

Recent works have focussed attention on the nature and extent of trade activity in Genoa, notwithstanding the restricted number of fully published contexts.

Analyses of the distribution of various artefacts, mainly storage containers, have indicated the trend in imports, although, at present, full quantitative comparative analyses of stratified assemblages, and sufficient calculations of relative percentages of each class per set period are unavailable.

Human presence in Genoa dates back to the Bronze Age, with meaningful but scarce evidence from the first Iron Age, suggesting some dispersed settlements along the bay. The fortified *oppidum* was founded at the end of 6th century BC on the Castle mount facing the bay (Milanese 1987; Melli 1999).

Recent excavations in the area of the Medieval Port, particularly in Portofranco, have provided evidence of the deep, undisturbed wet stratigraphy from the sea bottom. On preliminary analysis (Melli-Manganelli 1996), the deposit was referred to as a landing and discharge place, frequented since the archaic era, for its closeness first to the pre-Roman settlement and, in the Roman era, to the Forum.

Finds in the earlier layers of imported pottery, preliminarily dated to the first half of the 6th century BC, including Corinthian, Ionian cups, Etruscan amphorae, and coarse ware allow us to push back the site's origin. We suppose the coastal centre, about fifty years before the foundation of the *oppidum*, played a role for Etruscan penetration into south Piedmont, perhaps initially only as a halting place. The appearance of such rare items in the river markets lying along the Ticino waterway (Gambari and Colonna 1986; Gambari 1989; Gambari 1993,129; Gambari 1995, 44, fig.16), and in the Golasecca territories (De Marinis 1998, 63), shows that such vases must have arrived via *Genua*, which had meanwhile probably flanked, and later replaced, older markets such as Chiavari and Rapallo (Melli 1996d), which ceased to exist in the beginning of 6th century.

We cannot deal extensively with this subject hear, but it is important to note that the early stages may be related with the foundation of Marseilles, around 600 BC. The friendly relations between the Phocaean colony and Rome allowed a period of peaceful Tyrrhenian trade, which also benefited the Etruscans (Zevi 2000).

Domestic ware of the first phase of the settlement, within the first half of the 5th century BC, consists of imported goods (over 70% of the total), mainly amphorae and coarse ware from south and north Etruria, but also Attic fine pottery and a lesser quantity of wine amphorae from Corinth, eastern Greece and Marseilles (Milanese 1987; Melli 1999).

Throughout the 5th century BC, Genoa became a cosmopolitan commercial centre, strongly influenced by Etruscan culture and technology. The Etruscans brought iron metallurgy, and many finds of slags in the *oppidum* indicate smelting, even if we do not have adequate insight into the scale of production and its organization.

The wide range of goods displayed in the 5th and 4th centuries shows that the market was engaged in an exchange network which involved the mineral district in Etruria, where Populonia maintained a pre-eminent role: Colonna (1981, 115) followed by De Marinis (1998,70), conjectured that *Genua* was a colony of Populonia.

Grave goods included valuable imports, such as Attic and Faliscan red figured vases, Etruscan banqueting bronze vessels, alabaster unguentaria, and other luxury items and weapons of different production, all reflecting the high standards of living reached there.

The close similarity of grave goods assemblages suggests connections with the Etruscan centres in the Po river plane, and relationships between Genoa and the contemporary settlements linked in the so-called "port circuit" (Martelli 1985): Populonia, Aleria and Pisa, Marseilles and its contacts.

For most of these rich goods, Genoa appears to be a consumer rather than a conduit for trade north of the Apennine.

Although the regional area is very imperfectly known for the middle and late Iron Ages, it seems that at first the town wasn't strictly connected with the immediately surrounding territory, which does not show the same cultural and economic growth (De Marinis 1998, 69). Attic figured pottery is, for instance, absent in Liguria except in Sestri Ponente (Mannoni 1970-71, 15), near Genoa, along the way north.

It was suggested that a part of these goods reached, *via* Genoa, the so-called Inner Liguria - located in south Piedmont below the Po - and the mercantile settlements of the Golasecca culture, mainly Milan and Como, which served as an intermediary with the transalpine territories. Close similarities between some imports found in Genoa and the Trans-Apennine territories, as, for example, Etruscan bronze "*Schnabelkannen*" (Bouloumie 1973; Frey 1987, fig.191), might prove this. Such exotic goods could have been distributed as gifts, but were probably associated with the wine trade.

Even if a regularised, long distance trade and market exchange is still difficult to suppose, the appearance of

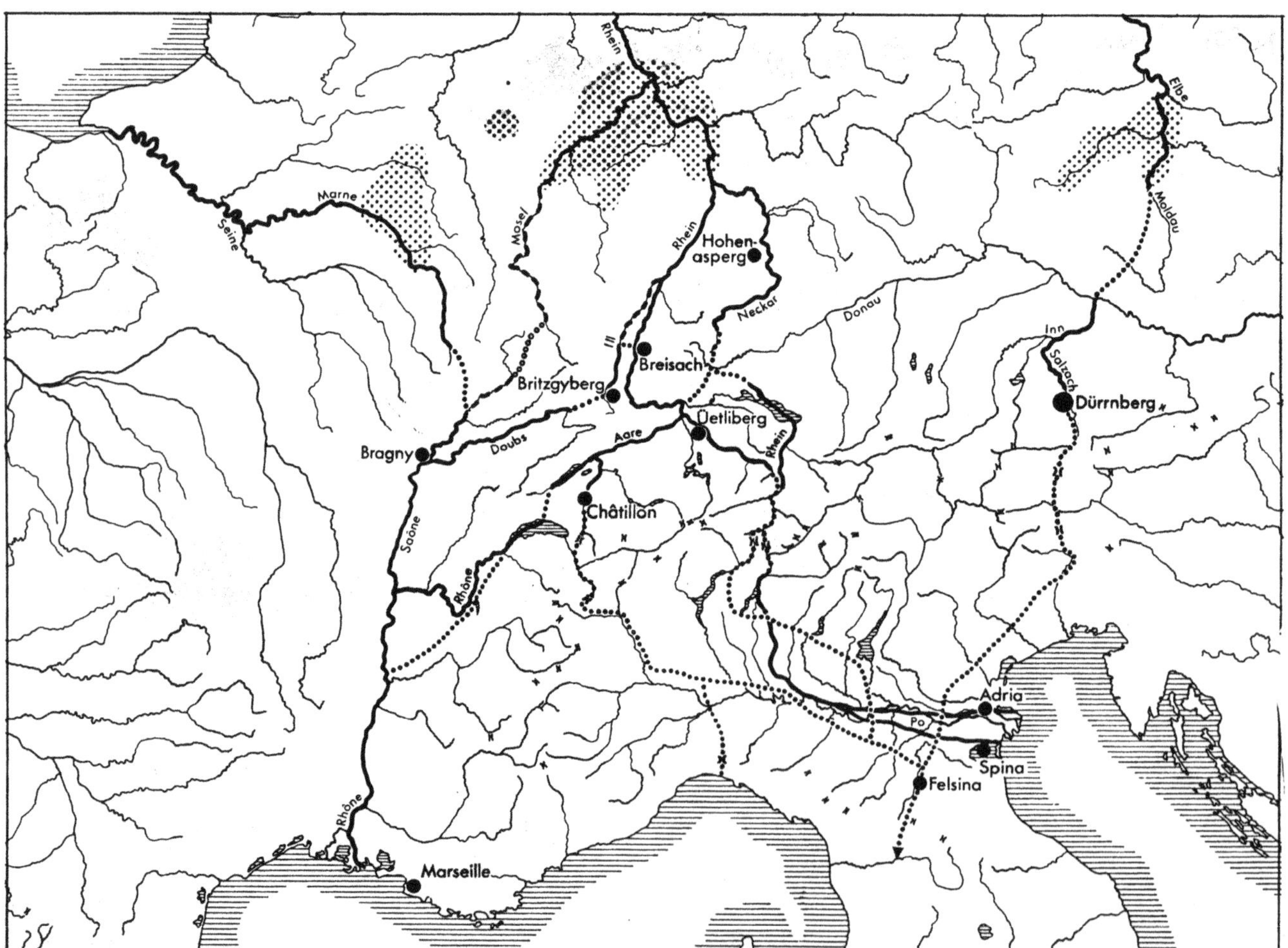

FIGURE 1. PRINCIPAL COMMERCIAL ROUTES LINKING NORTHERN ITALY WITH CENTRAL EUROPE IN LA TÈNE A (450-400 BC) (PAULI 1991, FIG.8)

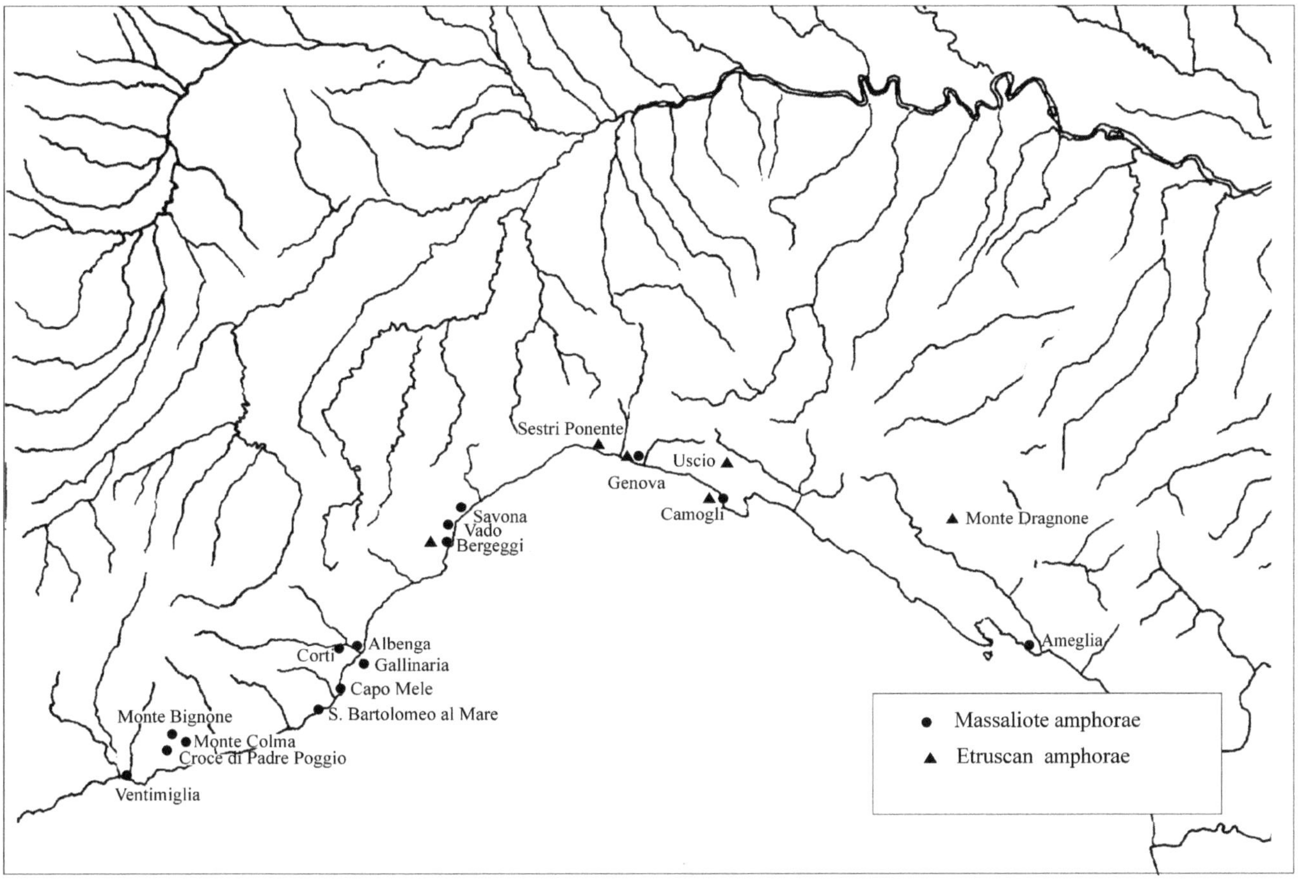

FIGURE 2. DISTRIBUTION OF ETRUSCAN AND MASSALIOTE AMPHORAE IN LIGURIA (APPENDIX 1)

rare classes of artefacts might bear witness to alliance-making activities, reinforced by the presentation of gifts and marriage alliances.

The site map of Certosa fibulae (De Marinis 1998, 68) shows clearly the route connecting Genoa with Golasecca territories through the Scrivia valley.

As agricultural resources were very limited, Genoa's prosperity is explained by its role as a market, involving both the redistribution and exchange of local products for imported goods, perhaps a toll system, as proved by historical sources for other contexts (Ampolo 1994). The Greek historian Strabo, who lived under Augustus and Tiberius, but using older sources too, refers (IV. 6.2) to timber of good quality "with trees so large that the diameter was found sometimes to be eight feet…suitable for ship-building", as in Pisa (V 2.5). Gras (1997, 165-66) has noted the great importance attached in antiquity, and especially in the archaic period, to timber supply for shipbuilding.

Trade in salt, slaves, and mercenary soldiers may also be argued. Ligurian mercenary soldiers, as referred to in the written sources, were appreciated, since the beginning of 5th century BC (Himera battle, 480 BC: Herodotus VII, 165), both by the Carthaginians and the Etruscans (Colonna 1988, 554; 1998, 265).

In the 4th century, the Celtic invasion of the Padane plain weakened, but did not interrupt, the trade contacts with the Po Valley settlements (Venturino Gambari, Traversone and Cattaneo Cassano 1996, 51-53); the grave goods bear witness (Melli in press c) that Genoa was still linked with the amber route (fig.1).

Owing to the international political events of the 4th century, and the consequent resetting of the trade balance in the Tyrrhenian, Etruscan imports to Genoa declined in favour of goods from Marseilles. From around 350 BC, wine from Marseilles almost completely replaced Etruscan wine, reaching with a widespread distribution many sites in Liguria. An exhaustive inventory of Massaliote amphorae found along the Ligurian coast was presented ten years ago by M. Milanese (1990) and not many finds have been added to his list. The distribution of amphorae from Marseilles (fig.2), from about 450 BC onwards, remains bordered on the coastal area or to the immediately adjacent hinterland. Except for Genoa, the finds have always been limited to single examples or very small quantities; Genoa is the most intensively excavated site, where amphorae are associated with Phocaean grey ware, "*céramiques à pâte claire*", and Massaliote black glaze pottery.

We may argue for an active role by Genoa in the political alliance and economy of the Phocaean Greek colony; the contemporary appearance in the Cisalpine region of coins imitating Massaliote *drachmas* may record such activity (Bats 1992, 273,275).

It was suggested (Piana Agostinetti 1995, 203-207) that a mint operated in Genoa, producing Ligurian "oboli", mostly distributed in Liguria, but no evidence of coin making has been found.

Until the middle of the 4th century BC, Genoa still received Attic red figured vases distributed along a western Tyrrhenian route, touching France and Spain (Rouillard 1992; Melli 1999, 180).

From the second half of the century, sea imports were made up of Etruscan, Roman and Campanian fabrics: black glazed pottery belonging to the so called "*Atelier des petites estampilles*", which is considered to have been produced in Rome and/or its vicinity, found in large quantities in central Italy and diffused extensively all over the western Mediterranean, the south of France and Spain; Caeretan "Genucilia plates", which may also have been manufactured in Rome; skyphoi of the "southern T.585 Ferrara" group; and vessels of Volterra and other north Etruscan products.

Long-established and active commercial relations with Marseilles and Rome explain subsequent events, when Genoa, according to historical sources, had a great strategic importance as a naval and military base, chiefly during the Roman war against Ligures and the second Punic War (218- 202 BC). Genoa's port was at Rome's disposal already by the year 218 BC, when P. Scipio landed there *en route* to the plains around Piacenza and Cremona.

It may be inferred that Rome had secured Genoa's friendship, and had perhaps even established a beachhead of its own there, when it began its first attempt to invade the Padane plain (Fraccaro 1956-7, 123; Toynbee 1965, II, 263).

According to Livy (XXVIII, 46), the town remained the only Roman ally between the other Ligurian tribes, and even if destroyed by the Carthaginians in 205 BC, it was soon rebuilt with Roman aid in 203 BC (Livy XXX, 1). The archaeological evidence does not confirm the date but shows that part of the *oppidum* was already destroyed from the first half of the 3rd century (Milanese 1987, 13-17; Milanese 1996).

Possibly from 200 BC the town was connected with Rome and the centres on the northern Tyrrhenian seaboard by a coastal continuation of the *Aurelia* road (Coarelli 1988, 23); by this time it appears to have been included in the Roman Commonwealth. In 148 BC the opening of the *Postumia* road, coast-to-coast from Genoa to Aquileia on the Adriatic side, crossing the Po Valley, had been originally intended for military purpose in order to conquer Cisalpina: it promoted, however, the renewal of trans-Apennine traffic (Gambari and Venturino Gambari 1988) and the circulation of ideas, habits, and Roman culture.

There is a lack of documentation between the end of the 3rd and the first half of 2nd century BC, whereas we have more information on the late-Republican period.

Although no contemporary harbour installations have been found, analysis of the ceramic material in Genoa shows a remarkable development (from the second half of the 2nd century BC) of the commercial activity of the port and its contacts with wider areas in the western Mediterranean basin. This confirms the records of Strabo (IV 6,1;6,2;V 1,3), cited above, who defines the town as "*emporion liguon*", where Ligurian products (timber, flocks, hides, and honey) were bartered with olive oil and Latin wine. Among the resources carried to Genoa, the author also mentions pack animals, horses or mules, called "*ginni*", and coarse wool (V 1,12) used to produce tunics and cloaks ("*sagi*").

Evidence for this phase comes principally from urban deposits (Melli ed 1996a, *passim*), some layers in the cited stratified sequence at Portofranco, and a store-house destroyed by fire on the Castle mound slope (Gambaro 1999, 149-158).

The pottery and other assemblages are dominated by Tyrrhenian fabrics, with a dramatic variety of black glaze pottery forms (Gambaro 1998; Melli-Gambaro 2000); they come from coastal sites and shipwrecks, and include Iberian vases that were part of homeward cargoes, widely diffused in many sites from France to Campania (Bruni and Conde 1991; Bruni 1992).

Also of interest is the appearance of some specimens of fine pottery from Asia Minor, such as Megarian bowls and Hellenistic lamps.

Among the coins belonging to this period should be noted a rare coin with Punic lettering from Cadiz, coined between 100 and 23 BC (Milanese 1993, 244, fig. 116,5), and confirming contacts with Spain, and a bronze *emicalco* from Marseilles dated to the 1st century BC (Milanese 1986, 15-18).

The large quantity of recovered Tyrrhenian amphorae and black glaze ware raises the hypothesis (Bruno 1998b; Melli 1998b) that these goods were not only intended for internal demand, but that a trade alliance was in force, at least between the port of Genoa and the centres lying along the first leg of the *via Postumia*, and some other minor sites on the coast, reached by coasting vessels. This assumption implies a degree of organisation and regularisation not perhaps fully justified by the evidence.

The impressive expansion in Italian wine exports to

southern France has been amply discussed (Tchernia 1986); map fig.3 shows the distribution of finds of Tyrrhenian amphora wrecks (Parker 1992, fig.8) and isolated items along the Ligurian coast.

Map of Tyrrhenian amphorae exports in Liguria (fig.4) records a distribution pattern in many coastal sites and along the major roads towards the interior. Comparison with Panella (1981, tav. XII), shows that the number of sites has reached a high figure.

The fact that the finds of amphorae decrease in number progressively towards the interior, notwithstanding the presence of sizable quantities of imported Tyrrhenian black glaze pottery, leads to a hypothesis for the redistribution of wine in skins, or barrels, after transhipment in the ports. Concerning river transports in the Padane plain, Strabo (V 1, 8) mentions “wooden jars”, containers well distributed in Gaul, and used in inner Liguria as proved by Piedmont stone reliefs, however their significant use is not certain before the 2nd century (Tchernia 1986, 285-292).

Dressel 1 amphorae, black glaze pottery, and other items of Tyrrhenian origin were found in the rural settlements and in the towns lying along the roads in the Polcevera and Scrivia valleys and Piedmont, for instance at “Costa Bottuin” (Davite et al 1992a), Costa Bastia (Davite et al 1992b), Campora (D’Ambrosio 1985b), San Cipriano (D’Ambrosio 1985a), *Libarna* (Bruno 1998, 334), Borghetto Borbera, close to *Libarna* (Gambaro 1998, 442); Villa del Foro (Facchini 1995) *Dertona* (Zanda and Vecchi 1994) and also Ivrea (Brecciaroli Taborelli 1987, 111-112, 113-121; Bruno 1998a, 333-334); Brecciaroli Taborelli 1988, 27-35) and Milan (Frontini 1991; Bruno 1998a, fig.1). Finds in Asti (Zanda 1986, pl.23, 9.1; Bruno 1998a, 333) and Alba (Bruno 1997, 517; 527-28) might be better explained as imports from other ports on the western Riviera, such as Vado.

Finds of Iberian pottery occur at Libarna and Casalcermelli (Bruni 1992), and late Punic amphorae are recorded (Bruno 1998a, 334) in several settlements in the western Padane plain.

It is interesting to note that - although different distribution mechanisms were in force - the limited importation of Tyrrhenian goods is recorded in the first phases of some important commercial sites connected by the *Postumia* road - Piacenza (Galli 1996, 70-71), Cremona (Galli 1996; Volontè 1998) and Calvatone-*Bedriacum* (Sena Chiesa 1998, spec. 351). Until now it has been suggested that vessels found in the Padane plain must have arrived from Adriatic ports, especially Adria, but the increasing number of finds call for a fresh discussion of the matter (Bruno 1998a; Gambaro 1998, 442; Morel 1998). It seems that different distribution methods were active, including transhipment in Ligurian ports.

Finds of clay fabrics from the immediate hinterland show contacts with minor neighbouring workshops: bricks, coarse ware and loom weights from the Polcevera valley (Milanese 1993,175), and *dolia* in gabbro clay from the Tigullio area.

The new prosperity reached by the upper and middle Genoese classes may also be witnessed by the improvement of domestic architecture: painted plaster walls and tessellated floors, and masonry buildings appear here as in other Italic sites. A great variety of building typologies, techniques, arts and crafts - of Roman origin - is well supported, at the same time as municipal growth, showing a good level of welfare and cultural development for the dominant classes.

Among the materials distributed *via* Genoa in the 1st century AD, it is possible that there were precious coloured marbles from Greece, Asia minor and Africa, as witnessed in the mosaics in Genoa (Melli in press b), and employed in large quantities in the floors of private houses and in the public monuments in Libarna (Finocchi 1996,113; 214); there may well also have been marble from the Luna quarries, as found in many Piedmont centres (Finocchi 1989, n.108).

Marble traffic along the Ligurian coast is proved by the discovery - in the harbour of Saint Tropez (Parker 1993, 376) - of gigantic architectural pieces of Luna marble, intended, as is suggested, for the rebuilding of the Capitolium of Narbonne. The stone is also found in other contexts, suggesting a minor trade in pre-cut pieces, ready to use and easy to transport.

In the 2nd and 3rd centuries, the *Aemilia Scauri* road, improved under Augustus and connecting Derthona to the *Vada Sabatia*, divided Genoa from the main traffic routes. The city seems to have suffered a period of inactivity, at the same time as other ports (such as Vado) were growing, but imports by sea never stopped. The material found came from a wide range of sources, including fine pottery and glasses from Po Valley workshops, table and coarse ware from Tyrrhenian, North African, and areas of southern Gaul, local or regional coarse ware, and amphorae (Bruno and Lavazza 1996; Storti 1996; Melli (ed) 1996, *passim*).

The third period of development for Genoa’s harbour was linked again to the evolution of the settlements in the Po Valley, mainly Milan - chief town and later imperial capital (AD 292-404) - with the reorganization under the Tetrarchy. A reference to the port, among a restricted number, occurs in *Edictum de pretiis* (35, 73.77 Giacchero), promulgated by Diocletian AD 301, as a major call along the routes from Sicily and Sardinia.

Since the late 3rd century, the archaeological evidence and historical sources indicate the restoration of the *Postumia* road as a thoroughfare north of the Apennine (Pasquinucci 1998; Melli 1998a; Cera 2000; Melli 2001).

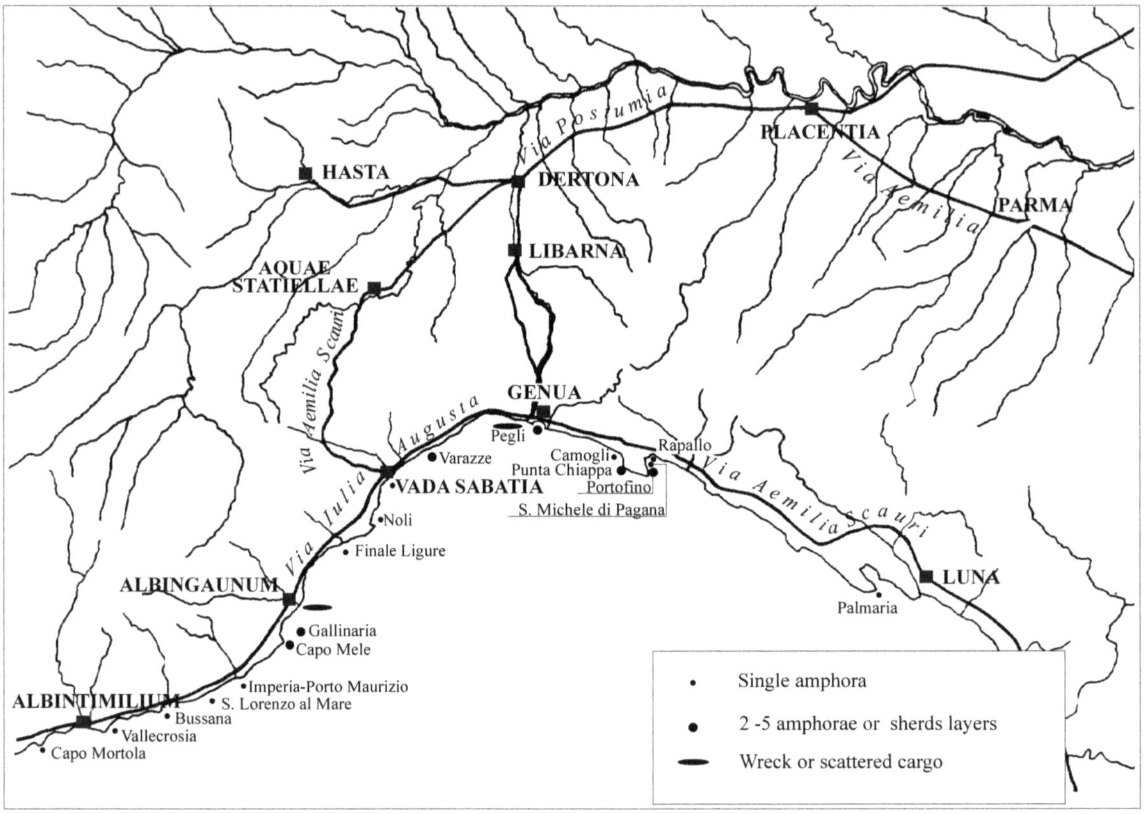

FIGURE 3. DISTRIBUTION OF TYRRHENIAN AMPHORAE WRECKS AND ISOLATED UNDERWATER EXAMPLES IN LIGURIA (APPENDIX 2)

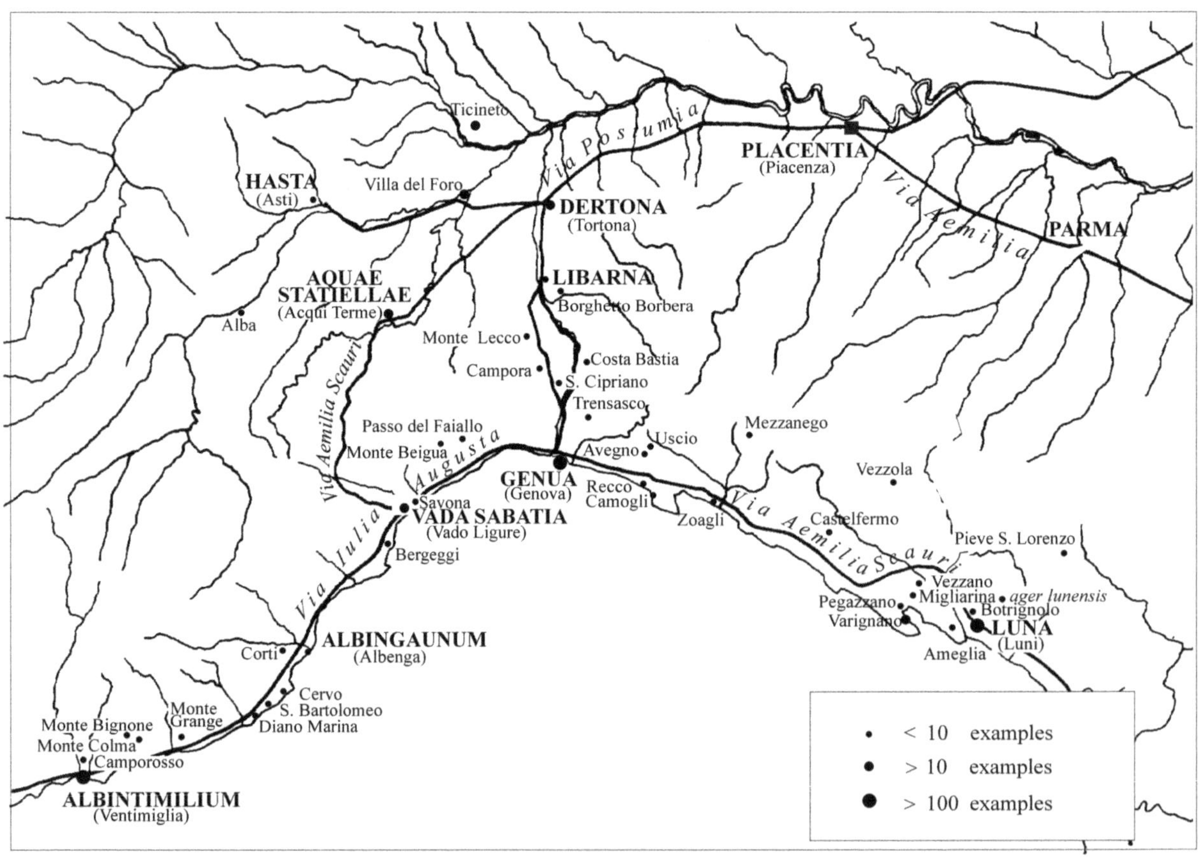

FIGURE 4. DISTRIBUTION OF TYRRHENIAN AMPHORAE IN LIGURIA AND SOUTH PIEDMONT (APPENDIX 3)

REPUBLICAN AFRICAN AMPHORAE

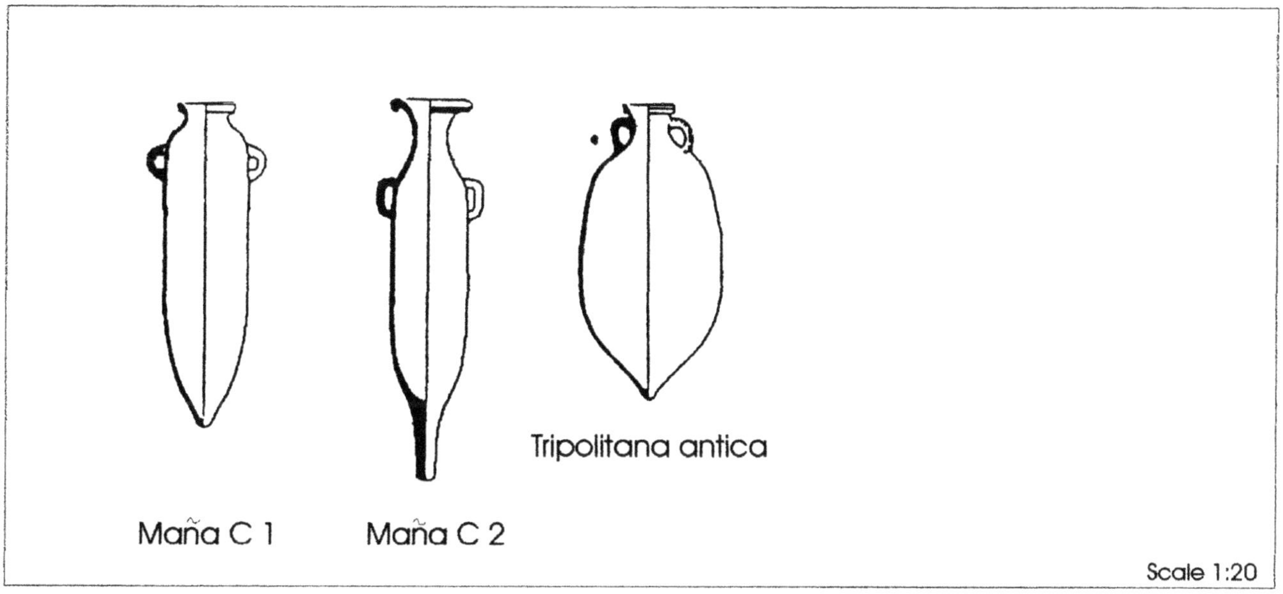

GRAECO - ITALIC

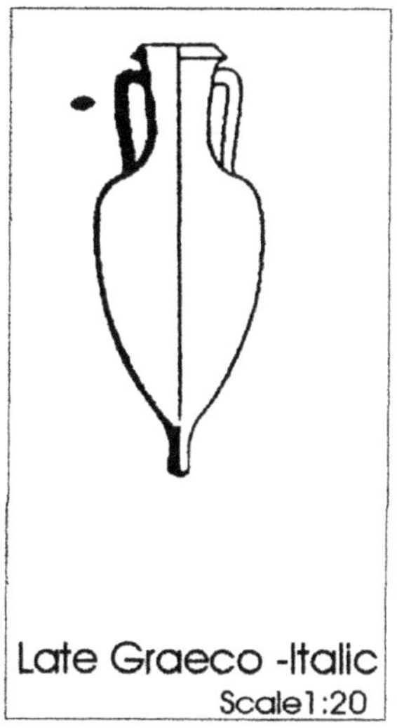

LATE REPUBLICAN ITALIAN AMPHORAE

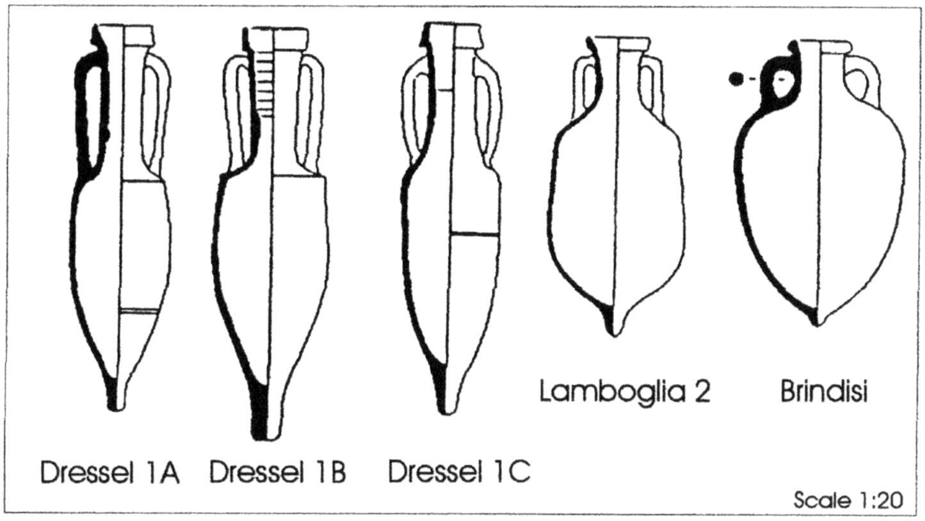

IMPERIAL ITALIAN AMPHORAE

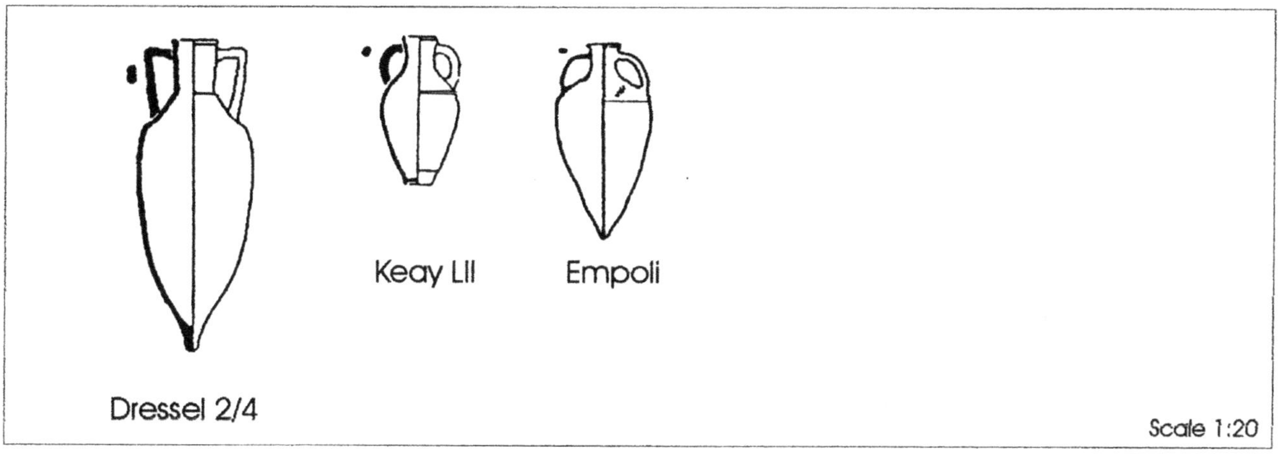

NORTH AFRICAN AMPHORAE

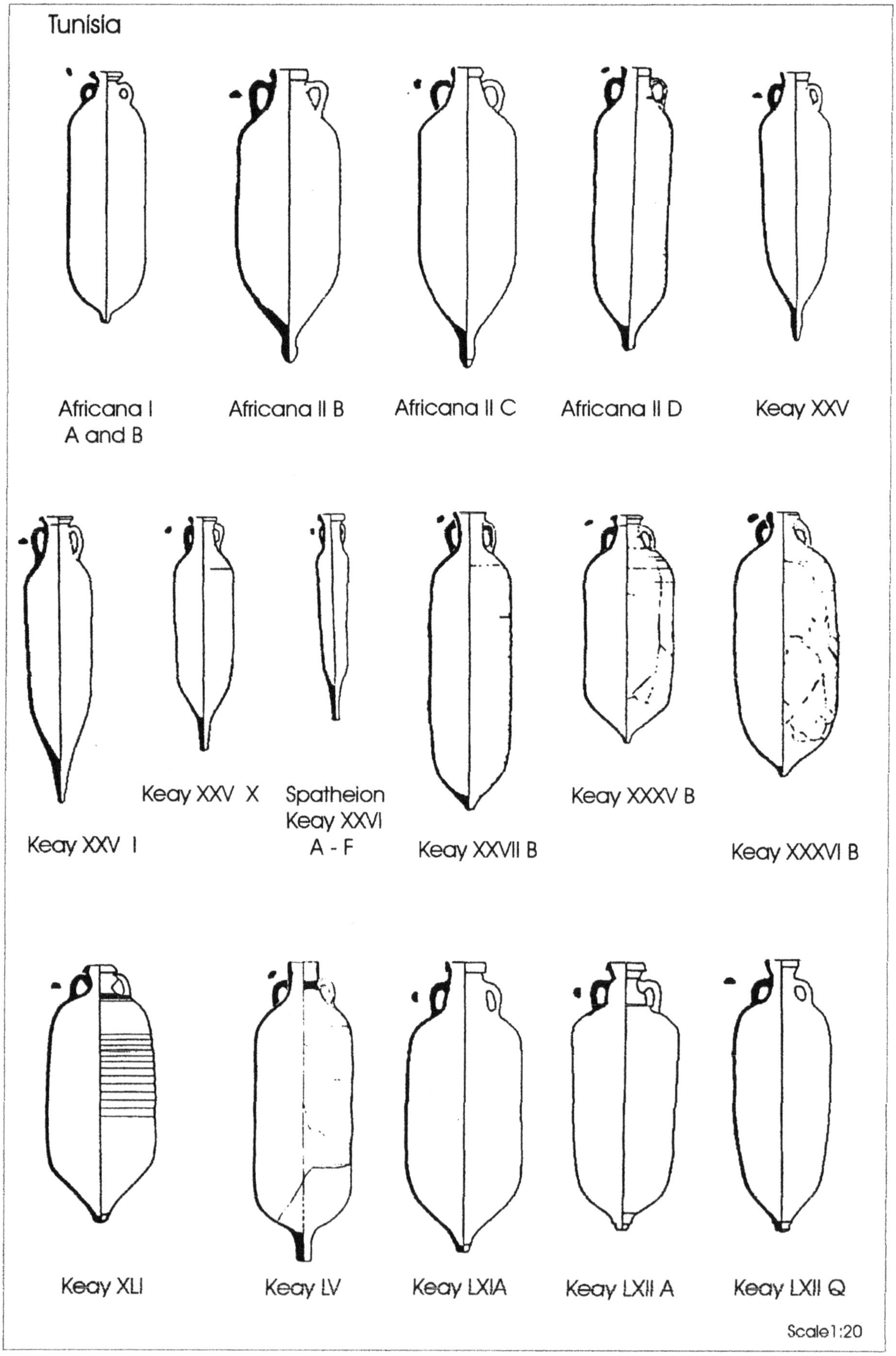

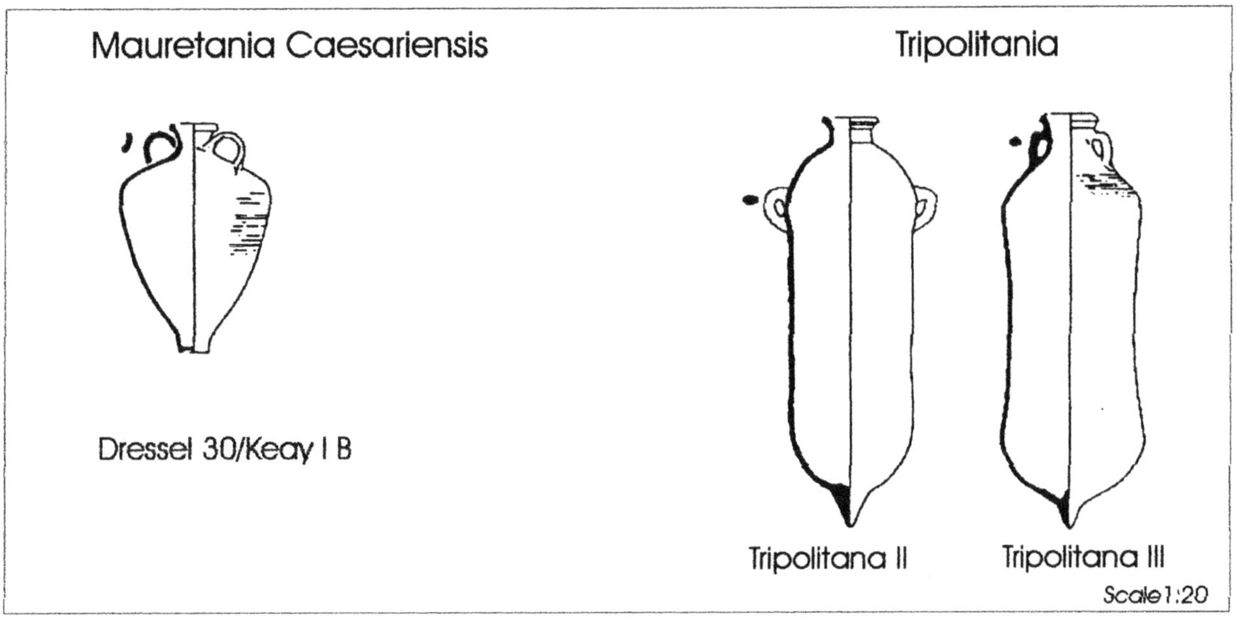

SPANISH AMPHORAE

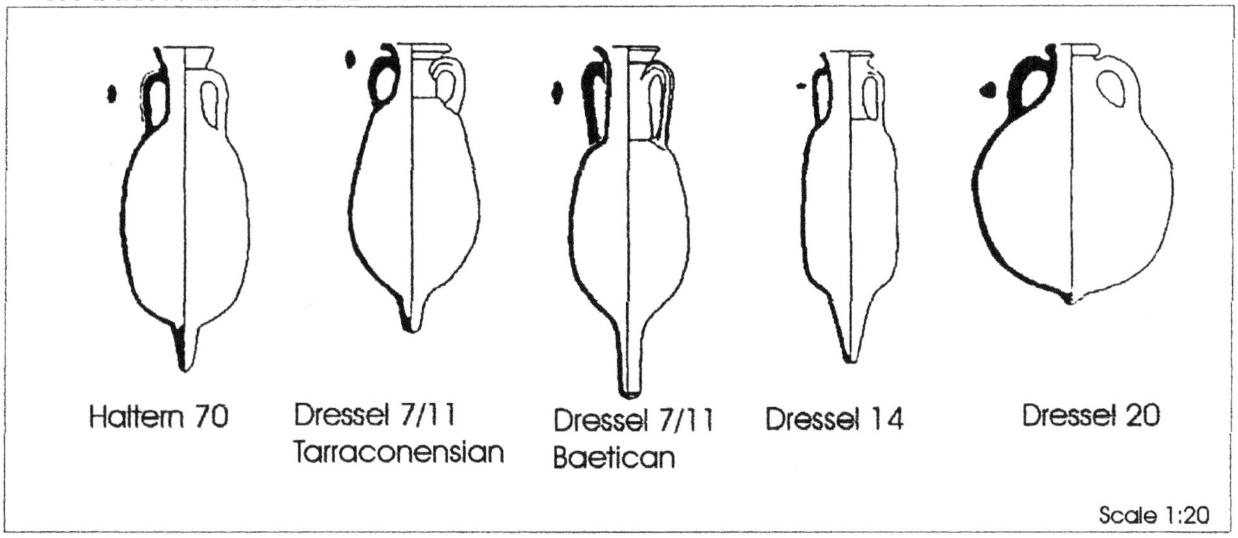

LATE SPANISH AMPHORAE

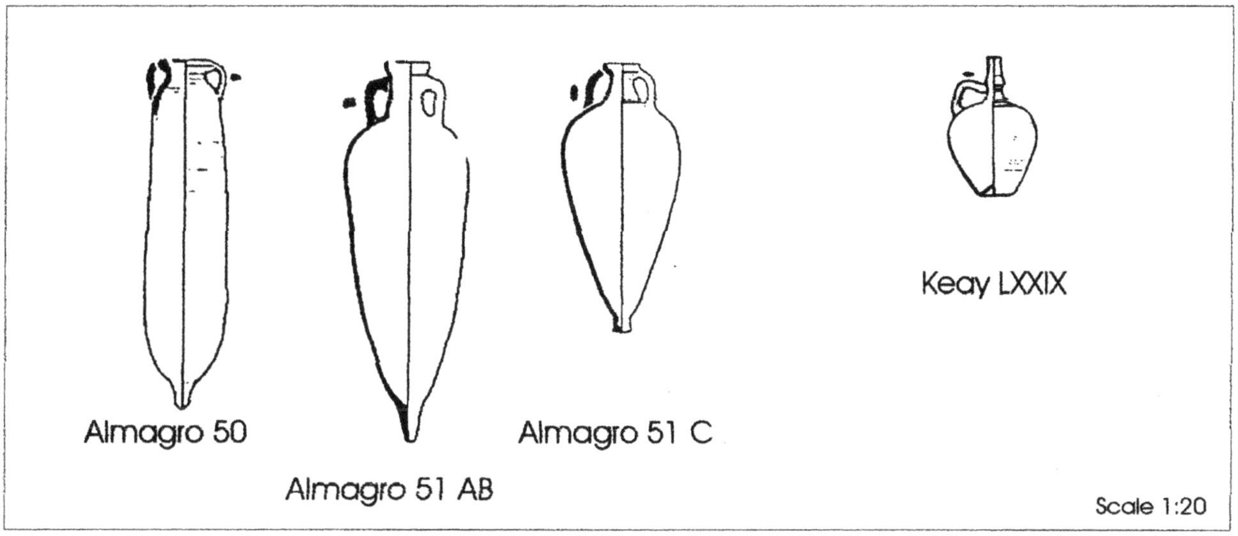

GAULISH AMPHORAE

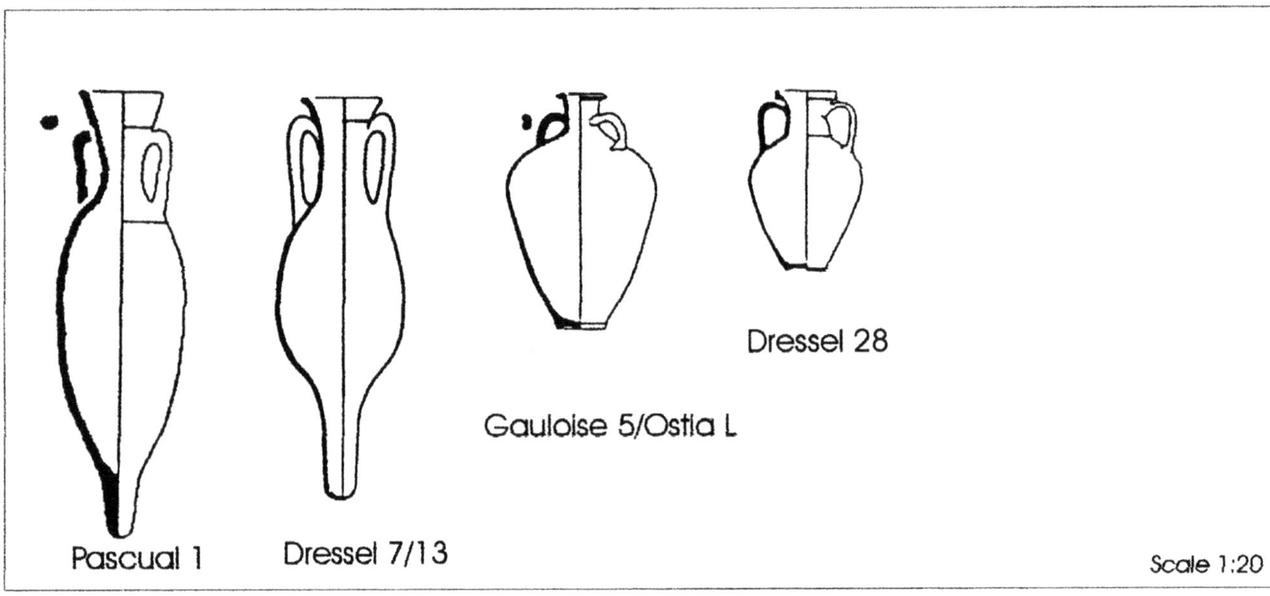

EASTERN MEDITERRANEAN / AEGEAN AMPHORAE

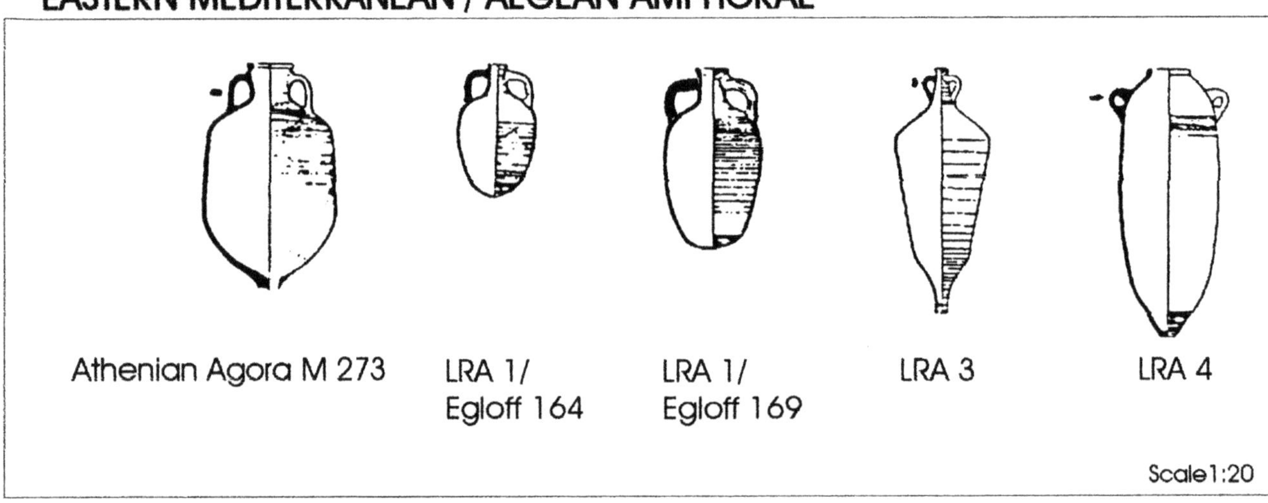

FIGURES 5-8. PRINCIPAL ROMAN AMPHORAE FOUND IN GENOA (P.MELLI AND B.BRUNO).

The port of Genoa became one of the main gateways receiving goods and foodstuffs from Sicily and African provinces, under the direct control of the praetorian prefect in Milan, on account of the new political and economical system of the Empire, for the purpose of the state *annona* supply, and perhaps owing to its growing role as an ecclesiastical centre (Formentini 1941; Frondoni 1996). Praetorian prefects had to supply the corn to feed the two capitals and some other leading cities of the Empire.

In the town lived a prosperous Jewish community, which plied, as in other centres of North Italy, trade in luxury items, slaves, and practised usury (Ruggini 1959, 222-223; Marcenaro 1993, 746-747) having a synagogue that was considered very old at the beginning of 6th century (Cassiod. *var*. II 27; IV 33).

The nature of evidence available includes a short number of very interesting stratified urban contexts (Melli and Torre 1996a; Melli 1996c; Biagini, Melli and Torre 1998), not fully published until now, and a large quantity of amphorae, found mostly during old excavations and reused in the extended late Antiquity cemeteries around the town (Gardini and Melli 1988; Gardini, Bellatalla and Bertino 1989; Gardini 1996; Bruno 1996). It seems important to note that analyses of amphora burials offer only a partial view, conditioned by amphora form selection.

Presently it is only possible to give a general overview, not yet a quantitative one, of the range of pottery that reached Genoa between the end of the 3rd and the 7th centuries, in order to assess its contribution to regional and long distance trade. Preliminary analysis demonstrates that Genoa received foodstuffs and fine wares from all over the western Mediterranean basin, and sometimes suggests a redistribution of items towards the north.

Redistribution from the Ligurian ports, and especially from Genoa, has been suggested, for instance, for the African fine ware diffused in Piedmont (Filippi 1995).

Recent surveys (Bruno 1996; Murialdo *et al.* 1999, 32-34) of the late Roman amphora forms imported in Genoa (fig. 5-7) show it was in firmly linked with the North African regions. Tunisian amphorae carrying oil and *garum* were imported since the end of 2nd century. Also well documented are oil amphorae from Tripolitania and Mauretanian wine containers (3rd - 4th century). Iberian area imports supplied fish-sauce, of different kinds, up to the 5th century.

From the 4th century onward, frequent imports from the East Mediterranean areas have been traced: amphorae from Syria, Cyprus, Rhodes, and a limited quantity from Aegean and Asia Minor kiln sites.

Only a small number of wine amphorae have been recognized as coming from South Italy, and a single Empoli amphora stamp (Bruno 1996, 324-26), showing contacts with the Arno Valley (Pasquinucci, Del Rio and Menchelli 1998,358-359).

Frequent imports of African red slip ware and Hayes' coarse ware (Milanese 1993, 96-104, 283-291; Storti 1996), almost certainly travelling together with grain and olive oil amphorae on the same ships, confirm links with African markets.

Among the imported commodities attested to in Genoa appear glazed pottery from the eastern Po Valley production centres (Gardini and Melli 1997) and luxury items such as the 4th-century engraved glass cup, attributed to a Rhineland workshop (Paolucci 1997, 142), and a rare gold-glass cup showing the early importance of the town as a stop for pilgrims (Melli in press a).

From various areas of the city come a great number of coins (Pera 1996), particularly 4th-century finds.

During Greek - Gothic war (AD 535-554), Genoa was a garrison town (Procop. *Goth.* II, 7, 36) with the main military harbour in Liguria.

In 569, during the invasion of Padane Liguria, the capture of Milan forced the city's nobility and clergy, headed by Archbishop Onoratus, to fly to Genoa. The Milanese community entrained continued communications with Rome (Formentini 1941, 18-27; 99-103).

Trade seems to have remained free from political difficulties: the town formed the administrative centre of the *Maritima Italorum*, the coastal land directly controlled by the Byzantine Empire (Christie 1989). In AD 599, under the reign of Maurice (582-602) a *vicarius* of the praetorian prefect was still stationed in Genoa (Greg. *Reg.* IX, 103).

The flow of imports did not cease and the port of Genoa was integrated into the trade exchanges dominated by the Byzantines, linking African markets to the north-Tyrrhenian ports. The historian, Procopius of Cesarea bears witness (*Goth.* II 12, 29; III 10,14) to the fact that Genoa was a port of call for the shipping lanes westwards to Gaul and Spain.

The archaeological evidence confirms the historical data. Various Byzantine coins, mainly coined under the reign of Justinian and Maurice, testify to the vivacity of the markets, and a rare coin of Domitian counter-struck by Vandals (Pera 2000); meanwhile relations with North Africa continued in the first half of the 6th century.

As late as the 6th, and up to the mid-7th century there were imports from Africa documented by late African red slip table ware and coarse ware, amphorae (Bruno and Lavazza 1996; Storti 1996; Bruno 1996; Biagini, Melli and Torre 1998) and lamps (Melli and Torre 1996a, 200-201). A good range of late pottery, including late Roman C/Phocaean ware, and glazed pottery, indicates that African red slip was only one component of fine ware assemblages. Eastern amphorae, a Palestinian container and sherds of vessels in *pietra ollare* from Alpine regions (Biagini, Melli and Torre 1998) show that the town was still linked with different sources.

About AD 641-643, King Rothari conquered Byzantine Liguria. The archaeological evidence does not confirm such destruction, but records a diffused decline, spoliation of buildings and abandonment of quarters: despite this the town survived.

The fact that from the Middle Ages Genoa became one of the main ports of the western Mediterranean and the natural means of communication between the Mediterranean and Europe (fig.9), is explained, at least in part, by its geographical position and the historical links, that the many invasions, wars and political events were unable to sever.

I would like to thank my colleagues F. Bulgarelli, L. Gervasini, G.P. Martino and B. Massabò in providing me with unpublished informations on Dressel 1 amphorae diffusion. Drawings by L.Tomasi.

FIGURE 9. *VON ITALIA* (*DIE COSMOGRAPH*, BASEL 1547-1551, FIG.)

References

Ampolo C. 1994, *Tra* empòria *ed* emporìa*: note sul commercio greco in età arcaica e classica*, in ΑΠΟΙΚΙΑ. Scritti in onore di Giorgio Buchner, "Annali di Archeologia e Storia Antica" NS 1, Dipartimento di studi del mondo classico e del Mediterraneo antico, Napoli, 29-36.

Bats M. 1992, *Marseille, les colonies massaliètes et les relais indigènes dans le trafic le long du littoral méditerranéen gaulois (Vie-Ier s.av.J.-C.)*, in *Marseille grecque et la Gaule*, Collection Etudes Massaliètes, 3, 263-278.

Biagini M. 1996a, *Scuole Pie. I materiali. Contenitori da trasporto*, in P.Melli 1996a, 296-298.

Biagini M., Melli P. and Torre E. 1998, *La ceramica comune in Liguria nel VI-VII secolo: Genova*, in L.Saguì (ed), *Ceramica in Italia: VI-VII secolo*, Atti del convegno in onore di John W.Hayes, Roma 1995, Edizioni All'insegna del Giglio, Firenze, 577-584.

Bouloumié B.1973, *Les oenochoés en bronze du type "Schnabelkanne" en Italie*, École française de Rome, Roma.

Brecciaroli Taborelli L. 1987, *Un contributo alla conoscenza dell'impianto urbano di* Eporedia *(Ivrea): lo scavo di un isolato a Porta Vercelli*, "Quaderni della Soprintendenza Archeologica del Piemonte" 6, 97-157.

Brecciaroli Taborelli L. 1988, *La ceramica a vernice nera da Eporedia (Ivrea). Contributo per la storia della romanizzazione nella Transpadana occidentale*, Orco Antropologica 6, Cuorgnè.

Bruni S. 1992, *Presenze di ceramica iberica in Etruria*, "Rivista di Studi Liguri" LVIII, 37-65.

Bruni S., and Conde M.J. 1991, *Presencia ibérica en Etruria y el mundo itálico a través de los hallazgos cerámicos de los siglos III-I a.C.*, in J.Remesal and O.Musso (eds), *La presencia de material etrusco en la Península Ibérica*, Barcellona, 543-576.

Bruno B. 1996, *Il commercio delle anfore a Genova in epoca tardo antica*, in P.Melli (ed), *La città ritrovata. Archeologia urbana a Genova 1984-1994*, 320-326.

Bruno B.1997, *Contenitori da trasporto: I consumi di olio, vino e di altre derrate*, in F.Filippi (ed.), *Alba Pompeia. Archeologia della città dalla fondazione alla tarda antichità*, Alba , Famija Albèise, 517-532.

Bruno B.1998a, *Importazione di merci e itinerari commerciali nella Liguria transappenninica*, in G.Sena Chiesa and E.Arslan (eds), *Optima via.* Atti del convegno internazionale di studi "Postumia. Storia e archeologia di una grande strada romana alle radici dell'Europa, Cremona 1996, Martellago (Venezia), 329-343.

Bruno B. 1998b, *Genova: le anfore tardorepubblicane*, in *Tesori della Postumia. Archeologia e storia intorno a una grande strada romana alle radici dell'Impero*, Catalogo della mostra Cremona 1998, Electa Milano, 440-441.

Cavalieri Manasse *et al.* 1986, Cavalieri Manasse G., Lavizzari M.P., Lusuardi Siena S., Ratti G., *The Roman Farmstead at Site 9- Appendix*, in Delano Smith C., Mills N., Gadd D., Ward Perkins B., *Luni and the ager lunensis. The rise and fall of a Roman town and its territory*, in "Papers of the British School at Rome", 116-117.

Cera G. 2000, *La via Postumia da Genova a Cremona*, «L'Erma» di Bretschneider, Roma.

Cimaschi L. 1961, *La prima campagna di scavo alla Pieve di S.Venerio (La Spezia)*, "Giornale Storico della Lunigiana" XII, 23-46.

Coarelli F.1988, *La fondazione di Luni. Problemi storici ed archeologici*, "Quaderni Centro Studi Lunensi" 10-12, 1985-87, I, 17-36.

Colonna G. 1981, *Presenza greca ed etrusco-meridionale nell'Etruria mineraria*, in *Etruria mineraria.* Atti del XII Convegno di Studi Etruschi (Firenze-Populonia-Piombino 1979), Firenze, pp.443-452.

Colonna G. 1988, *L'iscrizione etrusca del piombo di Linguadoca*, "Scienze dell'antichità. Storia archeologia antropologia" 2, 547-555.

Colonna G.1998, *Etruschi sulla via delle Alpi occidentali*, in L.Mercando and M.Venturino (eds), *Archeologia in Piemonte. I. La preistoria*, Soprintendenza Archeologica del Piemonte Torino, 261-266.

Christie N. 1989, *The* limes *Bizantino Reviewed: the Defence of Liguria AD 568- 643*, "Rivista di Studi Liguri" 55, 5-38.

D'Ambrosio B. 1985a, *L'insediamento di San Cipriano (Genova)*, "Studi e ricerche. Cultura del territorio", Comune di Campomorone, 1985, 49-69.

D'Ambrosio B. 1985b, *L'insediamento di Campora di Geminiano (Genova)*, "Studi e ricerche. Cultura del territorio"2, Comune di Campomorone, 70-72.

Davite C. et al.1992a, *Costa "Bottuin" di Trensasco*, in R.Maggi (ed.), *Archeologia preventiva lungo il percorso di un metanodotto*, Quaderni della Soprintendenza Archeologica della Liguria 2, Chiavari, 53-85.

Davite et al.1992b, *Costa Bastia*, in R.Maggi (ed.), *Archeologia preventiva lungo il percorso di un metanodotto*, Quaderni della Soprintendenza Archeologica della Liguria, 2, Chiavari, 87-92.

Dell'Amico P., *Albintimilium: le anfore del periodo augusteo provenienti dall'area dell'Officina del Gas*, "Rivista Archeologica dell'antica Diocesi di Como" 172, 103-142.

De Marinis R.1998, *I Liguri fra Etruschi e Celti*, in *Tesori della Postumia. Archeologia e storia intorno a una grande strada romana alle radici dell'Impero*, Catalogo della mostra Cremona 1998, Electa Milano, 59-75.

De Vingo P.1996, *I reperti della stratigrafia preromana. I contenitori da trasporto*, in *Lo scavo della contrada di S.Domenico al Priamàr (Savona). Relazioni preliminari sulle campagne di scavo 1989-1995*, "Archeologia Medievale" XXIII, 345-347.

De Vingo P. 2000, *I materiali dello scavo: la ceramica*, in E.M. Vecchi (ed), *La chiesa romanica di Santa Maria di Vezzano Ligure: un edificio ritrovato*, Atti del Convegno di studi Vezzano Ligure 1996,

"Giornale Storico della Lunigiana e del territorio lucense" n.s. XLVI-XLVIII, 1995-1997, 289-312.

Durante A.M.1995, *Necropoli di Ameglia- Cafaggio (La Spezia)*, in R.Maggi, F.Martini & L.Sarti (eds), *Toscana e Liguria*, Guide Archeologiche Preistoria e Protostoria in Italia, 6, Forlì, ABACO ed., 122-129.

Facchini G. 1995, *Alessandria, fraz. Villa del Foro. Via glareata in località San Damiano*, "Quaderni della Soprintendenza Archeologica del Piemonte" 13, 311-313.

Filippi F. 1995, *Una coppa di sigillata africana figurata con il mito di Eracle e Kyknos da una tomba tardoromana di Alba Pompeia*, "Quaderni della Soprintendenza Archeologica del Piemonte" 13, 59-72.

Finocchi S. 1984, *Acqui Terme (AL): contributo alla conoscenza della città romana. Scavi alla periferia urbana*, "Quaderni della Soprintendenza Archeologica del Piemonte" 3, 31-50.

Finocchi S. 1989, *Forum Fulvi*, in *Antichità ed arte nell'Alessandrino*, Atti del Convegno, Alessandria 1988, "B Torino" XLIII, 53-87.

Finocchi S.(ed.) 1996, *Libarna*, MAXMI ed., Castelnuovo Scrivia.

Formentini U. 1941, *Genova nel Basso Impero e nell'Alto Medioevo*, in *Storia di Genova dalle origini al tempo nostro*, II, Garzanti, Milano.

Fossati S. and Mannoni T. 1975, *Lo scavo della vetreria medievale di Monte Lecco*, "Archeologia Medievale" II, 31-97.

Fossati S., Messina W. and Milanese M. 1985, *Il castellaro di Vezzola (La Spezia)*, "Rivista di Studi Liguri" XLVIII, 1982, 178-192.

Fraccaro.P. 1956-7, *Opuscula*, Pavia, *Athenaeum*.

Francesetti A., Milanese M. and Rossi G.1984, *Ritrovamenti di anfore tardo-repubblicane al Monte Beigua (SV)*, " Studi Genuensi" n.s. II, 55-61.

Frey O.H., *I rapporti commerciali tra l'Italia settentrionale e l'Europa centrale dal VII al IV secolo a.C.*, in R.De Marinis (ed), *Gli Etruschi a nord del Po*, II, PubliPaolini, Mantova, 11-17.

Frontini P. 1991, *Ceramica a vernice nera*, in D.Caporusso (ed.), *Scavi MM3. Ricerche di archeologia urbana a Milano durante la costruzione della linea 3 della Metropolitana 1982-1990*, Edizioni ET, Milano, 23-39.

Galli G.1996, *La ceramica a vernice nera di Cremona: i "vecchi scavi"*, in G.M.Facchini, L.Passi Pitcher and M.Volontè (eds.), *Cremona e Bedriacum in età romana*, Edizioni ET, Milano, 69-81.

Gambari F.M.1989, *Il ruolo del commercio etrusco nello sviluppo delle culture piemontesi della prima età del ferro*, in *Gli Etruschi a nord del Po*. Atti del convegno Mantova 1986, Mantova, 211- 225;

Gambari F.M.1993, *Il bucchero etrusco nei contesti piemontesi della prima età del Ferro*, in Bonghi Jovino M. (ed.), *Produzione artigianale ed esportazione nel mondo antico. Il bucchero etrusco*, Atti del colloquio internazionale, Milano 1990, Edizioni ET, Milano, 127-134.

Gambaro L.1998, *La ceramica a vernice nera a Genova in età tardorepubblicana*, in *Tesori della Postumia. Archeologia e storia intorno a una grande strada romana alle radici dell'Europa*, Electa Milano, 441-443.

Gambaro L. 1999, *La Liguria costiera tra III e I secolo a.C.. Una lettura archeologica della romanizzazione*, Documenti di Archeologia 18, Società Archeologica Padana, Mantova.

Gandolfi D. 1986, in *La pietra ollare in Liguria*. Atti della giornata di studio in ricordo di Lella Massari, Finale Ligure, 22/6/1985, "Rivista di Studi Liguri" LII, 151-319.

Gardini A., Bellatalla and Bertino A. 1989, *Lo scavo dell'area suburbana di via San Vincenzo a Genova*, "Archeologia Medievale" XVI, 357-410.

Gardini A. and Melli P. 1988, *Necropoli e sepolture urbane ed extra urbane a Genova tra tardo antico ed Alto Medioevo*, "Rivista di Studi Liguri" XIV, 161-179.

Gardini A. and Melli P.1992, *Ceramiche invetriate tardoantiche e altomedievali da Genova*, in L.Paroli (ed), *La ceramica invetriata tardoantica e altomedievale in Italia*, Atti del seminario, Edizioni All'insegna del giglio, Firenze, 104-109.

Gervasini L. 1984, *Luni. La necropoli romana del Botrignolo*, in P.Melli (ed), *Archeologia in Liguria II. Scavi e scoperte 1976-81*, Tormena, Genova, 229-236.

Giannichedda E. 1995, *Dinamiche insediative e strutture sociali nel genovesato fra protostoria e romanizzazione*, in A.M.Pastorino, *La Tavola di Polcevera*, GGallery Ed., Genova, 39-51.

Gras M. 1997, *Il Mediterraneo nell'età arcaica*, Fondazione Paestum, Paestum.

Grasso L.1999, *Anfore*, in B.Massabò (ed), *Dalla villa al villaggio. Corti: scavo di un sito archeologico di età romana e altomedievale lungo il metanodotto del Ponente ligure*, Genova, Erga edizioni, 155-170.

Isetti G. 1960, *Due stazioni liguri dell'età del Ferro: Castelfermo e Cota (Comune di Carro, prov.della Spezia)*, "Giornale Storico della Lunigiana" XI, 3-4, 87-114.

Lamboglia N. 1934-35, *Anfore pescate lungo la riviera italiana: Capo Mele*, "Rivista di Studi Liguri" I, 133-134.

Lamboglia N. 1950, *Gli scavi di Albintimilium e la cronologia della ceramica romana. Parte prima. Campagne di scavo 1938- 1940*, Bordighera Istituto di Studi Liguri.

Lamboglia N. 1951, *Il castelliere di Monte Bignone (Sanremo)*, "Rivista Ingauna e Intemelia" N.S.VI, 3-4, 70-71.

Lamboglia N.1952a, *Nuova campagna di scavi a Monte Bignone*, "Rivista Ingauna e Intemelia" N.S. VII, 1952, 2-4, 61-62.

Lamboglia N. 1952b, *La nave romana di Alberga*, "Rivista di Studi Liguri" 18, 131-236.

Lamboglia N. 1955a, *Un'anfora pescata a Imperia*, "Rivista di Studi Liguri" 10, 88.

Lamboglia N.1955b, *Sulla cronologia delle anfore romane di età repubblicana (II- I sec.a.C.)*, Rivista di Studi Liguri" XXI, 211-270.

Lamboglia N.1956, *Primi risultati cronologici e storico-topografici degli scavi di Albintimilium (1948-1956)*, "Rivista di Studi Liguri" XXII, 91-152.

Lamboglia N.1959, *Prime osservazioni sugli strati preromani di* Albium Intemelium, "Rivista di Studi Liguri",

Lamboglia N.1966a, *Una nave massaliota nelle acque di Albenga?*, in "Rivista di Studi Liguri" XXXII, 3, 1966, 315-322.

Lamboglia N.1966b, *Postilla*, "Rivista di Studi Liguri" XXXII, 3, 322.

Lamboglia N. 1978, *La riscoperta dell'anfiteatro romano di Albenga*, "Rivista Ingauna e Intemelia" XXVIII-XXX, 1973-75, 89-92.

Mannoni T.1972, *La ceramica dell'età del ferro nel Genovesato*, "Studi Genuensi" 8, 1970-71, 3-26.

Marcenaro M.1993, *Note sulla presenza gota nella* Liguria *marittima in età teodericiana: la sinagoga di Genova e le epigrafi di Albenga*, in *Teoderico il grande e i Goti d'Italia*, Atti del XIII Congresso internazionale di studi sull'Alto Medioevo, Milano 1992, Spoleto 1993, 743-755.

Martino G.P. 1995-96, *Forma Maris Antiqui: Regio IX-Liguria*, "Bollettino di Archeologia Subacquea" II-III, 1-2, 113-125.

Massabò B. 1990, *San Bartolomeo al mare*, in P.Melli (ed), *Archeologia in Liguria III.2. Scavi e scoperte 1982-86*, Genova Tormena, 471-472.

Massabò B. and Gandolfi D. 1994, *Attività archeologiche nell'area di* Lucus Bormani, "Rivista Ingauna e Intemelia" XLVI –XLVII, 1991-92, 137-152.

Melli P. 1990, *Il castellaro di Uscio nel quadro del popolamento della Liguria centro-orientale nella seconda età del Ferro*, in R.Maggi (ed), *Archeologia dell'Appennino Ligure. Gli scavi del castellaro di Uscio*, Istituto di Studi Liguri, Bordighera, 291-296.

Melli P. (ed) 1996a, *La città ritrovata. Archeologia urbana a Genova 1984-1994*, Tormena Editore Genova.

Melli P. 1996b, *L'archeologia urbana in Italia e a Genova*, in Melli P. (ed) 1996a, 17-24.

Melli P. et al 1996c, *Scuole Pie,* in P.Melli (ed) 1996a, 283-303.

Melli P.1996d, *Il recupero della tomba di Rapallo: nuovi dati sul popolamento del Tigullio tra la fine del VII e gli inizi del VI sec. a.C.*, "Rivista di Studi Liguri" LXII, 1996, 95-114.

Melli P. 1998a, *La città e il suo territorio*, in P.Melli-M.Pasquinucci, *Prospettive di ricerca a Genova e nel suo territorio*, in G.Sena Chiesa and E.Arslan (eds), *Optima via.* Atti del convegno internazionale di studi "Postumia. Storia e archeologia di una grande strada romana alle radici dell'Europa, Cremona 1996, Martellago (Venezia) 1998, 417-425; 429-433.

Melli P. 1998b, *Genova: il grande porto del Tirreno*, in *Tesori della Postumia. Archeologia e storia intorno a una grande strada romana alle radici dell'Impero*, Catalogo della mostra Cremona 1998, Electa Milano, 433-439.

Melli P. 1999, *Nuove ricerche nel monastero di S.Maria in Passione*, in D.Gandolfi (ed), *Nel ricordo di Nino Lamboglia*, Atti del Convegno 1998, Istituto Internazionale di Studi Liguri Bordighera, 161-186.

Melli P. 2001, *La via Postumia*, in R.Luccardini (ed), *Vie romane in Liguria*, De Ferrari editore, Genova, 95-102; 227.

Melli P. in press a, *Vetri dalla necropoli di via XX Settembre a Genova*, in Atti del Convegno AIHV, Genova 2000.

Melli P. in press b, *Testimonianze di cultura figurativa a Genova: prospettive di ricerca*,

Melli in press c, *Il vino e il mirto. Considerazioni sui rituali funerari della necropoli di Genova*, "Prospettiva"

Melli P. and Gambaro L. 2000, *Considerazioni sulle produzioni tardo-repubblicane a vernice nera attestate a Genova*, in *La ceràmica de vernìs negre dels segles II i I aC: centres productors mediterranis i commercialització a la Peninsula Ibèrica*, Taula rodona Empuries 4-5 de juny 1998, Patronat Municipal de Cultura Mataró 2000, 19-29.

Melli P. and Manganelli C.1996, *La stratigrafia marina del Portofranco*, in P.Melli (ed) 1996, 83-86.

Melli P. and Starnini E. 1990, *I materiali dell'età del ferro*, in R.Maggi (ed.), *Archeologia dell'Appennino ligure. Gli scavi nel castellaro di Uscio*, Bordighera, Istituto di Studi Liguri, 261-290.

Melli P. and Torre E.1996a, *Mattoni Rossi. Lo scavo archeologico*, in Melli P. (ed) 1996a, 192-199.

Mennella G. 1996, *Il nome di Genova nelle fonti antiche*, in Melli P.(ed) 1996a, 28-32.

Milanese M.1984, *Camogli*, in P.Melli (ed), *Archeologia in Liguria II. Scavi e scoperte 1976-81*, Genova Tormena, 87-93.

Milanese M. 1986, *Rapporti fra Marsiglia e Genova dal V al I secolo a.C.: informazioni archeologiche dai recenti scavi di Genova*, in *Studi in memoria di T.O.De Negri*, "Bollettino Ligustico", 9-19

Milanese M. 1987, *Scavi nell'oppidum preromano di Genova*,"Studia Archaeologica" 48, «L'Erma» di Bretschneider, Roma.

Milanese M.1990, *La diffusione delle anfore massaliote in Liguria*, in M.Bass (ed), *Les amphores de Marseille grecque. Cronologie et diffusion (VIe-Iers.av.J.-C.)*, Actes de la table ronde Lattes 1989, Lattes/Aix-en-Provence, ADAM ed./Univ.de Provence (Etudes Massalietes 2), 217-222.

Milanese M.1993, *Genova romana. Mercato e città dalla tarda età repubblicana a Diocleziano dagli scavi del colle di Castello*, Studia Archaeologica 62, «L'Erma» di Bretschneider, Roma.

Milanese M. and Giardi M. 1986, *L'insediamento preromano di Monte Dragnone (La Spezia). Relazione preliminare*, in *Scritti in ricordo di Graziella Massari e Umberto Tocchetti Pollini*, Milano, Edizioni ET, 71-78.

Milanese M. and Mannoni T. 1985, *Gli Etruschi a*

Genova e il commercio mediterraneo, "Studi Etruschi" LII, 115-144.
Morel J.P. 1998, *Le ceramiche a vernice nera del Piemonte: tipologia, storia, cultura*, in L.Mercando (ed), *Archeologia in Piemonte. L'età romana*, Allemandi, Torino, 235-252.
Murialdo G. *et al.* 1999, *I contenitori da trasporto mediterranei in età tardoantica in Liguria (IV-VII secolo)*, in Atti XXX Convegno internazionale della Ceramica 1997, Albisola Centro Ligure per la Storia della Ceramica, 31-45.
Ognibene S. in press, *Anfore*, in Gervasini L., *Portovenere (SP). Zona archeologica del Varignano vecchio. Indagini archeologiche nel quartiere dei torchi oleari e nella zona residenziale della villa romana*, "Rivista di studi Liguri"
Pallares F. 1995, *La chiesa di S.Pietro di Camporosso*, "Rivista di Studi Liguri" LIX-LX, 1993-1994, 407-440.
Panella C. 1981, *La distribuzione e i mercati*, in A.Giardina and A.Schiavone (eds), *Merci, mercati e scambi nel Mediterraneo, Società romana e produzione schiavistica* II, Laterza Roma-Bari, 55-80.
Paolucci F. 1997, *I vetri incisi dall'Italia Settentrionale e dalla Rezia nel periodo medio e tardo imperiale*, Firenze.
Parker A.J.1992, *Ancient Shipwrecks of the Mediterranean & the Roman Provinces*, BAR International Series 580.
Pasquinucci M. 1998, *La val Polcevera*, in *Tesori della Postumia. Archeologia e storia intorno a una grande strada romana alle radici dell'Impero*, Electa Milano, 216-217.
Pasquinucci M., Del Rio A. and Menchelli S. 1998, *Produzioni di vino nell'Etruria settentrionale costiera*, in *El vi a l'antiguitat. Economia, producció i comerç al Mediterranei occidental*, Actes Badalona 1998, Monografies badalonines, 14, Museu de Badalona, 357-363.
Pauli L.1991, *Les Alpes centrales et orientales à l'âge du fer*, "Revue Archeologique de la Narbonnaise" Suppl.22, *Les Alpes à l'âge du fer*, 291-311.
Pera R. 1996, *Monete*, in Melli (ed) 1996a, 208-10; 221-2.
Pera R.2000, *Una moneta con contromarca vandalica dagli scavi di Genova*, in M.Khanoussi, P.Ruggeri and C.Vismara (eds), *L'Africa romana* XIII, Atti del convegno di studio Djerba 1998, Roma, 1455-1461.
Piana Agostinetti P. 1995, *La monetazione preromana dell'Italia nord-occidentale*, in "Rivista di Studi Liguri" LXI, 1995, 195-217.
Ricci M. 1953, *La seconda campagna di scavi al castellaro di Monte Colma*, in ""Rivista Ingauna e Intemelia" N.S. VIII, , 1-4.
Rouillard P. 1992, *La place de Marseille dans le commerce des vases attiques à figures rouges en Méditerranée occidentale (Ve-IVe s.av.J.-C.)*, in *Marseille grecque et la Gaule*, Collection Etudes Massaliètes, 3, 179-187.
Ruggini L.1959, *Ebrei e orientali nell'Italia settentrionale fra V e VI secolo d.C.*, "*Studia et Documenta Historiae et Juris*" 25, 186-308.
Storti S., *Scuole Pie. I materiali. Ceramica africana. Ceramica comune*, in Melli (ed)1996a, 294-296.
Surace A. 1984, *San Bartolomeo al mare*, in P.Melli (ed), *Archeologia in Liguria II. Scavi e scoperte 1976-81*, Tormena, Genova, 189-196.
Tchernia A. 1986, *Le vin de l'Italie romaine*, Ecole française de Rome, Roma.
Toynbee A.J. 1965, *Hannibal's legacy*, London, Oxford University Press.
Venturino Gambari M., Traversone B. and Cattaneo Cassano A. 1996, *Tortona prima di Dertona*, "Quaderni della Soprintendenza Archeologica del Piemonte" 14, 21-59.
Zanda E. 1991, *Ticineto. Materiali di età romana*, "Quaderni della Soprintendenza Archeologica del Piemonte" 10, 103-104.
Zanda E., Crosetto A., Pejrani L. 1986, *Asti. Interventi archeologici in centro storico*, in "Quaderni della Soprintendenza Archeologica del Piemonte" 5, 67-121.
Zanda E., Prosperi R. and Gabucci A. 1995, *Tortona. Interventi nel centro storico*, "Quaderni della Soprintendenza Archeologica del Piemonte" 13, 305-309.
Zanda E. and Vecchi A. 1994, *Portichetto della SS.Annunziata e Palazzo Guidobono*, "Quaderni della Soprintendenza Archeologica del Piemonte" 12, 265.
Zevi F.2000, *Roma arcaica e Ostia. Una riconsiderazione del problema*, in *Damarato. Studi di antichità classica offerti a Paola Pelagatti*, Electa Milano, 233-243.

Appendix 1 (fig. 2)

Massaliote amphorae

Ventimiglia: Lamboglia 1956, 99, fig.6, 12-13. (Py 5-6 and 7-8); Lamboglia 1959, 243 (Py 5-6); Milanese 1990, 218.
Croce di Padre Poggio(Sanremo, IM): Gambaro 1999, 52, n.15
Monte Colma (Sanremo, IM): Ricci 1963, 98.
Monte Bignone (Sanremo, IM): Lamboglia 1951, 70-71; Lamboglia 1952a, 61; Milanese 1990, 218.
***Capo Mele (Andora, IM)**: Lamboglia 1952b, 232 (Py 7-8); Navigia 1983, 37,26; Milanese 1990, 218.
San Bartolomeo al mare (IM): Gandolfi 1986, 281; Massabò 1990, 472, fig.604.
Gallinaria island: Lamboglia 1966a (Bertucchi 2-Bertucchi 3); Navigia 1983, 119, fig.139-140.
Albenga (SV): Lamboglia 1966b; Lamboglia 1978, 92.
Corti: Grasso 1999, 155, fig. 26, 1-2. (Py 6)
Castellaro di Bergeggi: Milanese 1990, 219; Del Lucchese et al.1991-1992, 78-84, fig.16, 1-2;19, 5-9. (Py 3, Py 6, Py 8)
Vado: F.Bulgarelli unpublished note.
Savona: Gandolfi 1986, 281; De Vingo 1996, 345-346, fig.31; Lavagna 1996, 33, fig.35.
Genova: Milanese 1990 (Py 2-3; 5-6; 7-8); Melli

1999,176 (Py 6).
Camogli: Milanese1984, fig.116,8. (Py 5-6).
Ameglia: Durante 1995.

Etruscan amphorae
Bergeggi: Del Lucchese et al. 1991-92, 84, fig.19, 11 (Py 4)
Sestri Ponente: Mannoni 1972, 5.
Genova: Milanese and Mannoni 1985; Milanese 1987, 279-280; Melli 1999 (Py 1-2; Py 3; Py 4; Py 4A; Py 5).
Camogli: Milanese 1984, 88, fig.116,6 (Py 4).
Uscio: Melli and Starnini 1990, 273-275, fig.162, 60,62-3 (Py 4 – Py 4a)
Monte Dragnone: Milanese and Giardi 1986, 74,6 (Py 4).

Appendix 2: Tyrrhenian amphora underwater discoveries in Liguria (fig.3)

Capo Mortola: Lamboglia 1971, 178; *Navigia* 1983, 33-34, 2-4. (Dressel 1)
Vallecrosia: *Navigia* 1983, 34, 6 (Dressel 1)
Bussana: Martino 1995-96, 117-118.
San Lorenzo al mare: *Navigia* 1983, 35, 16 (Dressel 1)
Imperia, **Porto Maurizio**: Lamboglia 1934-1935, 133-4; Lamboglia 1952, 235, fig.91, *Navigia* 1983, 35, 17; Parker 1992, 216 (Dressel 1B).
Capo Mele: Lamboglia 1952, 231-2, fig.86-87; Lamboglia 1955, fig.5; *Navigia* 1983, 37, 25; Parker 1992, 121 (Dressel 1C)
Gallinaria island: Lamboglia 1958, 63-65 (Graeco-Italic); Martino in press (Dressel 1).
Albenga: Lamboglia 1952; *Navigia* 1983, 45-68; Parker 1992, 49-50 (shipwreck: Dressel 1B; BGW *Campana* A)
Finale Ligure: Lamboglia 1952, 229-230, fig.85; *Navigia* 1983, 38,32 (Dressel 1).
Noli: Lamboglia 1952, 229, fig.84 (Dressel 1).
Vado Ligure: *Navigia* 1983, 39,43 (Dressel 1)
Varazze: Lamboglia 1952, 226-228, fig.81-82; Parker 1992, 444-45 (Dressel 1 B).
Genova Pegli: Lamboglia 1952, 213-223; *Navigia* 1983, 42,49; Parker 1992, 189 (shipwreck: late Graeco-Italic or Dressel 1A, BGW *Campana* A, Lamboglia form 6).
Genoa, port: Lamboglia 1952, 225-226; *Navigia* 1983, 42, 51 (Dressel 1)
Camogli: Lamboglia 1952, 224-225, fig.80; Navigia 1983, 43,55 (Dressel 1).
Portofino, **Punta Chiappa**: Lamboglia 1971, 190-191; Navigia 1983, 43,57; Parker 1992, 347 (Dressel 1).
Portofino: *Navigia* 1983, 43, 59 (Graeco-Italic sherds layer: shipwreck?).
S.Michele di Pagana (Portofino): information kindly given by G.P. Martino (Dressel 1)
Rapallo: *Navigia* 1983, 43, 61 (Dressel 1)
Palmaria island: information kindly given by G.P. Martino (late Graeco-Italic)

Appendix 3: Tyrrhenian amphorae distribution in Liguria and south Piedmont (fig.4)

Liguria
Ventimiglia: Lamboglia 1950, 251, fig.7 (late Graeco-Italic) 73-74, fig.32, 74-76; 85-86, fig.39, 89-92 (Dressel 1A); Lamboglia 1955b, 251-269. Dell'Amico 1990 (Dressel 1B).
Monte Colma: Gambaro 1998, 54 (late Graeco-Italic).
Monte Bignone: Gambaro 1998, 53 and n.19 (late Graeco-Italic).
Monte Grange/Monte delle Anime: Gambaro 1999, 54, n.31.
Diano Marina: Massabò and Gandolfi 1994, 142-146. (Dressel 1 B)
San Bartolomeo, loc. Rovere: Surace 1984, 192; Massabò Gandolfi 1994, 146-148 (Dr 1 B)
Cervo, Monte Castellaro: information kindly given by B.Massabò (Dressel 1).
Corti: Grasso 1999, 155, pl.26,3 (late Graeco-Italic); 155-156, pl.26, 4-12; 27,1 (Dressel 1A); 256, pl.27, 2-3 (Dressel 1B).
Albenga: information kindly given by B.Massabò (Dressel 1).
Camporosso, S.Pietro church: Pallares 1995, 425-426 (Dressel 1 A, B, C)
Bergeggi: Del Lucchese et al. 1991-92, 85, fig. 20,1; 21, 4 (late Graeco-Italic).
Vado Ligure: Lamboglia 1955b, 248-9, fig. 6 (Dressel 1C, one boring stamp SEXTIUS); Manacorda 1981, 11.
Savona: De Vingo 1996, 346, fig.31 (Graeco-Italic)
Monte Beigua (Urbe), Costa du Spinsu: Francesetti, Milanese and Rossi 1984 (Dressel 1 A)
Passo del Faiallo: Giannichedda 1995,46 (late republican Tyrrhenian amphorae)
Genoa: Biagini 1996a; Bruno 1998b (Graeco-Italic and Dressel 1A, B, C, A/C; stamps)
San Cipriano (GE): D'Ambrosio 1985a, 56-57, fig.16, 4 (late Graeco-Italic); 16, 1,3; 5 (Dressel 1A).
Campora di Geminiano (GE): D'Ambrosio 1985b, 70, fig.16,2 (Dressel 1A).
Monte Lecco- Passo della Bocchetta: Fossati and Mannoni 1975, fig. 114-117 (late Graeco- Italic)
Trensasco, "Costa Bottuin": Davite *et al.*1992a, 58-59, fig.9, 16-17 (Dressel 1).
Costa Bastia: Davite *et al.* 1992b, 90 (Italic amphorae sherds)
Recco: Melli 1990, 292 (Dressel 1)
Avegno, Testana and Monte San Pietro: Melli 1990, 293 (Tyrrhenian amphorae sherds).
Uscio, Castellaro: Melli and Starnini 1990, 273-275, fig.162, 61 (late Graeco-Italic).
Camogli: Milanese 1984, 88, fig.16,1-3 (Dressel 1A).
Zoagli: Gambaro 1999, 59 n.61, fig. 23 (Dressel 1)
Mezzanego, Porciletto: Melli et al., in press (late Graeco-Italic)
Castelfermo: Isetti 1960, fig.7 (Dressel 1 A)
Vezzola: Fossati, Messina and Milanese 1985, 182-183, fig.5, 53-54; 6, 64 (Graeco-Italic).

Pegazzano: Mannoni 1968, 302; Massari 1981, 107 (Graeco- Italic or Dressel 1).
Varignano, Roman villa: Ognibene in press (Dressel 1)
Migliarina: Cimaschi 1961, 31, fig.8 (Dressel 1)
Vezzano, Chiesa di S.Maria: De Vingo 2000, 290-294, 303-4, pl. I, 1,4,6-7; II, 8-11 (Dressel 1 A and B).
Ameglia, necropolis: Durante 1995 (Graeco-Italic)
Botrignolo, Luna's cemetery (Castelnuovo Magra): Gervasini 1984, 232, fig.267 (Dressel 1 B).
Luni: Luni II, 234, tav.141, 18 (Graeco-Italic); Luni II, 235-237, tav.142, 3-4, 6-22 (Dressel 1A); Bruno 1998a, 330-331, fig.3.
Ager lunensis site 9, farmhouse: Cavalieri Manasse et al. 1986 (Dr 1)
Pieve S.Lorenzo: Gambaro 1998, 61.

Piedmont
Alba: Bruno 1997, 517 (Dressel 1).
Acqui Terme: Finocchi 1984; Bruno 1998a, 333, n. 10 (Dressel 1).
Asti: Zanda *et al.*1986, 78-86, pl. XX, 32-34; XXI, 35 (Dressel 1)
Borghetto Borbera (AL): (Dressel 1A, black glaze pottery *Campana* A, B nord etruscan) Gambaro 1999, 182-186.
Libarna: Bruno 1998, 334 (Dr 1).
Tortona: Zanda and Vecchi 1994, pl. LXXVIIb,5; Zanda, Prosperi and Gabucci 1995, pl. CXX, CXXIII; Bruno 1998a, 333 (Dressel 1).
Villa del Foro: Finocchi 1989, 65, 75 (Dressel 1); Bruno 1998, n.10 (Dressel 1 A/C).
Ticineto: Zanda 1991, pl.LIV, 6 (Dressel 1 B).

Cagliari and its Hinterland from the Archaic to the Late Roman Age

Carlo Tronchetti

Abstract
The city of Cagliari (Italy), from the beginning of its settlement in historical times (at least from the 6th century BC) up to the Late Roman and Byzantine periods, is examined, with an attempt to trace commercial traffic arriving at its harbour in the different historical periods and its role as distributor of products to its hinterland.

The first stratigraphic evidence of the presence of a settlement in Cagliari in historical times goes back to a time not before the beginnings of the 6th century BC (Tronchetti 1990, 33; Chessa 1992a, 51). These remains, belonging to the Phoenician cultural sphere, were found on the eastern shore of the Santa Gilla Lagoon, thus in a position that can easily be connected with the existence of a good port or landing place well protected from the prevailing winds (north-west and south-east) which arrive with great force (especially the former) throughout the year. The existence in the area of beds of fresh water, exploited with wells up to the Middle Ages, is another element favourable to the birth of a settlement there. A vast hinterland created by the wide alluvial plains of the Campidano region, bordered by rolling hills, was a further element favourable to the growth of a settlement of great importance, as was the Cagliari of the Phoenicians, the Carthaginians and the Romans (Figure 1).

If the first stratigraphic traces go back to the beginning of the 6th century BC, a date based on Etruscan-Corinthian material associated with Phoenician shards (Chessa 1986), we are now in a position to advance the fairly reasonable hypothesis that Phoenician frequentation of the site, most probably with the founding of a settlement, began at least one century before. Decontextualised materials from the end of the 8th to the beginning of the 7th century BC (shards of Corinthian late geometric pottery) were found during excavations in Via Brenta in Cagliari on the shores of the lagoon (Chessa 1992b); other decontextualised materials from a later period are represented by shards of bucchero ware (end of the 7th, first half of the 6th centuries BC) and East-Greek cups (first half of the 6th century BC) (Usai and Zucca 1986, 165-166; Tronchetti 1992b; Chessa 1992c). Cagliari's hinterland has yielded similar imported materials, this time in indigenous contexts in accordance with the pattern of distribution of materials from Phoenician coastal settlements towards local populations, which is well documented in Sardinia (Tronchetti 1988, 63-88; Tronchetti 1995, 719-728).

Unfortunately, and this is true of all the periods we shall examine, Sardinia has almost never been the site of a territorial survey, except in very few cases in lands other than those we examine herein. Thus all the observations I present herein concerning such lands derive from random findings and limited investigations mostly due to contingencies: the data are thus for the most part indicative (Figure 2).

The site at the town of Settimo San Pietro, about ten kilometres from Cagliari, yielded Euboean and Corinthian fragments from between the end of the 8th and the beginning of the 7th centuries; the 7th and 6th centuries are represented by Etruscan bucchero ware and East-Greek cups. In the adjacent towns of Monastir and San Sperate, about sixteen kilometres to the north of Cagliari, findings are mostly from the 7th and 6th centuries, and are once again Etruscan and Corinthian pottery, with a small amount of East-Greek material. Phoenician pottery of the same period is found at all these sites of an indigenous matrix.

The introduction of imported goods among indigenous populations is attributed to the network of relations set up by Phoenicians living in the coastal towns for the purpose of gaining access to the sources of raw materials, first and foremost metals, as can be seen from the first Phoenician colonies set up in southern Sardinia along the "metal route" which, starting from *Pythecussai*, went as far as the Iberian Peninsula. This widespread presence of imported objects on the Campidano Plain can in all probability be traced to the Phoenician settlement in Cagliari because of the construction of a harbour and its being the gateway to an easy route penetrating inland.

The siting of the harbour in the Santa Gilla Lagoon in Phoenician times is, however, purely inductive; but this conviction is strengthened by the subsequent Punic period. Indeed, the Carthaginian town stretched along the eastern coast of the lagoon, covering and obliterating the few remains of the Phoenician settlement (Tronchetti 1990; Salvi 1991; Tronchetti 1992c). Between the end of the 19th century AD and the present, the bottom of the lagoon has yielded the remains of a good number of ships or barges, and a still greater quantity of archaeological material that had fallen into the sea, thus showing that the waterfront was heavily frequented, especially during the Punic period (end of the 6th century up to 238 BC) with an extension even into the first Republican Age (first decades of the 2nd century BC) (Zucca 1988).

Cagliari became quite prosperous in those centuries. There are few traces of the built-up areas; only some sectors near the lagoon have been investigated in recent years. Bringing together these data with those of the first half of the last century and in general the information we have concerning Cagliari's urban archaeology, it is safe to hypothesise that the principal nucleus of the Punic town was on the eastern coast of the Santa Gilla lagoon.

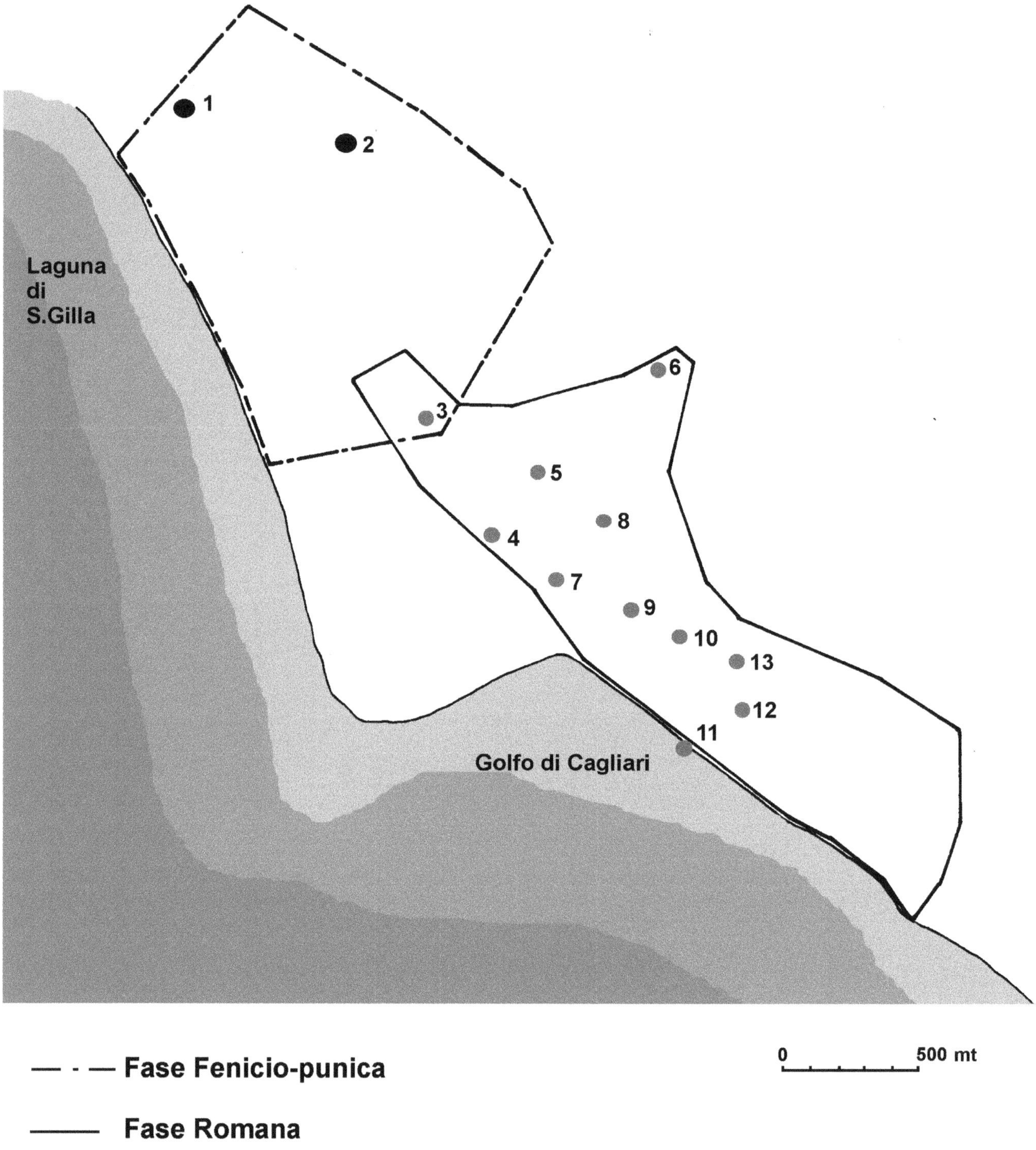

FIGURE 1. THE SITE OF CAGLIARI.
1 Phoenician-Punic settlement of via Brenta; 2 Necropolis of Tuvixeddu; 3 Lamps Workshop of via Zara; 4 Baths of Viale Trieste; 5 Houses called "Villa di Tigellio"; 6 Amphitheatre; 7 Forum (Piazza Carmine) and theatre-temple of via Malta; 8 Dump of pottery of Cripta di Santa Restituta; 9 Baths under Banca d'Italia; 10 Houses under the Church of Sant'Eulalia; 11 Supposed Site of the Harbour; 12 Fullonica; 13 Necropolis of Misenus Navy

FENICIO-PUNICO

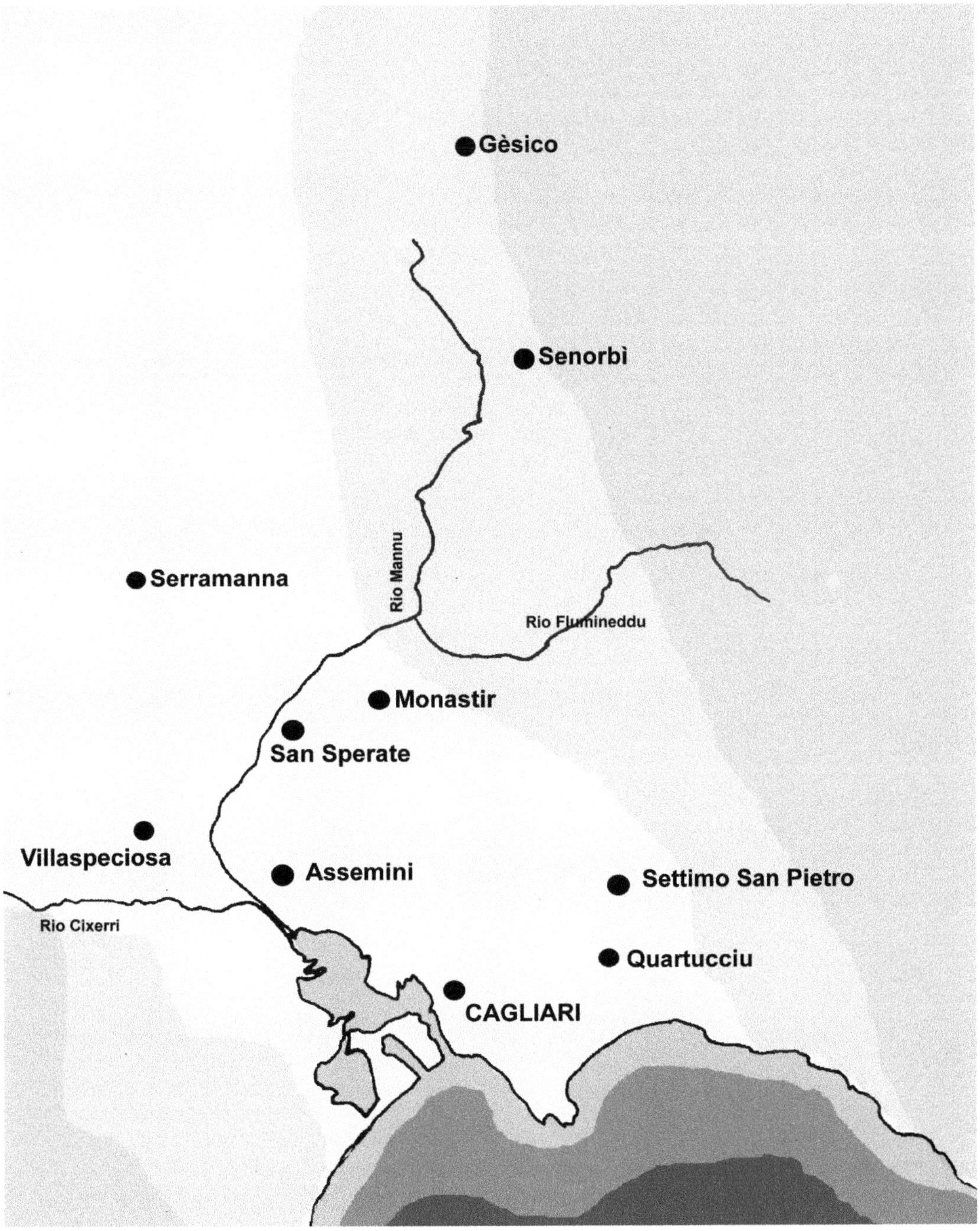

FIGURE 2. THE HINTERLAND IN PHOENICIAN-PUNIC AGE

Excavations in this sector of the built-up area in the 1980s (Tronchetti 1990; Salvi 1991; Tronchetti 1992a) have brought to light areas with dwellings and productive activities, including pottery making (findings of matrices, decantation tanks and clay deposits). In all probability, even lacking archaeometric analyses, these activities were connected with the cargoes carried by the ships or barges, in many cases composed of protomes and votive objects (Nieddu 1989; Moscati 1991); it is reasonable to suppose that productive activities were aimed not exclusively at the local market but were destined for export to other markets, which at present we are unable to locate.

If data on the built-up area are substantially few, excavations of the large Tuvixeddu necropolis help us to gain a better idea of the physiognomy and importance of Cagliari.

Starting from the beginning of the 5th century BC, the town presented a rich *facies* of imports from the Greek world, particularly Athens. Figured pottery, both black-figure and red-figure, is present in fairly small amounts and is of modest quality, especially in the case of black-figure pottery. The repertory is constantly dominated by tableware and, in the case of red-figure pottery, by receptacles for perfumed oil (Chessa 1992d, Tronchetti 1996a, 566). Of greater importance is the black-glaze Attic pottery which, starting from the end of the 5th century, became absolutely predominant. The formal repertory continues in its orientation towards kitchenware and containers for oil (*askoi-gutti*), as well as oil-lamps. Black-glaze pottery also came from the Latium area (*atelier des petites estampilles*) and Iberia (*gutti)* (Tronchetti 1985, 28-32; Tronchetti 1991a; Tronchetti 1994).

From the largest settlement, these and other materials spread to Cagliari's hinterland in a radius of some tens of kilometres, following the flatland of the southern Campidano Plain and the areas of low hills bordering it.

The massive take-over of the territory by the Carthaginians starting from the first decades of the 5th century BC, together with the serious lack of territorial analyses, makes it impossible to supply a detailed picture of the Cagliari *chora*, the exact extension of which is currently unknown. The clue to identifying the area of dependence on the town lies in the diffusion of locally produced pottery, which surely came from Cagliari; but even in this case the lack of archaeometric analyses forces us to base our ideas only on autoptic findings on clay and glaze, with all the obvious risks that this involves (Figure 2).

To mention only the most important findings, about thirty-five kilometres to the north of Cagliari the Senorbì site (the Monte Luna necropolis and the Santu Teru settlement) yielded red-figure Attic pottery starting from about 480 BC, followed by black-glaze pottery from Attica, from the *atelier des petites estampilles* and subsequently from Cagliari. Amphoras from Marseilles and Graeco-Italic amphorae mark the arrival of wine. The anonymous settlement, located in an excellent position in an area of flatlands and low hills at the beginning of a route of penetration into the more mountainous eastern interior, enjoyed a good level of prosperity, as can be seen from the fine gold jewellery of Punic and South-Italian origin (Tronchetti 1991b, 183-185) which come from Cagliari. The lack of jewels of the same kind in the vast Tuvixeddu necropolis in Cagliari is due to the fact that most of the graves were plundered in the remote past. Still farther north of Senorbì is the site at Gesico (about thirty-four kilometres from Cagliari) which has yielded Late Punic graves, with materials produced in Cagliari, and Sardinian-Punic coins minted in the 3rd century BC (Tronchetti 1997a).

To the northwest we find the very rich cemetery of Assemini (twelve kilometres from Cagliari) with numerous imports of Attic black-glaze pottery and some jewellery (unpublished excavations by Maurizia Canepa). At San Sperate (seventeen kilometres from Cagliari) a necropolis dating from the 5th to the 3rd centuries BC has been partially excavated, with the finding of Attic red-figure and black-glaze pottery, pottery produced in Cagliari and many Punic amphorae (Ugas 1993, 57-69). At the Serramanna site (twenty-seven kilometres from Cagliari) a necropolis has recently been excavated (unpublished excavations by Maurizia Canepa) with the usual materials coming from, or produced in Cagliari. Fewer traces have been found in the area of Villaspeciosa (Sanna 1984, 85-91).

To the east, even less research has been performed in any depth, owing not least to the lay of the land: the coastal area is marshy and, after a few kilometres, rises to become more and more rugged and irregular. The few investigations that have been performed have yielded no traces of frequentation in Punic times, except in Quartucciu (unpublished work by Donatella Salvi) about six kilometres from Cagliari, with modest graves dating from the 3rd century BC.

Carthaginian political attitudes in Sardinia, which were based on exploitation of the land and the widespread settling of the same, are to be seen clearly in this brief examination of Cagliari's hinterland. The coastal town represented a point of departure for distribution to the interior of fine goods such as pottery from Attica and Latium, wine and jewels, or was aimed at the less well-to-do, with the offer of "imitations" of imported black-glaze pottery manufactured, as stated previously, in the main town. On the other hand, we do not know what products left from Cagliari or what their destination was. We can only hypothesise that the harbour may have seen the exportation of the surplus food production (especially cereals) (Manfredi 1993), presumably in the direction of Carthage. It is also quite probable that Cagliari, in the light of its geographic position, was the point of departure of Sardinian mercenaries who we know were present in the Carthaginian army during the Sicilian campaign, which came to an end with the defeat at Himera in 480 BC.

Following the Roman conquest of Sardinia in 238 BC, Cagliari underwent a radical transformation which took place most probably during the first decades of the 2nd century BC. The strata excavated at the Santa Gilla Lagoon, together with those in other sectors, clearly show an eastward shift of the Roman town (Salvi 1991; Tronchetti 1992d). The centre is no longer on the lagoon and the new pole of attraction is shown strikingly by the building of the sanctuary in Via Malta, with a theatroid cavea, which dominated what has been recognised as the Forum of Roman *Carales* and which represented the nucleus of the new urban layout (Colavitti 1994). In a period that is most likely the same as that of the migration of the town's centre, the harbour also shifted, in all probability to what is now the eastern basin of today's harbour; evidence for this hypothesis is however from a later period and consists of some graves with inscribed cippi of mariners belonging to the fleet of Miseno stationed at Cagliari. These tombs, attributed to the 2nd century AD, were found at the end of the 19th century on the slope going down towards the supposed location of the Roman harbour (Figure 1).

The great importance assumed by the construction of an architectural form such as the theatre-temple in this work is beyond doubt: it reveals the conspicuous presence of Italic *negotiatores*. A fragment of an amphora sealed by *L. Lollius* bears witness to the frequentation of the *gens Lollia*, already known for their links to the sanctuaries of Delos (Colavitti 1999, 39-41); the world of trade is also represented by the Isiac statue found during excavations, even though it has been attributed to a later period (around 170 AD) (Eingartner 1991, 129-130). Among the votive offerings we find a fragment of a Campana B black-glaze cup (espéce Morel 1120) with part of an inscription *...M ADTIGI...* (Colavitti 1999, 40) which is probably linked to the material found both in the excavation of the sanctuary and in a large waste dump in the vicinity (the so-called Crypt of Santa Restituta). In Via Malta there have been found few shards of Dressel 1 amphorae, Campana A and B black-glaze pots and Iberian pottery (*sombreros de copa*) to remain in the Republican period; the rubble in the so-called Crypt of Santa Restituta contained a large amount of unstratified material. We have about two hundred shards of amphorae of Punic types Maña A, B3 and C2; nine shards of Rhodian amphorae with seals (unfortunately not published entirely) and some four hundred Dressel 1 amphoras, some of which with seals (Usai 1988, 117-121) bearing the letters *APO(LLONIUS)*, *MIIR,FLA(VIUS)*, *CK*; one Brindisi amphora has a seal with the letters*[AN]DRONICUS* (Colavitti 1999, 43). Together with the amphorae, which most clearly indicate the wine trade, there are also about seven hundred Campana A, Campana B and grayware shards of local production; compared to the others, there is a predominance of Campana B shards. Also present are some fragments of Italic-Megarian cups (also found in Via Malta and in the Tuvixeddu cemetery), thin-walled pottery and very few pieces of Italic sigillata with seals bearing the letters *ZOILI* and *L TETTI SAMIA*. Some graffiti on black-glaze pottery show a series of names which for the most part refer to the Campania and Latium regions, the same regions referred to by other epigraphic evidence found in Cagliari, as is clearly highlighted in the recent work on the Italic *negotiatores* in Sardinia (Colavitti 1999, in particular the table on page 55). The seal *SES* on a Dressel 1 amphora found in another part of Cagliari, near the forum and the theatre-temple in Via Malta, is another reference to the Etruscan area.

It is not out of place here to mention the well-known inscription in three languages (Latin, Greek and Punic) found in the interior (San Nicolò Gerrei) but commonly, and rightly, attributed to Cagliari and dated around 150 BC, in which a servile man *Cleon salari(orum) soc(iorum) s(ervus)* dedicates an altar to Aesculapius (C.I.L. X 7856). Still in the Late Roman Age we have an inscription, this time found at Donori, about twenty-five kilometres to the north of Cagliari, but no doubt to be ascribed to the latter, with names of *salt-workers* (Pani Ermini and Marinone 1981, 40, no. 53). Evidence of the *societas salariorum* at Cagliari shows that one of the most important products shipped from the Sardinian harbour, together with cereals (wheat) grown on the fertile Campidano Plain, was salt. It appears superfluous to mention the great deal of evidence on the large quantities of Sardinian wheat that were shipped to Rome, a trade mentioned by Cicero, Livy and others; the main ports from which grain reached Ostia were undoubtedly *Carales*, *Turris Libisonis* and *Olbia*. Universally known is the mosaic of a *statio* in the Piazzale delle Corporazioni in Ostia with the inscription of the *navicularii et negoziantes Karalitani*, dated between the second and third centuries AD.

Wheat-growing on the Plain must have been capillary, just as capillary is human presence in the area, to be seen from the small cemeteries and settlements in which the finding of the remains of baths, more likely in the case of small villages than of *villae*, are not infrequent.

It is not easy to indicate the farthest extension of the dependence of small and not-so-small villages in the hinterland of Cagliari; it is likely that its sphere of influence towards the north did not reach as far as today's Sardara, in ancient times known as *Aquae Neapolitanae*, with a clear reference to the town of *Neapolis*, situated in the southern part of the Gulf of Oristano; to the east the lay of the land has made investigations quite difficult, while to the west the vast Santa Gilla Lagoon, followed by an ample extension of marshes, makes it reasonable to believe that this swampy area marked the border between Cagliari and Nora, about thirty-five kilometres to the southwest (Tronchetti 1997b, 7) (Figure 3).

In this entire vast area are found imported products coming from different parts of the Mediterranean and common to the whole Roman world: from Italic sigillata to the South-Gallic to the different kinds of African red-slip ware; thin-walled pottery, lamps and commercial amphorae of the following kinds: Dressel 2/4, Dressel 20, Gallic, Tripolitan, African I and II, Late-Imperial cylindrical, Late Roman I and *spatheia*. The diffusion of such materials, both in the coastal town and throughout the hinterland, from which most of the evidence comes, makes it impossible to present a map of the distribution, which would in any case be no more than partial, in the light of the lack of published data and the continual updating of findings due mostly to contingent interventions.

We do not even know how these goods were distributed to the hinterland; that is, if the town acted as a market from which goods were sent to other settlements or if there were *nundinae aut similia* in internal settlements, or even whether the good were carried about by *circitores*. In any case, there is no doubt that the materials brought into the island and found in Cagliari's hinterland, in one way or another, came through Cagliari's harbour; *Carales* and its harbour were therefore at the head of commercial

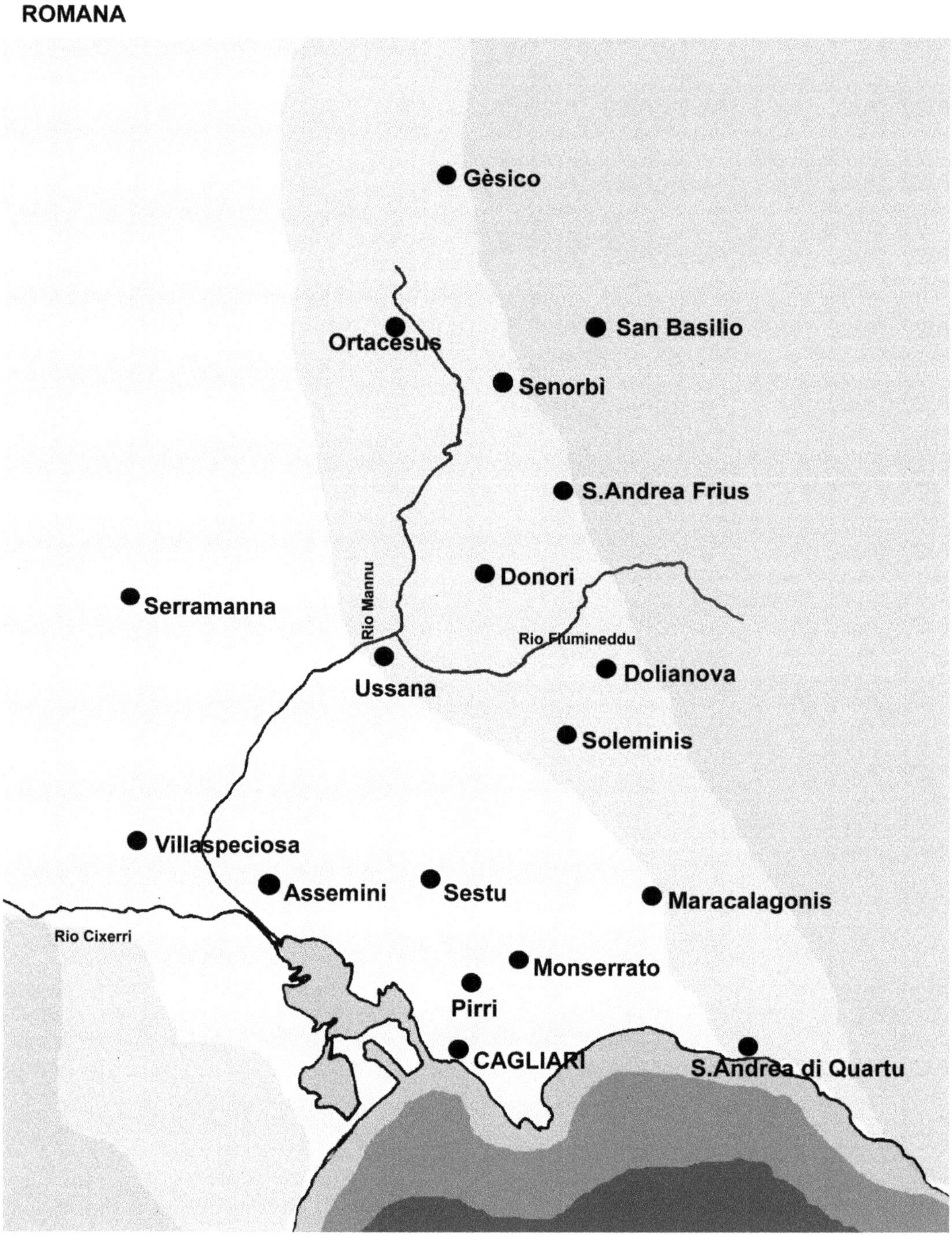

FIGURE 3. THE HINTERLAND IN ROMAN AGE

routes of two kinds: dendritic, oriented vertically, and distributive, oriented downwards (Ziccardi 2000, 139).

Although based on partial and not fully processed data, we can say that in the Imperial Age we have found, besides the Italic sigillata with the seals described above, the Late Italic (seal of *SEX. M. P.*) and the South Gallic as well. Concerning thin-walled pottery, no archaeometric investigations have ever been performed in an attempt to discover its provenance, but its shape and physical characteristics point in the direction of importations from the Etruscan, central Italic and Iberian areas.

The lack of publications on most of the excavations carried out in Cagliari in the past two decades is an obstacle to the tracing of a sufficiently homogeneous picture of the *facies* of importations at the height of the Imperial Age. We shall thus limit ourselves to reporting the presence of African red-slip ware A and D and the lamps, while the C appears to represent a small minority; on the subject of African red-slip ware we must mention, even though still unpublished, an extremely rare specimen from the workshop of *Navigius* which was found in the aforementioned Punic and Roman necropolis at Assemini. A special case of regional trade has been identified in Cagliari through the fairly conspicuous presence of so-called "fiammata" pottery (Tronchetti 1996b, 125-131), produced in Sant'Antioco between the third and fourth centuries AD with a diffusion thus far found exclusively in coastal areas, amply distributed along the southern coast of Sardinia and present at Tharros, Porto Torres and Olbia; outside the island it is represented by a single piece documented at Ostia.

In the hinterland, the examination of materials found for the most part through excavations in cemeteries, shows that fine table pottery had a fairly small market: in the first century AD. The Italic and South Gaulish sigillata were a minority compared to the production of "Sardinian" sigillata (by this term is meant the products of one or more shops that produced imitations of Italic sigillata recently identified and still under study), and again between the second and fourth centuries the African sigillata appear in substance to be the only imported products, but these were largely outnumbered by local production, this time for the most part not connected with external prototypes.

The data is even more episodic in relation to the Vandal and Byzantine epochs. We mentioned previously the presence of late commercial amphorae and also the African red-slip ware D_2 is fairly well represented in accordance with a *facies* common to the entire island, which in this period saw the arrival of fairly large numbers of African products. There is, however, a very important epigraphic document, the *lex portus*, which contains provisions on excises on goods going through the harbour of Cagliari issued by the Emperor Mauricius Tiberius (578-602) (Pani Ermini and Marinone 1981, 47, no. 77). The goods mentioned in this period, which offer an overview of the town's economic life, and in particular of its harbour, are: cereals, copper objects, cattle, vegetables and wine. The picture that emerges is that of a harbour that is still in full swing at the beginning of the seventh century AD.

References

Chessa I. 1986, *Ceramiche fenicie da Cagliari*, "Quaderni della Soprintendenza Archeologica di Cagliari e Oristano", 3, 19-25.

Chessa I. 1992a, *Lo scavo*, in Tronchetti (ed.) 1992a, 37-53.

Chessa I. 1992b, *La ceramica corinzia*, in Tronchetti (ed.) 1992a, 55-56.

Chessa I. 1992c, *La ceramica greco-orientale*, in Tronchetti (ed.) 1992a, 57.

Chessa I. 1992 d, *La ceramica attica a figure rosse*, in Tronchctti (ed.) 1992a, 62-67.

Colavitti A.M. 1994, *Ipotesi sulla struttura urbanistica di Carales romana*, in Atti del X convegno di studio "L'Africa romana ", Sassari, Editrice Archivio Fotografico Sardo, 1021-1034.

Colavitti A.M. 1999, *La presenza dei negotiatores italici nella Sardegna di età romana*, Oristano, S'Alvure.

Eingartner J. 1991, *Isis und ihre Dienerinnen in der Kunst der roemischen Kaiserzeit*, Leiden, Brill.

Manfredi L.I. 1993, *La coltura dei cereali in età punica in Sardegna e Nord-Africa*, "Quaderni della Soprintendenza Archeologica di Cagliari e Oristano", 10, 191-218.

Moscati S. 1991, *Le terrecotte figurate di S.Gilla*, Roma, Multigrafica.

Nieddu G. 1989, *Su alcuni tipi di terrecotte figurate da "Su Moguru"-S.Gilla*, "Quaderni della Soprintendenza Archeologica di Cagliari e Oristano" 6, 113-124.

Pami Ermini L. and Marinone M. 1981, *Catalogo dei materiali paleocristiani e altomedioevali del Museo Archeologico Nazionale di Cagliari*, Roma, Istituto Poligrafico dello Stato.

Salvi D. 1991, *Contributo per la ricostruzione topografica della Cagliari punica. Notizie preliminari sullo scavo di S.Gilla 1986-87*, in Atti del II Congresso Internazionale di studi fenici e punici, Roma, C.N.R., 1215-1220.

Sanna R. 1984, *Villaspeciosa. Censimento archeologico del territorio*, Cagliari, Castello.

Tronchetti C. 1985, *I Greci e la Sardegna*, "Dialoghi di Archeologia", 17-34.

Tronchetti C. 1988, *I Sardi. Traffici, relazioni, ideologie nella Sardegna arcaica*, Milano, Longanesi.

Tronchetti C. 1990, *Cagliari fenicia e punica*, Sassari, Chiarella.

Tronchetti C. 1991a, *La ceramica a vernice nera di Cagliari nel IV e III sec. a.C.: importazioni e produzioni locali*, , in Atti del II Congresso Internazionale di studi fenici e punici, Roma, C.N.R., 1271-1278.

Tronchetti 1991b, *Note di oreficeria punica*, "Quaderni della Soprintendenza Archeologica di Cagliari e Oristano", 8, 183-190.

Tronchetti C. (ed.) 1992a, *Lo scavo di via Brenta a Cagliari. I livelli fenicio-punici e romani, (= supplemento ai "Quaderni della Soprintendenza Archeologica di Cagliari e Oristano" 9)*, Cagliari.

Tronchetti C. 1992b, *La ceramica etrusca*, in Tronchetti (ed.) 1992a, 56-57.

Tronchetti C. 1992c, *L'età punica*, in Tronchetti (ed.) 1992a, 25-29.

Tronchetti C. 1992d, *L'età repubblicana*, in Tronchetti (ed.) 1992a, 30-33,

Tronchetti C. 1994, *La ceramica attica a vernice nera di IV sec. a.C. della Sardegna*, "Quaderni della Soprintendenza Archeologica di Cagliari e Oristano", 11, 165-194.

Tronchetti C. 1995, *Sardaigne*, in Krings V. (ed.), *La civilisation phénicienne et punique. Manuel de recherche (= Handbuch der Orientalistik, Erste Abteilung, Zwanzigster Band)*, Leiden-New York-Köln, Brill, 712-742.

Tronchetti C. 1996a, *The Greeks in Sardinia*, in Pugliese Carratelli G. (ed.), *The Western Greeks*, Milano,

Bompiani, 563-566.
Tronchetti 1996b, *La ceramica della Sardegna romana*, Milano, Ennerre.
Tronchetti C. 1997a, *La machaira e la kylix: note su alcune tombe puniche da Santa Lucia di Gesico (CA)*, in Acquaro E. (ed.) *Alle soglie della classicità. Il Mediterraneo tra tradizione e innovazione. Studi in onore di Sabatino Moscati*, Pisa-Roma, Istituti Editoriali e Poligrafici Internazionali, 993-1001.
Tronchetti C. 1997b, *Nora e il suo territorio in epoca romana*, Sassari, Poddighe.
Ugas G. 1993, *San Sperate dalle origini ai baroni*, Cagliari, Edizioni Della Torre.
Usai E. 1988, *Testimonianze di cultura materiale antica*, in AA.VV., *Domus et carcer Sanctae Restitutae*, Cagliari, Pisano, 107-145.
Usai E. and Zucca R. 1986, *Testimonianze archeologiche nell'area di Santa Gilla dal periodo punico all'età altomedievale*, in AA.VV., *S.Igia. Capitale Giudicale*, Pisa, ETS, 155-201.
Ziccardi A. 2000, *Il ruolo dei circuiti di mercati periodici nell'ambito del sistema di scambio dell'Italia romana*, in Lo Cascio E. (ed.), *Mercati permanenti e mercati periodici nel mondo romano*, Bari, Edipuglia, 131-148.
Zucca R. 1988, *S,Gilla. I nuovi ritrovamenti*, in Santoni V. (ed.), *Santa Gilla e Marceddì. Prime ricerche d'archeologia subacquea lagunare*, Cagliari, Trois, 20.

The Adriatic Amphora Type 1.2 Recovered from the Environment of Cartagena (Murcia, Spain)

José Pérez Ballester and Guillermo Pascual Berlanga

Abstract

This report regards about the presence of amphores type Lamboglia 2 in coastal sites, mines and shipwrecks in the area around Carthago Nova (Spain). The existence of direct relationships between this area and the North Adriatic one during the first third of the 1 century B.C. can be proved through the analysis of these sites, and the study of the stamps recorded and its parallels in Adriatic Italy and the Aegean area.

Introduction

The important presence of amphorae L-2 in the SE of Hispania, mostly in the Carthago Nova area, has been emphasised by J. Molina (1997 and 1999). He indicates that, probably, its presence proves the influence of this Roman City trade area. This hinterland may be extended approximately from Cabo de la Nao in the north of Alicante to Cabo de Gata in Almería (Molina, 1997). In the same way, he writes about the possible relationship between mines around Carthago Nova and the trade and consumption of Italic wine in the end of the 2nd century B.C. and during the first third of the 1st century B.C. The Thyrrenian wine was carried out on Dr. 1 amphorae, but the Adriatic one was carried on L-2 amphorae.

In this paper we discuss this problem and analyse the presence of L-2 amphorae in the city of Carthago Nova, in the mines of Loma de Herrerías (Mazarrón, Murcia) and Cabezo Agudo (La Unión, Murcia). We also studied Punta de Algas, Escombreras II and San Jordi shipwrecks, which are these that show an important presence of L-2 amphorae cargoes in the zone.

L-2 Amphorae found in the city of Cartagena

Molinete and Amphitheatre are the sites that provided us with an important number of Roman Republican amphorae in Carthago Nova. El Molinete is the biggest of the five hills of the ancient city. Polibius sets in this hill the Punic acropolis when he writes about the conquest of the city by Scipio.

C. Berrocal, J. Molina and G. Pascual studied amphorae from El Molinete. The whole group amounts to 1,494 fragments of diverse amphorae types. Amphorae from Apulia had a modest presence: 11.2%. The results of the study by J. Molina about relations between Thyrrenian and Adriatic amphorae reveals that 52.1% of them could be ascribed to Dr. 1 and the other 45.9% to the L-2 type. This method is applied also to other coastal sites of the SE and E of the Iberian Peninsula (Molina, 1997, 21-42).

The stamps that were recovered at El Molinete are REP·TO, SA (fig. 2.8 y 2.9) and SPA[E].

The Amphitheatre is located on the SE slope of Cerro de la Concepción where, according to Polibius, the Asklepios temple is also situated. In front of the amphitheatre there is a big square made of ancient anthropogenic layers that filled the small valley between Cerro de la Concepción and Despeñaperros. Excavations carried on in this main square between 1980 and 1991 (Pérez Ballester, Berrocal and San Martín, 1995; Pérez Ballester, 1995; Pérez Ballester and Berrocal, 1995) revealed the existence of successive habitat phases (1 and 2a). Other phases of grade layers (2b, 3, 4 and 5) have been dated between the last third of the 3rd century B.C. and 60/70 A.D.

The proportion between L-2 and Dr.1 amphorae is 4% and 96% respectively for amphorae that are theoretically contemporaneous. Percentages clearly indicate that the city of Cartagena should be considered as one large site and that the dates from it can change easily when new layers are analysed.

The study of different phases of the Amphitheatre allows us to have a more exact knowledge of the presence of Adriatic amphorae in Carthago Nova. Firstly type L-2 amphora is found in *phase 2b*. Anthropological fillings occupied the layers of this phase, and these contained materials dated to the end of the 3rd century B.C. and a great part of the 2nd century B.C. (130/120 B.C. *t.a.q.*). Thirteen rim fragments of L-2 amphorae have been recorded, which means 16.25% of the whole group of Thyrrenian and Adriatic amphorae of the same phase; all of these have a triangular rim. This characteristic and the fact of its early chronology allow us to think that these amphorae are type L-2/GrecoItalic, Baldacci I, Apani I or Group I of Bruno (Baldacci, 1972; Palazzo, 1989; Bruno, 1995, 50-55).

In phase 3, with artefacts from the 2nd century B.C. to 80/70 B.C., the percentage of amphorae type L-2 is 7.4% before Thyrrenian Dr. 1 (7 and 8 respectively).

In phase 4, with artefacts from the 2nd century B.C to 40/30 B.C., the percentage of amphorae type L-2 is 18.2% before Thyrrenian Dr. 1 amphorae.

In phase 5, with artefacts from the Augustan years to 60/70 A.D., the percentage of amphorae type L-2 is 12.5% before Thyrrenian Dr. 1 amphorae.

FIGURE 1. LOCATION OF SITES FROM MURCIA MENTIONED IN TEXT.

In short, it is possible to assert that for the Amphitheatre area the average percentages of type L-2 amphorae before Thyrrenian Dr. 1 are about 12.8%, which means they are too far from those of El Molinete. The average between both El Molinete and the Amphitheatre shows a relatively high index for amphorae type L-2 before Thyrrenian amphora type Dr.1 (29.3% and 61.7% respectively). This percentage is also present in other sites of the area, such as Loma de Herrerías, Mazarrón (49.6%) or in others located to the north, in Alicante, such as La Alcudia de Elche (44.2%), Tossal de Manises (57.6%), El Monastil de Elda (30.8%). All the above suggest the existence of an area of about 150 km near the coast where the concentration of amphorae type L.2 is the most important in the western Mediterranean.

Only one stamp was recorded before 1991; it is APPI and was impressed on a rim found in a layer of phase 3. This stamp's scarcity could be linked with the early presence of this type of amphorae in Carthago Nova, when probably the stamps of these amphorae were not common (Cipriano, 1994, 214-215).

In this paper we will also present other stamps recovered from the Amphitheatre. These were found in different excavations carried out between 1992 and 1998. The stamps are: ACAE; DAVOS; AI[... EV[... NIS[...(fig. 2.3) and Q·[.... From the same city but from an unknown provenience is another that was previously published: ABAR (Beltrán, 1970, 115).

Loma de Herrerías (Mazarrón, Murcia)

Loma de Herrerias is a settlement located near the coast, approximately 3 km away from the Mazarrón mines and 15 km. away from the city of Cartagena (fig. 1). It was a place dedicated to mineral workings, with houses in terraces that have been documented up to the top of the hill. Industrial structures, such as furnaces or storage sites, were recorded at the bottom of the hill (Ramallo, 1983).

The site was occupied between the last third of the 2nd century B.C. and the first half of the 1st century B.C., with the presence of some residual materials dating to the Augustan period. A large number of amphorae and amphora fragments of types Dr.1 and L.2 were recovered from a well, and the fill of a metal furnace provided a date, which we support, of around the middle of the 1st century B.C.

Molina studied all the 321 amphorae recovered there (Molina, 1997, 66-69). 94.5% of these could be dated between the end of the 2nd century B.C. and the first half of the 1st century B.C. (124 have been ascribed to type Dr. 1 and 136 to type L.2). Only 5.3% could be dated to the Augustan period.

The stamps found in Loma de Herrerías on L.2 amphorae are: SABINE (3 examples), SAL, ...] ALVIT, ME (M *retro*) and RVMA·C (2 examples). Belda has published other stamps recovered in Loma de Herrerías (PELLA, PA and VERSO. However, he is not precise on what type of amphora they were (Belda, 1975, 260); probably VERSO could correspond to a L. 2 amphora, but the others have a difficult interpretation.

El Cabezo Agudo (La Union, Mazarrón)

El Cabezo Agudo is located 5 km. to the north of Cartagena, beside the mines of El Cabezo Rajado (fig.1). It was excavated at the beginning of the 1940s (Fernández Avilés, 1942). For Avilés it was a settlement with houses aligned on the slope of the hill. The existence of furnaces in the area is also possible because of the high accumulation of lead, silver and copper slag in the zone. The majority of the artefacts that were found could be dated to the Republican period, and for him the site was abandoned in Augustan times, as has been documented in other sites of the mines of the Sierra de Cartagena (Domergue, 1990, 210). However the only dates for this chronology are two *asses* minted in Castulo and Gades (Vives, LXVIII. 11 and LXXIV.2) and one fragment of a volutes lamp (Avilés, 1942, 152, fig. 17). An exhaustive study of these materials reveals that the coins have to be dated to the 2nd century B.C. and that the lamp must be of another type. However a large number of Ricci G lamps and some Dr.2 were recovered. We propose that Cabezo Agudo was occupied during the 2nd century B.C. until the first half of the 1st century B.C. and probably only until the Sertorian War (80-75 B.C.).

F. Avilés writes about 14 stamps but neither specifies what type the amphorae are, nor draws them. Only with the identification of other similar stamps on amphorae L-2 listed from the area of Cartagena, helps us to pinpoint some of these containers of an Adriatic type even without knowing this beforehand. The stamps are: PLATOR (2), SABINA, SABINAN, L·PACONI, VERSO, B, GAS, NICIA, OPAL, (in Greek), SOLO, MIENTO, NAJOTO and APOLI.

Punta de Algas

Punta de Algas is a shipwreck located to the north of La Manga del Mar Menor, near one of the causeways connecting to the inner sea (fig. 1). It probably sank when it attempted to take refuge in Mar Menor. The ship lies at a depth of between 7 and 10 m (Más, 1971).

The majority of the cargo was of a type a L-2 amphora with five different variants. Approximately 50 of 500/700 amphorae were recovered. Más wrote that the rest of the cargo on the ship is dispersed in an area about 26 x 38 m However, we think that the ship was not as large as other authors state (Molina, 1997, 208), particularly if we bear in mind the cargo described before. We do not know too much about other materials transported in this ship. It is certain that a plate of Campanian C from Syracuse (Lamb. 5) and some fragments of Italic pottery were also transported.

The date postulated by J. Más for the Punta de Algas shipwreck was the second half of the 1st century B.C. Nevertheless, according to Ribera (Ribera, 1998, 353-354), and we agree, the ship must have sank in the second half of the first century B.C., since the amphorae type recorded there are quite similar to types 1 and 6 of Bruno. These are characteristic of the period between the end of the 2nd century B.C. and first decades of the 1st century B.C. (1995, 50-54 and 66-67). Even though the drawings by J. Más are not too precise, and it is not possible to make out the rims, it is sure that these are not of a triangular form. (Más, 1971, 410 fig.2). The presence of one Campanian C plate, the Italic pottery, and the study of the stamps indicate a shipwreck of about 100/80 B.C., such as those of San Jordi or Spargi.

Amphorae from Punta de Algas were marked with a repeated stamp: L·VIBI·L·C·L·LVC. To Hesnard and Gianfrotta (1989, 405) it refers to one *libertus* (L·LVC) who was *servvs comvunis* of two *patroni* associated with the business of wine trade (L·LVCEVS and L· VIBIVS). Basically, people from the LVCCEI and VIBII *gens* have been recorded in the Campanian area (Capua, Minturno and Pompeii) and also in Delos. These proofs for the existence of independent *negotiatores* in the mass production centres that loaded cargoes from different sites are actually stoppers with hallmarks of the same *gens* that have been found on Dr.1A and Dr.1B amphorae. The stamped stoppers of the libertus A·SAVFEI, recorded from the amphorae types Dr. 1A: 1B and 1C from the shipwreck Secca dei Mattoni of Ponza (Gianfrotta, 1994, 594-596), are a recent example of this.

On at least 36 of the 50 amphorae recovered in Punta de Algas, 14 different stamps have been recorded, signifying a high percentage of stamped amphorae. Julio Más published the following stamps: ABAR, CAI/GAI (3 examples), NEON, NICIA (6 examples), PLATO and PLATOQ (9 examples), ...]INA (Sabina?), S (1 example), SAL (4 examples) SIRA/ZIRA (3 examples), SPE, T·RE, TREBA, VIN. Belda (1975, 345) added A; Blázquez (1983, 65) added LVC and Desy reproduced it (1989, n. 286) where, in fact, it is a wrong interpretation of the stopper stamps described above.

Escombreras II

Escombreras II is one of the three shipwrecks that were found during the prospecting and excavation works carried out close to the island of Escombreras (fig. 1). At the moment we only know some information published as a result of an exhibition (Campillo, 1999), and through conversations with the excavators who carried out the underwater explorations, J. Pinedo and D. Alonso, to whom we are grateful for their collaboration.

It seems to be a shipwreck with a majority cargo of type Dr. 1A Thyrrenian amphorae, ten Adriatic L-2 amphorae and a pair of Brindisi-type Apani III amphorae. The cargo included a Campanian ware service of the type *Late Cales*, basically with forms Lamb. 1 and Lamb. 5, but also with some examples of Lamb. forms 2, 3 or 10. About 40 lamps of type Ricci G were recorded in the same way.

Although some of the stamps were indecipherable, other finds of L-2 amphorae were stamped: DAVOS (1), [S]IANDA[E] (1). Amphorae of type Apani III were also stamped on both handles (C·ANINI on one and SOTERIX on the other). These stamps have been interpreted as *dominus* and *servus* respectively from the Apani factory in the Brindisi area. Two of the Dr. 1 amphorae recovered still had puzzolana stoppers marked as GRAECI. The shipwreck is dated around the first half of the 1st century.

San Jordi (Mallorca)

Cerdá published the San Jordi shipwreck in 1980; in 1987 it was revised by Colls. The ship lies at a depth of 4 m in a bay to the south of Mallorca, near the coast and the little island known as Na Guardis, where a Punic factory was situated (Colls, 1987, 7-9 and 16). Because of the shallowness of the water it is quite possible that sport divers have removed some of the cargo. About 53 amphorae have been recorded: 9 of type Dr.1A, 30 of type Dr. 1C, 11 of type L-2, 2 of Greek type (Cos and Cnidos) and at least 1 of type Mañá C2.

Some black glazed Campanian ware finds from the on-board service are of prime importance among the artefacts recovered. These are four of type Lamb.1, two of types Lamb.2 and Lamb. 3, six of type Lamb. 5: F-2943, F-2566, one of types Lamb. 10, Lamb. 11 and MP. 127, whose chronology has been established between 100-80 B.C., according to Late Cales black glazed ware (late Campanian B). Among the other finds there were examples of forms Lamb. 6 and Lamb. 7, made of Campanian C ware from Syracuse, as well one oriental *lagynoi*, two *italo-megaric* bowls, and some pieces of Italic pottery.

Cerdá established the date of the shipwreck at around 100 B. C; to us (and Colls) the chronology must be between 100 and 80 B.C.

The presence of this ship in the Balearic Islands can be explained in relation to their position as a stop for the provision of water and food, or as a place of refuge; it is difficult to think of Mallorca as a commercial objective (Colls, 1987, 92-93). Likewise, it is probable that the route of the ship that sank at San Jordi began on the Thyrrenian coast, probably in Campania, and continued to the Straits of Boniface, from where it continued to the Hispanic Coast, stopping in the Balearics, where it sank. This was a well-known route in antiquity to avoid the Lyon Gulf (Molina, 1997, 211-220; Ruiz de Arbulo, 1990). A logical destination for that ship crew would have been a port to the South of Cabo de la Nau, possibly Carthago Nova.

Amphorae type L.2 had 6 different stamps on 7 amphorae: APOLO, DACVS, PLV[..., (*retro*), SA[..., SAB[..., SIRAZ and VERSO.

Stamps recovered from the environment of Cartagena

Table I shows the sites and the number of times that different stamps have been recorded in each site. This is the list of stamps (with parallels) that have been recovered from the environment of Cartagena:

ABAR[... Recorded in Punta de Algas. We know of another from the port of Cartagena (Beltrán, 1970, 115).
ACAE. (Fig. 2.2). Recovered from the Amphitheatre of Cartagena. This stamp is identical to another recorded in Montedoro (Taranto), impressed on a handle with a circular section and classified by Desy as an indeterminate type (1989, 152, n. 1184).
APOLO. Recorded in San Jordi (Colls, 1987, 48; Desy, 1989, n. 296). Two identical stamps on L-2 amphorae are known from Delos (Desy, 1989, n.325 and 326) and another from Narona (Croatia), but in this case the affiliation also appears: APOLO·F (Blanc-Bijon, 1998, n. 602). From Monte Erice one APOLONI on type L-2 was found (Desy, 1989, n. 213). Clearly it is a *nomen* that must be not confused with stamps where it is abbreviated or with the ones that have two L: APOL, APOLLO, APOLLON, which are frequent on other types of amphorae and can be referred to Apollonides, Apollonius etc. (Bruno, 1995, 172).
APPI. Recovered in phase 3 of the Cartagena Amphitheatre (before 80/70 B.C.), in Grao Vell (Sagunto), and recorded on another APPI stamp (Aranegui, 1982, 154, lám. 1,1). Bruno (1995, 123) recorded another identical stamp from Magdalensberg, probably recovered in the Roman Republican layers of this Germanic settlement.
CAI/GAI. Three examples recovered in the Punta de Algas shipwreck. Other similar stamps on L-2 amphora have been recorded in Torre la Sal, Castellón ([G]AII, Blázquez, 1983, 59) and in Exmés, France (GAI in Greek, Desy, 1989, n. 236).
DACVS. Listed in San Jordi. There is another similar stamp on L-2 amphorae in Denia, Alicante (Gisbert, 1998, 386, fig. 3, 5-6). Outside Spain it has been recorded

FIGURE 2. STAMPS FOUND IN THE AREA OF CARTHAGO NOVA.

in Peripato (Taranto), Sevegliano (Adriatic coast of Italy) and in Delos (Desy, 1989, 56, 153 and 328).

DAVOS. (Fig. 2.4). Recorded on L-2 amphorae in Cartagena Amphitheatre (*retro*) and in the Escombreras II shipwreck. **L·PACONI.** Recorded in Cabezo Agudo. Fernández Avilés writes about another stamp found in Tarragona that probably refers to a person from the same gens: this stamp is Q·PACO[... (1942, 148, C.I.L. II, 4970, 366). Beltran described a L·PACONI stamp on Dr. 1 amphorae found in Mesas de Asta (Jerez) (1970, 156, n. 240b). The frequent presence of people of this *gens* on pottery stamps since the 3rd century B.C. was emphasised by Bruno when writing about an identical stamp on amphorae L-2 found in Milan (1955, 223-224). On the one hand he writes that one Q. Paconius, who had lands and vineyards in the 1st century B.C., has been recorded on black glazed Cales ware, Dr. 1, L-2 and Dr. 6 amphorae, even though on Terra sigillata ware. On the other hand, people from the same *gens* have been recorded in the East and in Greece, always related to business activities. Pedroni (unpublished) has done exhaustive research on this *gens* of Cales origin. In this way this *gens* has been especially recorded in Delos in the late Roman Republican period. The stamp that we show here could also be related to a Dr. 1 amphora, but the stamp recorded in Milan on a L-2 amphora allows us to include it in our list.

LVIPOR. (Fig. 2.5). Recorded in the Amphitheatre area (EU: 20515, 1988); it is difficult to read. Some VIPOR stamps are known on Brindisi amphorae recovered in Ampurias (Beltrán, 1970, 196, n. 486). Other stamps of this type have been recorded in Marmorelle and in the Giancola factories that were active about 50 B.C. and were located near Brindisi (Manacorda, 1994, 4-9; Desy, 1989, n. 977). Another reference to this stamp was recorded on L-2 amphorae found on Hvar (Croatia): AOLIPOR (*retro*) (Blanc-Bijon, 1998, n. 600).

ME. Recorded in Loma de Herrerías. The M is inverted (*retro*). Probably the punch used to print this stamp was used to print others recorded in Montedoro (Taranto), Margherita de Savoia (Puglia) (Blanc-Bijon, 1998, n. 651) and in Via Falcone (Milan), always on L-2 amphorae and all of these dated to the 1st century B.C. Other similar stamps have been recorded in Syracuse and Mont Beuvray (Bruno, 1995, 235). Finally, the stamps ME/METR, LVC and RVMA that have been interpreted by Manacorda as servi of M·BETILIENI, even though they do not have a stratigraphic context and were made in the factory of La Rosa, near Brindisi, are frequent (Manacorda, 1994, 30).

NICIA. Recorded alone, with a palm or with another imprint of a gem where is represented *Nike* wearing a crown. This stamp has been recorded in Punta de Algas (6) and in Cabezo Agudo. Outside Spain it has been recorded in the north of the Adriatic Sea: Aquileia (3), Dortona and Marano-Lagunare (Bruno, 1995, 142; Blanc-Bijon, 1998, n. 664 and 665) and in the East Mediterranean Sea: Alexandria, Athens and Delos (3 examples dated before 80 B.C.) (Desy, 1989, n. 349, 350 and 359). The same stamp has also been found on oval amphorae produced in Piceno (Cipriano and Carre, 1989, 77), which allows us to consider a north Adriatic, or central Adriatic origin.

PLATO. 8 examples of PLATO and 1 of PLATQ stamps on L-2 amphorae were found in Punta de Algas. Likewise 1 PLATOR has been recorded in Cabezo Agudo; and another in Elche (Márquez y Molina, 2001, 123, n. 17). Outside Spain we only find one PLATO, in Fos Gulf, on a L-2 amphora (Amar and Liou, 1984, 142), and probably another which was listed in Dertona (Blanc-

STAMP	Cartagena	Escombreras II	Cabezo Agudo	Punta de Algas	Loma de Herrerías	San Jordi
A				1		
ABAR	1			1		
ACAE	1					
APOLO						1
APPI	1					
CAI/GAI				3		
DACVS						1
DAVOS	1	1				
GAS			1			
L.PACONI			1			
LVIPOR/LNPOR	1					
ME					1	
NEON				1		
NICIA			1	6		
PLATO/PLATOR			1	9		
REP.TO	1					
RVMA.C					2	
SA	1					
SABINA/E			2	1?	3	1?
SAL				4	1	
[S]IANDA[E]		1				
SIRA/ZIRA/ZIRAS			2	3		1
SPA[E]	1					
SPE				1		
T.RE/REC				2		
TREBA				1		
VERSO			1		1	1
VIN/VINI				1		
AI[...	1					
B[...			1			
EV[...?	1					
NIS[...	1					
PLV[...						1
Q·[...	1					
SA[...						1
...]ALVIT				1	1	

TABLE I. LIST OF STAMPS RECOVERED FROM THE ENVIRONMENT OF CARTAGENA AND THE NUMBER OF TIMES THAT DIFFERENT STAMPS HAVE BEEN RECORDED IN EACH SITE.

Bijou, 1989, n. 676).

RVMA·C. 2 examples recorded in Loma de Herrerías. Surely it corresponds to one of the slaves of M·BETILIENI. ME·RVMA RVMA·C are stamps that have been recorded on the Adriatic coast: Aquileia, Rivigiano (Gomezel, 1994, 533; Bruno, 1995, 145), also in Taranto, Montedoro (Desy, 1989, n.52) and in Rome. Another stamp [RVM]ABETIL[IENI] was recorded in Mesas de Asta (Jerez), which seems to have been made in the same factory at La Rosa, even though Beltrán thought that it was impressed on a Dr. 20 amphora (Beltrán, 1970, 115). This stamp has also been recorded in Narbone and Ensérune (Desy, 1989, n. 69 and 946). RVMA is a stamp that has been found on different types of Adriatic amphorae, specifically on L-2 and oval Brindisi amphorae (Cipriano, 1994, 213).

SABINA/E. This stamp has been recorded in Cabezo Agudo and Loma de Herrerías. It is also possible that the stamps ...] INA from Punta de Algas and SAB [... from San Jordi were referred to SABINA. Outside Spain SABIN[... has been recorded in Peripato, Taranto (Desy, 1989, 296, n°. 58). The SABINA *nomen* is usual on other types of amphorae, such as Dr.1 (Hesnard and Carre, 1998, 296), on oval Brindisi amphora recorded in Ensérune and Narbone (Desy, 1989, n°. 947 and n°. 960), examples of Dr. 20 recorded in Acinipo and Testaccio, or on indeterminate amphorae recorded in Tarragona (Fernández de Avilés, 1942, 148).

SAL. This stamp has been documented in Punta de Algas and Loma de Herrerías. SAL stamps also have been recorded in the shipwreck of la Ciotat, one on a L. 2 amphora (Bouches du Rône) and another on an indeterminate amphora recovered in Alexandria, which probably is a L.2 type (Desy, 1989, n°. 266 and n°. 1272).

SIRA/ZIRA/SIRAZ. Punta de Algas, SIRA/ZIRA (3); San Jordi, SIRAZ/ZIRAZ (1); Cabezo Agudo, ZIRA/NIRA (2); another was recorded in Elche, the ancient Ilici (Márquez y Molina, 2001, 127, n. 21). Outside Spain we have only recorded one ZIRA in Athens (Desy, 1989, n°. 319).

SPA [... (Fig. 2.6) (*retro*). Cerro de El Molinete (1). It could be read as SPA[E]. Same stamps have been recorded in Brindisi and Taranto (Desy, 1989, nº. 40 and nº. 66).
SPE. Punta de Algas (1). Outside Spain this stamp has been recorded in Santa Lucía (Taranto) and also in the destruction layers, dated to 86 B.C., which were documented in Athens (Desy, 1989, nº. 67 and nº. 317).
TREBA. Punta de Algas (1); Valentia 1 stamp recovered in the destruction layers of the city (destroyed by Pompey in 75 B.C.) (López et *alii,* 1994, 94-95; Ribera, 1987, 123). Outside Spain this stamp has been recorded in Aquileia (1) (Bruno, 1995, 149) and in Delos (5) (Desy, 1989, nº. 354 and nº. 355).
VERSO. This is one of the most usual stamps recorded on the Mediterranean Spanish coasts. Cabezo Agudo (1); Loma de Herrerías (1); San Jordi (2), Villaricos (Almería) and in Les Sorres (Barcelona) (Desy, 1989, nº. 302 and nº. 358). It is also especially common on the north Adriatic coasts of Italy, in the Po Valley (Ivrea, Altino, Milan (2), and on the Ilyrian coasts (Dyrrachion and Kryemdhej) (Bruno, 1995, 150; Faccini, 2000; Blanc-Bijon, 1998, nº. 691; Desy, 1989, 116 and 118).

At least 3 different punches of VERSO stamp of Illyrian origin have been recorded. Bruno (1995, 69-72) mentions that one of these stamps is marked on a L.2, group 7 amphora dated to the second half of the 1st century B. C.; the example from Ivrea has been dated to the middle of the 1st century B.C. He also studied a VERSO stamp that was recorded on an oval Brindisi amphora recovered at Luni. All the above data offer a further approach to the variability of punches, chronologies and origins of this usual stamp.

AI[... (Fig. 2.1) Cartagena Amphitheatre (1 example, which could be read as AIDI); Belo (1 example, which is also difficult to be read) (Desy, 1989, 53, nº. 276).
S]IANDA[E. Escombreras II (1). Outside Spain this stamp has only been recorded in Lombardia, in Milan (2 on L.2 amphorae) and in Lodi (1 example on an indeterminate amphora).
EV[... Cartagena Amphitheatre (1 example on a handle fragment, which probably was part of a Brindisi amphora). No stamp starting with EV is recorded on L.2 amphorae. But these letters have been recorded on oval amphorae from the Apani factory EVTVC, EVTYCHI in Brindisi (Desy, 1989, nº. 490-492).
Q·[... (Fig. 2.7). Cartagena Amphitheatre (1 example recovered from EU 30557, which is part of the name of a freeman or a *libertus nomen* (QUINTVS). In Sa Nau Perduda (Foerster and Pascual, 1970, 290) and Cremona (Bruno, 1995, 254) stamps only with a Q. have been found. However, Q· as a *praenomen* has also been recorded in Bouthrote, Albania (Q·FA, Desy, 1989, nº. 99), in Milan (Q·AQU[..., Bruno, 1995, 255-256) or from Marano Lagunare, Friuli-Venezia (Q[..., Blanc-Bijon, 1998, nº. 679).

The chronology

If we bear in mind only the context of the shipwrecks in which these stamps have been recorded and the anthroponomy, it is very difficult to date some stamps or L-2 amphorae. The reuse of this type of amphora containing other products such as puzzolana in the La Chretienne A shipwreck (Gianfrotta and Hesnard, 1989, 398), sand, nuts and raisins in the Pisa ship B (Bruni, 2000, 42-43), or resin from the Cap Caveaux shipwreck (Long, 1998, 341-343) is well known. Another example of the reuse of this type of amphora has been documented in the Planier 3 shipwreck, where a chronological difference exists of about 30/40 years between the L-2 amphorae and the rest of the cargo (Panella, 1998, 548-549). The same chronological difference has been noted for the L-2 amphorae listed for Cap Caveaux 1 and Pisa ship B, both dated to the Augustan period.

The majority of names stamped on L-2 amphorae have a slave origin. Generally these names are *nomina* alone, or appear abbreviated, many of these people are of Greek origin and the stamps with these names appear on other types of amphora from different periods and origins, such as SABINA or VERSO.

In the area of Cartagena we checked four terrestrial and three underwater sites where stamps on L-2 amphorae have been recorded. Their chronology is the following:

El Molinete (Cartagena)	without a precise date
Amphitheatre (Cartagena)	before 80/70 B.C.
Loma de Herrerías (Mazarrón)	first half of the 1st century B.C.
Cabezo Agudo (La Unión)	first third of the 1st century B.C.
Punta de Algas (S. Pedro del Pinatar)	first third of the 1st century B.C.
Escombreras II (Cartagena)	first half of the 1st century B.C.
Sant Jordi (Mallorca)	first fourth of the 1st century B.C.

We have other chronological references from various sites where similar stamps have been recorded:

Delos. Previous or contemporary phases to 80 B.C. (DACVS, VERSO and TREBA)
Athens. From the Sulla destruction layers of 86 B.C. (SPE and may be ZIRA)
Valentia. From the Pompey destruction layers of 75 B.C. (TREBA)
Ivrea. From the layer of the 50 B.C. (VERSO)
Milan. In Via Falcone store dated to the 1st century B.C. (ME and L·PACONI)

In this way, we think it possible to date some of the described stamps to a time before, or contemporary to 80/70 B.C.:

APPI, which was recovered from phase 3 of the

Cartagena Amphitheatre;
DACVS, SAB[... SIRA/ZIRA, VERSO, recovered from the San Jordi shipwreck;
SABINA, GAS, NICIA, PLATOR, ZIRA, VERSO and L·PACONI?, listed in Cabezo Agudo;
ABAR, CAI/GAI, NEON, NICIA, PLATO, PLATOQ, ...]INA (Sabina?), SAL, SIRA/ZIRA, SPE, TREBA, recorded in Punta de Algas;
And SABINE, SAL, ME, RVMA·C and VERSO, catalogued in Loma de Herrerías.

The contrast of these archaeological contexts confirms to us the earliest chronology that was postulated for the Punta de Algas shipwreck. In the same way parallels of the stamps discovered in the Adriatic Sea (NICIA, PLATO, SAL, TREBA), or in regions such as Delos or the Spanish coast (SIRA/ZIRA, CAI/GAI, SPE), could indicate a possible central- or mid-Adriatic origin for the ship that sank in Punta de Algas.

We want to pay special attention to the VERSO stamp that is so frequent along the Spanish coasts. It seems clear that different persons used this stamp over a long period of time (from the beginning of the 1st century B.C. to Augustan ages on L-2 amphora and on other types of Adriatic amphorae).

The ME stamps recorded in Loma de Herrerías, and L·PACONI in Cabezo Agudo (if it is on a L-2 amphora), are nowadays vaguely dated to the 1st century B.C., thanks to the Via Falcone depot. We think that L·PACONI is a person, related to the *gens* PACONIA from Cales, who was involved with wine production and trade in the first third of the 1st century B.C.

The examples of RVMA·C stamps catalogued in Loma de Herrerías may help us to date the factory of M·BETILIENI in La Rosa (Brindisi) (Manacorda, 1994; Cipriano, 1994), which probably was in operation from the beginning of the 1st century B.C. For the moment, both RVMA·C and LVIPOR, are two of the rare indicators of links between Carthago Nova and the factories of Brindisi. The majority of the stamps recorded came from the mid-Adriatic (Piceno) or north Adriatic coasts (Adria-Venezia).

Other stamps from the same locations

Not to mention San Jordi, there are a total of 34 different stamps catalogued on L-2 amphora, representing one of the highest concentrations of these types of amphorae and stamps recorded in the western Mediterranean (Table I).

More interesting is the fact that some of the studied stamps have been recorded on different sites. Six different stamps catalogued in Punta de Algas were also listed in Cartagena (ABAR), Loma de Herrerías (SABINA, SAL, SIRA/ZIRA) and Cabezo Agudo (NICIA, PLATO, SABINA, ZIRA). In the same way, SIRA/ZIRA and VERSO have been recorded in San Jordi; the latter was also listed in Cabezo Agudo and Loma de Herrerías. PLATO and SIRA have also been recorded in Elche. What does this phenomenon tell us?

On the one hand, as we have shown, the majority of the sites may be dated to the first half of the 1st century B.C., more probably in the first quarter of this century, except for Loma de Herrerías. After the systematic prospecting carried out in Loma de Herrerías and Cabezo Agudo, it has been possible to demonstrate a very high percentage of amphorae type L.2 in the Mazarrón and Cartagena mining areas. Both sites are settlements and both were involved in processing minerals from the nearby mines. On the other hand, the data recorded in Cartagena varies from one excavated area to another (Cerro de El Molinete or The Amphitheatre); this confirms a middle/high percentage of L.2 amphorae in one of the most important redistribution ports of Hispania at the time.

Wine, mineral and slaves

At least 35/37 of the shipwrecks listed in the Mediterranean were transporting substantial cargos of amphorae type L-2. 60% (23) of these have been recorded in the Adriatic (Illyria and Dalmatia). On Sicily and the nearby islands 4 have been listed, in the Aegean, which was the traditional destination of Adriatic wines, only 2 cargoes of L-2 amphorae have been recovered. 1 in the Straits of Boniface, and approximately 4/6 shipwrecks of this type have been recorded in the western Mediterranean and along coasts of Spain.

Amphorae type L-2 was more produced in the northern and mid-Adriatic area (Adria-Venezia) than in Apulia (Cipriano and Carre, 1989, 80-55; Panella, 1998, 545). In 1986, Tchernia drew attention to the fact that L-2 amphorae were the most suitable and comprised the cargo that accompanied slaves, marble, and works of art from the eastern Mediterranean to Rome. Panella proposed that the abundant presence of shipwrecks with L-2 cargoes along the coasts of Croatia and Albania coasts testified to the exchange of wine for slaves, pelts, and livestock (Panella, 1989, 550). It would be easy to explain the presence of Italic wine (Thyrrenian and Adriatic) in such a centre of redistribution as the port of Carthago Nova, especially if we think of the fact that at this time the city was in a period of expanding economy and the silver mines were at their most productive. In the same way, as Molina has proved, it is easy to justify the direct arrival of ships to Carthago Nova from the Adriatic (Molina, 1997, 219-222). However, to explain why L-2 amphorae are concentrated in specific areas around the mines of Cartagena, and at some of the principal coastal points between Cartagena and Cabo de San Antonio (off Ibiza), is quite difficult. On the one hand, Molina suggests that Italic-Adriatic ships went with slaves from Delos to Adriatic ports, such as Brindisi and Taranto, where the human cargo was exchanged for wine to transport to Hispania (Carthago Nova). In Hispania they exchanged this wine for minerals (first silver and later lead) to

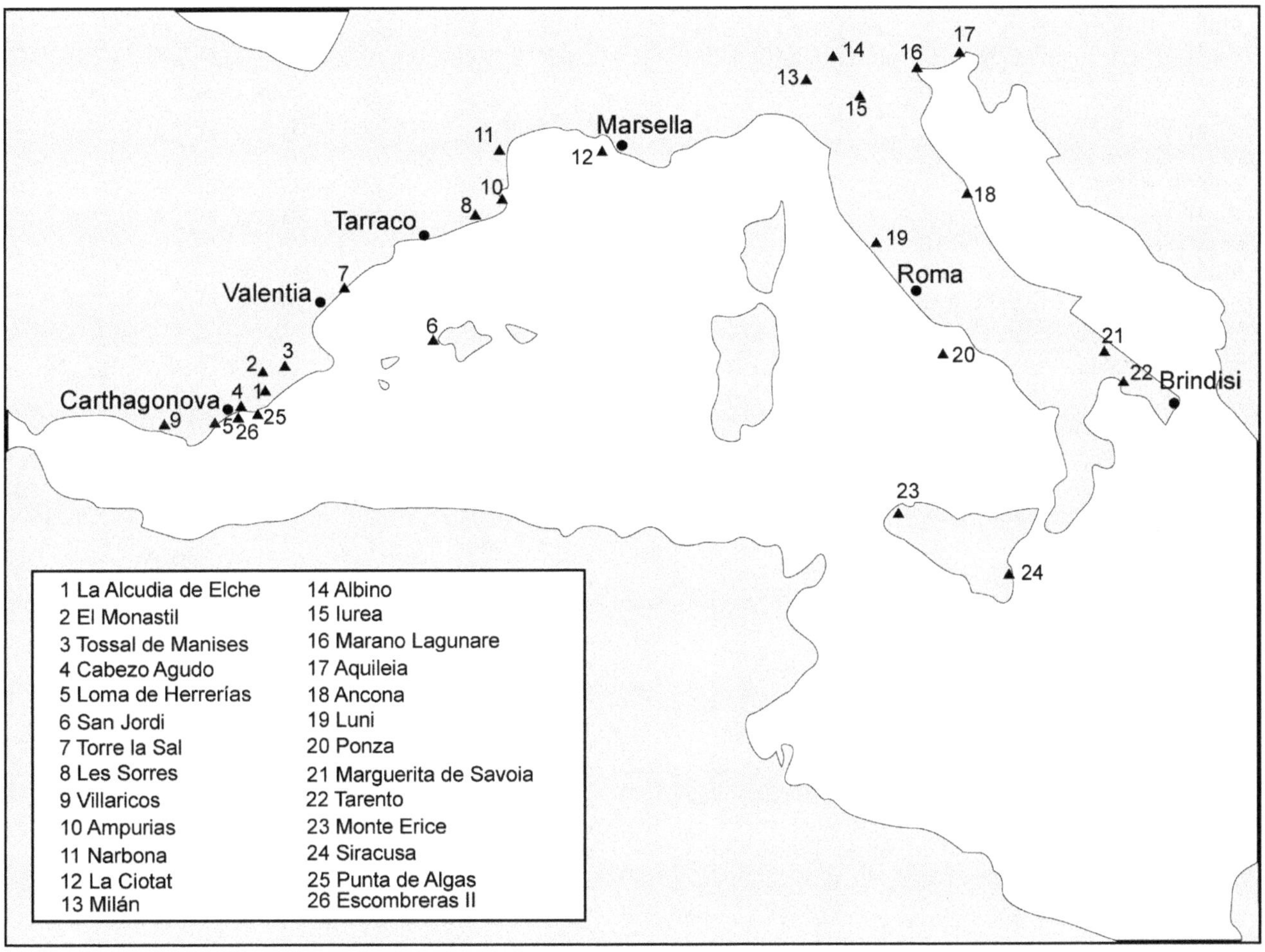

FIGURE 3. SITES MENTIONED IN TEXT.

transport to the Italic ports. On the other hand, he suggested that the coast described was under the commercial control of Carthago Nova and its coastal shipping (Molina, 1999, 523).

The frequent presence in Carthago Nova of eastern pottery and other objects (white painted *lagynoi*, Hellenistic bowls with reliefs, Rhodian amphorae, etc.) which are also common on Delos (Pérez Ballester, 1994; *idem*, 1998), allows Molina to form a direct link between Carthago Nova and Delos, via Brindisi or Taranto, at least if we compare this with other cities of the western Mediterranean; for him the slaves, Apulian wine, and the trade in metals from Carthago Nova are the same phenomenon (Molina, 1999, 523).

The relationship between the mine workings, undertaken by slaves, and the consumption of wine is obvious. On the one hand it is possible that wine was exchanged for labour or materials (Pérez Ballester, 1988, 255), or, of course, the wine could have been be used as an energetic stimulant for the workers (Molina, 1999, 521). The majority of the sites around the Carthago Nova mines have a predominant percentage of Thyrrenian Dr.1 amphorae. However, only at certain sites is a high percentage of Adriatic amphorae listed (Cabezo Agudo and Loma de Herrerías). This must be put in relation with a very precise intention that may be related to the Italic *publicani* who had properties in the Adriatic area and economic interests in the Carthago Nova mines; this might be possible, but a full study of the Republican prosopography of the Cartagena area is necessary (Abascal and Ramallo, 1997). However, we do not have to exaggerate the presence of Adriatic merchants in Carthago Nova. It is necessary to understand this presence within the important EW and WE commercial traffic that developed between Hispania Citerior and Italy from the end of the 2nd century B.C. to the first half of the 1st century B.C.

References

Abascal, J.M. and Ramallo, S., 1997, *La ciudad de Carthago Nova: la documentación epigráfica.* Murcia.

Amar, G., and Liou, B., 1984, Les estampilles sur amphores du Golfe de Fos, *Archaeonautica*, 4, 145-211.

Aranegui Gascó, C., 1982, Las ánforas del tipo Lamboglia 2" en el País Valenciano, in *Estudios dedicados a Juan Peset Aleixandre*. Universidad de Valencia, Valencia, 153-158.

Baldacci, P., 1972, Importazioni cisalpine e produzione apule, in Recherches sur les amphores romaines, *Mélanges École Fr. de Rome*, suppl.10, Rome, 7-28.

Belda, C., 1975, *El proceso de romanización en la provincia de Murcia*, Murcia.

Beltrán Lloris, M., 1970, *Las ánforas romanas en España*, Zaragoza.

Blanc-Bijon, V. et alii, 1998, *Recueil de timbres sur amphores romaines*. II. Travaux du Centre Camille Julian, 20, Aix-en-Provence.

Blázquez, J.M., 1983, Ultimas aportaciones a los problemas de la producción y comercio del aceite en la Antigüedad, in *IV Congreso Internacional "Producción y comercio del aceite en la Antigüedad"*, Sevilla, 19-99.

Bruno, B., 1995, *Aspetti di storia economica della Cisalpina romana. Le anfore di tipo Lamboglia 2 rinvenute in Lombardia,* Studi e Ricerche sulla Gallia Cisalpina, 7, Roma.

Campillo, R., 1999, *Metamorfosis. El Puerto de Cartagena ante el Tercer Milenio* (Catálogo de la Exposición), Madrid.

Carre, M.B. et alii, 1995, *Recueil de timbres sur amphores romaines*. I. Traveaux Centre Camille Julian, 16, Aix-en-Provence.

Cerdá, D., 1980, *La nave romano-republicana de la Colonia de Sant Jordi (Ses Salines, Mallorca)*, Palma de Mallorca.

Cipriano, M.T., 1994, La raccolta sulle anfore italiche trovate in Italia, in Epigrafia della produzione e della distribuzione, *Coll. de l'École Fr. de Rome*, 193, Rome, 205-218.

Cipriano, M.T., and Carre, M.B., 1989, Production et typologie des amphores sur la côte adriatique de l'Italie, in *Amphores Romaines et Histoire Economique*, (Siena, 1986), Paris, 67-104.

Colls, D., 1987, *L'épave de la Colonia de Sant Jordi 1*, Publ. Centre P. Paris, 16, Paris.

Desy, Ph., 1989, *Les timbres amphoriques de l'Apulie républicaine,* B.A.R. International Series 554, Oxford.

Domergue, Cl., 1990, *Les mines de la péninsule Ibérique dans l'Antiquité Romaine*, Coll. de l'École Fr. de Rome, 127, Roma.

Facchini, G.F., 2000, Aspetti del commercio nella Cisalpina Romana tra l'età repubblicana e l'età augustea, in *Atti Convegno "Milano tra l'età repubblicana e l'età augustea"*, Milano, 255-274.

Fernández de Avilés, A., 1942, El poblado minero iberorromano del Cabezo Agudo, en La Unión, *Archivo Español de Arqueología*, XV, 46, Madrid, 136-152.

Foerster, F., and Pascual, R., 1970, La nave romana de "Sa Nau Perduda", *Rivista di Studi Liguri*, XXVI, 1-3, 273-306.

Gianfrotta, G.P., 1994, Note di epigrafia maritima, in Epigrafia della produzione e della distribuzione, *Coll. de l'École Fr. de Rome*, 193, Rome, 591-608.

Gianfrotta, P., and Hesnard, A., 1989, Les bouchons d'amphore en pouzzolane, in *Amphores Romaines et Histoire Economique,* (Siena, 1986), Coll. De l'École Fr. de Rome, 114, Paris, 393-441.

Gisbert, J., 1998, Anfores i vi del territorium de Dianium (Denia), in *El Vi à l'Antiguitat*, 2, Museu de Badalona, Badalona, 383-418.

Gomezel, C, 1994, Nuovi bolli su anfora dal territorio aquileiese, in Epigrafia della produzione e della distribuzione, *Coll. de l'École Fr. de Rome*, 193, Rome, 525-541.

Hesnard, A., and Carre, M.B., 1998, Les timbres DIO... sur amphores Dr.1 et Lamb. 2, in Blanc-Bijon, V. *et alii, Recueil de timbres sur amphores romaines.* II. Travaux du Centre Camille Julian, 20, Aix-en-Provence, 295-299.

Hesnard, A., and Gianfrotta, P., 1989, Les bouchons d'amphores en pouzzolane, in *Amphores Romaines et Histoire Economique*, (Siena, 1986), Paris, 394-441.

Long, L., 1998, Lvcivs Volteivs et l'amphore de 4° type. Découverte d'une amphore atypique dans une épave en baie de Marseille, in *El Ví a l'Antiguitat, 2*, Museu de Badalona, 341-349.

López, I., Marín, C., et alii, 1994, *Hallazgos arqueológicos en el Palau de Les Corts*, Valencia.

Manacorda, D., 1988, Per un studio dei centri produttori delle anfore brindisine, in C. Morangio (ed.), *La Puglia in età repubblicana*, Galatina (Lecce), 91-117.

Manacorda, D., 1994, Produzione agricola, produzione ceramica e proprietà della terra nella Calabria romana tra Repubblica e Impero, in *Epigrafia della produzione e della distribuzione*, Coll. de l'École Fr. de Rome, 193, Rome, 3-59.

Márquez, J.C y Molina, J., 2001, *El comercio en el territorio de Ilici*. Universidad de Alicante. Alicante.

Mas, J., 1971, La nave romana de Punta de Algas, *Noticiario Arqueológico Hispánico*, XIII-XIV, Madrid, 402-427.

Mas, J., 1985, Excavaciones en el yacimiento submarino de San Ferreol (Costa de Cartagena), in *Actas del VI Congreso Internacional de Arqueología Submarina* (Cartagena, 1982), Madrid, 189-224.

Molina, J., 1997, *La dinámica comercial romana entre Italia e Hispania Citerior*, Inst. de Cultura Juan Gil Albert, Alicante.

Molina, J., 1999, Vinculaciones entre Apulia y el área de influencia de Carthago Nova en época tardorepublicana, *Latomus*, 58, fasc.3, Bruxelles, 509-524.

Parker, A.J., 1992, *Ancient Schipwrecks of the Mediterranean and the Roman Provinces*, B.A.R. International Series, 580, Oxford.

Panella, Cl., 1998, Anfore e Archeologia Subacquea, in G. Volpe (ed.), Archeologia Subacquea, Univ. de Siena, Firenze, 531-559.

Pedroni, L. (En prensa), *Ceramica calena a vernice nera. Produzione e diffusione*, Napoli.

Pérez Ballester, J., 1994, Asociaciones de lagynoi, boles de relieves y ánforas rodias en contextos mediterráneos (siglos II y I a.C.), *Huelva Arqueológica,* XIII, 2, Huelva, 347-366.

Pérez Ballester, J., 1995, La actividad comercial y el registro arqueológico en la Carthago Nova republicana. Los hallazgos del área del Anfiteatro, *Verdolay*, 7, Murcia, 339-349.

Pérez Ballester, J., 1998, El "Portus" de *Carthago Nova*. Sociedad y comercio tardo-helenísticos, in Pérez Ballester and Pascual (Coords.), *Actas III Jornadas de Arqueología Subacuática*, Valencia, 249-262.

Pérez Ballester, J., and Berrocal, C., 1995, Prospecciones geofísicas en el Anfiteatro de Cartagena y la Plaza del Hospital. La campaña de excavaciones de 1990, *Memorias de Arqueología,* 5 (1991), Murcia, 188-202.

Pérez Ballester, J., San Martín, P., and Berrocal, C., 1995, *El Anfiteatro Romano de Cartagena*, in *El Anfiteatro en la Hispania Romana*, Mérida, 91-118.

Pesavento, S. et alii, 2000, *Anfore della nave B*, in C. Bruni (ed.), *Le Navi Antiche di Pisa*, Firenze, 131-134.

Ramallo, S., 1983, *El horno romano de fundición de la Loma de Herrerías (Mazarrón, Murcia), I. Estudio histórico arqueológico*, XVI Congreso Nacional de Arqueología, Zaragoza, 925-936.

Ramallo, S., 1985, *Mosaicos Romanos de Carthago Nova*, Murcia.

Ribera, A., 1998, *La fundació de València*, Inst. Alfons El Magnánim, Valencia.

Ruiz de Arbulo, J., 1990, *Rutas marítimas y colonizaciones en la Península Ibérica*, "Itálica", 18, Madrid, 79-115.

Tchernia, A, 1986, *Le vin de l'Italie romaine*, Roma.

Volpe, G., 1988, *Primi dati sulla circolazione delle anfore repubblicane nella Puglia Settentrionale*, in C. Morangio (ed.), *La Puglia in età repubblicana*, Galatina (Lecce), 77-90.

Two major trading routes of the Roman Antiquity in Southern Gaul: The Narbonne-Toulouse road and the Rhône way towards Arles

Alexis Gorgues, L. Long, Christian Rico

Abstract
This paper gives the present state of research and reflects on the conditions that led to the development of the two most important commercial axes of Southern Gaul in the Roman period: the Narbonne-Toulouse route, which was the main axis for the penetration of Italic then Hispanic wine into inner Gaul and the Rhône route towards Arles, which was the gateway to the north and the important markets of the military camps on the Rhine.

Narbonne and Arles, two cities with a different background, are in the heart of the two main networks of great Mediterranean commerce set up with the Roman conquest of Southern Gaul. Even if their geographical location is different (the former on the coast, the latter more continental), they nevertheless function in a similar way, as two exchange bases strategically located between the centre of Empire and its Iberian and Gallic territories. The Roman conquerors understood it well first when they created what was to become, as Strabo puts it, 'the biggest commercial site' in Gaul, the city of *Narbo Martius*, which functioned in close relationship with the indigenous town of Toulouse which had secured access to inner Gaul; and then when they gave privileges to *Arelate*, an old Hellenized city and relay of Massaliote commerce, which was to play a leading role in the fluvial trade routes towards the northern parts of the Empire. Field archaeology and the study of the marks on Italic amphorae on the one hand, and underwater archaeology on the other, can contribute to our knowledge of the two commercial axes each city controlled in Southern Gaul: two different methods of approach we thought useful to present in parallel in the following pages.

1 The Narbonne-Toulouse route and the Mediterranean trade structures in the 2nd and 1st centuries BC

Until the first years of the 2nd century BC, the commercial contributions from the Mediterranean world were restricted to the coastal towns. In the Aude Valley, the eastern part of the region - the areas of Pech-Maho (Sigean, Aude), Montlaurès, probably the *Naro* of the ancient authors, the hypothetical capital city of the Elysic people), of Cayla (Mailhac, Aude), and, or still the Moulin à Peyriac-de-Mer (Aude) - was particularly influenced by the maritime commercial trends coming from the Greek world (that Marseille or Empúries took over from), the Iberian world or, more sporadically, from the Phoenician and then the Punic worlds. Inland, the evidence is rarer (Passelac *et al.*, 1990, 139-152) and the archaeological data transmits an image of anecdotal commercial contributions, almost nonexistent beyond Toulouse, perhaps pointing at inner exchanges made by the natives. Only the coastal area was directly in contact with exogenous commerce and it was a voracious consumer of the produce of sea traffic.

Not until the beginning of the 2nd century BC and the arrival of Italic products, did continental spaces open to major trade. That opening took place twice and materialized in two quantitative advances, reported by M. Bats (1986, 413-414), in the traffic of wine imported from Italy: the first occurring between 175 BC and 150 BC, and the second around the 120 BC.

The quantitative increase in commercial activity, of which wine is a good example, ties in well in this region of Languedoc with a certain reorganization of the territory as a whole (Figure 1). In the area of the lagoons at the mouth of the river Aude, the small native habitat of Pech-Maho disappears at the end of the 3rd century BC, annihilated by a military operation carried out by one of the powers fighting at that time for supremacy in the Eastern Mediterranean, whereas the important indigenous *oppidum* of Montlaurès seems to reappear (De Chazelles 1997, 40-42; essay on microregional synthesis in Gorgues, forthcoming). Throughout the 2nd century BC, between the Aude and Garonne, many raised settlements are developed or expanded: *Carcaso* (Carcassonne, Aude), *Eburomagus* (Bram, Aude), *Sostomagus* (Castelnaudary, Aude), *Elusiodunum* (Montferrand, Aude) (synthesis in Passelac 1983). Finally, at the other end of the corridor formed by the Aude valley and the Lauragais plain, the significant Gallic township of *Tolosa* (Toulouse, Haute-Garonne), capital city of the Tectosage people develops during the first half of the 2nd century B.C (synthesis in Pailler, *Toulouse antique 2*, forthcoming).

The conjunction of these two facts is striking, even if it is still difficult to make any statement on the chain of causality. All along an axis linking the low Aude valley with the bend of the river Garonne, a trade of goods and varied products coming from the Mediterranean world is beginning to develop. Its quantitative aspects are now getting to be better known thanks mainly to the works cited above: the real "birth" of a particular trade in the first half of the 2nd century BC is no longer apparent. However the "structure" of any trade is still poorly known.

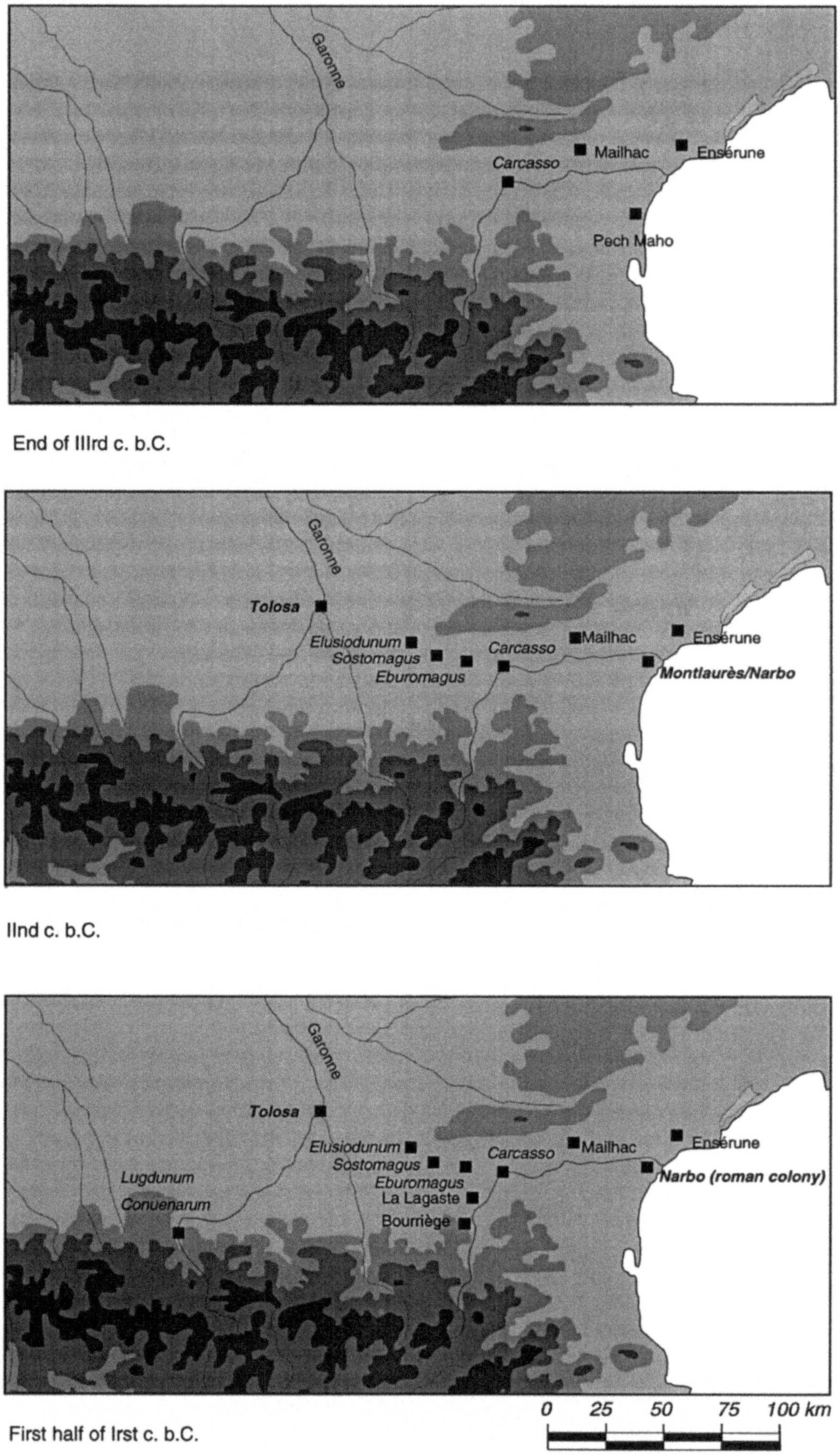

FIGURE 1. THE STRUCTURATION OF THE HINTERLAND OF OCCIDENTAL LANGUEDOC AT THE END OF THE IRON AGE.

We mean here to ponder on the issue.

Two types of data allow us to approach the structural aspect of ancient trade: that concerning merchants and their dealings, and that concerning the means they had for trade. However, on this last point, the regional archaeology is particularly scarce. As to sea trade, just the sites from the region of Gruissan (Solier *et al.* 1981) provide rather frustrating and indirect information about trade at the time. The excavations of Montlaurès have not revealed any structure that can definitely be attributed to the supposed harbour and site of trading activity. And if we can imagine that the route later to become the Aquitaine Way already existed, then no post, no depot, in short nothing that can be associated with commercial activities has yet been identified along its length, at least as far as those times are concerned.

We might explain this absence by means of the commercial practice of that time, protohistoric tradition, and special practices in antiquity based on currency and the centralized management of space; the available information is focussed on the tradesmen themselves. This data can usually be gleaned from two sources: the old texts – and we do not have any from this period – and the so-called commercial epigraphy: painted marks, amphoric stamps, commercial letters on lead, and so on. At the beginning of the era we are concerned with, most of this kind of information is produced in Iberian writing.

We have noticed the relative abundance, from the years 250-200 BC, of such documents in the low Aude valley (Gorgues, forthcoming) and their presence a few decades later in *Tolosa.* We will just take a look at the documents from this last site that throw light on the way the trade relationships used to work between the region of Narbonne and this wealthy inland region which includes Toulouse and its surrounding area. In 1983, M. Vidal and J.-P. Magnol (Vidal-Magnol 1983) published 30 inscriptions painted on Graeco-Italic amphorae discovered in the fills of several "funerary wells"[1] on the site of Vieille-Toulouse. They presented the particularity of being written in Iberian characters; the inscriptions are subdivided in two parts: an anthroponymic element followed by a series of signs, which are generally interpreted as figures. In one example the name was written in Latin characters: Q. Ofeli(us). Out of 30, 24 were legible and mentioned names evoking different ethnical horizons, according to the authors, who took advantage of wise advice from J. Untermann. According to them, six inscriptions related to the Italic ("Babirgi"-*Papirius*, "Curti"-*Curtius*, "Seste"-*Sestius*, "*Q. Ofeli"(us)*, each appearing in one single example, and "Binugi"-*Vinucius*, which was found in two examples). Six were attributed to the Iberian ("Usi", in one example, and "Rupa…Sacar" appears five times), two to the Celtiberian ("Carbi"et "Ol"), eleven to the Celtic area ("Iu", in two examples, "Anbi"in four and "Ka"in five).

For the scholars, the names appearing on Graeco-Italic amphorae referred to the addressees, who might have lived in Vieille-Toulouse. Recently, A. Tchernia (1999) proposed a different reading of these inscriptions, taking back all the names to the Italic. Therefore they would be the genitive form of Italian tradesmen's names established either on the Narbonne coast or, and that is the hypothesis which the author subscribes to, on the Tarragona coast, and in Empúries. Yet, it seems to us that the first interpretation is the most logical due to certain elements that let us see in those people, as the first publishers did, the addressees, residing in Toulouse, of amphorae,[2] the only satisfactory way to explain the unicity of the phenomenon. A restitution of the trade (Gorgues, forthcoming) linking Toulouse with the coastal suburbs of the Narbonne region, probably Montlaurès, which could be reached at that time by ship without interruption, is suggested (Strabo, IV, 1, 14).

At the beginning of the continental trade, indigenous elements were probably in force, using the Iberian writing as conventional writing with commercial usage, whereas the Iberian usage in this context seems to fade away to the south of the Pyrenees. It is the first structured distribution network of Mediterranean products to be known inland. It centres on the city of the *Neroncen* as another network, favouring the Greek, based on Marseille, a city that developed a more important axis with a continental bias, moving up the Rhône valley. The origins of Italic trade in Gaul were those of the intermediaries who were already settled there: the natives, or Greeks, who have been living for more than four hundred years.

Given these conditions, what is this multiethnic community doing in Toulouse? What are these Italians doing, since, obviously, the consignees of wine amphorae distributed by authoctonus networks play no part in the business of vineyard products? Their activity is possibly linked with the position of *Tolosa*, both named on the far borders under Mediterranean influence, and the main base of the Tectosages people.

The Romans and the Iberians were aware of the coinage at this time on two levels: the Celtic and Aquitanian worlds did not. *Tolosa* also appears as being situated at the far end of the 'monetized' world; the numeral marks on the inscriptions of Toulouse are perhaps the last testimony of an advanced form of economic abstraction, to hand for a rare elite of immigrants coming from the Mediterranean aristocracy, or, why not, native businessmen from western Mediterranean countries. Between the Mediterranean world, in which Montlaurès is to be found, and the native continental world, the "iberianscripters" probably also took on the role of

[1] The function of these structures has caused much ink to flow. Such a problem does not worry us right away, so it helps us avoid the obstacle.

[2] The elements of the dossier will be developped in another article: Gorgues, to be published 2.

intermediaries, exchanging coins for raw materials in Narbonne and bartering in Toulouse: genuine tradesmen, undertaking activities with chrematistic vocation, free to work in a region which was not monetized enough to attract the attention of Italian tradesmen.

Who, then, are the people mentioned in the inscriptions? First of all let us forget the hypothesis that requires us to give them all the same type of activity, the differences of ethnic order covering possibly differences of social and working conditions (the Italians were probably tradesmen, the Gauls more likely local notables), and let us concentrate on a single case, rather explicit, that of Q. Ofelius, a man endowed with an unusual gentilic.[3] This name, of Campanian origin, is possibly Capouan (for the distribution of the gentilic, D'Isanto 1993, 148. Its diffusion is restricted to time of the Republic: we know some in Capoua, Toulouse, and also Delos (as well as in other Eastern cities some time later, generally in the 1st century BC: Hatzfeld 1912, 58-60); as for the best known Ofelius, M. Ofelius Ferus, and the statue which was dedicated to him in the "agora of the Italians" Queyrel 1991, Marcadé 1999). The relative rarity of the gentilic makes us propose the hypothesis that the Ofelius from Toulouse and the one from Delos are from the same family (the character from *Tolosa* seems to predate that from Delos by at least 25 years), and that they would be two members from a same *gens*, both having business at the confines of the "Italic world". The name of Quintus Ofelius would have been written in Latin because, of all the consignees, he was perhaps the only one who was born in Italy. Indeed we may believe that the other Italian names (we ignore their forenames, contrary to Ofelius), written in Iberian, are those of liberated slaves of Iberian origin representing in Toulouse the interests of their *patronus* (an idea that has already been set forth by Bats 1986, 409-410). The *patronus* perhaps belonged to this great number of expatriate Italians, mainly from Campania, whose names on ingots of the Carthagena region (Domergue 1990, table X, 254-257) are found elsewhere.

Two questions come out of all this: what were the Italians living in Toulouse doing there, and, above all, what was their connection with the natives, whose names also feature on the inscriptions of Vieille-Toulouse, in this body of "wine importers " who are supposed to be wealthy? As to the first question, we may probably eliminate all money-lending activities due to the economic context. There is a still further hypothesis brought about by the case of Ofelius: slave trading. Indeed, the ancient sources (Strabo, XIV, 5, 2) evoke the intensity of human merchandise going through the Delos market. If the relationship that was established between the *Ofelii* from the East and that of Toulouse is valid, we may consider that their economic activity was the same. The situation of Toulouse particularly favours the acquisition of such a "commodity": situated both at the far end of the Mediterranean world and of the Tectosage territory, it benefits from a wide access to continental lands, rich in men and easy to plunder. But this hypothesis is just valid for Ofelius, and, eventually, for other characters with Italian names. We may imagine that what linked the Gauls, the Iberians, and the supposed Celtiberians, to Ofelius and the Italian businessmen working in the forefront of new trade activity, was the access to products stemming from the undertakings of the *Tolosates*, providing an access by means of exchange for the Italians, and perhaps as a result of the large agricultural estates of the natives – if we accept the idea that we are here talking of 'aristocrats'.

The 2nd century BC is very much the time of ascending power of the Mediterranean trade from a quantitative point of view. The model is based on an interface area, represented by coastal redistribution networks of products inland: indigenous structured networks, whose nature is clear in comparison with the sporadic diffusion of inland Mediterranean imports that were observed in the previous century. In this sense it was just at this time that a coastal settlement on the Aude delta, Montlaurès from all evidence, becomes, in terms of commercial functionality, a real port; whereas from the 6th to the 3rd centuries BC it was only an area for the consumption of goods coming from sea trade. The Aude sea area becomes in the first half of the 2nd century BC a conduit for the exchanges that from then on connect the Gauls' continental spaces with the sea, via native tradesmen who undertook the redistribution of products between a commercial port and the wider regions inside the country. The structures of a more federal type that were put into practice (like those constituted by the Tectosage people), apparently due to the progressive Celticization of the more southerly regions, presumably very much accelerated this process of structuring the commercial framework on a territorial scale. From then on the coastal interiors comprise a network of distinct regions relating a measure of their economic activities to their capacity for redistribution. This system is already a forerunner of the model that the Roman colonizers will develop from 118 BC, as deduced from a colony in Narbonne.

Contemporary with, and very possibly the origin of, at least in the region under discussion, of the second quantitative leap in the trade of Italic amphorae, as signalled by M. Bats, was the foundation of the Roman colony of *Narbo Martius,* the biggest Roman trading post (*emporion*) in the area (Strabo, IV, 1, 6), and the start of Roman control of the previously mentioned interface area. The rapid inland progress (we find by 106 BC a Roman garrison in Toulouse) achieved during Marius's campaign against the Cimbres and the Teutons (the seizing of the *hegemon* of the Tectosages Copillos in 106 by Sylla: Plutarcus, *Sylla*, IV, 1), presaged Roman dominance of the whole area by the final years of the 3rd century BC at the latest.

[3] The *CIL* VI gives 16 occurences of the name, covering all the possible variables, in Rome during the whole imperial time.

Therefore a time of extreme change begins in the economic life of Transalpine Gaul, affecting also the trade structures. The plea made by Cicero in defence of the *propraetor* Fonteius is probably the clearest testimony of that time. He pictures a situation in Gaul, though somewhat coloured by his rhetoric, radically different from the image provided by the scant archaeological data for the previous era. Gaul is full of dealers (*referta Gallia negotiatorum est*) and Roman citizens; no Gallic trader could operate without a Roman citizen as intermediary; no silver coin could circulate around Gaul without first being registered in the accounts of the Roman citizens. Further on in the same passage of his accusations he declares: "... from all the dealers (*ex toto negotiatorum*), colonists, publicans, countrymen, cattle raisers, not one single witness could be identified." Later on, in another passage referring directly to our region (IX, 19), he gives the list and fees of the tolls (*portoria*) and taxes due on wine between Narbonne and Toulouse, taxes amounting to between two denarii and a *victoriat* and six denarii. The conclusion we can draw from these passages is clear. The references to coins inform us of the first changes occurring at that time to trade dealings, the use of money, and other drivers, among which the demands of the colonists to satisfy the treasury are paramount. This phenomenon finds an echo in the development, at that time, of indigenous mints of silver or bronze coinage, with Greek or Iberian legends, on the coastal areas, and of coins with the "cross" of the Midi Toulousain. Moreover, the list of jobs done by Transalpine Roman citizens shows very well that they have taken control of all the most profitable sectors of the local economy, including commerce.

From then on we observe the exclusion of native elements, not only in the commercial sector but also in all economic sectors. The growth of the Narbonne colony brings about the rapid decline of the native area of Montlaurès, which is unfortunately situated further up the Aude (De Chazelles 1997). The structures initiated by the natives are quickly set aside by those introduced by the Romans. They are based on a network of secondary living sites (among which we may mention the example of Bram-*Eburomagus*: Passelac 1971) in order to export successfully into the interior the products arriving in Narbonne. A proportion are consumed by the Italians attracted by the riches in the Gallic raw materials, and if the taxes mentioned in the text are perhaps exceptional, and probably related to the necessity to find funds to finance Pompey's campaigns in Spain, the control on the wine traffic (a control bestowed on the *publicani*) is nevertheless strict. From that moment on, the exchanges in eastern Languedoc between the now Roman port of Narbonne and the city of the *Tolosates* are monetary exchanges, from which the Roman citizens mainly benefit. Toulouse, still a city within confines, but now within the confines of a Roman province, sees its economic role change bit by bit. As the final intermediary in the field of Mediterranean commerce, Toulouse becomes a full player, sending Italian products[4] to the areas of the Gallic isthmus. In this way its economic status became standardized and, step by step, the city became part of the Empire.

The transition from the 3rd and the 2nd centuries BC marks a time of development in the continental exchanges of the western Languedoc, a situation facilitated by revisions to existing spatial organisation, in which the living areas become especially concentrated within their territories to the detriment of inter-community exchanges, resulting in a social structure where a certain hierarchy takes place. In this new situation, native networks of exchange acting as trade posts develop between those areas in contact with Italian sea traffic and those from the interior. These traders speak Iberian, which has for some time already been the language for commercial transactions along the coast. From an early date, their activities favoured the establishment of foreign dealers in the federal capital, *Tolosa*, situated on the boundaries of the continental and Mediterranean worlds. Some of these traders perhaps belonged to great *gentes* who were expanding their influence from one end of the new world to the other; a world "tamed" by the Italians and which provided them with an access to resources that could be readily exploited in the great centres. Most of the activities of redistribution were probably carried out from the native oppidum of Montlaurès, which then becomes a commercial hub through which important quantities of merchandise can circulate. It is only from this time that we can talk of a possible "port", a term distorted by proto-historians. Indeed, the previous condition to the existence of a port (from a structural point of view) is the existence of regular sea traffic, which did not seem to be the case beforehand.

The establishment of the *Narbo Martius*,[5] in 118 BC, happens as the Italians implicate themselves more and more in the regional economy (although it is difficult to make out a chronology relating the two phenomena). So, the native economic and commercial conditions flourish, and the Italians gain control of the markets, which are monetarized. Here again it is impossible to say whether monetarization happened before or after the great interventions of the newcomers. Yet it seems to us that this degree of economic abstraction was necessary to cause the intervention of Italian tradesmen. Barter, typical of the previous era, was left to the locals. The setting up of the colony marks the beginning of Roman-like trade:

[4] Therefore it is undoubtely at that time that we can attribute the real beginnings of an important traffic on the Gaulish isthmus, even if the recent historiography has perhaps overevaluated the importance of that "economic axis "(Roman 1972) as far as the Republican time is concerned. Indeed, when Strabo talks about traffic between the river Aude and the river Garonne, he means that it sill active, "especially nowadays "(Strabo, IV, 1, 14), that is during the Augustian time.

[5] A creation, as J.-M. Pailler pointed it out to one of us (A.G.), which is not probably connected only with a commercial position of the city, but also with its position at the very center of a fertile territory. As a matter of fact there is an agricultural crisis, and the Gracques' episode is far from being forgotten.

whereas Montlaurès, an indigenous area, was the focal point of native networks, *Narbo Martius* was to be lead the way for the Italian trading system.

2 Sea and river trade at the mouth of the River Rhône in Antiquity (1st century BC/1st century AD). The role of the city of Arles

During Antiquity, the mouth of the river Rhône always constituted an area for the handling of freight flowing between the great sea routes, and the riverine diffusion of raw materials and consumables in Gaul. Recent underwater excavations on the riverbed at Arles, and off the Camargue, confirm the strategic importance of this city at the head of a very well organized network of redistribution, using, when needed, the Marius Canal or the natural branches of the river. The ancient authors were not always unanimous as to the extent of the river delta, which might indeed vary from one season to another according to the spates (Long 1997a, 273). Their testimonies, often contradictory, talk in fact about successive changes; Strabo tries to put them in order (Benoit 1965, p. 117), so Polybius (XXXIV, 10, 5, b, - W), in the 2nd century BC, contradicts Timeus (around 350 BC) and maintains that the Rhône has not five mouths but two. Artemidorus, on the other hand, says three and Diodorus goes as far as five: Posidonius (135-50 BC), who had seen the place, says six.

Strabo attributes successively two, three, five, and even seven. This opinion might derive from an counting the *Fossae Marianae* and the *Stomalimné* (the Estomac pond, in Fos-sur-Mer) as a sixth and seventh branch. But Timeus, who had also inspired Appollonios of Rhodes (*Argon.*, IV, 634), preceded Marius, probably on the hearsay of a Massaliote. But, for the period we are interested in, Pliny's opinion (*HN*, III, 5), who only tells of three branches, tallies with the later account of *Statio* 27 of the Forum of Corporations, in Ostia, attributed to the Arles naviculars' *schola*, and with the view of Peutinger's Round Table (Nat. Austrian Lib., Viena). In the interval Ptolemy gives the coordinates of two branches.[6] Evidently navigators found the delta far from easy and often had to put up with significant variations in depths across the "graus" (*gradus*).

By the end of the 2nd century BC, Marius temporarily solved the problem of the alluvial bar which limited the crossing of high-tonnage ships, using his troops to make canals among the ponds between Arles and Fos-sur-Mer. Therefore at the decline of Marseille in 49 BC, Arles, reorganized since Julius Caesar founded a colony there in 46 BC, saw an immediate rival disappear in the competition for economic and political supremacy. The main successor to the Greek city dispossessed by Caesar, Arles benefited from the canal works and quickly assumed coastal supremacy. Moreover, if the trading improvements in Gaul were also developed inland, the road network, soon to be improved by Agrippa, would also be beneficial to the young city. Under Augustus its steady growth weakened somewhat at the end of the first century BC, although this was the period of its major walls and monuments. In effect, even if the geographic situation does not look very suitable for a sea harbour, the river connected the city with all the lands of its valley, the Saône valley, and also north to the Seine basin, the Meuse, the Moselle, and the Rhine valley. This exceptionally promising location was praised by many authors into late Antiquity, and has since been confirmed by excavations.

For the last twelve years, underwater operations carried out on the river bed around Arles have revealed the existence of several very large deposits of amphorae, most of them on the right bank (Long 1998, 86) (Figure 2). There, near the Trinquetaille suburbs, five sites have been traced. They are directly related to the remains of docks and other port premises which show the importance of the harbour and its naval dockyards. These yards were justly famous, as Caesar, when at war against Pompey, had been able to have twelve galleys built in a very short time. The first feature to be found among the five underwater deposits was a bank made exclusively of Gaul 4 amphorae, still linked by a thin concrete tile covering (*Arles-Rhône 1*). Slightly further up, the second site revealed a partly preserved, inverted wooden hull, possibly a specialized sea/river boat (remains *Arles-Rhône 2*). It is a flat-bottomed vessel, without freight, and the dendrochronology suggests that the trees were felled between 114 and 137 (Guibal 1992). The keel-built construction and materials are clearly based on Mediterranean tradition. Further up, on the same riverside, level with the cemetery of Trinquetaille, rubble remains spread over 50 m indicate the existence of an 8 m deep abutment with a fragment of Gaul 4 amphora, inserted in the concretion, perhaps dating from the end of the first century AD (Long 1994, 56). This discovery recalls Arles' magnificent and famous *pons navalis*, well known from the literary and iconographic sources[7]. The structure, with stone piers at each end, maintained 16 or 17 ships and used drawbridges on both ends to accommodate vessels with masts. Therefore, the waterways and land routes ways developed without problems (Sintès 1999-2000). The first work of this type probably dates from early Empire times, judging by the blocks still visible in 1921 on the left side (Constans 1921, 343). Therefore we think that this work is part of the town's second phase, linked with an intense economic activity and prosperity as well as an increase in population. An amphitheatre is erected around 80 AD, followed a few decades later by the great circus with 20,000 seats. At the same time, the suburb of Trinquetaille is transformed into a huge residential area surrounded by an equally large space for crafts and trade

[6] *Cosmographia tabulae*, editions of the Latin manuscript plates VF. 32 (15th century), Nat. Lib of Naples, Booking International, 1990.

[7] Statio 27 from the Forum of Corporations, Ostia.

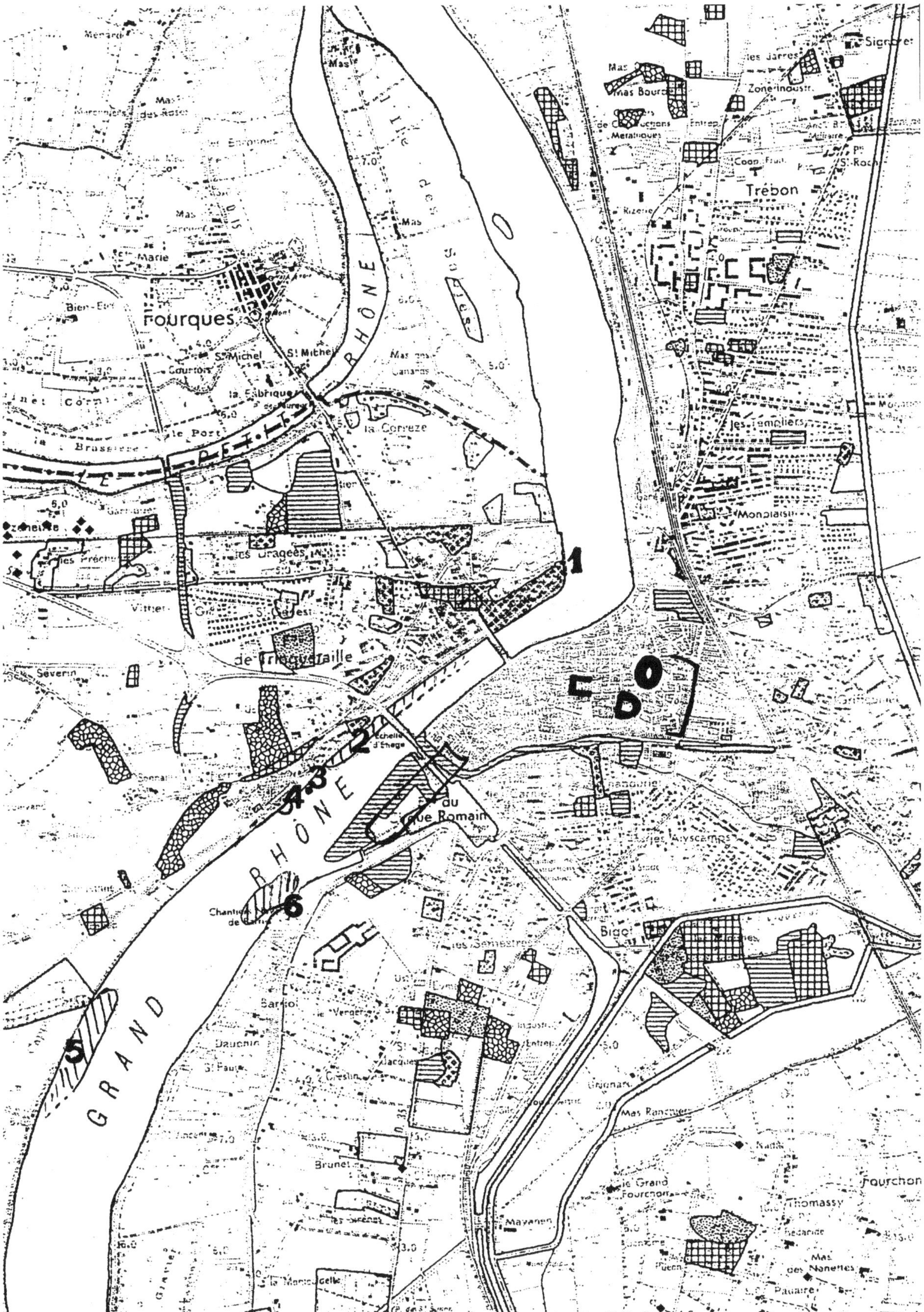

FIGURE 2. ARLES, RHÔNE DEPOSITS. ON THE RIGHT RIVERSIDE:
1. Remains of a Roman bridge abutment; 2. Deposit A; 3. Arles-Rhône 2 wreck; 4. Gallic amphorae deposit (Arles-Rhône 1); 5. Deposit B. On the left riverside: 6. Hauling area deposit. (L. Long).

(Rouquette, Sintès 1989).

On the same side there is a series of very rich deposits that spread along the riverbed over several kilometres at a depth of 7-8 m. The first, deposit A, lies by the house estates from Trinquenaille bridge to the harbour, found as late as 1967, when concrete beams were set up to hold the motorway bridge (Billo 1991). It revealed a rich assemblage of amphorae and vessels indicating uninterrupted activity in this area between the Augustan period and the 6th century AD. In the same sector, the discovery in 1874, when the modern harbour was being built, of a Roman dock standing on pillars and a *dolium,* gives backing to the idea of docks here for unloading and warehouses situated all along the river (Nicolas 1877, 83).

Situated in front of the Roman circus, the second deposit (B) is then upstream, 2 km from the city centre. If this site is wider, its features are relatively spread out as they were possibly separated from deposit A by flooding and then settled in the bend of the river where the current loses strength.

Finally, on the left side and 4 m deep, the deposit near the Barriol naval dockyard makes a sixth deposit. It is not as wide as the others but it revealed a fairly large assemblage of amphorae, similar to those on the opposite side.

From the economic point of view, the study of around 700 containers collected from the river, from all the sites, clearly shows the predominance of Gallic production (32% of the total), between the 1st and 3rd centuries AD, with an overwhelming majority of G4 wine containers.[8] Like F. Laubenheimer (Laubenheimer 1990, 99), we are of the opinion that if Gallic amphorae were to have an archetype, then it would be the G4, and that if they were to be linked with only one port in the Empire, then that port would be Arles. Amphorae from the Iberian peninsula were also abundant and diverse under the early Empire, but were secondary to Gallic output. From the Spanish provinces, the Andalusian vessels (for oil and preserved fish[9]) are the most common, followed by Lusitanian[10] and then Tarraconensis examples.[11] After Spanish products, the Italian wine amphorae are most numerous[12] and then the African cylindrical amphorae (with particular forms developed from interior types) on the embankment of the Roman circus (Piton 1998).[13] Finally, from the 1st to the 6th centuries, smaller Greek and Eastern Mediterranean amphorae are found in even quantities but to a lesser extent than the previous examples.

These recent discoveries serve to reinforce the many plaudits heaped on the city of Arles at the crossroads of the sea and inland waterways. They indicate a port of considerable dimension where the contents of the amphorae, recently unloaded, were probably transferred to other containers for the needs of local consumption and to facilitate the redistribution of goods inland. Attributed to the Durance flotilla, the bas-relief from Cabrières d'Aigues (Vaucluse), which depicts a boat loaded with barrels being towed, illustrates this type of container and the important role it played in river traffic (Lapidary Museum, Avignon). It was easy to unload those barrels and to transfer immediately their contents to Gallic amphorae. The bas-relief also shows Gallic amphorae neatly ordered on shelves (G4) over the boat, as if they were about to receive the precious cargo for distribution upriver. With thousands of litres of wine, these barrel vessels probably became, from the end of the 1st century AD, the heirs to the *dolia* boats on the river. As for these vessels, we have to wonder, having read R. Etienne (Etienne 1989, 131-132), whether they could easily have crossed the Rhône up to Lyon, with a sea keel and a load of around 50 tons.[14]

Approximately 30 km further south, the excavations carried out at sea for ten years off the Camargue, have lead to the discovery and study of around 30 wrecks. Most are located near Saintes-Maries-de-la-Mer, off an ancient branch of the Rhône St-Ferréol. Its old course, from the south of Arles through the northwest of the Vaccarès lagoon, has been traced by sedimentologists; it has disappeared into the present-day lagoon system (Arnaud-Fasseta 1996). As a result of the constant retreat of the bank since Antiquity, these vessels are today located 3 km out to sea at an average depth of 14 or 15 m; they clearly ran aground on bars in front of the coast. Their ill fate is indeed attributed to the presence of a regular series of sand bars running parallel to the coast at a depth of 2 or 3 m. The largest bank, under 2.5 m of water, is still 300 m from the shore, whereas the bank in between lies 100-150 m offshore, at a depth of 1.5 m (Long 1997b, 109). Sometimes, just where the river starts, these high, muddy banks, called "theys", emerge a few centimetres above the low water and determine islands into which the Rhône flows. These semi-circular strands are frequently submerged, either by the river itself, or by huge waves (Durrenmatt 1993).

All these wrecks are memorable for their diverse cargoes of amphorae, bronze objects, marble blocks or other raw materials, such as the Cenevole lead from the wreck *SM1* (Long, Domergue 1995) that revealed a long list of finds. Recent work has focussed on a series of seven wrecks loaded with iron ingots whose several forms, from the flat bar to the short ingot, often bear rubber stamps. They are

[8] In a lesser number the G3, G1, G5 et G7 come afterwards.
[9] In decreasing order : Dressel 7-11, Dr. 20, Beltrán IIA et B, Haltern 70, Pompéi VII amphoras.
[10] Almagro 51 C and Almagro 50 amphoras.
[11] Amphoras Dr. 2-4 and Pascual 1 amphoras.
[12] Dr. 1 amphoras, major number with scarcer Graeco-Italic, Dr. 2-4, Dr. 6, Forlimpopoli et Keay LII.
[13] Keay XXV, African 1, *spatheia* and African 2 amphoras.

[14] About this point, the research which is being carried out by S. Marlier, will probably bring some precisions.

still legible and the producers' names are sometimes associated with a nautical symbol: a sea anchor. These homogeneous and rather contemporary cargoes, sometimes a 100 m away from each other, provide evidence of a regular trade in iron, despite the risks, between the Augustan and Flavian eras.

The geographical situation of these wrecks, in a very small area off the Camargue, indicates that the ships were trying to locate the correct entrance to the river and went aground on the labyrinth estuarine bars. The river water has always coloured the sea at a great distance from its mouth; far offshore it shows up cloudy white, while nearer the beaches it goes a darker colour, turning almost yellow (Baudin 1840, 241). Only by noticing these colours in the water can one avoid the coastal dangers. Other routes were available. For example, we know of a sea axis, linking Narbonne with Rome, further away and crossing the deeper sea-lanes, where wrecks lie at depths of several hundred metres. One such wreck is the *Arles Plage 5*, full of La Graufesenque vessels; she probably connected Narbonne with Rome, via Cap Corse (Long 1997 b, 81).

The recent underwater finds by L. Bonnamour of iron ingots similar to ours at Montbellet (Saône-et-Loire) and Ouroux (Saône), reinforce the hypothesis of some metals being distributed by sea to Gaul. The presence also of Andalusian and Tarraco amphorae, which were common on these ships, first lead us to believe that this iron came from Spain. While awaiting the results of the analysis, the very important iron and steel district of the Montagne Noire, working at contemporary date to our ships, represented an even more interesting hypothesis. On the Grand Ferrier site, in the place of Les Martys (Aude), the production was evaluated over three centuries at a minimum of 80,000 tons (Decombeix, Domergue, Fabre, Tollon 1998). Communicating with the river Aude, the barges from the extraction zone (De Izarra 1993, 56) could have reached Narbonne, where other ranges of merchandise, such as Spanish amphorae, were stored for redistribution. The city, which exported products from inland and received merchandise from far away into its warehouses, was considered by Strabo as the first *emporion* in Gaul (IV, 3, 2). The discovery of bars and flat ingots similar to ours in the Gruissan lagoon complex, on the eastern end of the Narbonne estuary, is worth mentioning (Solier 1981). Moreover, all the gentilics on the Camargue ingots are to be found in Narbonne, and they are either quite rare or very dispersed in the closest areas of Spain (Long, Domergue, Rico 2001).

Among the wrecked cargoes, the *SM10* finds suggest a relatively small ship, not more than 9-10 m long, with a load of 5-6 tons of iron. However wrecks *SM2* and *SM9* should be included among the lists of bigger and heavier ships. *SM2*, whose keel remains are large, is supposed to be 15-18 m long, for a load of about 20 tons of iron; her additional freight consisted of about 40 Spanish amphorae, principally Dressel types 2-4 from Tarraco (1st century AD). *SM9* is more impressive and dates to a time from Augustus to Claudius. The ship was approximately 18 m long and loaded with 30-50 tons of iron. With such loads we should ask whether these *naves,* whose bottoms are dotted, are provided with a system of traditional construction of keels, keelsons and even stanchions, were really able to cross the alluvial bar of the Rhône, which has always been an obstacle to navigation. In spite of all the channelling works it was not possible to get more than 3.5 m of water above the bar, and very often ships of 2 m draught could not venture up (Durrenmatt 1993, 45). The study of trade in Marseille from the archives of the 17th and 18th centuries, highlights the awkwardness of access (Rambert 1966, 7 note 1). According to his author, the Great Rhône had four branches. To the west, the 'Iron Branch' had already been abandoned by navigators because of its sinuosity, whereas to the east, the 'Dead Branch' had closed up many years before. In between, the Great Rhône ended up in three canals of which the one situated more to the west remained navigable for sea craft, but the bar often reduced the depth to 4 or 5 feet (1.28 m - 1.60 m). Concerning this point, calculations made on the Roman wreck *La Cavalière*, a 13 m long coaster that ran aground around 100 BC, have provided us with the boat's draught (Charlin, Gassend, Lequément 1978). For a theoretical load of 20 tonnes, to which the accumulated weights of the keel (5 tons) and superstructure and rigging (5 tons) should be added, the draught has been established as 1.25 m. Consequently the wrecks *SM2* and *SM9* must have greatly exceeded their clearance limits and risked running aground at any time. It is of interest to compare *SM9* with the wreck from Port Vendres (5th century AD). This vessel drew 1.89 m with a total length of 17 m and a hypothetical cargo of 68 tons (Roman 1997 159).

Curiously, the positions of the Camargue wrecks throw some light on the conditions of the shoreline in Antiquity. If we connect the ancient wrecks that ran aground, roughly between the years 50 BC and 50 AD, off the Rhône St-Ferréol with a dotted line on the map we get a good outline of the ancient river mouth and the banks that enclosed it (Figure 3). To the east this route corresponds to a line of a linear coast, but to the west the characteristic form of an alluvial lobe reminds us of the cartographic surveys made on the Beauduc bank by the Arles Consuls in the 18th century (Figure 4). This form of natural mouth coincides pretty well with the reconstructions elaborated by the geologists and sedimentologists (L'Hommer *et alii* 1981) (Figure 5). In between, an area of anchorage situated off the old river mouth reveals no remains, but a large number of lead anchor stocks and innumerable broken pieces of amphorae. We may imagine that this vast anchorage was used for the transfer of merchandise from sea boats to flat-bottomed barges capable of going up upriver, as another mosaic in the Forum of Corporations in Ostia (Le Gall 1954, n° 9) shows (with African cylindrical amphorae). According to the sources of the 16th and 17th centuries, these boats with shallow

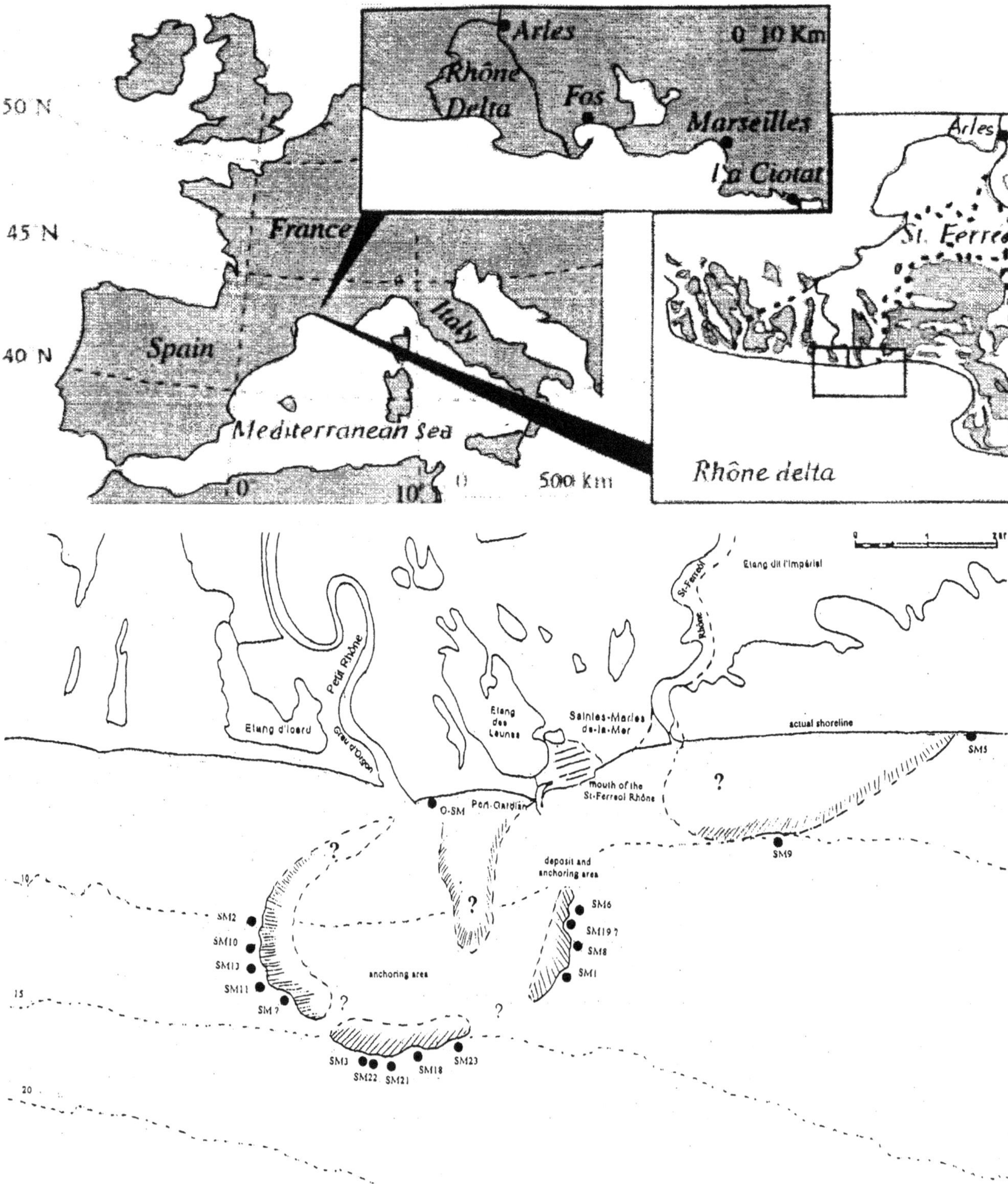

FIGURE 3. THE POSITION OF ROMAN WRECKS GIVES A GOOD REPRESENTATION OF THE ANCIENT SHORELINE ON THE TWO SIDES OF THE MOUTH OF THE RHÔNE (L. LONG).

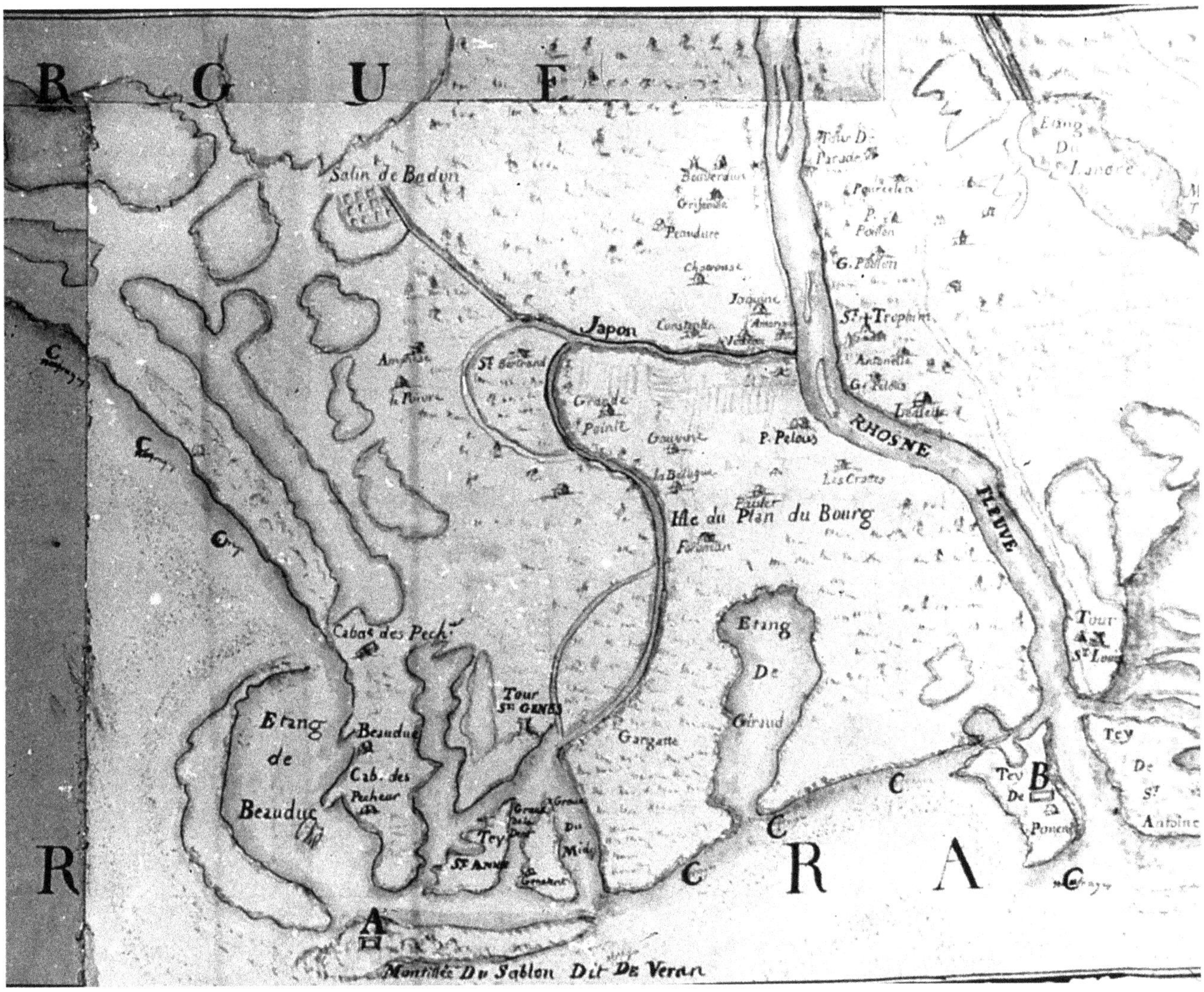

FIGURE 4. DETAIL OF THE SHORELINE MAPPED IN 1783 BY THE ARLES CONSULS. ON THE LEFT THE BEAUDUC LAGOON LOBE WITH THE REPRESENTATION OF SAND BARS ALL AROUND IT AND THE POSITION OF MODERN WRECKS MARKED BY A C CAN BE SEEN. (AD, B-D-RH, SÉRIE 200 E 1010, PHOTO L. LONG).

draughts did not exceed a cargo of 60-70 tons, the average tonnage being around 30-40 tons. From the 18th century, a few large boats could be noticed crossing the Rhône carrying 80-120 tons.[15] In fact, the Roman *Comacchio* wreck, in the Pô delta, shows quite well the performance of this type of barge in Antiquity. 21 m long and about 6 m wide, the ship was able to load 92 tons with a 1.70 m draught (Bonino 1990). Except for the periods of low waters, only that type of boat could avoid the hazards and ratify Strabo (IV, 1, 14), who speaks of enormous cargoes going up the river.

Indeed, during Imperial times, several types of navigation existed in the region of Arles and particularly on the Lower Rhône. The *navicularii marini arelatenses* sometimes formed a single body, or sometimes five different groups. In charge of the transfer and carrying of merchandise, these men, who had their own houses in Ostia, were mostly foreigners - especially Greek. With the help of sea boats, they would play their part in supplying of Rome and many other cities. Among their prestigious masters, several notables are known by theirnames in the funerary epigraphy.[16] Curators of the Arles sailors' *schola* ran other sub-corporations at the same time, especially the Durance boatmen's corporation and the *Ernaginum utricularii*; they nearly all belonged to the population of Arles. (Admittedly the latter, furthest down the catalogue of ships, practised their art across the lagoons and the swamps on rafts fixed to wineskins. The Rhône Nauts, whose mighty corporation was associated with wine merchants, had their ships towed on the Rhône, the Durance and the Saône by *homines trahentes,* and

[15] As for the 17th century we refer here to the Arles barges loaded in 1636 and 1637 against the Spaniards. P. Rigaud, project on Arles barges, Arles Town Archives, p. 18, note 18 ; for the 18th century : ACC, HH232, A . Illouze's research.

[16] *Dominius Claudius Boethus* (*CIL*, XII, 672) ; *Lucius Secondius Eleutherus* (*CIL*, XII, 704) ; *Marcus Frontonius Europus* (*CIL*, XII, 982).

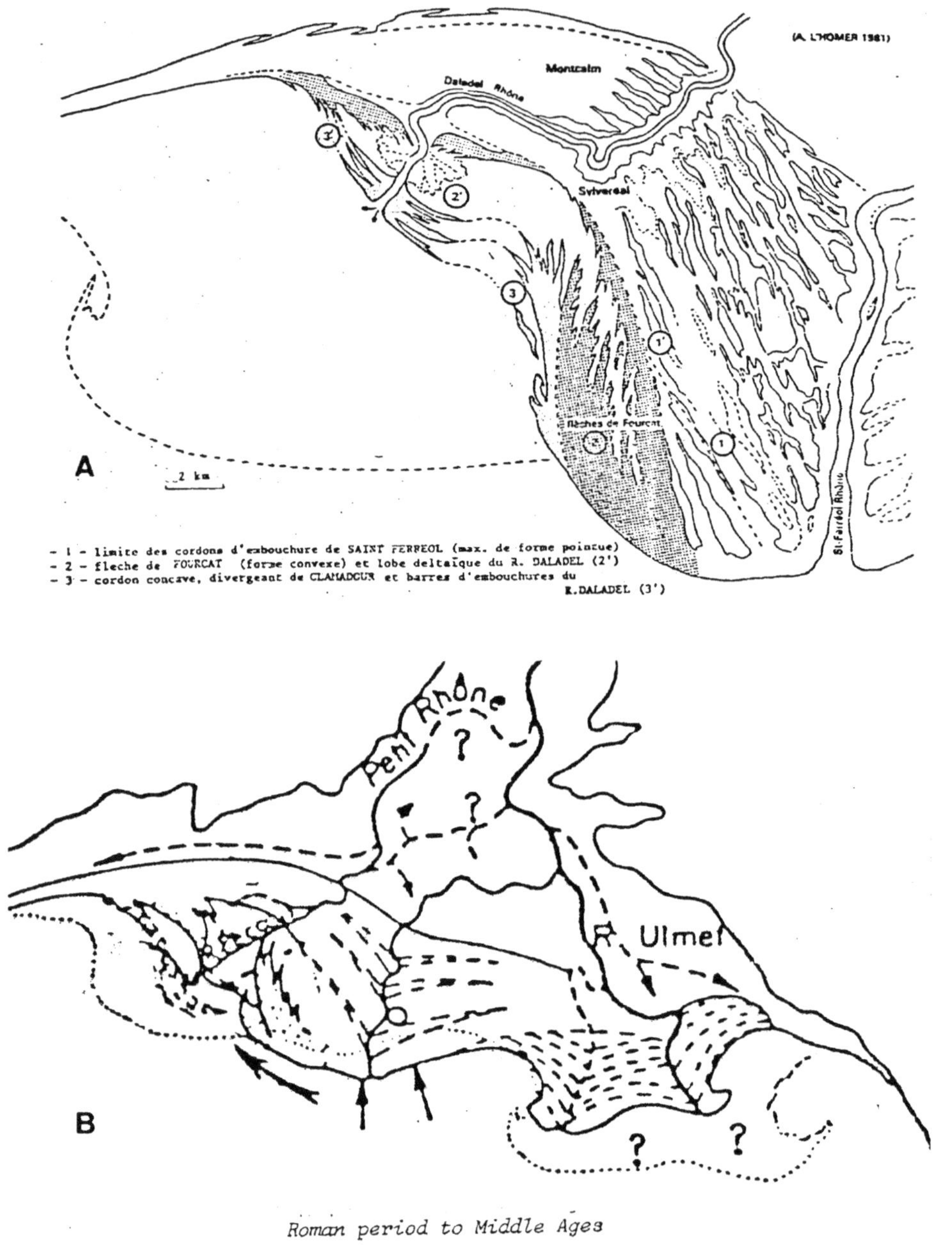

FIGURE 5. GEOLOGICAL, MAPPING SURVEYS SHOWING THE ST-FERREOL MOUTH. A : POINTED STAGE BETWEEN 6000 AND 5700 BP ; B : ROMAN SHORELINE (FROM L'HOMER *ET ALII* 1981, FIG. 6 & 7).

were also in charge of the land transport from one river to the other (Durrenmatt 1993, 154). In Trinquetaille, an arcade partially used again in the Middle Ages for the construction of Baux Castle, perhaps served as a forum for the sea- and river-men's colleges (Benoit 1954).

Before the recent discoveries, about 50 km west of Fos-sur-Mer, there was a general tendency to consider the Marius Canal as the Rhône's main navigable branch at that time: in fact the only navigable branch. If ever true, Strabo's evidence must modulate this opinion since at that time access to the *Fossae Marianae* had become difficult because of silting.[17] It is highly probable, as J. Rougé (1966, p. 145) points out, that the development of the sea trade under the Empire increased the capacity and number of trading ships to such a degree that the importance of the traffic would need new and substantial harbours capable of receiving such fleets. Called *duplex* by Ausonius (*Ordo urbium nobilum*), the city of Arles must have expanded on both sides, and we can imagine that this must have meant a sea harbour further down the boat-bridge, by the lagoons, and a water port further up (Rougé 1966, 155). Others thought that the poet was referring to both Arles and Fos (Liou, Sciallano 1989),

[17] Strabo, Geography, IV, 1, 8, c 188-189.

but in this case the new findings in the Camargue would make a triple city of Caesar's creation and the Sixth Legion in Augustinian times and under the early Empire.

Covered with sand by a century of silt (Vella 1999, 159),[18] Fos harbour, at the time we are interested in, was certainly bigger than Marseille, but it perhaps it was not as well suited as before to the huge movement of goods and traffic in both direction between Gaul and the northern countries, along the Rhône-Saône. It is interesting to compare the coded data on wine amphorae collected in Arles, on the Rhône (Long 1998, 93), together with examples from the river mouth in Fos-sur-Mer (Liou, Sciallano 1989, 157), at that period at the end of the chain, from northeast Gaul, and Germania (Baudoux 1992). The material from Arles is rather continental and similar to the northern sites where the Gallic amphorae prevail, whereas Fos preserves a more marine character, that of a port of call and redistribution point between Spain and Italy. The stamp representing it on Peutinger's map is of a similar importance to that of Ostia, and, perhaps, rightly so, with its extent, installations, and *horrea*, making it one of the biggest and safest harbours on the coast between Marseille and Narbonne.

Narbonne and Arles thus functioned as conduits for maritime traffic in the Western Mediterranean. As the harbour from which Italic wine entered into inner Gaul by the end of the Republic, Narbonne confirmed its position in the early Empire by distributing the wine produced in the north-eastern part of Hispania Citerior, and became a port of call for goods from the nearby Hispanic provinces. The port also acted as a point of departure for products from the interior - wine and metal, iron from the Black Mountains, and *sigillata* from the kilns of La Graufesenque. Under the Principate, Arles sees her role confirmed as a relay stage for commerce towards northern Gaul, and most probably the military markets of the Rhine. Both locations had to include important reception and storage capacities for the products passing through; modern archaeology has only begun to explore these features. The two great ports in southern Gaul thus retained their status under the Empire. Moreover, they kept their true maritime vocation, making them major players in the great export markets of the Principate. So, in the famous forum of the corporations in Ostia, the offices of the marine *navicularii* from Narbonne and Arles stand alongside the big maritime corporations from Sardinia and, above all, Africa (*stationes* 27 and 31), a fact that highlights the key rôle undertaken by the carriers from southern Gaul in the Roman *annona* of the early Empire.

Acknowledgments

We would like to very warmly thank Professoressa Marinella Pasquinucci (university of Pisa) for the opportunity to participate here. Our gratitude also extends to Thierry Rico and Bertrand Goffaux for helping with the translation of this paper.

[18] In Fos Gulf, the coastline moved forward over approximately 600 metres between the beginning of our era and the 3rd century AD.

References

Arnaud-Fasseta G. 1996, *Variabilité des flux hydriques-solides rhodaniens et dynamique de l'occupation du sol à l'échelle pluri-millénaire (Ve s. av. J.-C.-XVe s. ap. J.-C.). In* : "Delta du Rhône, Programme collectif de recherche 1996-98 : rapport intermédiaire", 1. SRA-PACA, 93-106.

Bats M. 1986, *Le vin italien en Gaule aux IIe-Ier s. av. J.C. Problèmes de chronologie et de distribution*, "Dialogues d'Histoire Ancienne", 12, 391-430.

Baudin L.-S. 1840, *Manuel du Pilote de la Mer Méditerranée*, I, 2ème édition, Toulon, éd. Laurent.

Baudoux J. 1992, *La circulation des amphores dans le Nord-Est de la France*, in F. Laubenheimer. *Les amphores en Gaule : production et circulation* (table ronde de Metz, 1990), (ed), Paris, Les Belles Lettres, 163-169. (Annales littéraires de l'Université de Besançon, 474).

Benoit F. 1954, *Arles*, collection Alpina.

Benoit F. 1965, *Recherches sur l'hellénisation du midi de la Gaule*. Aix-en-Provence, éd. Ophrys. (Annales de la faculté des lettres, 43).

Bonino M. 1990, *Tecnica costruttiva e architettura navale, proposte per la ricostruzione*, in F. BERTI, *Fortuna Maris : la nave romana di Commacchio*. Bologne, Nuova Alpha Editoriale.

Billo M. 1991, *Ponts et ouvrages d'arts en Arles*, Regards sur le Patrimoine. Aix-en-Provence, Edisud.

Charlin G., Gassend J.-M., Lequément R. 1978, *L'épave antique de la baie de Cavalière (Le Lavandou, Var)*, "Archaeonautica", 2, 9-93.

Constans L.-A. 1921, *Arles antique*, Paris.

De Chazelles C.-A. 1997, *Montlaurès (Narbonne, Aude). Le bilan de six années de fouilles (1989-1994)*, in "Languedoc Occidental Protohistorique. Fouilles et recherches récentes, VI e-IV e s. av. J.C .", travaux du Centre Camille Jullian, 23-44.

Decombeix P.-M., Domergue C., Fabre J.-M., Tollon F. 1998, *Évaluation du volume des ferriers romains du domaine des Forges (Les Martys, Aude), de la masse de scories qu'ils renferment et la production de fer correspondante*, "Révue d'Archéométrie", 22, 77-90.

De Izarra F. 1993, *Hommes et fleuves en Gaule romaine*. Paris, éd. Errance (coll. des Hespérides).

D'Isanto G. 1993, *Capua Romana. Ricerche di prosopografia e storia sociale*, Vetera, 9, Rome, Quazar.

Domergue C. 1991, *Les mines de la Péninsule Ibérique dans l'Antiquité Romaine*, Collection de l'Ecole Française de Rome, 127, Rome.

Durrenmatt G. 1993, *La mémoire du Rhône*, Pont-Saint-Esprit.

Etienne R. 1989, *Lyon, emporion des Gaules : la ville et le fleuve chez Strabon, géographe du Ier siècle après*

Jésus-Christ, "La ville et le fleuve : actes du 112e Congrès national des sociétés savantes"Lyon, 123-134.

Gorgues A. to be published, *Agglomérations littorales et négoce maritime dans la région de Narbonne à l'Age du Fer (VI e s. av. n.è .- II e s. av. n.è.)*, in *"Actes de la table ronde sur les ports de Narbonne Antique (décembre 1999)"*.

Guibal F. 1992, *First dendrochronological dating of a shipwreck in western Mediterranean area*, "Dendrochronologia", 10, 147-156.

Hatzfeld J. 1912, *Les Italiens résidant à Délos mentionnés dans les inscriptions*, "Bulletin de Correspondance Hellénique", XXXVI, 1-218.

Laubenheimer F. 1990, *Le temps des amphores en Gaule, vins, huiles et sauces*, Paris, éd. Errance. (coll. des Hespérides).

Le Gall J. 1954, *Graffites navals du Palatin*, "Mémoires de la Société des Antiquaires de France", 41-52.

L'Homer A. Bazile F., Thommeret J., Thommeret Y. 1981, *Principales étapes de l'édification du delta du Rhône de 7000 BP à nos jours ; variations du niveau marin*, "Océanis ", 7, 4.

Liou B., Sciallano M. 1989, *Le trafic du port de Fos dans l'Antiquité : essai d'évaluation à partir des amphores*, in "SFECAG, Actes du Congrès de Lezoux ", 153-167.

Long L. 1994, *Prospections et sondages archéologiques dans le Rhône, à Arles et ses environs*, in "Histoire du Rhône en Pays d'Arles, Actes du colloque du 7 nov. 1994", Arles : Groupe Archéologique Arlésien, 45-71.

Long L. 1997a, *Le Rhône et Arles à travers les textes antiques*, in "Paléographie, Le Rhône d'Arles, Textes et Histoire", Arles, Archives Communales, 273-276. (De la Paléographie à l'Histoire n°3).

Long L. 1997b, *Inventaire des épaves de Camargue, de l'Espiguette au Grand Rhône, des cargaisons de fer antiques aux gisements du XIXème siècle : leur contribution à l'étude du paléorivage*, in M. Baudat "Crau, Alpilles, Camargue, Histoire et Archéologie", Arles, Groupe Archéologique Arlésien, 59-115.

Long L. 1998, *Inventaire des amphores du Rhône à Arles : un aspect des échanges à l'époque impériale*, in "SFECAG, Actes du Congrès d'Istres", 85-95.

Long L., Domergue C. 1995, *"Le véritable plomb de L. Flavius Verucla" et autres lingots : l'épave 1 des Saintes-Maries-de-la-Mer*, "MEFRA", 107, 2, 801-867.

Long L., Domergue C., Rico Chr. 2001, *Les épaves antiques de Camargue et le commerce maritime du fer en Méditerranée nord-occidentale (Ier siècle avant J.-C./Ier siècle après J.-C)*, in "L'Africa Romana,actes du XIV convegno di studi (Sassari, 2000)", à paraître.

Nicolas M. 1877, *Etude préhistorique sur la basse vallée du Rhône*, in "Congrès archéologique de France, XLIIIème session", 1876, Arles, 50-124.

Pailler J.-M. (ed), *Toulouse antique 2*, Collection de l'Ecole française de Rome, to be published.

Passelac M. 1970, *Le* vicus Eburomagus. *Eléments de topographie. Documents archéologiques*, "Revue Archéologique de Narbonnaise", 3,71-102.

Passelac M. 1983, *L'occupation du sol en Lauragais à l'âge du Fer et pendant la période romaine : acquis, problèmes et méthodes*, in *Le Lauragais, Histoire et Archéologie*, Actes du LIVe congrès de la FHLMR, Montpellier, 29-64.

Passelac M., Rancoule G., Solier Y. 1990, *La diffusion des amphores massaliètes en Languedoc Occidental et sur l'axe Aude-Garonne et ses abords*, "Etudes Massaliètes", 2, 131-152.

Piton J. 1998, *Contexte amphorique du début du Vème siècle à Arles (Bouches-du-Rhône)*, in "SFECAG, Actes du Congrès d'Istres", 107-115.

Queyrel F. 1991, *C. Ofelius Ferus*, "Bulletin de Correspondance Hellénique", CXV, 389-464.

Rambert G. 1966, *Histoire du commerce de Marseille*, VIII, 1660-1789, Paris.

Roman R. 1997, *Etude architecturale comparative de sept navires de commerce gréco-romains et byzantins*, Thèse de doctorat, université Aix-Marseille 1.

Rougé J. 1966, *Recherches sur l'organisation du commerce maritime en Méditerranée sous l'empire romain*, Paris, Ecole Pratique des Hautes Etudes.

Rouquette J.-M., Sintès C. 1989, *Arles antique, Monuments et sites*, Paris, éd. Imprimerie Nationale. (Guides archéologiques de France, 17).

Sintès C. 1999-2000, *Le pont de bateaux d'Arles*, in R. Bedon et A. Malissard, *La Loire et les fleuves de la Gaule romaine et des régions voisines*, "Caesarodunum" XXXIII-XXXIV, 153-175.

Solier Y. 1981, *Les épaves de Gruissan*, "Archaeonautica" 3, Paris, CNRS.

Tchernia A. 1999, *Une autre hypothèse sur les inscriptions peintes en caractères ibériques de Vieille-Toulouse*, in *Mélanges C. Domergue*, 2, "Pallas ", 101-107.

Vidal M., Magnol J.-P. 1983, *Les inscriptions peintes en caractères ibériques de Vieille-Toulouse (Haute-Garonne)*, "Revue Archéologique de Narbonnaise", XVI, 1-28.

Vella C. 1999, *Perception et évaluation de la mobilité du littoral holocène sur la marge orientale du delta du Rhône*, thèse de doctorat, université Aix-en-Provence.

Commercial flows, ports and hinterlands in North Coastal Etruria (late Republican- late Roman period)

Marinella Pasquinucci and Antonella Del Rio

Abstract

This paper studies the ancient Pisa and Volterra territories, local resources and manufacturing activities from the late Republican period to late Antiquity. Import and export trades are examined, which concerned mainly foodstuffs (wine, oil, fish sauces, honey, preserved fruit), wares, timber, stone and marble. The study of the imports shows a diachronic evolution in trade patterns: in the late Republican period the bulk of goods came from the central Tyrrhenian area, in the early Empire it was foodstuffs from the Iberian Peninsula then from the 3rd century A.D. goods from North Africa. Trade with the Eastern Mediterranean remained steady through the whole period.

The ancient *Pisae* (Pisa) and *Volaterrae* (Volterra) territories extended across the lower Arno and Serchio, Fine and Cecina river valleys, in North coastal Tuscany (fig.1).

The area is currently being studied in an integrated fashion, incorporating geomorphological research, remote sensing and non-destructive techniques applied to landscape and settlement archaeology, archaeological research (intensive survey and monitoring, stratigraphic excavations, underwater archaeology), archaeometric and other studies of artefacts, bioarchaeology, palaeoecology and documentary research (Pasquinucci, Menchelli, Mazzanti, Marchisio, D'Onofrio 2001).

Proceeding from North to South, the studied territory includes:

- lower Versilia and Lake Massaciuccoli;
- the Arno coastal plain (an alluvional Holocenic plain, mostly formed by sand and silt, bordered by hills: Monti Pisani in the North and Colline Livornesi in the South);
- the rocky coast stretching from Leghorn to Castiglioncello;
- the sandy littoral of the Fine and Cecina coastal plains and its hinterland.

The plains and the lower hill slopes were and still are mainly exploited for agriculture; Mediterranean scrub covers most of the strip, while woods cover the highest slopes of the reliefs.

Coastal Tuscany is characterized by rocky and sandy littorals. The sandy ones in the areas reached by the main rivers (Magra, Arno/Serchio, Ombrone), began to grow westwards from the 8th century B.C. At present, the other soft littorals with no wide rivers (the Vada - Cecina and the Piombino - Follonica districts) lie behind the 8th century shoreline (Pasquinucci, Menchelli, Mazzanti, Marchisio, D'Onofrio 2001).

In general, the growth of beaches depends on both the sea-level position, subsidence and solid fluvial deposits. In the Tuscan littoral we find evidence of all three factors. There is no direct evidence of the causes that produced the great fluvial deposits. The phenomenon came to an end around 1830, when the solid transports began to be diverted in order to fill marshlands. Erosion of the Arno and Ombrone deltas began at the end of the 19th century (Mazzanti 1994) (fig.2).

From Etruscan times *Pisae* and *Volaterrae* had a harbour system along the ancient coastline, well integrated with the Arno waterways and with the road network Pasquinucci 2003). For the late Republican and Imperial period the Roman roads are documented by archaeological, epigraphical, ancient literary and medieval documentary evidence (Pasquinucci, Ceccarelli Lemut 1991).

The harbour system included a number of locations of varying importance (ports and calls) sited a) in coastal lagoons, b) close to river mouths, c) along the major rivers.

In the *Pisae* and *Volaterrae* territories the main ports were *Portus Pisanus* and *Vada Volaterrana*.

Portus Pisanus was located North-North-East of the Livorno promontory, in a coastal lagoon later progressively silted up. It was situated in the area now called Gronda dei Lupi.

Evidence for the location is provided by ancient sources (*Itinerarium Maritimum*, 501, mentioning *Portus Pisanus* 18 *milia* far from *Vada Volaterrana* and 9 from the Arno mouth: *Pisae fluvius*), by medieval toponymy, by a mid 18th century description of the site (Targioni Tozzetti, 1768) and by geomorphological research.

In this area a multidisciplinary team, which includes archaeologists and geomorphologists, is currently studying remarkable geomorphologic changes dating from the end of the 2nd millennium B.C. to the Middle Ages. The area NNE of Livorno was partially occupied by a large coastal lagoon, that prograded westwards, as emerges from Etruscan, Roman and Medieval evidence. In the classical and medieval periods it was connected with the sea by a natural channel, kept clear by the water flow, while the sediments transported by the Arno River and minor streams formed submerged and progressively emergent sandy barriers.

The Gronda dei Lupi (see above) coastline was set SW-

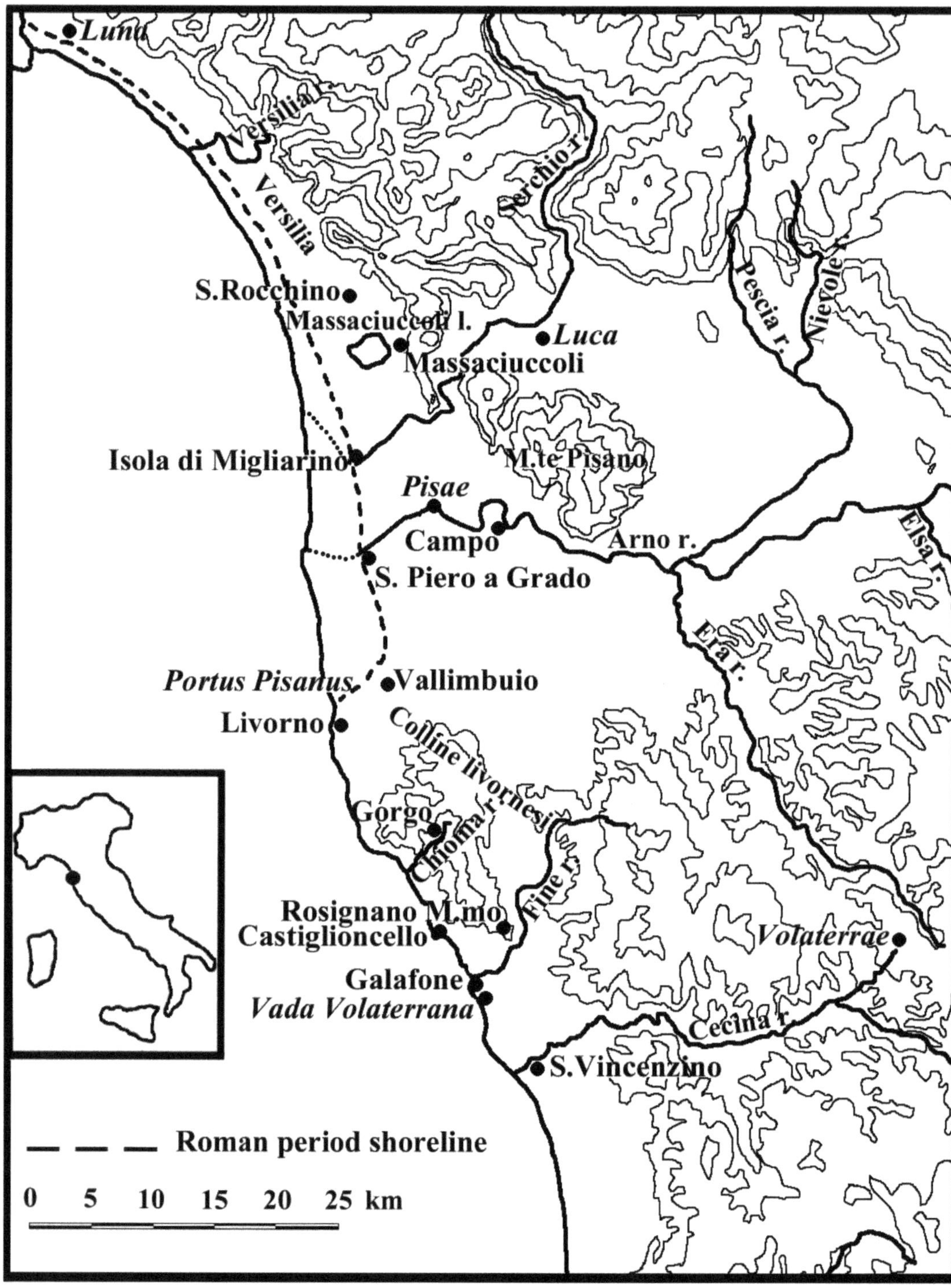

FIGURE 1.

NE, that is in the direction of the prevailing wind ("Libeccio"). Storms were damped by wave refraction near the coast; moreover, it originated around the Meloria Shoals located in the offing, 10 km SW of the Gronda. When sea storms were too violent, ships could shelter in the Southern part of the area (now "Stagno"), where the Roman and later the Medieval *Portus Pisanus* were located, the latter to the west of the former.

In the 18th and 19th centuries remarkable archaeological evidence of the Roman harbour settlement was visible in the Gronda dei Lupi area, dating from the 3rd – 2nd centuries B.C. to late antiquity (T. Tozzetti 1768, 407 ss.; Banti 1943, 107-112; Ciampoltrini, Cianferoni, Romualdi 1982, 18 ss.). A long sector (about 9 km) of the *Portus Pisanus* aqueduct has recently been identified. It was constructed with curved tiles and departed from the Colline Livornesi (Galoppini, Mazzanti, Menchelli, Taddei 2004 c.s.). A manufacturing quarter for production of wine amphorae (Dressel 1 and Dressel 2-4:

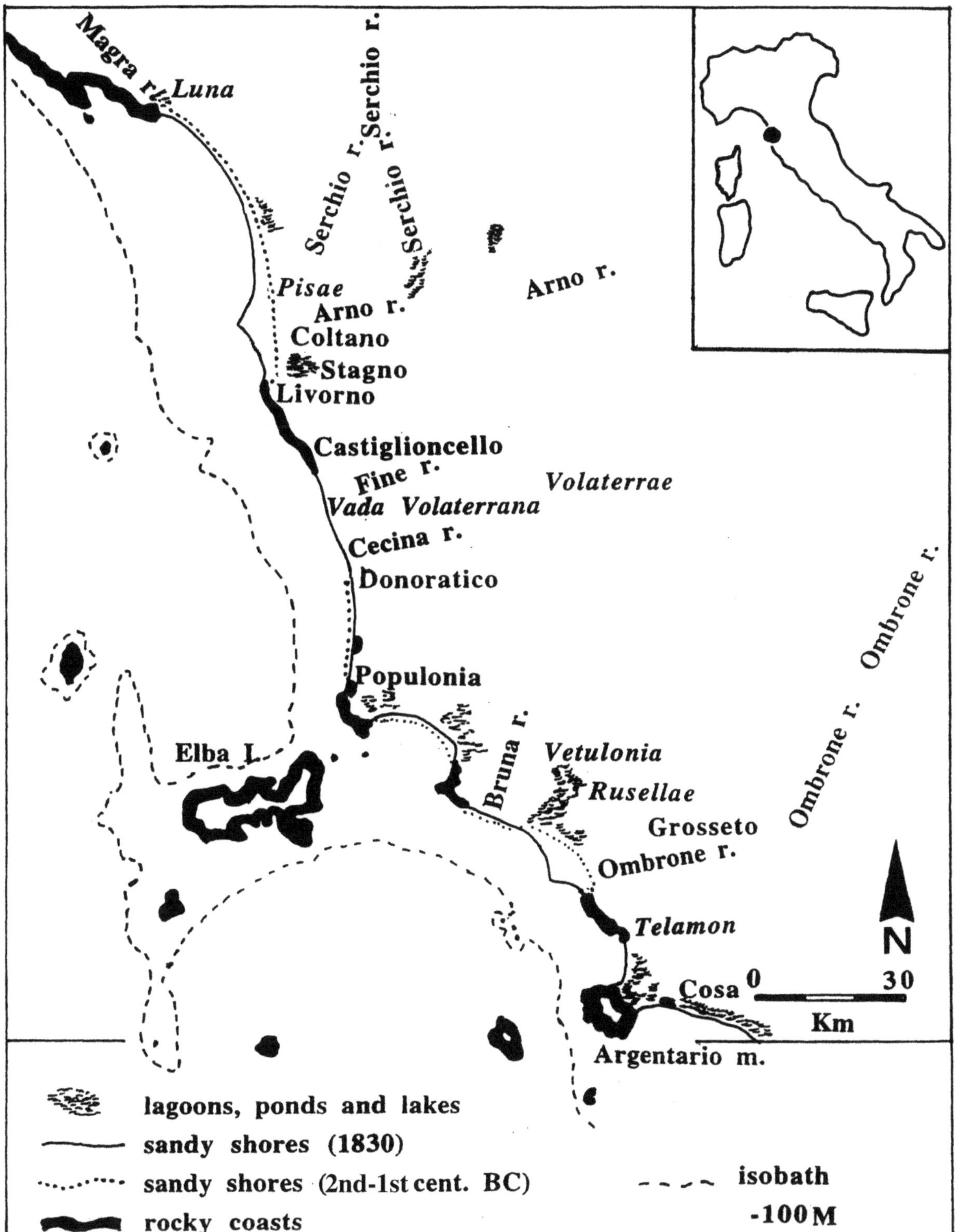
Magra r.
Luna
Serchio r.
Serchio r.
Serchio r.
Pisae
Arno r.
Arno r.
Coltano
Stagno
Livorno
Castiglioncello
Fine r.
Volaterrae
Vada Volaterrana
Cecina r.
Donoratico
Ombrone r.
Populonia
Ombrone r.
Elba I.
Bruna r.
Vetulonia
Rusellae
Grosseto
Ombrone r.
Telamon
N
Cosa
0
30
Km
Argentario m.
lagoons, ponds and lakes
sandy shores (1830)
sandy shores (2nd-1st cent. BC)
rocky coasts
isobath
-100M

FIGURE 2.

I century B.C.- I century A.D.) has been excavated in the *Portus* hinterland (at Vallin Buio) (Pasquinucci, Del Rio, Menchelli, 1998, 357-363).

In the early 5th century A.D. *Rutilius Namatianus* still referred to *Portus Pisanus* as well sheltered and very active (*de red.* 1. 559). Archaeological, archive and literary sources document the *Portus* activity through the medieval period, which conformed to the shoreline geomorphologic evolution (Pasquinucci, Menchelli, Mazzanti, Marchisio, D'Onofrio 2001; Pasquinucci 2003).

The lagoon progressively silted up. The sandy littoral between Luni and Livorno shows a shoreline progradation (about 7 km in correspondence of the Arno mouth) from the 8th century B.C. up to around 1830.

The remarkable fluvial solid transport was probably due to anthropic causes, mainly the deforestation linked with manufacturing and agricultural activities (Pasquinucci, Menchelli 1999). The former developed mostly from the 7th century B.C. onwards (AA.VV. 1985); the latter were increased by the *centuriatio* carried out in the Triumviral-Augustan period (see below).

By means of the Roman network of highways and centurial roads *Portus Pisanus* was well linked to the coastal sites and the hinterland (Pasquinucci, Ceccarelli Lemut 1991).

The harbour of *Vada Volaterrana*, already established in Hellenistic times, is mentioned by late Republican and Imperial sources. The Roman harbour settlement, built in the 1st century A.D. (Pasquinucci-Menchelli 1999, 126) is located North of present day Vada, in a coastal district protected by an extensive rock shelf.

In the early 5th century B.C. *Rutilius Namatianus* described the ships approaching the coast through a channel in the shoals. Posts equipped with bushes marked the channel banks.

In the Vada stretch of sea four shipwrecks have been identified (Pasquinucci, Menchelli, Del Rio 2003). Geomorphological research and an underwater archaeological survey are currently being carried out by a team including our Dipartimento, the Soprintendenza per i Beni Archeologici della Toscana and the Pisa CNR.

Along the coast, in the S. Gaetano di Vada area, part of the Roman town has been excavated, including two *thermae*, *horrea*, a *macellum* (?), a *schola* . The buildings were constructed towards the end of the 1st century A.D. They underwent renovation in the 4th century and were in use until the early 7th century (Pasquinucci, Menchelli, Del Rio 2003).

Other ports and calls were active along the *ager Pisanus* and *Volaterranus* coasts (fig. 3). Among these landing-places, one was close to the ancient Versilia river mouth; San Rocchino (Campo Casali, Massarosa) was active from at least the end of the 8th century B.C. (Pasquinucci and Menchelli 1995, 209-217).

On the ancient coast and close to the mouth of a river (perhaps a branch of the Serchio called *Auserculus*) was a call or port whose earliest activity is documented from 6th-4th century B.C. It was frequented till the 6th century A.D., receiving goods from Etruria, Lazio, Campania, the Eastern and Western Mediterranean, which it redistributed to inland towns and cities by road and river transport. In the Augustan era and up to the middle of the 2nd century A.D., it was an important centre for the production of terra sigillata (Menchelli *et alii* 2001; Pasquinucci, Menchelli 2003), exported to the whole Roman Empire.

As for inland navigation, the main branch of the Serchio river flowed into the Arno at Pisa (Strabo 5.2.5; Plin. *N.H.* 3. 50; Rut. Nam. 1. 566; Schol. Ptol. 3.1.4) (Pasquinucci and Menchelli 1995, 209-217).

In the first half of the 6th century A.D. both rivers were still navigable (Cassiod. *Var.* 5.17. 6; 20. 3).

On the NW outskirts of Pisa (S. Rossore Railway Station) remarkable evidence of this inner navigation has been partially excavated. Some crafts have been identified including three *onerariae*, one oared craft, three boats for inland navigation dated between the end of the 1st century B.C. and the Imperial period and a later ship (AA. VV. 2003): here sunk coasters, inland navigation ships and boats used to carry goods to and from the ships that were anchored in the sea ports or close to the coast (Pasquinucci, Del Rio, Menchelli 2002, 770; Pasquinucci and Menchelli 1995, 209-217).

East of Pisa, an Arno landing place has been identified in a sandpit near Campo.

Southwest of the town, close to the ancient Arno mouth, berthing is documented at San Piero a Grado. The landing place was relevant from at least the 7th century B.C. Located not far from the mouth of the Arno river, it served as junction point between maritime and river shipping routes (Pasquinucci-Menchelli 1995, 209; Bruni 1998, 153 ss).

Between *Portus Pisanus* and *Vada Volaterrana* several calls and minor ports are understood or documented. Among them, the natural one at Castiglioncello was particularly notable in the Hellenistic period, as documented by rich necropolises (AA.VV 1999).

Both *Pisae* and *Volaterrae*, with their territories, flourished during the 3rd century B.C. due to the fertility of the agricultural soil, that produced mainly grain and wine, cattle breeding (Liv. 35.3.1 concerning *the ager Pisanus)*, along with commercial and manufacturing

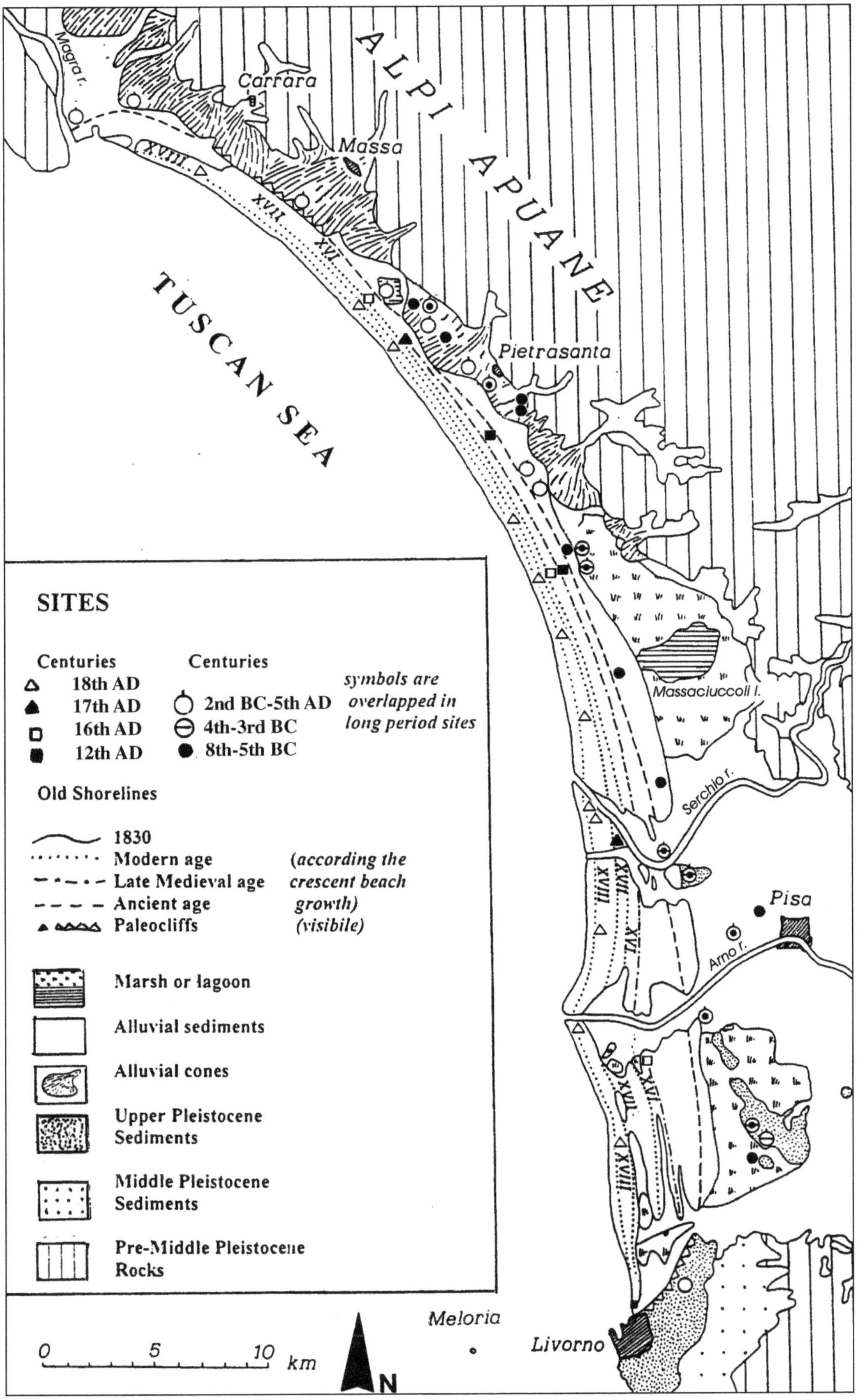
Magra r.
Carrara
Massa
ALPI APUANE
TUSCAN SEA
Pietrasanta
Massaciuccoli l.
Serchio r.
Pisa
Arno r.
Meloria
Livorno
SITES
Centuries
18th AD
17th AD
16th AD
12th AD
Centuries
2nd BC-5th AD
4th-3rd BC
8th-5th BC
symbols are overlapped in long period sites
Old Shorelines
1830
Modern age
Late Medieval age
Ancient age
Paleocliffs
(according the crescent beach growth)
(visibile)
Marsh or lagoon
Alluvial sediments
Alluvial cones
Upper Pleistocene Sediments
Middle Pleistocene Sediments
Pre-Middle Pleistocene Rocks
0 5 10 km
N

FIGURE 3.

activities, including shipyards (Strabo 5.2.5, concerning *Pisae,* based on Posidonius), stone quarrying (Strabo 5.2.5 based on Posidonius), production of pottery (wares, amphorae, bricks and tiles, etc.) (see below) and Volterran cinerary urns (AA.VV. 1985; Bonamici 1990, 97-124).

Intensive survey campaigns have identified settlements mostly located along the coast, main rivers and roads. In the late Republican period the countryside was largely populated by smaller settlements and there were isolated farmsteads (Pasquinucci and Menchelli 1999, 122-141); *oppida* of the 3rd-1st century B.C. on the lower slopes of the Monte Pisano (Bonamici 1990, 122) and on Monti d'Oltre Serchio (Pasquinucci *et al.*1998a). Further south, in the lower Cecina river valley, one large settlement, probably a village or *mansio/statio*, has also been identified (Cherubini, Del Rio 1995).

The establishment of the colonies *Opsequens Iulia Pisana* and *Iulia Augusta Volaterrae* caused great changes both at urban sites and in their territories. In the *ager Pisanus* a vast area in the plain was centuriated; farmsteads were set up along the *limites*, often coinciding with or close to Hellenistic sites which seem to have been abandoned or reoccupied (Pasquinucci-Menchelli 1999, 130). There were also some villas with a rich *pars urbana:* only one is preserved, near the Eastern shore of Lake Massaciuccoli (Ciampoltrini 1994, 119-130).

In the coastal territory of Volterra no evidence of centuriation has yet been found. Here, from the second half of the 1st century B.C., there was a more complex settlement pattern: small and medium-size farmsteads, villas and villages, alongside surviving earlier settlements. Villas, with a wealthy *pars urbana* adorned by mosaics, columns and statues were numerous both along the coast (chiefly between Castiglioncello and the Cecina river mouth), and on the hills overlooking the coastal plain (Cherubini-Del Rio 1995).

Roman re-organisation both of the land and of the economic and social systems certainly improved agricultural production, chiefly in grain and wine, and commercial and manufacturing activities.

The local economy does not appear to have been affected by the Italic crisis of the late 2nd and 3rd century; a significant continuity in the pattern of settlement is attested until the late Roman period when the landscapes around Pisa and Volterra were dominated by large villas the rich owners of which were members of the Roman aristocracy (Pasquinucci and Menchelli 1999).

Imports

From the archaic period, north coastal Etruria was well connected to Mediterranean trade routes (Del Rio *et al.* 2000, 449-457; Pasquinucci, Menchelli 2003). In the 3rd-2nd century B.C., during Roman expansion to the northwest, the Etruscan ports and calls played a very important role. Pisa was a military base for land and maritime warfare.

Large amounts of wares, including foodstuffs, reached the ports and calls and were redistributed in the hinterland via inland navigation and/or the road network (Pasquinucci, Del Rio, Menchelli 2002; Pasquinucci, Menchelli 2003).

Here, only in a few cases percentage data will be specified concerning the various foodstuffs (wine, oil, fish sauces, etc.), since they were traded in amphorae that could be used as containers for different products. For example, it has been proved that African amphorae usually interpreted as oil containers, were frequently smeared with pitch inside, therefore they could contain fish sauces or wine (Bonifay 2002 c.d.s). The Dressel 6 amphora usually carried wine produced along the Adriatic coast, but other foodstuffs too, e.g. fish sauces are documented by tituli picti at Salzburg (Massa 1993). Therefore only general drifts will be provided.

Wine

Wine reached the territories studied from the archaic/late archaic period, but in rather limited quantities, given the local wine production (see below). Pisa and other coastal settlements imported wine from South Etruria and the Eastern Mediterranean (Del Rio *et al.* 2000).

From the 3rd century B.C. until the 1st-2nd century A.D., North coastal Etruria was well connected with the wine trade from Central and South Italy to Gallia and Iberia. Our area received wine from South Etruria, Latium and Campania in amphorae documented in harbours, in the *domus* of Pisa e Volterra, in the farms scattered in the territory, in burial grounds, in two shipwrecks (south of the Fine and the Cecina River mouths respectively) and in occasional underwater finds in the stretch of sea in front of *Vada Volaterrana* (Pasquinucci, Menchelli, Del Rio 2003).

Wine from the Adriatic district reached our territory in minimal quantities both in the late Republican period and in the early Empire: Adriatic amphorae were found in Pisa, in the coastal settlements and in occasional underwater finds (AA.VV. 2003; Menchelli 2003).

Adriatic wine reached the Etruscan coasts by means of the commercial flows that carried the Eastern Mediterranean wares too.

From the late Republican period, in fact, small but significant quantities of renowned, and therefore expensive Eastern Mediterranean wine was imported. Eastern Aegean wine was held to be a high quality product for the privileged few. Ordinary people drank the local wines (see below). The earliest evidence, dated 2nd-1st century B.C., is urban only and provided by *Pisae,*

Volaterrae, Luni, *Luca*, Populonia (Del Rio *et al.* 2000, with previous bibliography).

The Pozzino shipwreck (Populonia: 140-120 BC) carried a mixed cargo including amphorae, wares, spices and ointments from the East, amphorae and wares from Western Tyrrhenian Italy (Firmati, Romualdi 1998, 184-192). Evidently goods from the Eastern Mediterranean and Italic wines were shipped on the same cargoes, evidence of ships stopping along the Tyrrhenian coasts.

Eastern Mediterranean wine was imported throughout the Imperial age from numerous areas: archaeometric analyses prove that the *horrea* at *Vada Volaterrana* and Pisa received amphorae manufactured in the districts of Rhodes, the *Issicus sinus*, Ephesus, the Meander Valley, Gaza and Palestine (Del Rio et al. 2000).

Eastern wine imports were definitely increased from the mid-3rd century A.D. and became substantial in late antiquity for political reasons. The eastern wine is actually found in the cities (Luni, Lucca), in ports and calls, in the wealthiest villas and in the Tuscan Archipelago islands, that is in the Byzantine trade flows favouring their main strategic sites (Del Rio *et al.* 2000).

From the early Empire until the 4th century A.D., wine from Gaul reached our territory only in minimal quantities, evidently because the district produced medium/low quality wine, similar to the Gallic: only 6% of the 1st-2nd century A.D. imports is Gallic amphorae, as shown by the study of finds from surveys in sample areas of the Pisan-Volaterran territory (cfr. Tab. 1 in Pasquinucci, Del Rio, Menchelli 2000).

In the early and middle Empire, fairly high quantities of wine from *Tarraconensis* and *Baetica* reached the main cities and the farmsteads in our district through maritime trade: 11% of a specimen formed by 293 Iberian amphorae from the *Vada Volaterrana horrea* can be assigned to wine amphorae (cfr. Tab. 2 in Pasquinucci, Del Rio, Menchelli 2000). Moreover, a shipwreck carrying most probably Iberian wine amphorae was recovered in the westernmost area of the Vada shoals (Massa 1980-81).

In the 3rd-4th century A.D. *passum* from *Mauretania Caesarensis* is documented in *Pisae* and *Volaterrae*, as well as in shipwrecks (Capraia) (Pasquinucci, Menchelli 2003).

It is possible that wine from other areas of North Africa reached the North Etruscan coasts, since the same amphora type could be used to ship various foodstuffs and a very high number of North African amphorae reached North Etruria. In the *Vada Volaterrana horrea* 42.5% of the 1740 excavated amphorae were manufactured in North Africa (Pasquinucci *et al.* 2004 in print).

From the last quarter of the 4th century A.D. and during the 5th, wine from Calabria and/or Sicily reached at least *Vada Volterrana* in small but significant quantities, over the same trade routes that carried imports from the Eastern Mediterranean basin (Del Rio, Vallebona 1996).

Olive oil

In the Archaic period oil from the Eastern Mediterranean reached North coastal Etruria, in limited quantities.

In the Imperial age olive oil mainly from *Baetica* and North Africa reached our district in high quantities.

From Augustus onwards, oil from *Baetica* is widespread throughout ports and calls in the urban *domus* and in the farmsteads all over our territory but mainly in the coastal *ager Volaterranus*. Imports decreased from the 2nd /early 3rd century A.D. and ceased in the 4th/5th.

Much Iberian oil was imported from several sites. Archaeometric analyses of oil amphorae from Baetica show many different fabrics, evidence of raw materials supplied from different areas, if not of different manufacturing centres (Pasquinucci, Del Rio, Menchelli 2000).

The numerous shipwrecks loaded with Baetican oil amphorae identified in the stretch of sea in front of the Tyrrhenian coasts, the Tuscan Archipelago Islands and North Corsica confirm the large amount of oil imports (Pasquinucci, Del Rio, Menchelli 2000).

Oil from North Africa began reaching North Etruria in the 1st century A.D., when it is documented in fairly low quantities all over the territory. Imports increased in the 2nd century A.D. and mainly in the 3rd (as confirmed by data provided by the finds in the *horrea* at *Vada Volaterrana*) and remained remarkable to the 5th century.

At *Vada Volaterrana,* in particular, imports of amphorae types prevalently used as oil containers increased strongly after the mid-5th century (Pasquinucci *et al.* 1998b).

The food supplies needed by Rome meant continuous trade routes from North Africa; private enterprises run by *mercatores, negotiatores, navicularii* (cfr. Rouge 1966) joined the *annona* trades and shipped the Tunisian goods along the North Tyrrhenian sea-routes towards the markets in Gallia and the Iberian Peninsula.

As for the North African oil that reached our district, the archaeometric analysis of 33 samples from African amphorae (a small amount, compared to the high number of fabrics so far identified) has highlighted several, often identifiable manufacturing areas in central coastal Tunisia (Pasquinucci *et alii* 2004, in print).

Until the 6th-7th century A.D., oil from North Africa and the Eastern Mediterranean continued to reach the port of

Vada Volaterrana and the Tuscan islands in fairly large quantities, in the historical context of the Byzantine conquest of coastal North Africa and the defensive system of the Etruscan and Ligurian coast.

Fish sauces

From the Augustan period until the 3rd century A.D. fish sauces were the largest foodstuff import from *Baetica*. Iberian amphorae of the type used for such storage and transport are widespread all over the territory. A shipwreck whose load included fish sauces from Baetica was identified seawards from the Vada shoals (Pasquinucci, Del Rio, Menchelli 2000).

As was remarked above, concerning the oil from Baetica, the large amount of imported sauces and of manufacturing centres are noteworthy. The places of origin are discernable from the large number of fabrics and by different amphora types. Small quantities from *Lusitania* in fact also reached our territory.

In the 4th century A.D. Iberian imports decreased; in the 5th they ceased completely (Pasquinucci, Del Rio, Menchelli 2000). Underwater archaeology in the Ligurian and Tyrrhenian Sea provides evidence of Iberian cargoes including both wine and fish sauces.

From the 3rd century A.D. Iberian fish sauces were partially substituted by the Tunisian ones that reached our territory in massive quantities until the late 5th-6th century A.D. Quantitative data cannot be provided because of the already-mentioned difficulty in identifying for sure the contents of North African amphorae.

Oil and fish sauces were certainly imported in high quantity. Local production of olive oil is attested by decanting tanks excavated in two villas located in the northern territory of Pisa, at Capezzano Pianore, and in the coastal territory of Volterra, at San Vincenzino (Pasquinucci and Menchelli 1999, 132).

During the Empire other goods (olives; pine resin; perfumed oils; legumes?) reached our district from North Africa and the eastern Mediterranean basin in unremarkable quantities; these cannot be precisely defined since these goods were traded in amphorae normally used as wine and olive oil containers.

Honey and preserved fruit

In the late Republican period and early Empire, preserved fruit and/or honey from the Iberian Peninsula are documented by *kalathoi* or *sombreros de copa* found in the coastal district both in towns and rural sites, and in underwater finds. They document precocious links between the Iberian Peninsula and North Etruria (Pasquinucci, Menchelli 2003).

In the late Republican period honey reached our coasts from Corsica too. This island was renowned for producing honey and other goods including wax, pine resin, pitch, shellfish (Pasquinucci *et al.* 2000).

In the Early Empire, very small quantities of preserved fruit reached *Pisae*, apparently from *Campania* (Massa 1993, 360). Therefore, we may consider it as a subsidiary commodity, travelling with more consistent cargoes, e.g. wine amphorae from *Campania.*

Pottery

Between the late Republican period and late Antiquity, a large amount of pottery reached the settlements of North Etruria as a subsidiary cargo, stowed among amphorae.

Black-glazed pottery has been discovered both in rural and urban settlements, in ports, calls and underwater deposits. It reached our districts from several manufacturing areas located in Lazio ("Genucilia" and *petites estampilles*) and Campania (Calenian pottery, "Campana A", "B-oide" pottery) (Pasquinucci et *alii* 1998a). Cooking ware manufactured in the same areas is also well documented (Menchelli, in this volume).

In the late Republican period, the so-called "Ampurias jugs" reached our coasts from the western Mediterranean. They were often associated with *kalathoi* or *sombreros de copa,* mainly in the necropolis at Castiglioncello (AAVV. 1999). Very likely they were goods distributed through the existing busy maritime traffics, not Iberians moving westwards (Pasquinucci, Menchelli, Del Rio 2002).

In the late Republican period, Corsica, being well linked to local and long distance sea routes, had a relevant role. Hellenistic Corsican beakers reached the coasts of North Etruria and Elba.

They were traded by the ships calling at Corsican ports, most probably with other goods of no archaeological evidence (Picchi 2003).

From the late Republican period, Eastern Mediterranean wares were traded with the Eastern Aegean wine. They included Eastern Terra Sigillata A, Megarian bowls, *lagynoi,* manufactured in various sites of Greece, Asia Minor, Syria and the islands opposite. During the Imperial period Eastern wares reached the studied territory in much smaller quantities. Few pieces of Eastern sigillata A, B, C, Cypriot and coarse ware, in particular trefoil mouth jugs (Menchelli and Pasquinucci, 2000).

As for the sea routes from Gallia to Rome, South Gallic wares (1st-2nd century A.D.) have been discovered in the ships excavated at Pisa (Stazione Pisa- S.Rossore). They were traded alongside the amphorae, but were unsuccessful compared to the Italic and Late Italic sigillata: in the *horrea* at *Vada Volaterrana* the South Gallic wares are less than 0.5 % of the excavated sigillata

(Pasquinucci , Menchelli , Del Rio 2003).

A small amount of wares from North Italy reached our district. The evidence includes the very few fragments of sigillata and *Firmalampen* traded by sea or land (trans-Apennine) (Pasquinucci, Menchelli, Del Rio 2002).

Large amounts of Wares from North Africa were imported in the early centuries of the Empire and became prevalent from the end of the 2nd-early 3rd century, in conformity with assessments concerning the whole Roman world. A high percentage of thin-walled pottery, terra sigillata, cooking ware, coarse pottery and lamps reached all the settlements in the territory, e.g., the African lamps from the *horrea* at *Vada Volaterrana* actually constitute 42.8% of the typologically identifiable samples. In particular, tableware and lamps continued circulating, even though in slightly decreasing quantities, in the 6th and early 7th century (Pasquinucci *et al* 1998a).

Alongside North African wares, Pantellerian pottery reached North Etruria. It consisted in cooking ware (pans; bowls) manufactured by specialized workshops using fireclay. It reached coastal Tuscany in small amounts but was widespread mainly in Late Antiquity.

Marbles

Precious marble reached the studied district in the Imperial period from the Aegean area, Egypt and various sites of North Africa. It was used for architectural decoration and for floors in the *villae* and baths at *Vada Volterrana.* These were decorated by Verde Antico from Thessaly, Portasanta from Chios and Porfido rosso from Egypt.

In the late Republican period other goods, for which archaeological evidence is unavailable, reached our territory from Gaul. According to literary sources, the Gaulish aristocracies exchanged Italic wine and wares for raw metals, wool, hides, hams and slaves (Strabo 4.4.3; 5.2; 6.12; Diod. Sic. 5.26; Varro *R.R.* 2.4.10; L. Afr., *Comoedia Togata Fragments,* ed. Daviault A., Paris 1981, 236-7; Tchernia 1983). In North Etruria there were ports of discharge of *pueri venales ex Gallia* (Cic. *pro Quinct.* 6.2: slaves from Gaul landed at *Vada Volaterrana* and were taken to Rome to be sold).

From the late Republican period very valuable goods reached our coasts but left no archaeological evidence. These products were associated with the wine and wares of the Eastern Mediterranean; they included pearls, gems, spices, perfumes, purple, frankincense, linen cloths and slaves (Cic. *Verr.* II.5.56.146).

During the Empire, our territory must have seen imports of wheat, esparto, cloth, horses, and wild beasts for games from North Africa. Evidence of this trade is provided by literary and epigraphic sources (Pasquinucci *et alii* 1998b).

Export

From the archaic period to late Antiquity the numerous ports and calls of North Etruria were well connected with the sea trade and through them local produce was largely exported.

Wine

Wine production of northern coastal Etruria is documented by literary sources and by a considerable number of wine amphorae kilns discovered through excavation, intensive surveys and petrographic analyses.

About 20 kilns, active between the late Republican and the late Imperial period, have been identified. They were often located close to shipping sites or roads able to foster trade (e.g., the manufacturing centres located at Vallin Buio (close to *Portus Pisanus*), at Il Galafone (close to the port of *Vada Volaterrana*), at Il Gorgo (close to the banks of the Chioma stream; a call was located at its mouth) (Cherubini and Del Rio 1995; Cherubini and Del Rio 1997; Menchelli 1990-91; Esposito 1992; Pasquinucci, Del Rio, Menchelli 1998).

The local wine, reputedly of medium quality, was exported from the late Republican period. At present only a sub-regional trade connected with coastal navigation is documented, as shown by wine amphorae manufactured in *Pisae/Volaterrae* found at Luni (Gambaro 2000,108-111).

The Roman territorial reorganization and the development of viticulture seem to have caused a *surplus* of wine production and consequently an increase in local wine exports. Some of the local wine was shipped with North Etruscan sigillata (see below) from *Portus Pisanus* and probably *Vada Volaterrana* to the *castra* of the Roman *limes.* Archaeometric analyses of Dressel 2-4 provide evidence of wine amphorae manufactured in the coastal *ager Volaterranus* and exported to the military camps at *Augusta Raurica* and probably *Aventicum* (Thierrin-Michael 1992, 50-51). At least a small percentage reached the markets in Rome through Tyrrhenian and Mediterranean trades induced by the *annona civilis* (Pasquinucci, Del Rio, Menchelli, 1998), most probably sailing from the port at *Vada Volaterrana* with other goods (e.g. locally produced salt). In the Vada *horrea* large numbers of locally manufactured wine amphorae have been discovered, destined for regional or extra-regional trade (Del Rio and Vallebona 1996, 490).

In the 4th-5th centuries and probably in the 6th, the numerous *villae* scattered over the territory still ensured adequate wine exports, proved by the Empoli type amphorae used, from the end of the 2nd century A.D. to the end of the 5th, probably the 6th, to trade North Etruscan wine.

Wine production may have been stimulated by the

annona distribution needs. Significant is the passage in *Flavius Vopiscus* (SHA, 48) concerning *Aurelianus*, the emperor intending to cultivate the *agri fertiles ac silvosi* in North coastal Etruria in order to meet the demand for wine to be distributed to the *plebs* (Pasquinucci, Menchelli 2004). The plan was most probably unaccomplished, but in Rome the Empoli type amphorae occur in meaningful frequency in several contexts (Pasquinucci and Menchelli 1999 with previous bibliography). In the 4th century *vinum Tuscum* was one of four productions mentioned by the *Expositio Totius Mundi* (*Exp.* 55) and was widely traded. Empoli-type amphorae are attested in numerous coastal sites of the North Tyrrhenian coast and among the Tuscan Archipelago, in *Carthago* and mainly in *Tarraco* (Pasquinucci, Del Rio, Menchelli 1998). The success of the North Etruscan wine trade along the Iberian coasts is confirmed by imitations of the North Etruscan amphorae at *Dianum*, in the Valencia territory (Gisbert, 1998).

Pottery

Between the late Republican period and the 2nd century A.D., vessels produced in workshops located in the territories of Pisa and Volterra were largely exported on a sub-regional and extra-regional scale.

During the 3rd century B.C., Pisa, Volterra and their territories produced large quantities of black-glazed pottery. To date only one kiln has been found (De Marinis 1977, 200-12; Castiglioni and Pizzigati 1997, 26-27), but wares produced in Volterra and in this part of Etruria, such as red-figured, black-glazed Malacena, "anses en oreille" and Campana B are well known. Moreover, some black-glazed "Pisan" fabrics have been characterized by petrography (Pasquinucci *et Alii* 1998a).

The pottery manufactured in the Volterra district could be exported along three trade routes:

a) through the Era and Elsa river valleys to the Arno; following this river they reached the ports of the Pisa territory.
b) Along the Cecina river valley, that linked Volterra to its port, *Vada Voalterrana*.
c) The route Era-Elsa and Auser-Pescia-Nievole linked Volterra with the Apennine passes and the Po Plain. Volterran pottery was exported to these areas (Pasquinucci and Menchelli 2003).

Finds of black-glazed pottery "B" in Delos and *Carthago* (Morel 1986; Morel 1998, 511) and the presence of Volterran and B black-glazed pottery along the Iberian coasts (Bianchini, Cibecchini, Pasquinucci 2000, 7-17) confirm that North Etruria was well connected with the Mediterranean trade routes in the late Republican period. River and coasting navigation and the road network fostered trade on a sub-regional scale. Black-glazed pottery and cooking ware manufactured in the *Pisae* and *Volaterrae* territories reached *Luna* through coastal trade (Gambaro 2000, 108-111).

From the 1st century B.C. until the middle of the 2nd A.D. particularly remarkable was the export of terra sigillata Italica which, from Arezzo and later from Pisa reached the whole Romanized world and beyond (Oxé, Comfort, Kenrick 2000).

In Pisa the terra sigillata Italica and late Italic manufacturing centre was located in the northern suburbs, along the branch of the *Auser*, not far from its merging with the Arno. Another relevant manufacturing centre was at Isola di Migliarino, the already mentioned call at the *Auserculus* mouth. Archaeometric analyses prove that (a) sigillata was locally produced and (b) sigillata manufactured in the hinterland, along the *Auserculus*, was conveyed to Isola di Migliarino in order to be traded on an extra-regional scale. The stamps on the vessels belong to *Cn. Ateius* and his slaves/freedmen and to late Italian potters (Menchelli *et alii* 2001).

In the first half of the 1st century A.D. the *gens Ateia* dominated the markets thanks to their political connections: the potter *Cn. Ateius* belonged to the same *gens* as *Cn. Ateius Capito* (Sangriso 1998), *consul suffectus* in A.D. 5 and *curator aquae* since A.D. 13 or 15 to A.D. 22. (Tac. *Ann.* 1.76; 3.75; Frontin. *de aquaeductu* 102). Thanks to these political links the *gens Ateia* was able to dominate the market mainly along the Rhine-Danubian *limes* in connection with the *annona militaris.* Some of the Pisan wares were added to merchandise sent to, or coming from, the Roman market. Vivid documentation of commercial flow heavily conditioned by the *annona civilis* is provided by the Punta Ala wreck (Bargagliotti, Cibecchini, Gambogi in this volume) which provided Iberian amphorae side by side with Gaulish, late Italic Pisan terra sigillata and Forlimpopoli-type amphorae.

Pisan terra sigillata reached the chief ports and frontiers of the Roman Empire (Menchelli 1997); one cup was found at Arikamedu in south-eastern India, where a *conventus* of Roman mercatores is documented (Comfort 1991, 137-39, fig.8.7).

After A.D. 50 the Ateian workshops were replaced by workshops run by potters linked with the Pisan aristocracy: *L. Rasinius Pisanus, C.P. ( ) Pi(sanus), Sex. Murrius Festus, Sex. Murrius (T), L. Su ( ) M ( ),* and *L. Nonius Florus.* The distribution of Pisan terra sigillata around the Mediterranean continued until the first half of the 2nd century (Menchelli *et alii* 2001).

During the early Imperial era, other *gentes* belonging to the Pisan and Volterran aristocracies (*Venulei Aproniani, Rasinii, Petelii, Caecinae*) produced bricks and tiles exported to North Etruria, the Tuscan islands, Corsica and Sardinia. The area covered coincides significantly with that of common North Etruscan ware: bricks and tiles and common earthenware exported along very busy commercial routes did not have much intrinsic value, they were unsuitable for exportation beyond regional exchange, probably also because of competition from central Italic goods (Menchelli 2003a; Menchelli 2004 in print).

Other exports from our area: literary sources ((Liv. 4.25; 4.52; Plin. *NH.* 18.86-87; 18.109) often mention wheat, which must have been exported in large quantities, often to Rome.

In the early Imperial period we have also evidence at Pisa of shipyards, stone quarrying and timber that was exported to Rome (Strabo 5.2.5; CIL XI 1436 on *fabri navales* and *fabri tignarii*; CIL XI 1415 on *marmoraii*). In the early 7th century Pisa continued to supply the shipyards with wood to build the *dromoni* for an expedition that challenged the truce between the Lombards and Byzantines (Gregory M., *Ep.* 13.26).

The wreck of a *navis marmoraria,* loaded with dressed marble blocks, and what is perhaps part of a column, has been detected on the bottom at the Meloria shoals, not far from *Portus Pisanus,* but as yet there is no evidence to establish whether it is one of the ships that in the Imperial era exported marble from Luni to the Capital or otherwise (Bargagliotti, Cibecchini, Gambogi 1997).

Salt

Salt production is documented at *Vada Volaterrana* by late Imperial literary sources (Rut. Nam. *de red.* 1.475-490) and Medieval documents (until the 12th century). Historical maps dated at the end of the 18th century document the toponyms "Saline" (salt marshes) and "Prato delle Saline" in the area North of Vada and East of S. Gaetano di Vada (Pasquinucci, Menchelli, Del Rio 2003).

Given the importance of salt, we may assume that it was exported at least on a sub-regional scale.

Salt was produced southwest of Pisa, in the Coltano area, according to archaeological evidence (briquetage) dating from the Bronze Age (Pasquinucci, Menchelli 2002).

References

AA.VV. 1985, *Artigianato artistico: l'Etruria settentrionale interna in età ellenistica*, Maggiani A. (ed.), Milano, Electa.

AA.VV. 1999, *Castiglioncello. La necropoli ritrovata*, Gambogi P. and Palladino S. (edd.), Rosignano Solvay.

AA.VV.2003, *Pisa ed il Mediterraneo. Uomini, merci, idee dagli Etruschi ai Medici*, Tangheroni M. (ed.), Milano Skirà.

Banti L. 1943, *Pisae,* "MemPontAcc", ser. III, 6.1

Bargagliotti S., Cibecchini F., Gambogi P. 1997, *Prospezioni subacquee sulle Secche della Meloria (LI): alcuni risultati preliminari,* Atti del I Convegno Nazionale di Archeologia subacquea, Bari, 43-53

Bianchini S., Cibecchini F., Pasquinucci M. 1998, *Aspetti e problemi della ceramica a vernice nera del II-I sec. a.C. nell'Etruria nord-occidentale,* in *La ceràmica de vernís negre dels segles II i I a C.,* Taula rodona, Mataró, 7-17.

Bonamici M. 1990, *L'epoca etrusca:dall'età del Ferro alla Romanizzazione,* in *San Giuliano Terme. La storia, il territorio,* Pisa, Giardini, 97-124.

Bonifay M. 2002 in print, *Les Amphores Africaines de l'Antiquité tardive, nouvelles donnée sur la typologie, la chronologie et le contenu,* I International Conference on Late Roman coarse wares, cooking wares and amphorae in the Mediterranean: archaeology and archaeometry, Barcelona, in print.

Castiglioni M., Pizzigati A. 1997, *Preliminari ad un'indagine topografica sulla Valdera in età romana,* in *Contributi della Scuola di Specializzazione in Archeologia dell'Università degli Studi di Pisa,* 1, Pisa, 13-38

Cherubini L., Del Rio A. 1995, *Appunti su fabbriche del territorio pisano e volterrano,* "Annali Scuola Normale Superiore Pisa" 25.1-2, 351-388.

Cherubini L., Del Rio A. 1997, *Officine di età romana nell'Etruria settentrionale costiera: impianti, produzioni, attrezzature,* "Rei Cretariae Romanae Fautorum Acta", 35, 133-41

Ciampoltrini G, Cianferoni, Romualdi A. 1982, *La raccolta Archeologica e Numismatica Enrico Chiellini, il Museo di Livorno ed i materiali dal Portus Pisanus,* "Rassegna di Archeologia", 3, 183-241

Ciampoltrini G. 1994, *Gli ozi dei Venulei: Considerazioni sulle "Terme" di Massaciuccoli,* "Prospettiva", 73-74, 119-130.

Comfort H. 1991, *Terra sigillata at Arikamedu,* in Bergley V., and De Puma R. D. (eds.) *Rome and India. The ancient sea trade,* Madison, WI, 134-50.

De Marinis G. 1977, *Topografia storica della Val d'Elsa in periodo etrusco,* Firenze

Del Rio A., Vallebona M. 1996, *Le anfore (I - VII sec. d.C.) rinvenute negli horrea di S. Gaetano di Vada (Rosignano M.mo, LI),* "Archeologia e calcolatori" 7, 487-96

Del Rio A., Menchelli S., Capelli C., Puppo G. 2000, *Le anfore orientali nell'Etruria settentrionale costiera (II secolo a.C.- VII secolo d.C.),* "Rei Cretariae Romanae Fautorum Acta", 36, 449-457

Esposito A. M. 1992, *Presenze etrusche nel territorio livornese,* Atti I Seminario, Storia del Territorio Livornese, Livorno, 23-28

Firmati and Romualdi A.1998, *Il relitto del Pozzino a Baratti,* in Poggesi G. and Rendini P. (eds.), *Memorie sommerse: Archeologia subacquea in Toscana,* Pitigliano, 184-192.

Galoppini R., Mazzanti R, Menchelli S., Taddei M. 2004 in print, *Un acquedotto romano a Portus Pisanus,* "Rassegna di Archeologia", in print

Gambaro L., 2000: *Commercio e produzione*, "Quaderni

Centro Studi Lunensi", 6, 108-111.

Gisbert, J. A. 1998, *Amfores i vi al territorium de Dianum (Dénia): una proposta de sistematizació de la producció d'amfores al Pais Valencià*, in *El vi a l'Antiguitat.* Atti 2 Col.loqui Internacional d'Arquelogia Romana, Badalona, 383-417

Massa M. 1980-81, *Le anfore del Museo Civico di Rosignano M.mo (Livorno),* "Rassegna di Archeologia", 2, 223-257.

Massa M. 1993, *Anfore commerciali,* in AA.VV., *Pisa .Piazza Dante. Uno spaccato della storia pisana. La campagna di scavo 1991*, Bruni S. (ed.), Pisa, 345-375.

Mazzanti R. (ed.), *La pianura di Pisa e i rilievi contermini*, Roma, 183-204.

Mazzanti R., Menchelli S., Taddei M. 2004 c.s., *L'acquedotto romano di Portus Pisanus*, "Rassegna di Archeologia", in print.

Menchelli 1990-91, *Una fornace di anfore di Dressel 2-4 nell'ager Pisanus ed alcune considerazioni sui contenitori vinari prodotti nell' Etruria settentrionale in età romana,* "Opus", 9-10, 1990-91, 169-184.

Menchelli S. 1997, *Terra sigillata pisana: forniture militari e libero mercato,* "Rei Cretariae Romanae Fautorum Acta", 35, 191-98.

Menchelli S. 2003a, *Il commercio marittimo dei laterizi: alcune considerazioni per le rotte alto-tirreniche,* in Atti II Convegno Archeologia Subacquea, Castiglioncello 2001, Bari 2003, 167-174.

Menchelli S. 2003b, *Pisa nelle dinamiche commerciali mediterranee (III sec. a.C.-VII sec. d. C.)*, in *Pisa ed il Mediterraneo. Uomini, merci, idee dagli Etruschi ai Medici*, Tangheroni M. (ed.), Milano, Skirà, 99-103.

Menchelli S., 2004 c.s., *Nuovi reperti per le figline nell'Etruria settentrionale costiera*, "Studi Classici Orientali", 2004.

Menchelli S., Capelli C., Del Rio A., Pasquinucci M., Thirion –Merle V., Picon M. 2001, *Ateliers de céramiques sigillées de l'Etrurie septentrionale maritime: données archéologiques et archéométriques,* "Rei Cretariae Romanae Fautorum Acta", 37, Lione, 89-105.

Menchelli S., Pasquinucci M. 2000, *Ceramiche orientali nell'etruria settentrionale costiera (II sec. a.C. – VI sec. d.C.)*, "Rei Cretariae Romanae Fautorum Acta", 36, 371-378

Menchelli S., Picchi G. 2001, *Ceramiche nord-Etrusche di eta' romana in Corsica*, in Actes du Congrès Environnement et Identité en Mediterranée, Corte 2000, Biguglia, 129-135.

Morel J. P. 1986, *Céramiques à vernis noir d'Italie trouvées à Délos*, "Bulletin Correspondence Hellénique", 110, 461-493

Morel J. P. 1998, *Le commerce à l'èpoque héllenistique et romaine et les enseignements des épaves,* in G. Volpe editor *Archeologia subacquea,* Siena, 508-510

Oxé A., Comfort H., Kenrick Ph. 2000, *Corpus Vasorum Arretinorum, 2°edition,* Bonn.

Pasquinucci M. 2003, *Pisa e i suoi porti in età etrusca e romana*, in *Pisa ed il Mediterraneo. Uomini, merci, idee dagli Etruschi ai Medici*, Tangheroni M. (ed.), Milano, Skirà, 93-97

Pasquinucci M. 2003, *Pisa romana,* in *Pisa ed il Mediterraneo. Uomini, merci, idee dagli Etruschi ai Medici*, M.Tangheroni editor, Milano, Skirà, 81-91

Pasquinucci M. *et alii* 1998a, *Ceramica a vernice nera dall'Etruria settentrionale costiera,* in Frontini P. and Grassi M.T. (edd.), *Indagini archeometriche relative alla vernice nera. Nuovi dati sulla provenienza e diffusione*, Milano, 101-118

Pasquinucci M. *et alii* 1998b, *Circolazione di merci africane nel Tirreno settentrionale,* "L' Africa Romana", 12, 1401-1421

Pasquinucci M. *et alii* 2000, *La fascia costiera dell'Etruria settentrionale: paleogeografia, porti, attivita' produttive, dinamiche commerciali,* in Attivita' scientifica delle Universita' di Pisa e di Corte, Progetto Interreg II Toscana-Corsica 1997-1999, Pisa 25-31.

Pasquinucci *et al.* 2004 in print, *Analisi archeologiche ed archeometriche sulle anfore nord-africane rinvenute a Vada Volterrana (I-VII sec. d.C.)*, "L'Africa Romana", in print.

Pasquinucci M., Ceccarelli Lemut M. L. 1991, *Fonti antiche e medievali per la viabilità del territorio pisano*, "Bollettino storico Pisano", 38, 111-138.

Pasquinucci M., Del Rio A., Menchelli S. 1998, *Produzioni di vino nell'Etruria settentrionale costiera in età romana,* 2on Col.loqui Interacional d'Arqueologia Romana, *El vi a l'Antiguitat*, Badalona, 357-363.

Pasquinucci M. , Del Rio A., Menchelli S. 2000, *Dalla Baetica all'Etruria settentrionale costiera: le dinamiche commerciali dall'età augustea al tardo-antico,* Congreso Int. Ex Baetica Amphorae, Siviglia 1998, Ecija 2000, 853-860.

Pasquinucci M. , Del Rio A., Menchelli S. 2002, *I Porti dell'Etruria settentrionale costiera (ager Pisanus* e *Volaterranus) e le dinamiche commerciali mediterranee (III secolo a.C. – VI sec d.C.*, "L'Africa romana", 14, 768–778).

Pasquinucci M., and Menchelli S. 1995, *Paesaggio agrario e produzioni artigianali nell'Etruria settentrionale costiera*, in N. Christie (ed.), *Papers of the fifth Conference of Italian Archaeology*, Oxford, 209-217

Pasquinucci M., Menchelli S.1999, *The Landscape and Economy of the Territories of Pisae and Volaterrae (Coastal North Etruria)*, "Journal Roman Archaeology", 12, 1, 1999, 122-141

Pasquinucci M., Menchelli S. 2001, *Agri fertiles ac silvosi: landscape, production and trade in North coastal Etruria,* in *One Land Many Landscapes*, Darvill T. and Gojda M. (edd.), BAR Int. Ser. 987, Oxford, 157-164.

Pasquinucci M., Menchelli S., *The Isola di Coltano Bronze Age village and the salt production in North coastal Tuscany (Italy),* in *Archéologie du sel, Techniques et sociétés dans la Pré - et Protohistoire européenne*, O. Weller editor, Rahden/Westf. 2002,

177-182.

Pasquinucci M., Menchelli S. 2003, *Porti, approdi e dinamiche commerciali nell'ager Pisanus e nella valle dell'Arno (III sec. a.C.-VI sec. d.C.)*, in *Puertos Fluviales Antiguos: Ciudad, Desarollo e Infraestructuras*, IV Jornadas de Arqueología Subacuática, Valencia , 237-249.

Pasquinucci M., Menchelli S. 2004, *Vina Graeca, Vina Tusca,* in *Miscellanea in Onore di Orlanda Pancrazzi*, Bruni S., Caruso T., Massa M. (edd.), Pisa, 310-316.

Pasquinucci M., Menchelli S., Del Rio A. 2003, *Archeologia subacquea a Vada Volaterrana: il porto, i relitti, i commerci alla luce delle recenti acquisizioni,* Atti II Convegno Archeologia Subacquea, Castiglioncello 2001, Bari 2003, 35-42.

Pasquinucci M., Menchelli S., Mazzanti R., Marchisio M., D'Onofrio L. 2001, *Coastal Archaeology in North Etruria. Geomorphologic, archaeological, archive, magnetometric and geoelectrical researches,* in "Revue d'Archéométrie", 25, 187-201.

Picchi G. 2003, I rapporti *commerciali fra Etruria centro-settentrionale e Corsica: alcune evidenze per le rotte mediterranee (IV sec. a.C.-VI sec. d.C.),* Atti II Convegno Archeologia Subacquea, Castiglioncello 2001, Bari, 295-301.

Roncioni R. 1844, *Delle Istorie Pisane, Libri XVI,* "Archivio Storico Pisano", I, 17-18

Rouge J. 1966, *Recherches sur l'organisation du commerce maritime en Méditerranée sous l'Empire Romain,* Paris

Sangriso P. 1998, *Terra sigillata e politica augustea: alcune note su Cn. Ateius,* "Studi Classici e Orientali", 46, 3, 919-932

Targioni Tozzetti G., 1768: *Relazioni d' alcuni viaggi fatti in diverse parti della Toscana*, II, Firenze.

Tchernia A. 1983, *Italian wine in Gaul,* in Garnsey P., Hopkins K., Whittaker C.R. (eds.), *Trade in the Ancient Economy,* London, 87-117

Thierrin-Michael G. 1992 , *Römische Weinamphoren,* Freiburg.

The Mediterranean coarse ware pottery trade (3rd century BC-7th century AD)

Simonetta Menchelli

Abstract
This paper focuses on the coarse ware pottery trade from the 3rd century BC to the 7th century AD. Some case studies are shown concerning local, regional and Mediterranean traffics and their political, economic and social relationships.

It is well known that Roman coarse ware pottery consists of all vessels used for preparing and cooking foods, for domestic purposes, for serving at table and preserving food in the pantries and cellars. In these vessels the functional aspects prevail over aesthetic ones. (For the definition of the term "coarse pottery" and the history of research see Olcese 1993 and Panella 1996).

In the specialized literature until recently ordinary merchandise was thought not to have been traded in the Roman period, except on a small scale. Nowadays this opinion is changing thanks to many archaeological and archaeometric studies and to the progress of underwater archaeology which has discovered a remarkable quantity of coarse pottery in several shipwrecks.

At present we know that coarse wares could be traded throughout the Mediterranean if endowed with good technical characteristics. These characteristics were necessary especially for kitchen ware, since the vessels had to be refractory in order to permit thorough cooking of the food. Particular clays were necessary also for the *mortaria*, as their big handles were difficult to form (Olcese 1993, 104). We shall see that high quality was necessary but not sufficient: specialized vessels could travel successfully on long distance exchanges only thanks to a combination of political and economic factors.

Latium and Campania - in the late Republican and in the first Imperial periods - and then North Africa up to the Late Roman period, produced and exported a great quantity of coarse pottery in a wide range; also Eastern Mediterranean wares travelled in the long distance trade.

These regions shipped a great deal of foodstuffs throughout the Mediterranean; exports were controlled (partly at least) by the State and the coarse pottery accompanied grain and amphorae in the holds of the ships.

As for coarse ware from Lazio and Campania, many specialized workshops have been identified in the Tiber valley, at Rome, in its outskirts and in the gulf of Naples (Olcese 1994; Di Giovanni 1996; Gasperetti 1996). At the moment it is very difficult to distinguish, either by morphological or by archaeometric standards the products of the many workshops working in this great area (Olcese 1996, 438-440). These ateliers produced high quality vessels, especially cooking ware (*caccabi*, *ollae*, *patinae*) and *mortaria* (Gianfrotta-Pomey 1981, 182). Their fabrics were characterized by volcanic inclusions, giving the vessels their excellent refractory quality for cooking food.

The export of coarse wares from Lazio and Campania reached its peak from the 2nd century B.C., up to the Augustan period, and this trade was strictly connected with the wine sea-routes directed towards regions undergoing Romanization.

The Mandrague de Giens shipwreck is a good illustration of this economic phenomenon. This ship sailed from Lazio, probably from Terracina about 60-50 B.C., and it was wrecked along the Gallic coasts near Tolone (Tchernia *et al.* 1978). Its cargo consisted of Dressel 1 amphorae; piles of black glazed and coarse vessels were set in the free spaces among them: proving that all merchandise was loaded at the same time. In total 891 fragmentary vessels have been salvaged; they were dishes, pans, pots, lids. Every form was manufactured in different size standards, confirming the "industrial" activity of these ateliers.

The remarkable presence of this pottery in the *castra* and colonies founded in the 2nd century B.C. confirms that its trade was closely connected with the process of Romanization.

We have also archaeometric and quantitative data concerning *Albintimilium* (see fig.2) and *Luna* (Ratti Squellati 1987, pp. 465-495)

The coarse ware from *Latium* and *Campania* was common in the Gallic *oppida*, together with the Tyrrhenian wine amphorae and the black glazed vessels, which constituted the wine service. In this case the presence of imported ware is an important cultural marker. It shows that the local elite wished to acquire various aspects of the Roman lifestyle, such as symposium and Roman cooking. For example, the success of the Italian red slipped pans in Gallia was due to the acquired habit of baking hardtacks and cakes, according to the Roman-Campanian style (Bats 1988, 202).

Along the same sea-routes, the quantities of imported coarse wares might change according both to the location (coastal or inland site, with or without river links etc.) and to the socio-economic context (rural or urban centre, production, consumption or redistribution site). In this

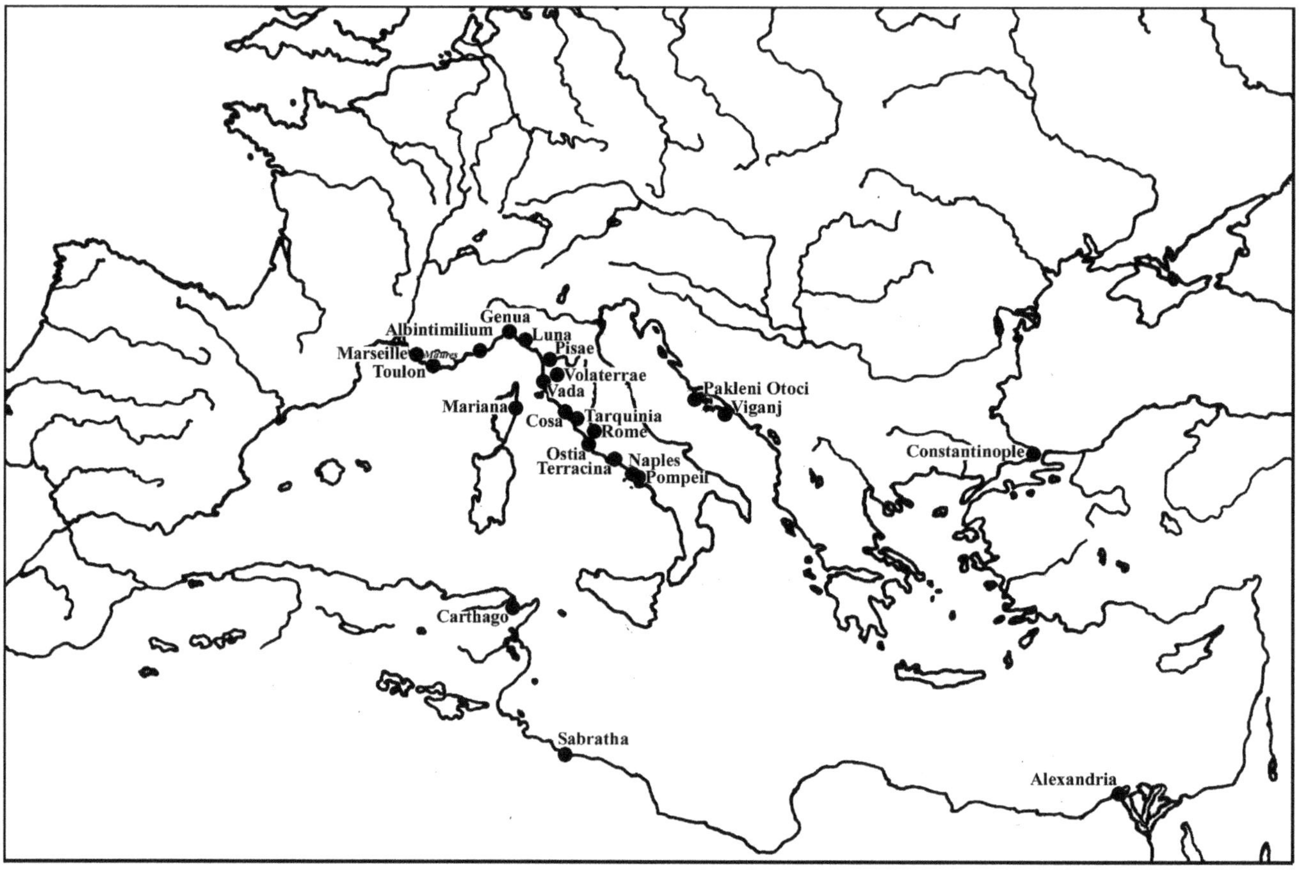

FIGURE 1.

respect the comparison between the Roma and Ostia contexts is very meaningful: the provenances of the imported coarse pottery show very different quantitative data (Pavolini 1996).

Another factor that influenced the success of the imported pottery was the presence of local specialized workshops. For example, at *Luna* the imported wares predominated from the foundation of the colony up to the 5th century A.D. (Rossignani, Bruno, Locatelli 2002), whereas at *Pisae*, whose pottery production is well known, the imports are less abundant, at least in the *domus* known at present (Pasquinucci-Storti 1989) (fig. 3,1). Obviously, in the 1st century A.D. at Pompeii the imported coarse ware was very unusual (less than 3%: Di Giovanni 1996, 72).

As regards the well-known North-African coarse ware, this pottery was plentifully distributed throughout the entire Roman world, especially in the Western Mediterranean coasts, from the 2nd to the 5th century A.D. (Reynolds 1995, 102-103).

It was mostly kitchen ware (casseroles, pans, dishes/lids) produced with characteristics which technically improved its cooking quality (e.g. blackened surfaces; grooves both in the inner wall and in the exterior bottom: for technical aspects see Schuring 1988). Other forms were *mortaria,* flanged bowls, and other bowls for various purposes.

This pottery travelled along with the other North African exports: grain, olive oil and *garum* amphorae, terra sigillata, lamps and marble. The commercial flows from North Africa were conditioned by the *annona*, and in particular by the grain supplies to Rome (Fulford 1987, 71; Lo Cascio 1990; Tomber 1993, 144). The foodstuff imports to Rome influenced the movement of goods in general, exerting what G.E. Rickman calls a gravitational pull on the main grain growing areas of the Mediterranean and on the organisation of shipping and other resources (Rickman 1980, 262-263; Lo Cascio 1991, 329; 349-351). State and private trade were closely intertwined: we know that the *navicularii* (financiers and shipowners) involved in the *Annona* trade let spare capacity on their ships for the cargos of other merchants (*mercatores, negotiatores*) (Rougè 1966, 245-294; Tomber 1993, 145). From the 3rd century onwards, *Navicularii* of Africa were exempted from the port charges on the goods they carried for their own trade (Warmington 1954, 61-62).

Several shipwrecks containing African merchandise have been identified: one example is the Trincere shipwreck, near Tarquinia (Pontacolone-Incitti 1991) (Fig 3, 2).

In this ship 75.96% of the cargo consisted of kitchen wares and 10.58% of *mortaria* and bowls. The amphorae amounted to only 12.50%, but there is the suspicion that many items had been stolen before the excavations.

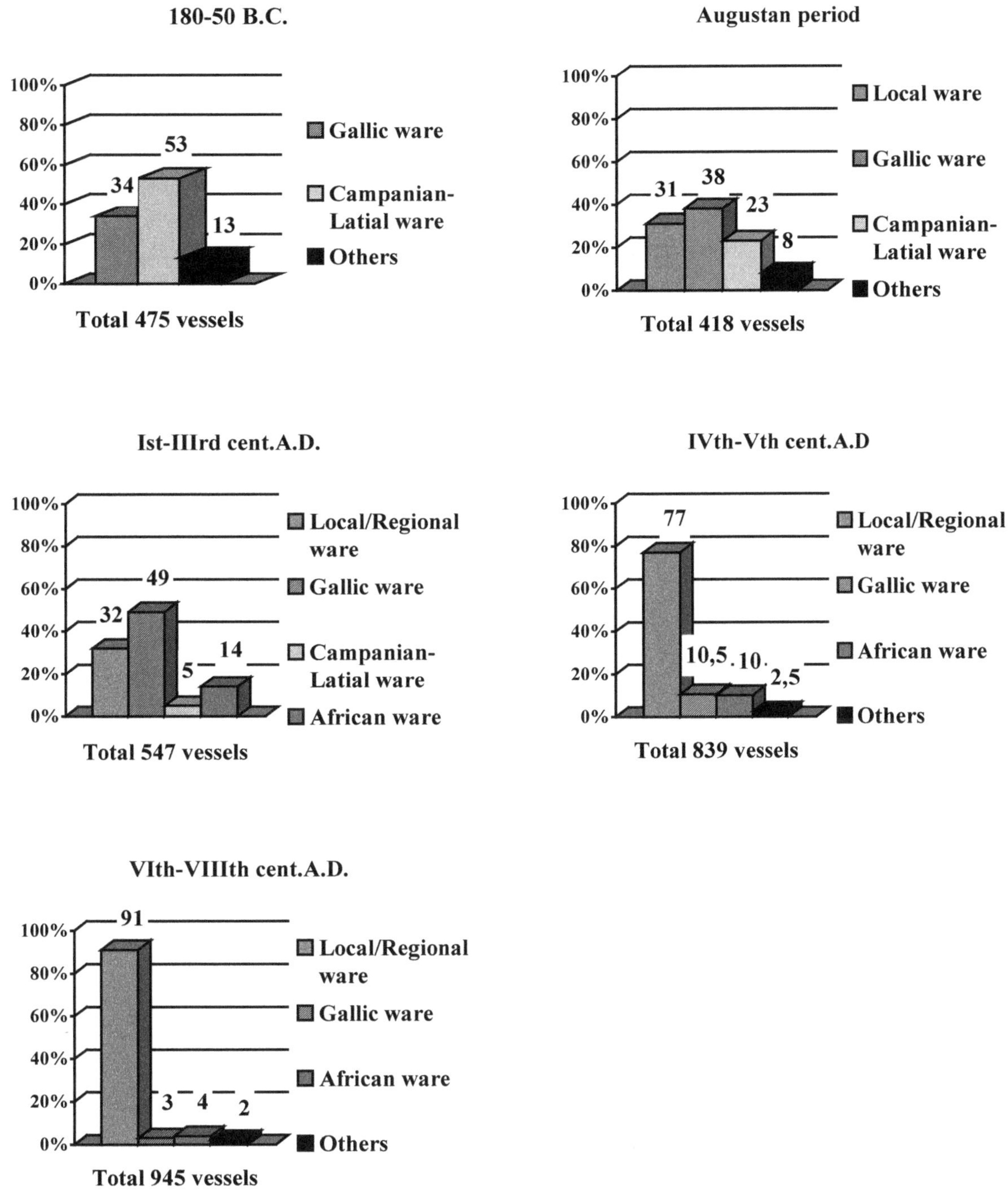

FIGURE 2. *ALBINTIMILIUM* (*CASTRUM* FOUNDED IN 180 B.C.)
After G. Olcese, *Le ceramiche comuni di Albintimilium*, Firenze 1993

The location of the wreck north of Rome shows that ships loaded with African merchandise could sail independently of urban *Annona* business. North African coarse ware vessels were shipped along the main sea-routes Carthago-Rome but, as they were endowed with good technical characteristics, after being unloaded in the harbours, they could follow their own pattern of distribution and thus stimulate the demand still further.

Many Italian and provincial workshops imitated African ware (in general see Fontana 1995): this is further evidence that these vessels commanded a certain value in the markets of the Roman world.

Obviously, African imports were abundant particularly in the redistribution centres: in the *horrea* excavated at *Vada Volaterrana,* the harbour serving both *Volaterrae* and a rich hinterland, African coarse pottery amounted to 30.70% (fig. 3,3), whereas at *Albintimilium* it was a maximum of 14% in the 1st-3rd century levels (fig. 2). At

1) *PISAE*. ARCIVESCOVADO *DOMUS*
After M. Pasquinucci - S. Storti, 1989.

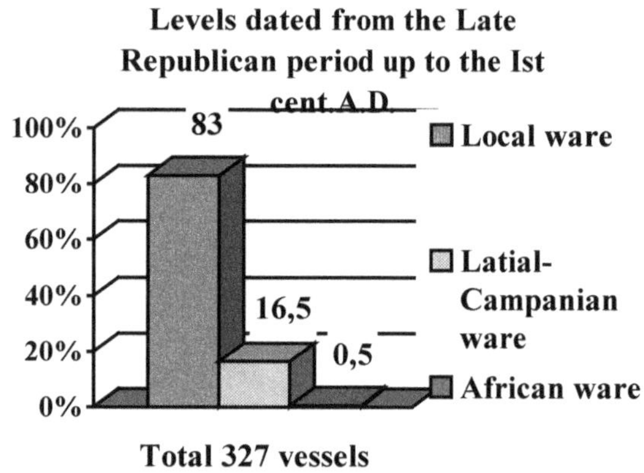

2) TRINCERE SHIPWRECK
After L. Pontacolone - M. Incitti 1991, pp.543-570

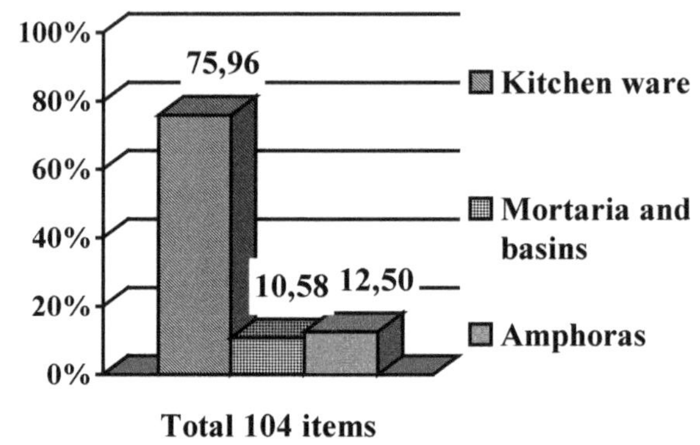

3) *VADA VOLATERRANA. HORREA.*
After M. Pasquinucci - S. Menchelli (Editors), *Vada Volaterrana. I. Gli Horrea. Stratigrafie, Strutture, Materiali*, forthcoming.

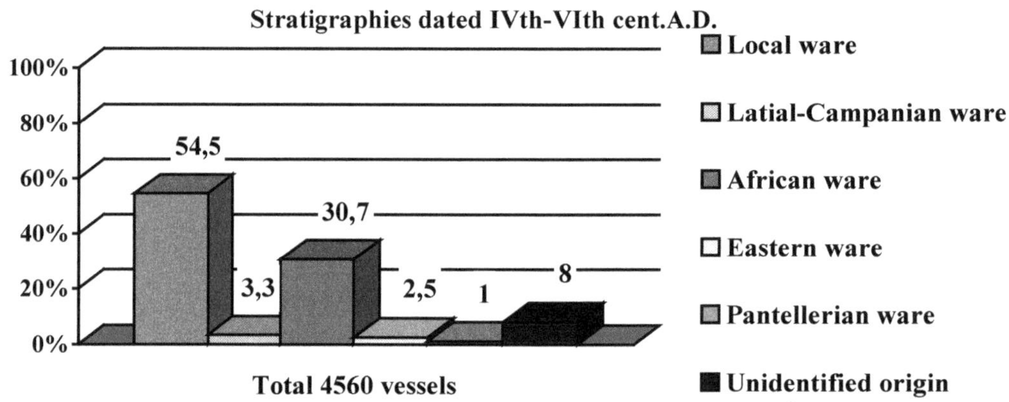

4-5) OSTIA. TERME DEL NUOTATORE. AREA NE.
After L. Anselmino - C.M. Coletti - M.L. Ferrantini - C. Panella, 1986, pp. 45-81.

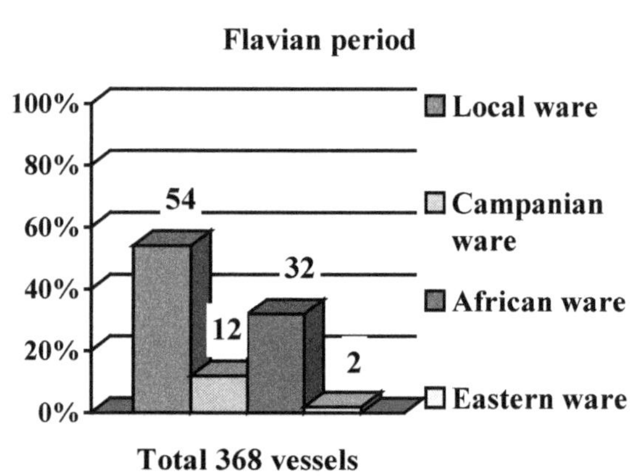

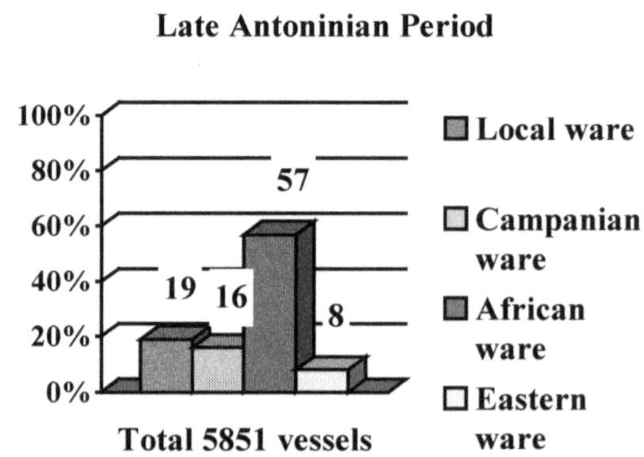

FIGURE 3.

Ostia in the Late Antonine period the African pottery even amounted to 57% of the cooking ware (Anselmino et Al., 1986) (fig. 3,5).

As far as the Eastern coarse pottery is concerned, this was another ware whose distribution was connected with the *Annona* trade, in particular with the grain sea-route Alessandria-Roma. A direct route was probably taken from Rome to Alexandria, whereas the journey to Rome was an indirect one: from Cyprus, to the southern coasts of Asia Minor and then westwards to Crete, Sicily and the west coast of Italy (Rickman 1980, 266). Besides grain, Eastern regions exported to the West precious wines. From the 4th century onwards, Constantinople's demand for consumer goods drove the agricultural and manufacturing production in the Eastern regions. The Late Roman amphorae 1-7 provide evidence of the distribution of Eastern wine throughout the whole Mediterranean basin (Panella 1993).

Eastern coarse wares were produced in several workshops in Asia Minor, in Attica and Crete. They were widely distributed along the Mediterranean coasts from the 2nd century A.D., but its quantity is not comparable to the Campanian-Latial and African wares: also in the 4th and 5th century contexts its percentages do not reflect the remarkable presence of Eastern amphorae (Reynolds 1995, 103).

At Ostia the Eastern fabrics amounted to 2% in the Flavian period and 8% in the late Antonine period (fig.3, 4); at *Vada Volaterrana* they were at 2.5%. The items included cooking and table wares (pans, pots with wide sloping rim, casseroles); in the table ware the most common form was the trefoil-mouthed pitcher, produced in morphologic and dimensional variants by several Aegean workshops (in particular in Attica and Crete) in the 1st-4th centuries A.D. (Coletti-Pavolini 1996). This form reached the Western Mediterranean coasts as far as Marseille (Pasqualini 1998, 297, forms 16 and 17).

Several of these pitchers appear to be manufactured in the same fabrics of thin walled jugs, in particular of jugs Ricci I/122, characterized by ridged ribbons: it is clear that they both were part of the same table service (Coletti-Pavolini 1996, 400; Menchelli-Pasquinucci 2000, 376).

The great variety of fabrics suggests that these pitchers could have been used also as cooking vessels (perhaps as boilers), as well as table ware. Because of their abundant presence at Ostia, it has been thought that they might also be carriage vessels, which added the worth of the content (most probably precious wine) to the technical quality of the table vessels (Coletti-Pavolini 1996, 400).

Local factors conditioned the markets receptivity: at Ostia, besides the pitchers, the Eastern pots and casseroles are well represented, at *Vada Volaterrana*, instead, this cooking ware was not successful, evidently it could not face up to the competition of local and African coarse pottery; at Napoli, in the Carminiello ai Mannesi context, Eastern table ware was absent, in favour of many imported Eastern kitchen vessels and amphorae (Arthur 1994, 218).

In two shipwrecks identified along the Croatian coasts (Pakleni Otoci = Isole Infernali and S. Ivana Cape, near Viganj in the Pelješac Channel) only coarse and thin walled vessels appear to be found. The forms (casseroles, pots, pans, trefoil-mouthed pitchers, jugs with ridged ribbons) are peculiar to the Eastern workshops (Ilakovac 1968; Istenic 1988).

At the moment we do not know whether they can be considered as evidence of imports from eastern regions or from the Italian Adriatic coasts, as some Apulian workshops imitated Eastern forms (Leone-Turchiano 2002). It is very likely that these vessels travelled together with grain, since amphorae have not been found. Anyway the Eastern coarse pottery both in original and in imitated forms appear to have a significant presence along the Adriatic sea-routes.

Till now we have focused on those regions which exported huge quantities of goods, including coarse pottery as secondary or tertiary cargos. In these cases the distance travelled by coarse wares depends on the value of the primary cargo, on the frequency of its exports and on a special "political" orders at the final destination (Fulford-Peacock 1984, 256-257; Reynolds 1995, 128).

The case of the Pantellerian cooking ware is clearly different as it was produced by a small island which did not export foodstuff. However, especially in the late Roman period, it had great commercial success along the African coast from Carthage to Sabratha, on the main sea-routes from Carthage to Marseille and along the Iberian coasts. This ware is black, sometimes varying to reddish buff inside; the surfaces are smooth and sometimes show evidence of light burnishing (Fulford-Peacock 1984). It appears to have been made mostly by hand, but the turntable was also used (Santoro 2000, 561). The forms were designed for efficient stacking during transport: the most successful vessels were bowls, handled bowls, and casseroles. As regards minero-petrographic aspects, this ware is clearly characterized because it contains inclusions originating in peralkaline volcanic terrains which are very rare in the Mediterranean basin, but well known on Pantelleria.

This coarse pottery was particularly proof against thermic shocks and, of course, it had an intrinsic value. According to Peacock the Pantellerian ware production was driven by urgent need: the island was not suited to farming (Ovid called Pantelleria *sterilis*: Fasti, III, 567) and the inhabitants were able to acquire the necessary foodstuffs by means of trading the specialized vessels (Peacock 1982, 79-80).

Evidence of this traffic is provided by the shipwreck (or most likely a lost cargo or a discharge) identified near the Scauri harbour, in the southwestern area of the island. About 700 Pantellerian vessels have been salvaged; they appear to have been produced expressly for export (Santoro 2002).

The privileged trade with the territories of Sicily and Carthago favoured the entry of this pottery into the main sea-routes. The most remarkable quantities of finds are just in these regions and in southern Italy (Reynolds 1995, fig.166). Further north the Pantellerian ware was distributed in small quantities: R. Tomber presents the trade of these vases as an example of peripatetic shipping, that is, small quantities of pottery unloaded harbour after harbour along the Western Mediterranean coasts (Tomber 1993, 148). At *Vada Volaterrana*, for example, the Pantellerian was only 1% (fig. 3, 3).

Besides these wares, that were successful in long distance exchange, we also know of coarse pottery of good technical quality that was involved in small and medium scale trading.

Now we shall focus on the case studies of Provençal micaceous pottery and North Etruscan gabbric ware.

The Provençal pottery is a black handmade cooking ware; its fabric is rich in micaceous inclusions; the exterior surfaces were pocked in order to make the vessels both lighter and more fire-proof at the same time (Olcese 1993). The forms were pots, pans and bowls (Olcese 1993, fig. 18); they were produced in a region not particularly renowned for agricultural surplus, that is in the Maures Massif area and in the Argens Valley. From the 2nd century B.C. up to the 4th century A.D. it was capillarily distributed along the coastal sites between the Rhone and Western Liguria: at *Albintimilium* it was found in high quantities (fig. 2).

The Roches d'Aurelle (Var) shipwreck gives evidence of the trade mechanisms of the Provençal coarse pottery. This small ship has been completely excavated: it has been estimated to be loaded with 160 *tegulae*; from 100 to 150 imbrices; 50 wine amphorae Gauloises 5; 850 micaceous vessels (R. Lequement - B. Liou, 1975, pp.76 ss.; A. Pollino et al., 1987, 25-49).

This presence in the same cargo of different goods coming from the same region was due to wholesale dealers, who bought goods from various ateliers and retailed them along the coasts. In this small scale cabotage trade great quantities of coarse pottery could not reach sites too far away from the production centres.

Another case study we would like to focus on is the gabbric North Etruscan coarse pottery. It was produced in many workshops identified in the Fine and Cecina river valleys, belonging to *ager Pisanus* and *Volaterranus.* The most frequent forms were pots and pans (Cherubini-Del Rio 1997; Menchelli 2003B c.s.).

The kitchen ware was of good technical quality thanks to the gabbros which can absorb heat and release it slowly, thus permitting a careful even cooking.

These vessels were manufactured from the Hellenistic period up to the Late Roman. A great quantity of this pottery has been found in the *Vada Volaterrana horrea*, which is in a redistribution context; it indicates the wide circulation of this pottery in the local markets and beyond. Archaeometric analyses prove that the gabbric kitchen ware was traded along the coastal strip between *Luna* and *ager Cosanus.* As regards the table ware, north Etruscan forms, in particular jugs, have been identified at Mariana in Corsica (Menchelli-Picchi 2001).

It is possible that the diffusion of the North Etruscan coarse pottery overlapped with the distribution of the bricks and tiles stamped by Pisan-Volterran *gentes (Rasinii, Caecinae, Venuleii Aproniani, Nonii).* These bricks and tiles were distributed along the Tyrrhenian coast from *Lunae* to central Etruria, and in the islands of Elba, Sardinia and Corsica (Menchelli 2003A c.s.). While other North Etruscan goods, such as terra sigillata and wine amphorae, were widespread throughout the Mediterranean (Menchelli *et al.* 2001; Pasquinucci-Del Rio-Menchelli 1998), the local coarse pottery was less successful.

At this time we do not know whether North Etruscan brick and tiles and coarse pottery were loaded in the ships along with terra sigillata and wine amphorae or (as in the Provençal case) their distribution was organized by small ships specialized in cabotage trading along a limited coastal strip. It is very likely that both situations occurred, nevertheless North Etruscan coarse pottery was unable to exceed the boundaries of small/middle scale trading. This was probably due to the competition of the Campanian-Latial and African wares, which, as we saw, were widely distributed along the Tyrrhenian coasts.

After reviewing these case studies we can conclude that from the 3rd century B.C. up to the Late Roman period the coarse pottery trade was not at all rare, and was accompanied by various economic aspects.

The highest success was guaranteed by the accompanying factor of high technical quality and political and economic elements (e.g. export of foodstuffs to Rome or regions undergoing Romanization, military supply, etc.). The main sea-routes connected with *annona* and those of the cabotage trading were intertwined (Tomber 1993, 144): coarse pottery was distributed by both the great *navicularii* of long distance trade and by petty merchants and hawkers through local markets and fairs.

Pottery, and coarse pottery in particular, was secondary or tertiary cargo in the hold, but this does not diminish a certain intrinsic value of the coarse ware. Above all, commercial success depended on the pottery's technical characteristics: packing vessels in the holds full of foodstuffs reduced carriage prices, but pottery had to possess a minimum of technical qualities, in order to be bought. No Iberian coarse pottery was involved in middle/long-distance exchanges, despite the enormous export of metals and Dressel 20 and Dressel 7-13 amphorae from Spain during the early Empire (Fulford-Peacock 1984, p. 256). Evidently this ware did not possess the characteristics necessary to survive long distance exchanges.

Other wares were exported on a regional and extra regional scale: high quality was necessary but not sufficient: specialized vessels had to be supported by political and economic factors to travel successfully on the long distance exchanges.

In conclusion, even if conditioned by various elements, the coarse ware pottery trade appears not to have been completely parasitic: it gained a certain autonomy and retained its own economic value.

References

Anselmino, L. *et al.* 1986, L.Anselmino, C.M.Coletti, M.L. Ferrantini, C.Panella, *Ostia. Terme del Nuotatore*, in *Societa' Romana e Impero Tardoantico,* III, A.Giardina ed., Roma-Bari , 45-81.

Arthur, P. 1994, *Ceramica comune tardo-antica ed alto-medievale*, in Il Complesso Archeologico di Carminiello ai Mannesi, Napoli (Scavi 1983-1984), P. Arthur ed., Lecce , pp. 181-220.

Bats, M. 1988 *Vaisselle et alimentation à Olbia de Provence (v. 350 -v. 50 a. C.)*, Paris.

Bats, M. (editor) 1996, *Les céramiques communes de Campanie et de Narbonnaise (Ier siècle av. J.C.-IInd siècle apres J.C.)*, Napoli.

Cherubini, L., Del Rio, A. 1997, *Officine di età romana nell'Etruria settentrionale costiera: impianti, produzioni, attrezzature,* RCRFActa 35 1997, 133-141.

Coletti, M.C. and Pavolini, M. 1966, *Ceramica comune da Ostia,* in Bats 1996 editor, 391-419.

Di Giovanni, V. 1996, *Produzione e consumo di ceramica da cucina nella Campania romana (II a.C.-II d.C.)*, in Bats 1996, pp. 65-103.

Fontana, S. 1998, *Le imitazioni della sigillata africana e le ceramiche da mensa italiche tardo-antiche.* In Colloquio in onore di J.W. Hayes, Ceramica in Italia: VI-VII secolo , Saguì, L. editor, Firenze, All'Insegna del Giglio, pp. 83-100.

Fulford, M. 1987 *Economic interdependence among urban communities of the Roman Mediterranean,* World Archaeology 19,1, 58-75.

Fulford, M.G. and Peacock, D.P. S. 1984, *Excavation at Carthage: the British Mission,* I, 2, Sheffield, pp. 157-159.

Gasperetti, G. 1996, *Produzione e consumo della ceramica comune da mensa e dispensa nella Campania romana.* In Bats 1996, pp. 19-63.

Gianfrotta, P.A., and Pomey, P. 1981, *Archeologia subacquea,* Roma 1981.

Ilakovac, B. 1968, *Keramika iz antičkog broda potonulog Kod Paklenih Otoka,* Diadora 4, 1968, pp.183-202.

Istenič, J. 1988, *Kuhinjsko posuđe egejskih tipova na nalazištu Rodik-Nekropola pod Jezerom,* Diadora 10, pp.99-110).

Leone, D. and Turchiano, M. 2002., *L'Apulia e le rotte commerciali di eta' tardo-antica attraverso le testimonianze archeologiche,* L'Africa Romana, XIV Convegno Internazionale di Studi, 857-890.

Lequement, R. and Liou, B. 1975, *Les epaves de la cote de Transalpine*, in Cahiers Ligures de Prehistoire and Archaeologie, XXIV, 1975, pp.76 ss.

Lo Cascio, E. 1990, *L'organizzazione annonaria*, in S.Settis, Civilta' dei Romani, Milano 1990, 229-248.

Lo Cascio E., 1991, *Forme dell'economia imperiale.* In Storia di Roma II, 2. Torino 1991, 313-365.

Menchelli, S. 2003A, c.s. *Il commercio marittimo dei laterizi: alcune considerazioni per le rotte alto-tirreniche,* in Atti Convegno Archeologia Subacquea, Castiglioncello 2001, in stampa.

Menchelli, S. 2003B, c.s., *Per un catalogo delle ceramiche comuni nell'Etruria settentrionale costiera*, RCRFActa 38, in stampa.

Menchelli, S. *et al.* 2001, S. Menchelli, C.Capelli, A.Del Rio, M. Pasquinucci, M.Picon, and V. Thiron Merle, *Ateliers de céramiques sigillées de l'Etrurie septentrionale maritime: données archéologiques et archéométriques,* RCRFActa 37, Lione 2001, pp. 89-105.

Menchelli, S. and Pasquinucci, M. 2000, *Ceramiche orientali nell'Etruria settentrionale costiera (II sec. a.C.-VI sec. d.C.),* RCRFActa 36, pp. 371-378.

Menchelli, S. and Picchi, G. 2001, *Ceramiche nord-Etrusche di eta' romana in Corsica*, in Congrés Environnement et Identité en Mediterranée, Actes du Congrès Corte 2000, Biguglia 2001, pp. 129-135.

Olcese, G. 1993, *Le ceramiche comuni di Albintimilium,* Firenze.

Olcese, G. 1994, *La produzione ceramica a Roma in epoca repubblicana e nella prima eta' imperiale: notizie preliminari sulle analisi di laboratorio,* in Ceramica Romana e Archeometria: lo stato degli studi, a cura di G. Olcese, Firenze 1994, pp. 237-246.

Olcese, G. 1996, *Ceramiche comuni di origine tirrenica centro-meridionale tra il II sec. a.C.e il I sec. d.C.: problemi aperti. L'evidenza dei reperti di Albintimilium,* in Bats 1996, pp. 421-445.

Panella, C. 1993, "*Merci e scambi nel Mediterraneo tardoantico*", *Storia di Roma,* III, 2, (Torino), 613-697.

Panella, C. 1996, *Lo studio delle ceramiche comuni di eta' romana: qualche riflessione,* in Bats (editor), pp. 9-15.

Pasqualini, M. 1998, *Les céramiques communes en basse Provence (I ^{er}-IIIe s.). Essai de classification.* In Fouilles à Marseille. Les mobiliers (Ier-VIIe s.ap. J.-

C.). Études Massaliètes 5, 1998, 293-308.

Pasquinucci, M., Del Rio, A. and Menchelli, S. 1998, *Produzioni di vino nell'Etruria settentrionale costiera in età romana,* 2[on] Colloqui Interacional d'Arqueologia Romana, El vi a l'Antiguitat, Badalona, pp. 357-363.

Pasquinucci, M. and Storti, S., *Pisa antica. Scavi nel giardino dell' Arcivescovado,* Pontedera 1989.

Pasquinucci, M. *et al.* 1998, M. Pasquinucci, D.Alessi, S.Bianchini, A.Del Rio and S.Menchelli, Circolazioni di merci africane nel Tirreno settentrionale (I-VII sec. d.C.), L'Africa Romana 12, 1998, 1401-1421.

Pavolini, C. 1966, *Mercato ostiense e mercato romano: alcuni contesti ceramici a confronto.* In "Roman Ostia Revisited", Edited by A. Gallina Zevi and A.Claridge, Roma, pp. 223-242.

Peacock, D.P.S. 1982, *Pottery in the Roman World, an Ethnoarchaeological Approach,* London 1982

Pollino, A. *et al.* 1987 *L'épave des Roches d'Aurelle,* in Cahiers d'Archéologie Subaquatique, 6, 1987, pp. 25-49.

Pontacolone, L. and Incitti, M. 1991, *Un relitto con carico di merci africane di eta' imperiale alle Trincere (Tarquinia),* Africa Romana VIII, 1991, pp. 543-570.

Ratti Squellati, G. 1987, *Produzioni locali e materiali d'importazione nella ceramica di uso comune,* Quaderni Centro Lunense 12, pp. 465-495.

Reynolds, P. 1995, *Trade in the Western Mediterranean , AD 400-700: the ceramic evidence,* BAR Int. Ser. 604 (Oxford).

Rickman, G., 1980, *The Grain Trade under the Roman Empire,* MAAR 36, pp. 261-275.

Rossignani, M.P., Bruno, B. and Locatelli, D. 2002, *Insediamenti ed economia nell' area di Portus Lunae nella prima meta' del II secolo A.C.,* L' Africa Romana 12, 2002, 753-765.

Rougè, J. 1966, *Recherches sur l'organisation du commerce maritime en Méditerranée sous l'empire romain,* Paris.

Santoro, S. 2000, *"Pantellerian Ware": il Progetto di Ricerca (1998-2000),* RCRFActa 36, 2000, pp. 561-566.

Santoro, S. 2002, *Pantellerian Ware: produzione di ceramica da cucina di Pantelleria diffusa in tutto il Mediterraneo occidentale,* in L'Africa Romana, XIV Convegno Internazionale di Studi.

Schuring, J. M. 1988, *Terra sigillata africana from the San Sisto Vecchio in Rome,* Bullettin Antieke Beschaving, 63, pp. 1-68.

Tchernia, A. *et al.* 1978, *L'épave romaine de la Madrague de Giens (Var),* Gallia, suppl. 34, Paris.

Tomber, R. 1993, *Quantitative approaches to the investigation of long-distance exchange,* JRA, 142-166.

Warmington, B.H. 1954, *The North African provinces from Diocletian to the Vandal conquest,* Cambridge.

Inland navigation in ancient Northern Italy: The port of *Ticinum*

Rodolfo Bargnesi

Abstract
The importance in antiquity of the inland waterway system of the river Po and its affluents is supported by considerable literary, epigraphic and archaeological evidence. *Ticinum* (Pavia) was a land and river junction connecting the western Alpine passes and the Adriatic Sea, thus playing a significant role well into the Middle Ages.

I. The hydrography of northern Italy is characterized by the great waterway system formed by the river Po and its affluents from left and right, through which the region is widely accessible. In the basin there also lie Prealpine lakes (west to east, Lake Maggiore, Lake Como, Lake Iseo, Lake Garda), which stretch to the foot of the central Alpine passes (Figure 1).

The earliest extant description of the Po waterway system dates back to the middle of the 2nd century B.C., when historiographic reflections on northern Italy were being made in Rome for the first time:[1] I refer to Polybius 2. 16. 6-12. In the text we find the first reference to navigation on the waters of the Po.[2] According to Polybius, the river was navigated from one of its two mouths (Volano) for 2000 stadia, (about 350 km): the approximate distance to the confluence of the rivers Tanaro and Po,[3] on the border between today's regions of Piemonte and Lombardia. The Polybian measure has been considered "unrealistic"[4] because it is a round number, however, being the Greek translation of 240 Roman miles it may well originate from a positive measurement for itinerary purposes.[5]

A century and a half after Polybius, Strabo in his *Geography* often emphasized the wealth of waters of Cisalpine Gaul, including this among the factors determining the famous prosperity of the land:[6] in the fifth book there are no few references to the waterways of the most important towns in the region.[7] In particular, concerning navigation of the Po, which is considered the main artery,[8] Strabo supplies significant information about the duration of the journeys: he mentions a sailing service, probably included in the *cursus publicus* organized in the Augustan age,[9] taking two days and two nights from Piacenza to Ravenna.[10]

In Strabo's view, the presence of waters is really prominent in the *Venetia* area: "Now this whole country is filled with river and marshes, but particularly the part that belongs to Heneti" (Strab. 5. 1. 11; transl. Jones 1923). The northwestern Adriatic coast, into which the Po Delta branches and the Veneto River flow, was to a greater extent in antiquity than today a land of marshes and lagoons. The area had been the object of hydraulic operations since Etruscan times,[11] yet not till the Augustan age was the problem really tackled of cross connecting the stretches of rivers whose waters mingle in the lagoons. These are generally parallel, running perpendicular to the coastline.

The canals (*fossae*) built between the 1st century B. C. and the 1st century A. D. made the north-south shore axis from Aquileia to Ravenna fully navigable.[12] Among them the well known *fossa Augusta*, as seen in Strabo, connected inland Po navigation and the Adriatic harbour of Ravenna, making use of a dry branch of the Po Delta, named *Padusa*.[13] Vitruvius says larch-wood was carried along such a waterway, from the Alpine production area to Ravenna and thence to various Adriatic towns.[14]

Further data concerning inland navigation in northern Italy are supplied by Pliny the Elder and Tacitus: the former, the author of the most highly articulated and detailed description of the Po hydrographic system to have come down to us from antiquity,[15] mentions the role of the waterways in connection with trade, and identifies Turin as the point at which the Po became navigable;[16] the latter constantly mentions the Po in his descriptions of the battles and movements of troops during the military

[1] See Tozzi 1976.
[2] Pol. 2. 16. 10-11: "It (scil. Po) is navigable for about two thousand stades from the mouth called *Olana*; for the stream, which has been a single one from its source, divides at a place called *Trigaboli*, one of the two mouths being called *Padua* and the other *Olana*. At the latter there is a harbour, which affords as safe anchorage as any in the Adriatic" (transl. Paton 1960).
[3] See Philipp 1942, c. 2188; Walbank 1957, 179.
[4] Boffo 1977, 627 note 16.
[5] See Uggeri 1987, 321-322 and note 83.
[6] See Strab. 5. 1. 12.
[7] See Strab. 5. 1. 7 for *Patavium*; 5. 1. 8 for *Opitergium*, *Concordia*, *Hadria* and *Vicetia*; 5. 1. 8 for *Aquileia*. See also Tozzi 1988 and Bargnesi 1997, 93-94.
[8] See Strab. 5. 1. 5: "As for all the cities that are situated above the marshes in the interior, the inland voyages afforded thereto by the rivers are wonderful, but particularly the *Padus*" (transl. Jones 1923). See also Alfieri 1981.
[9] See Uggeri 1987, 322-323; 330-331.
[10] See Strab. 5. 1. 11: "Of the distance from *Placentia* to *Ariminum* I have already spoken; there is also a voyage thence to by the *Padus* down to Ravenna which takes two days and nights" (transl. Jones 1923).
[11] See Plin. *NH*. 3. 120. See also Uggeri 1991.
[12] There's a large number of recent studies on the subject. See at least Uggeri 1978; Rosada 1984; Uggeri 1987, 337-347; Marchiori 1990; Uggeri 1997.
[13] See Plin. NH. 3. 119: *Augusta fossa Ravennam trahitur (*scil. *Padus), ubi Padusa vocatur, quondam Messanicus appellatus.*
[14] See Vitr. 2. 9. 14: *Larix vero, qui non est notus nisi iis municipalibus, qui sunt circa ripam fluminis Padi et litora maris Hadriani* .... 16*: Haec (*scil. *materies) autem per Padum Ravennam deportatur; in colonia Fanestri, Pisauri, Anconae reliquisque, quae sunt in ea regione, praebetur*. See also Corso 1983.
[15] See Plin. *NH*. 3. 117-122.
[16] See Plin. *NH*. 3. 123: *Transpadana appellatur ab eo (*scil. *Pado) regio undecima, tota in mediterraneo, cui marina cuncta fructuoso alveo importat. Oppida Vibi Forum, Segusio, ... Augusta Taurinorum – inde navigabili Pado* - ...

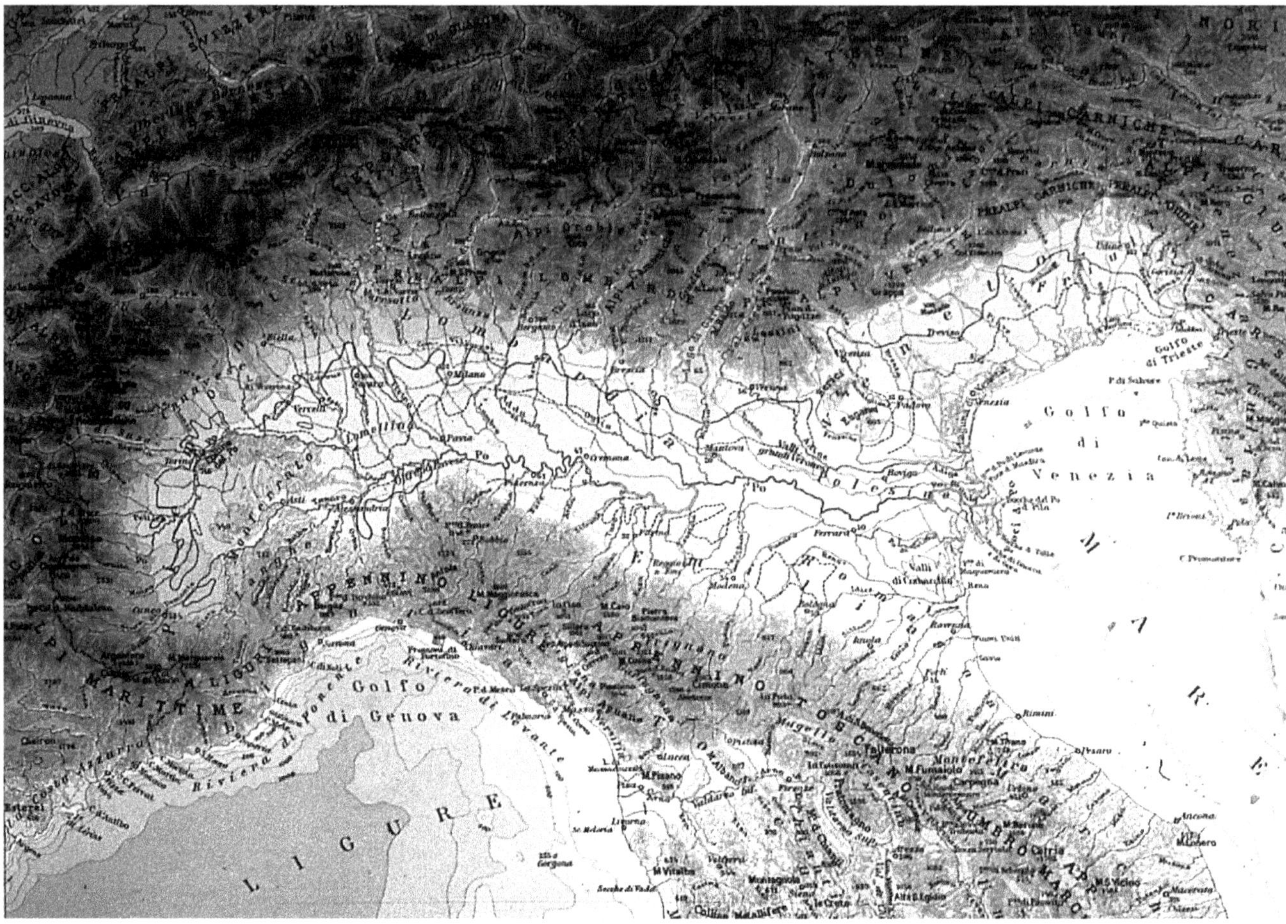

FIGURE 1: GEOGRAPHY AND HYDROGRAPHY OF NORTHERN ITALY.

campaigns of the year 69.[17]

A long period of silence follows. We find further documentation in the 5th and 6th century authors, mentioned later in this paper in connection with Pavia. The fairly exiguous literary evidence, relative generally just to the Po's course and dispersed in time over centuries, is insufficient for a history of riverborne trade on the branched waterway system of northern Italy. A different kind of evidence then comes into play.

The *Tabula Peutingeriana*, the famous medieval copy of an *itinerarium pictum* from Roman imperial age[18] mentions a connection *per Padum* between Ostiglia on the left bank of the Po slightly below the Mincio, and Ravenna.[19] Significantly, this is the only instance of a navigable river in Italy given for certain in the *Tabula.*[20]

Thanks to inscriptions containing references to *collegia nautarum* (corporations of boatmen)[21] we are informed, for example, of ancient boating on Lake Garda, otherwise unknown: the waterway Mincio-Garda-Sarca was a useful alternative to the Claudia Augusta way from Ostiglia to Trento and to navigation on the upper river Athesis, leading to the Resia and Brennero Alpine passes.[22]

Archaeology provides valuable information through the identification of harbour structures (for example, on the shores of Lakes Garda[23] and Como,[24] in Brescia[25] and Milan[26]) and the discovery of boats.[27] Fit for inland and lagoonal navigation, sewn plank boats (*sutiles naves*) were made most use of, owing to their moderate size, lightness and flat keel: the greatest number of ancient Roman relics found in the whole Mediterranean sea are concentrated along the Adriatic coast.[28]

With all due caution we can determine the use of inland waterways on the basis of the diffusion of various types

[17] See Tac. *Hist.* II, 23; 35; 43; 100; III, 12; 52. See also Tozzi 1970.

[18] For general surveys see Miller 1916; Levi and Levi 1967; Bosio 1983.

[19] Tab. Peut. III. 5 – IV. 1: Hostilia – Ab hostilia per Padum – Ravenna.

[20] For the outline of northern Italy and Po basin in the *Tabula* see Tozzi 1995, 22-27; Bargnesi 1998.

[21] For general surveys see Boffo 1977; De Salvo 1992, 138-139; 633-634; Bargnesi 1997.

[22] See Frézouls-Fasciato 1962; Rigotti 1974-1975; Mosca 1991; Bargnesi 1997, 101-103.

[23] See Massensini 1973; Uggeri 1990, 185.

[24] See Butti Ronchetti 1995.

[25] See Mirabella Roberti 1963, 278-280; Cera 1995, 192-193.

[26] See Caporusso 1990; Cera 1995, 189-191.

[27] See Alfieri 1968; Bonino 1978; Uggeri 1990; Cera 1995.

[28] See Beltrame 1996-1997.

of manufactures: in spite of the fact that in antiquity the faster and less expensive transport by water was generally preferred, it is not always possible to establish whether goods were carried by land or water, or exactly what routes they followed.[29] However, heavy or bulky materials, such as stones, and fragile freight, such as glasses and fine pottery, were nearly always transported by water.

II. Ancient *Ticinum*, today's Pavia, was built after 89 B.C.[30] on a diluvial terrace projecting above the left bank of the river Ticino, from which the town got its name.[31] The site is a few kilometres north of the Ticino and Po confluence. From this brief description it is clear how advantageous the position is in terms of road connections.[32]

Figure 2, a picture taken by the *R.A.F.* during World War II, shows the survival of the Roman orthogonal town plan close to the Ticino and, at the bottom, the traces of a paleomeander of the Po.

In a letter to his friend Heronius, Sidonius Apollinaris, bishop of Clermont-Ferrand, gives an account of his journey from Lyon to Rome in 467, at the head of an embassy to the neo-emperor Anthemius.[33] After crossing the western Alps Sidonius arrived by land in *Ticinum*, where he boarded a *cursoria*, i. e. a craft used in *cursus publicus*, which took him down to Ravenna along the Ticino and Po, stopping en route at Cremona and *Brixellum*. There was a change of crew at *Brixellum*, at the border between the provinces of *Venetia et Histria* and *Aemilia*.[34]

The itinerary shows clearly the significant role played by ancient Pavia as a road junction. Two great Transalpine land roads reached the town from the west:[35] the first, descending from the pass of Monginevro, ran beside the rivers Dora Riparia and Po and passed through Turin (*Augusta Taurinorum*);[36] the second, further north, descended from Little Saint Bernard and passed through Aosta (*Augusta Praetoria*) and Vercelli (*Vercellae*).[37] The latter was probably the one Sidonius travelled along, although this is impossible to infer with certainty from his letter.[38] At the same time *Ticinum* was the terminal of Po navigation, which comes to an end eastward, in Ravenna. The town therefore became the focal point in a land and waterway system connecting the western Alpine passes and the Adriatic sea.

With a letter in Cassiodorus' *Variae*, written about forty years after Sidonius' text, the Gothic king Theodoric ordered the Gothic *comites*, the *defensores* and *curiales* of *Ticinum* to send some Heruli barbarians on a boat to Ravenna, providing them with five days' provisions, probably to last the length of the journey:[39] this comes in confirmation of the regularity of the water transport service.

At the beginning of the 6th century Ennodius, bishop of Pavia, dwells on the lack of comfort and the inconvenience of such a journey, recalling his predecessor Epiphanius' passage to the Theodorician court at Ravenna in these terms: "cold, rains, the Po, hunger, sailing, danger, thunder, shelterless nights, unsafe landings on flooded river banks" (*Vita Ep.* 184; transl. Cook 1942).[40]

The documentation above explains the apparently odd item in Stephanus of Byzantium's geographical lexicon (6th century A.D.): "*Ticinum*, town of Italy near Ravenna" (*Ethn.* p. 624 Meineke).

When the imperial court moved to Milan at the end of the 3rd century, *Ticinum*, which is only 30 kilometres from the city, became a sort of military and administrative satellite, a detached base for armies and civilian staff. Then, when the emperor moved to Ravenna in 402, *Ticinum* gained more autonomy and became seat of *palatium* in the age of the Gothic king Theodoric.[41] The

[29] See Uggeri 1987, 314: "Né l'archeologia può darci risposte definitive, dal momento che molti generi sono deperibili e non emergono dallo scavo e altri non forniscono indicazioni sicure sulla via seguita per giungere da lontani centri di produzione".

[30] The *terminus post quem* consists of the so called *lex Pompeia de Transpadanis* (which we know from Asconius *in Pisonianam* p. 3 Clark): this grants *ius Latii* to the allied communities north of the Po which became Latin colonies, though often said by modern scholars to be "fittizie", since no population migration was involved (as Asconius writes: *Pompeius enim non novis colonis eas constituit, sed veteribus incolis manentibus ius dedit Latii*). It is, however, highly probable that planning and organization of territory and city took some time, and indeed the most considerable of the oldest archaeological remains are of the late Republican or Augustan periods. Over recent years there has been a wide ranging debate on the complex problems concerning the *lex Pompeia*: see at least Tibiletti 1973; Luraschi 1979, 139-214; Gabba 1984, 220-223.

[31] See Gabba 1984, 222: "Il caso di *Ticinum*, vale a dire di un nome di città derivato da quello del fiume (*Ticinus*), che l'attraversa o le scorre accanto, si riconduce ad una tradizione romano-italica già applicata per altri insediamenti coloniari" (e. g. *Ariminum, Aternum, Liternum, Pisaurum, Sarnum, Volturnum*).

[32] See Tozzi 1984, 184-185.

[33] For a recent commentary see Köhler 1995, 183-215.

[34] Sid. Ap. *Ep.* 1. 5. 3-5: *Ticini cursoriam (sic navigio nomen) escendi, qua in Eridanum brevi delatus cantatas semper comissaliter nobis Phaethontiadas et commenticias arborei metalli lacrimas risi. Ulvosum Lambrum caerulum Adduam, velocem Athesim pigrum Mincium, qui Ligusticis Euganeisque montibus oriebantur, paulum per ostia adversa subvectus in suis etiam gurgitibus inspexi .... Atque obiter Cremonam provectus adveni, cuius est olim Tityro Mantuano largum suspirata proximitas. Brixillum dein oppidum, dum succedenti Aemiliano nautae decedit Venetus remex, tantum ut exiremus intravimus, Ravennam paulo post cursu dexteriore subeuntes.*

[35] See Tozzi 1998.

[36] Sources: Strab. 5. 1. 11; Tac. *Hist.* 2. 27-30; 65-70; *CIL* 11. 3281-3284; *Itin. Ant.* p. 51 Cuntz; pp. 53-54 Cuntz; *Itin. Burdig.* p. 87 Cuntz; Amm. Marc. 15. 8. 18; 10. 3-8. For the epigraphic evidence on this road see Banzi 1999, 14-41.

[37] Sources: *Itin. Ant.* pp. 52-53 Cuntz; *Tab. Peut.* II. 3 – III. 1. For the epigraphic evidence on this road see Banzi 1999, 54-70.

[38] See Köhler 1995, 192.

[39] Cassiod. *Var.* 4. 45: ... *Itaque praesenti iussione commoniti et navis eis usum usque ad Ravennatem urbem et annonas dierum quinque sine aliqua dilatione praeparate...*

[40] Another uncomfortable journey on the Po waters is the subject of *Carm.* 1, 5 (423 Vogel).

[41] For the history of Pavia in late antiquity see Cracco Ruggini 1984.

FIGURE 2: THE TOWN PLAN CLOSE TO THE TICINO COURSE IN A PICTURE TAKEN BY THE *R. A. F.* ON THE SEPTEMBER 1ST 1943, DIPARTIMENTO DI SCIENZE DELL'ANTICHITÀ, UNIVERSITY OF PAVIA, PAVIA.

question therefore arises as to whether the significance of the northern Italian waterway system was a new phenomenon for the town, related to its good fortune in late antiquity.

Epigraphical and archaeological data seem to give evidence against such a supposition.

An incomplete inscription on the fragment on the side of a sarcophagus found in Pavia mentions the patron of a *collegium nautarum* which was, in all probability, active in the town. The role of such an epigraph as evidence has been shown above. The date of the inscription is probably around the end of the 2nd or beginning of the 3rd century.[42]

In the south-eastern zone of the town, below the Ponte

[42] See Boffo 1977; Boffo and Ambaglio 1992, number 24.

Coperto, built in the last century close to the original site of a Roman bridge, the remains of a rectangular plan structure with apse and a series of small rooms along the sides were unearthed 45 metres away from the bank of the river.[43] According to a plausible hypothesis this could have been a storehouse connected with the harbour structure. Cassiodorus informs us of the existence on the banks of Ticino in the 6th century of state storehouses (*horrea*), for army provisions.[44] The investigator of the building in Pavia ascribed it to the Theodorician period,[45] but an earlier date, the 1st century A.D., has subsequently been proposed on the basis of the wall structures and the pottery found in the excavation.[46]

A great many of the stones used in the buildings in *Ticinum* came from *Venetia* and the eastern Prealpine area as early as the Augustan age.[47] Research on the rare findings of fine pottery, dating back to the 1st century A.D., emphasizes the analogy with samples from *Venetia* and the northern Adriatic area.[48] As was already suggested, trade in such materials very probably travelled along the waterways.

All these signs lead to the supposition that, in the early imperial age, *Ticinum* had already been a port complementary in function to the land road junction.

Little is known of navigation along the Ticino above Pavia in antiquity, or of the connections of the town with Lake Maggiore. In recent years excavations on the lake shore at Angera (*Sebuinus Vicus*) have brought to light both the homogeneity of the material culture in the Verbano-Ticino area and the existence of privileged trading in materials with the north Adriatic coast and the eastern Veneto area during early imperial age. These phenomena have been explained as the "consequence of the development of a wide network of river traffic on the Ticino-Po-Adriatic axis".[49] Contacts between *Ticinum* and the Lake area seem to account for examples of stone manufacture in white granite from Lake Maggiore, gneiss from Val d'Ossola and marble from Candoglia found in Pavia and surrounding areas;[50] the paucity of the finds, however, makes caution advisable.[51]

III. During the early Middle Ages the town under the name of *Papia* (of disputed origin) in place of the Roman name of *Ticinum,*[52] first became the Lombardic capital and then, until the destruction of the royal palace during the revolt of 1024, that of the *regnum Italiae*. Pavia was thus not only a political and administrative centre, but also a vitally important crossroads and trade hub. During the Carolingian and post-Carolingian periods it is said to have been "the only continental emporium where most of Europe could procure luxury goods from the Orient".[53]

The economic well-being of the town depended on the amount of river traffic stopping there. Originally it was the Comacchiesi as intermediaries between East and West who dominated international traffic, as is attested by the Liuthprand charter of 715.[54] The Venetians then took over, but during the 10th century merchants from northern Europe (*gens Anglicorum et Saxonum*) and from the cities in the Campania (Salerno, Gaeta and Amalfi) also met there.[55] According to the anonymous compiler of a Life of Saint Maiolus, abbot of Cluny, who in the last thirty years of the 10th century visited Pavia on several occasions, the city was not unworthy of comparison with Tyrus and Sidone.[56]

While international trade was in the hands of the Venetian *negotiatores*, trade on a regional scale was under ecclesiastical control.

Monasteries owned land spread over various areas of the Padana region of Italy. They needed to ensure that there were no obstacles, either economic or material, impeding the free circulation necessary to collecting the produce of their various *curtes*, and from the time of the Lombardic monarchy were frequently granted rights over the rivers.[57]

The concessions granted by the crown also concern landing stages. Documentation for the early Middle Ages does not suggest that Pavia had a single harbour, but

[43] See Mirabella Roberti 1973-75; Saletti 1983, 134.

[44] See Cassiod. *Var.* 10. 27; 28; 12. 27, years 535/36. See also Cracco Ruggini 1961, 325-327.

[45] See Mirabella Roberti 1973-1975, 163.

[46] See Tocchetti Pollini 1984, 45-46.

[47] See Tozzi-Oxilia 1981; Zezza 1982.

[48] See De Masi 1999, 115: "L'analisi dei materiali ha evidenziato analogie con il panorama di ritrovamenti ceramici delle zone veneta e alto-adriatica, zone con le quali *Ticinum* era collegata grazie a una rete integrata di vie di terra e di vie d'acqua e che per la loro posizione geografica fungevano da centri di smistamento per le produzioni nord-italiche e arretine verso le regioni danubiane".

[49] Sena Chiesa 1985, 19.

[50] See Zezza 1982, 56-57.

[51] See Tozzi-Oxilia 1981, 21-22: "È piuttosto deludente, invece, la possibilità di definire il rapporto di Pavia con la regione del lago Maggiore, che si presenta, almeno su un piano teorico, eccezionalmente favorevole per l'abbondanza del materiale lapideo e per la brevità e opportunità del percorso fino a *Ticinum*. Il Ticino ... rappresentava il legame più naturale, ma mancano significative testimonianze di uno sfruttamento di qualche rilievo delle cave". Of differing opinion Sena Chiesa 1995, LVI: "Le pietre d'Angera giungevano fino a *Mediolanum* e forse a Cremona, certamente per via d'acqua. La loro massima diffusione dovette avvenire nel I sec. d. C., quando la richiesta di pietra da costruzione o da taglio dovette essere più forte per l'espandersi delle grandi città padane".

[52] See Gabba 1987.

[53] Settia 1987, 119.

[54] With this *pactum* the Lombardic king Liuthprand granted the *milites* of Comacchio the right to transport salt along the Po and sell it in the towns along the banks. The document also established the tributes due to the *Camera regis*, which the Comacchiesi had to pay to royal officials in the ports indicated. For the text see Hartmann 1904, 123-124. See also Mor 1977 and Racine 1986, 11.

[55] See *Honorantiae civitatis Papie* ll. 38-53; 67-71, pp. 18-19 Brühl – Violante. The document, of years 1010-1020, established the tributes which various *ministeria*, professional associations closely related to the court, owed the *Camera regis*. See Brühl and Violante 1983.

[56] See Anon. Silviniac. *Vita S. Maioli* 18: *Quae (scil. Papia) multiplicibus populorum referta turbis, nobilium et diversarum mercium speciebus insignis, quasi quaedam Tyrus et Sidon videtur remansisse, quibus complacet ad sui mercimonii comparationem et venditionem venire* (from Romano 1911, 317 note 1).

[57] See Racine 1986.

FIGURE 3: SAINT AUGUSTINE'S MARBLE TOMB, DETAIL, ABOUT 1370, BASILICA OF SAN PIETRO IN CIEL D'ORO, PAVIA.

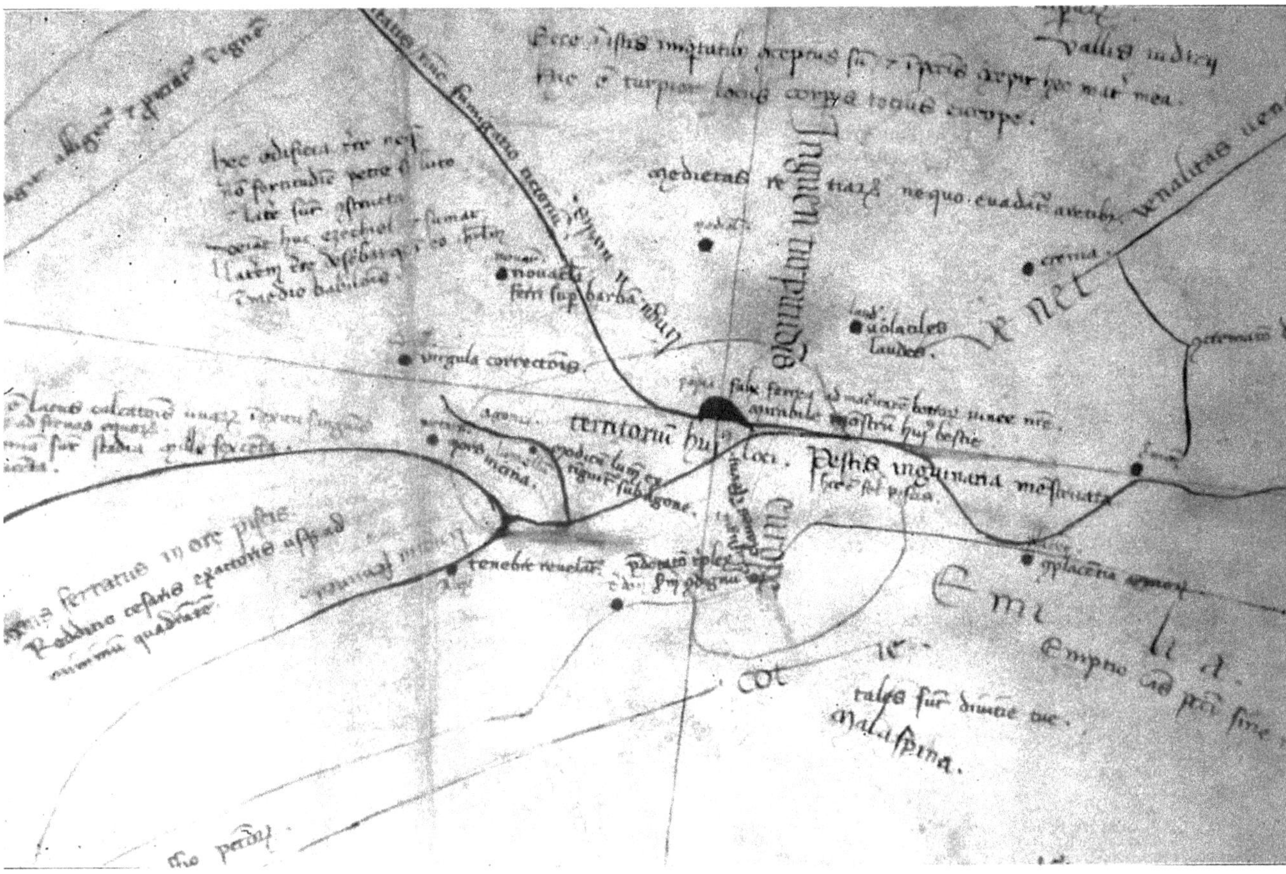

FIGURE 4: *CODEX PALATINUS LATINUS* 1993, F. 3R, BIBLIOTECA APOSTOLICA VATICANA, CITTÀ DEL VATICANO.

rather a series of landing stages owned by external church bodies and monasteries within the city, placed at various points along the left bank of the Ticino above and in particular below the town and at not great distance from it.[58]

Liuthprandus, bishop of Cremona, supplies information on the duration of water trips in the Padana region during this period, which can usefully be added to that of Sidonius and Cassiodorus mentioned above: his journey from Pavia to Venice at the beginning of August 949 took three days.[59]

Rather than entering into details of the history of the development of the port of Pavia during the late Middle Ages and in more recent times, it is of interest to cast a glance over the iconographic documentation, an opportunity which antiquity does not offer.

Between 717 and 725 the catholic Lombardic king Liuthprand transferred the body of Saint Augustine, endangered by Saracen invasions, from Sardinia to Pavia.[60] The body was set in the basilica of San Pietro in Ciel d'Oro. Figure 3 shows a detail of Saint Augustine's marble tomb, of the second half of the 14th century: it represents the transfer of the mortal remains of the saint by sea and their entrance into the town by river.

The priest of Pavia Opicino de Canistris, who lived in the first half of the 14th century in Pavia, Genoa and the papal court of Avignon, left two manuscripts, preserved in the Biblioteca Apostolica Vaticana, containing suggestive geographical drawings, anthropomorphical world outlines, sketches of "Lombardy" (in its medieval meaning and extent) and maps of Pavia, sometimes superimposed for the purpose of revealing new relationships between places.[61] In the drawing in Figure 4, from *Codex Palatinus Latinus* 1993, Pavia, depicted as a red semicircle, intented to represent the shape of the town plan, appears in the middle of north-western Italy, covering a central area and surrounded by the most important towns in the region, like a crown. Above all, the town lies close to the rivers Po and Ticino, dominating their confluence, which is the core of the

[58] E. g. a royal charter of year 916 documents that the abbey of Santa Giulia in Brescia owned part of a harbour called *Sclavaria, in ripa Ticini*. Another share of the same harbour was granted at the end of the 10th. century to the monastery of San Martino in Pavia, together with part of a harbour located on the opposite bank. In a charter of 925 to the Church of Pavia were granted, among other things, *portus qui dicitur Navicella Episcopi et in Ticinum portus Caballaricius, ut sint in potestate et iure ipsius ecclesie*. See Zimolo 1940, 500-509; Settia 1987, 122-123.

[59] See Liudpr. *Antapodosis* 6, 4: *Die quippe Kalendarum Augustarum Papia exiens per Heridani alveum triduo Venetiam veni...*

[60] See Beda, *Chr.* 593 p. 321 Mommsen; Paul. Diac. *Hist. Lang.* 6, 48.

[61] See Salomon 1936; Tozzi 1990; Tozzi 1996.

FIGURE 5: VIEW OF PAVIA WITH SAINT ANTHONY ABBOT, BY BERNARDINO LANZANI, 1522, BASILICA OF SAN TEODORO, PAVIA.

representation.[62] The image recalls the celebration of commercial life in his town, to be found in Opicino's *Liber de laudibus civitatis Papie*: Pavia is the point at which goods coming by river converge from all over the world.[63]

I come finally to a conclusion showing the view of Pavia found in a fresco by Bernardino Lanzani from 1522 (Figure 5). It's in the basilica of San Teodoro in Pavia. The view is from the south. The great vertical axis of Strada Nuova, the ancient *kardo* of *Ticinum*, stands out as the main line of the town plan. In the foreground appear the Ticino and the medieval Ponte Vecchio, raised on an original Roman structure. Below the bridge, in an area to the south-east, not far from where the remains of the probable ancient storehouse mentioned above were found, ships and floating mills are moored. The craft, which have long narrow hulls curved at each end, flat bottoms and the cabin aft, are of the type known in Venice as "nave de Pavia" (ship of Pavia), in existence until the 19th century.[64] Further downstream, floating mills are to be seen, recognisable by their double hulls and great wheels: documentation confirm the existence of water mills on the bank of the Ticino from at least the

[62] See Tozzi 1990, 62 and Figure XII; Tozzi 1996, 89-91 and Figures 97-99.

[63] See Opicin. *Liber de laudibus* 12: *Ad civitatem illam papiensem, cum duorum ex maioribus Lombardie fluminibus portus obtineat, ex diversis partibus mundi mercimonia deferuntur: usque illuc enim de Adriatico mari, ubi est Venetiarum civitas per multas illinc dietas distans ab oriente, naves cum sale et aliis mercimoniis per Padum et Ticinum ascendunt. Illuc tam de suo territorio quam de Monteferrato cum preciosis et rubicundis vinis et aliis rebus per Padum ab occidente descendunt. Similiter descendunt illuc cum optimis vinis de Novariensium et Mediolanensium partibus per Ticinum.*

[64] See Vaccari 1987, 81; 123-132.

beginning of the 10th century. They were to be found at the points where large consignments of cereals were unloaded.[65]

This is perhaps the oldest illustration of the harbour of Pavia in existence.

Acknowledgements

I wish to express my gratitude to Prof. M. Pasquinucci, of the University of Pisa, for giving me the opportunity to present a paper on such an important occasion as the Annual Meeting of the European Association of Archaeologists, and to Prof. P. Tozzi, of the University of Pavia, for having directed me to the study of ancient topography and for his constant interest in my work. My thanks also go to Dr. A. Gibbon, of the University of Urbino, for helping me with my English.

Bibliography

Alfieri N. 1968, *Tipi navali nel delta antico del Po*, in *Atti del Convegno Internazionale di Studi sulle Antichità di Classe, Ravenna 14-17 ottobre 1967*, Ravenna, Longo, 187-208.

Alfieri N. 1981, *Strabone e il delta del Po*, "Padusa", 17, 3-11.

Banzi E. 1999, *I miliari come fonte topografica e storica. L'esempio della XI regio (Transpadana) e delle Alpes Cottiae*, Roma, École Française de Rome.

Bargnesi R. 1997, *La testimonianza dell'epigrafia sulla navigazione interna nella Cisalpina romana*, "Rivista Archeologica dell'Antica Provincia e Diocesi di Como", 179, 93-108.

Bargnesi R. 1998, *Il bacino del Po nella Tabula Peutingeriana*, "Syngraphé", 1, 143-154.

Beltrame C. 1996-1997, *Sutiles naves e navigazione per acque interne in età romana*, "Padusa", 32-33, 137-143.

Boffo L. 1977, *Per la storia della antica navigazione fluviale padana*, "Rendiconti della classe di scienze morali, storiche e filologiche dell'Accademia dei Lincei", series 8, 32, 623-632.

Boffo L. and Ambaglio D. 1992, *Regio XI Transpadana – Ticinum – Laumellum et vicinia*, "Supplementa Italica", 9, Roma, Quasar, 212-347.

Bonino M. 1978, *Archeologia e tradizione navale tra la Romagna e il Po*, Ravenna, Longo.

Bosio L. 1983, *La Tabula Peutingeriana*, Rimini, Maggioli.

Brühl C. and Violante C. 1983, *Die "Honorantiae civitatis Papie"*, Köln – Wien, Böhlau.

Butti Ronchetti F. 1995, *I materiali dal porto di Como*, in G. Frigerio, G. Luraschi, D. Martello Frigerio (eds.), *L'antica via Regina*, Como, Società Archeologica Comense, 215-234.

Caporusso D. 1990, *La situazione idrografica di Milano romana*, in *Milano capitale dell'impero romano. 286-402 d. C.*, Milano, Silvana Editoriale, 94-96.

Cera G. 1995, *Scali portuali nel sistema idroviario padano in epoca romana*, in L. Quilici and S. Quilici Gigli (eds.), *Agricoltura e commerci nell'Italia antica (Atlante Tematico di Topografia Antica, supplemento 1)*, Roma, "L'Erma" di Bretschneider, 179-198.

Cook G. M. 1942, *The Life of Saint Epiphanius by Ennodius*, Washington D. C., The Catholic University of America Press.

Corso A. 1983, *Territorio e città dell'Italia settentrionale nel De Architectura di Vitruvio*, "Archeologia Veneta", 6, 49-69.

Cracco Ruggini L. 1961, *Economia e società nell'Italia annonaria*, Milano, Giuffré.

Cracco Ruggini L. 1984, *Ticinum: dal 476 d. C. alla fine del Regno Gotico*, in *Storia di Pavia*, 1, Milano, Banca del Monte di Pavia, 271-312.

De Masi C., *Ceramica fine da mensa a Pavia: un ritrovamento lungo il corso del Ticino*, in C. Maccabruni, E. Calandra, M. G. Diani, L. Vecchi (eds.), *Multas per gentes et multa per aequora. Culture antiche in provincia di Pavia: Lomellina, Pavese, Oltrepò. Atti della giornata di studi (Gambolò, 18 maggio 1997)*, Milano, Edizioni ennerre, 113-124.

De Salvo L. 1992, *I corpora naviculariorum. Economia privata e pubblici servizi nell'impero romano*, Messina, Samperi.

Frézouls-Fasciato M. 1962, *Note sur Vérone, Brescia et la batellerie du lac de Garde aux trois premiers siècles de notre ère*, in M. Renard (ed.), *Hommages à Albert Grenier*, 2, Collection "Latomus", 58, Brussels, 689-706.

Gabba E. 1984, *Ticinum: dalle origini alla fine del III sec. d. C.*, in *Storia di Pavia*, 1, Milano, Banca del Monte di Pavia, 205-247.

Gabba E. 1987, *Il nome di Pavia*, in *Storia di Pavia*, 2, Milano, Banca del Monte di Lombardia, 9-18.

Hartmann L. M. 1904, *Zur Wirtschaftsgeschichte Italiens im frühen Mittelalter*, Gotha, Perthes.

Jones H. L. 1923, *The Geography of Strabo*, 2, London, William Heinemann - New York, G. P. Putman's sons.

Köhler H. 1995, *C. Sollius Apollinaris Sidonius Briefe Buch I*, Heidelberg, Universitätsverlag C. Winter.

Levi A. and Levi M. 1967, *Itineraria picta. Contributo allo studio della Tabula Peutingeriana*, Roma, "L'Erma" di Bretschneider.

Luraschi G. 1979, *Foedus Ius Latii Civitas. Aspetti costituzionali della romanizzazione in Transpadana*, Padova, Cedam.

Marchiori A. 1990, *Sistemi portuali della Venetia romana*, "Antichità Altoadriatiche", 36, 197-225.

Massensini G. 1973, *Note sui resti di un antico porto a Padenghe sul Garda*, "Benacus", 1, 43-49.

Miller K. 1916, *Itineraria romana*, Stuttgart, Strecker und Schröder.

Mirabella Roberti M. 1963, *Archeologia ed arte di Brescia romana*, in *Storia di Brescia*, 1, Brescia,

[65] See Vaccari 1987, 81; Settia 1987, 117.

Morcelliana, 233-320.

Mirabella Roberti M. 1973-1975, *Un edificio tardo romano lungo il Ticino a Pavia*, “Sibrium”, 19, 161-167.

Mor C. G. 1977, *Un'ipotesi sulla data del “Pactum” c.d. Liutprandino coi “milites” di Comacchio relativo alla navigazione sul Po*, “Archivio Storico Italiano”, 135, 493-502.

Mosca A. 1991, *Caratteri della navigazione nell'area benacense in età romana*, “Latomus”, 50, 269-284.

Paton W. R. 1960, *Polybius. The Histories*, 1, London, William Heinemann – Cambridge Massachusetts, Harvard University Press.

Philipp H. 1942, s. v. *Padus*, “Paulys Real-Encyclopädie der classischen Altertumswissenschaft”, 18, Stuttgart, J. B. Metzler, cc. 2178-2202.

Racine P. 1986, *Poteri medievali e percorsi fluviali nell'Italia padana*, “Quaderni Storici”, 61, 9-32.

Rigotti A. 1974-1975, *I collegia nautarum Benacensium*, “Atti dell'Accademia Roveretana degli Agiati”, series 6, 14-15, 117-125.

Romano G. 1911, *Pavia nella storia della navigazione fluviale*, “Bollettino della Società Pavese di Storia Patria”, 11, 311-328.

Rosada G. 1984, *Funzione e funzionalità della Venetia romana: terra, mare, fiumi come risorse per un'egemonia espansionistica*, in *Misurare la terra: centuriazione e coloni nel mondo romano. Il caso veneto*, Modena, Panini, 22-37.

Saletti C. 1983, *L'urbanistica di Pavia romana*, “Athenaeum”, 61, 126-147.

Salomon R. G. 1936, *Opicinus de Canistris. Weltbild und Bekenntnisse eines Avignonesischen Klerikers des 14. Jahrhunderts*, London, Warburg.

Sena Chiesa G. 1985, *Introduzione*, in G. Sena Chiesa (ed.), *Angera romana. Scavi nella necropoli 1970-1979*, 1, Roma, Giorgio Bretschneider, 7-27.

Sena Chiesa G. 1995, *Angera romana: il vicus e l'indagine di scavo*, in G. Sena Chiesa and M. P. Lavizzari Pedrazzini (eds.), *Angera romana. Scavi nell'abitato 1980-1986*, 1, Roma, Giorgio Bretschneider, XXXI-LXIII.

Settia A. A. 1987, *Pavia carolingia e postcarolingia*, in *Storia di Pavia*, 2, Milano, Banca del Monte di Lombardia, 69-158.

Tibiletti G. 1973, *Ravenna Populus Foederatus e le zone della Cisalpina rese “latine” nell'89 a. C.*, “Studi Romagnoli”, 24, 25-31, then in G. Tibiletti, *Storie locali dell'Italia romana*, Como, New Press, 285-293.

Tocchetti Pollini U. 1984, *Le città in età romana. L'inizio del fenomeno urbano e le sue trasformazioni*, in *Archeologia urbana in Lombardia*, Modena, Panini, 34-47.

Tozzi P. 1970, *Tacito e la geografia della valle del Po*, “Athenaeum”, 58, 104-131.

Tozzi P. 1976, *Gli inizi della riflessione storiografica sull'Italia settentrionale nella Roma del II secolo a. C.*, in *L'Italia settentrionale nell'età antica. Convegno in memoria di Plinio Fraccaro (Pavia 8-10 settembre 1975)*, “Athenaeum fascicolo speciale”, Pavia, Tipografia del libro, 28-50.

Tozzi P. 1984, *L'impianto urbano di Ticinum romana*, in *Storia di Pavia*, 1, Milano, Banca del Monte di Pavia, 183-203.

Tozzi P. 1988, *L'Italia settentrionale di Strabone*, in G. Maddoli (ed.), *Strabone e l'Italia antica*, Napoli, Edizioni Scientifiche Italiane, 25-43.

Tozzi P. 1990, *Opicino e Pavia*, Pavia, Libreria d'Arte Cardano.

Tozzi P. 1995, *Viabilità romana nell'Italia settentrionale*, in G. Frigerio, G. Luraschi, D. Martello Frigerio (eds.), *L'antica via Regina*, Como, Società Archeologica Comense, 11-28.

Tozzi P. 1996, *La città e il mondo in Opicino de Canistris*, Varzi, Guardamagna.

Tozzi P. 1998, *Pavia e le vie delle Gallie*, Varzi, Guardamagna.

Tozzi P. and Oxilia M. 1981, *Le pietre di Pavia romana*, “Bollettino della Società Pavese di Storia Patria”, 81, 3-45.

Uggeri G. 1978, *Vie di terra e vie d'acqua tra Aquileia e Ravenna in età romana*, “Antichità Altoadriatiche”, 13, 45-79.

Uggeri G. 1987, *La navigazione interna della Cisalpina in età romana*, “Antichità Altoadriatiche”, 29, 305-350.

Uggeri G. 1990, *Aspetti archeologici della navigazione interna nella Cisalpina*, “Antichità Altoadriatiche”, 36, 175-196

Uggeri G. 1991, *Interventi idraulici nell'Etruria padana*, in M. Bergamini (ed.), *Gli Etruschi maestri di idraulica*, Perugia, Electa Editori Umbri, 69-72.

Uggeri G. 1997, *I canali navigabili dell'antico delta padano*, in S. Quilici Gigli (ed.), *Uomo acqua e paesaggio (Atlante Tematico di Topografia Antica, supplemento 2)*, Roma, “L'Erma” di Bretschneider, 55-60.

Vaccari G. 1987, *Quando Pavia navigava*, Pavia, Luigi Ponzio e figlio.

Walbank F. W. 1957, *A historical commentary on Polybius*, 1, Oxford, Clarendon Press.

Zezza M. G. 1982, *I materiali lapidei locali impiegati in età romana nell'area compresa tra il Ticino e il Mincio*, Milano.

Zimolo G. 1940, Pavia nella storia della navigazione interna, in Atti e Memorie del IV Congresso Storico Lombardo (Pavia, 18-19-20 maggio 1939), Milano, Giuffré, 493-534.

Ports and Trade in the *ager Cosanus* and on Giglio Island from the Mid to Late Imperial Age

Giulio Ciampoltrini and Paola Rendini

Abstract
By an extensive analysis of recent works (mainly of the authors) in the archaeology of Albegna valley and on Giglio Island, an attempt is made to sketch an outline of port system and trade in this area from Mid- to Late Imperial Age.
As a consequence of a late Republican and Augustan re-organisation, a network of ports protected by concrete wharves (portus Cosanus, but also Domitiana positio and Giglio Porto), is completed by minor harbours, mainly at the mouth of rivers (Albinia). By the end of 1st century A.D. down to the years of Hadrian, great maritime villas in terra firma and in the Giannutri Island were built to improve the ancient port system; this great effort, aided by Imperial funds, with evidence from underwater archaeology, suggests that the coastal and sea-routes from Gaul, Spain, Africa, supplying Rome with various goods, converged at this point of the northern Tyrrhenian coast. The Giglio Porto Severan age wreck may indicate the growing role of African routes in this trade system.
The Torre Tagliata and Albinia Late Roman layers show the continuing vitality of these ports down to the mid-5th century, the trade routes being supplied by the end of 4th century also by East Mediterranean wares. By AD 460, in relationship with the new political situation in the Western Mediterranean, the landing places are connected to protected settlements; so the only partially deserted villa of Saraceno at Giglio Porto, the Cosa arx, the ancient hilltop of Telamon, shape a network whose final crisis was a consequence of Longobard conquest of Ligurian coast in the middle 7th century.

A series of land and underwater excavations along the coastline of the Ager Cosanus, in the Albegna valley, in the Villa del Saraceno area at Giglio Porto, during the 1980s and early 1990s, together with a review of previous land and underwater finds, have provided a large amount of material, allowing us to trace (particularly for some periods) the development of coastal settlements and related trade in this area (fig. 1) from the Late Republic Age to the Early Middle Ages.

In the Late Republic it seems to be a well-established network of ports in which portus Cosanus, at the foot of the southeastern slope of the plateau on which the city of Cosa stands, has a decisive place. An investigation of the second century B.C. necropolis, with its monumental tombs along the road linking the town and the port (Ciampoltrini 1991a), has confirmed that a close relationship between city and port is fundamental to the fortunes of Cosa up to the early decades of the first century B.C. Minor ports, including those on Giglio Island (Ciampoltrini and Rendini 1992), are distributed around the portus Cosanus, the next port to the north being the ancient portus Telamonis (Ciampoltrini 1995). So archaeological evidence supports the "pilots' book" cited by Pomponius Mela, seemingly written in the Late Republican Age (Ciampoltrini 1994-95).

The earliest re-organisation of this port system seems to be due to the new settlement pattern displayed in the years immediately following the civil war between Sulla and Marius partisans. Telamon and the portus Telamonis disappear, replaced by the Torre Saline positio at the mouth of the Albegna River, strictly linked to the road system (Ciampoltrini 1997).

The founding of the first maritime villas, at Santa Liberata (Domitiana positio) and at other positions dominating the northern Argentario coast (Ciampoltrini 1998; Ciampoltrini and Rendini 1996) as well as on Giglio Island and on Giannutri (Rendini 1995a; Rendini 1995b) completes the network of 'minor' ports. The portus Cosanus seems to have a special role, being provided with navalia built-up in a beach sector protected by a series of concrete moles (Felici 1998, 275 ff.; Ciampoltrini, Iezzi and Agricoli 1999, 219 ff.); a separate landing place for Cosa is arranged on the other side of the town hill, on the beach of the Feniglia (Cavallo, Ciampoltrini and Shepherd 1992). The new system of concrete moles is also used to protect the fishery and the port area of the Domitiana positio (Ciampoltrini 1998), while the quay of Giglio Porto – where the great 'villa del Saraceno' became established in the Julio-Claudian Age – was provided with a continuous wharf, recently detected in the 18th century cartographic evidence (Ciampoltrini and Rendini 1998).

From the final years of Domitian's rule to the beginning of Hadrian's, the network of ports and landing places, built in the years between the Civil Wars and the Julio-Claudian age, undergoes another transformation giving it the shape which was to last until Late Antiquity. Great maritime villas are built under the Emperor's direct intervention, i.e. at Talamone, which recuperates the earlier role of portus Telamonis on the opposite side of the bay, at Madonna delle Grazie, connected via a diverticulum to the via Aurelia (Ciampoltrini 1993; Ciampoltrini 1994, 2 ff.); at the portus Cosanus (Ciampoltrini 1991b); at Giannutri. This island is provided by a double array of ports, Cala Maestra and Cala Spalmatoio (Cavazzuti 1998; Rendini 1999).

If the Late Republican Age port system was planned to favour the heavy commercial traffic between Central Italy and Gallia and (to a lesser extent) the Iberian Peninsula, as the many wrecks laden with Graeco-Italian and Dressel 1 amphorae, recovered from the stretch of sea

FIGURE 1. PORTS AND LANDING PLACES IN THE AGER COSANUS.

between the Albegna valley, Giannutri, Giglio, the Formiche of Grosseto, indicate (Rendini 1998a), it has been suggested that its re-organisation under Augustus, with ports defended by concrete moles, would have been better suited for ships carrying supplies of construction material from Luni and Pisa to Rome, as well as ships fitted with dolia (Ciampoltrini 1994-5).

On the other hand the re-organisation of the landing system around maritime villas, designed perhaps under Domitian but constructed under Traianus and completed under Hadrian, as the brick stamps from the villa at Torre Tagliata, in the portus Cosanus, show (Ciampoltrini 1991b, 74 ff.), is definitely aimed at serving the routes that were carrying to Rome increasing supplies of goods from the provinces in the western Mediterranean, i.e. Gaul, Spain and north Africa. Second and third century wrecks, documented or systematically explored, in the waters of Giglio, Giannutri and the Formiche islands, signal the meeting point of routes from southern Gaul along the Tyrrhenian coast, and by high sea from Spain (through the Bocche di Bonifacio) and Africa (via Sardinia), traversing the Tyrrhenian sea across the 'bridge' provided by the Tuscan archipelago (Rendini 1998a). The African route becomes ever more important from the time of Severan dynasty, with the increasing demand for African goods, not only victuals; the wreck explored in Giglio Port, laden with large IIA and IIB African amphorae, is from the early phases of this growth in African trade and production (Dell'Amico and Rendini 1995).

Excavations in the Albinia positio at Torre Saline and in the Tagliata maritime villa in portus Cosanus, carried out between 1983 and 1989, show that, with the exception of slight touches of an unclear nature under Severus, the early 2nd century A.D. structures went largely unchanged up to the time of Theodosius (Ciampoltrini 1991b, 76 f.). A similar picture emerges from excavations in the area of the villa del Saraceno at Giglio Porto (Rendini 1995b; Rendini 1998b). In the period between the late 3rd century A.D. up to Constantine, the erection of a cycle of imperial statues at Torre Saline (of which only the one of Gallienus survives), and the sumptuous Polverosa necropolis in the immediate hinterland of Albegna valley which, apart from jewellery, yielded a rare example of African made Navigiusbecher (Ciampoltrini 1985), combine with evidence from the wrecks to testify the vitality of the port system in the area and particularly the extremely close links to routes connecting Italy to north Africa.

The abandonment layers of the first half of the 5th century A.D. at Torre Saline, found in the small area excavated (Ciampoltrini 1997, 283 ss.) agree perfectly with the huge transformations undergone by the portus Cosanus at the

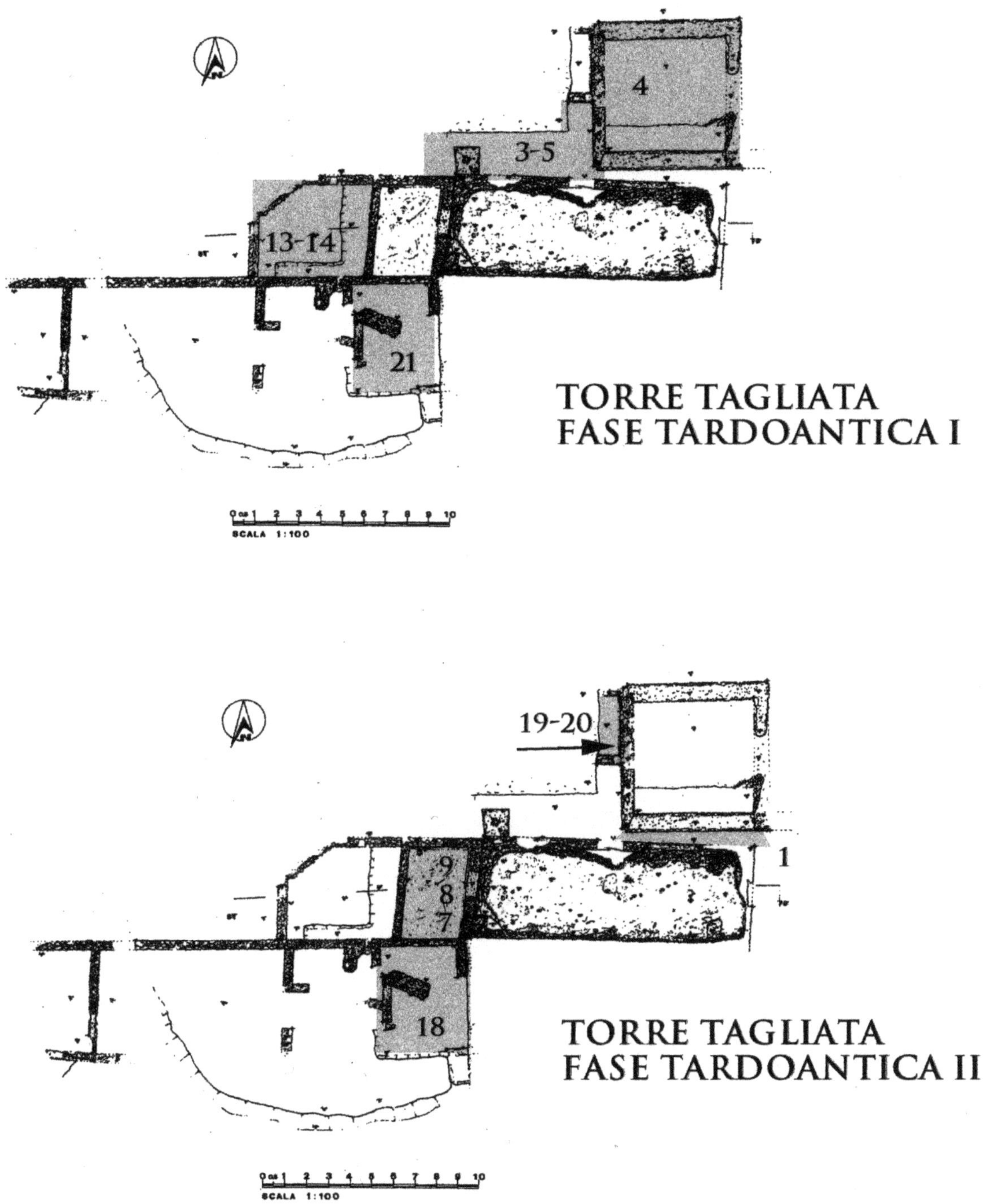

FIGURE 2. TORRE TAGLIATA: EXCAVATION AREA WITH LATE ROMAN LAYERS.

beginning of the 5th century (fig. 2; Ciampoltrini and Rendini 1988; Ciampoltrini and Rendini 1990).

The villa of the Tagliata is probably still fully functional in the 4th century, with a necropolis arranged in the eastern beach, a discreet distance away. When Rutilius Namatianus docked and stayed at the portus Cosanus, he saw a landscape largely unchanged over three centuries.
Only a few years later, during the early decades of the 5th century – as the copious findings of African sigillata testify – many of the buildings still in use were entirely or partly levelled using mixed waste (fig. 2: 3-5, 4, 13-14, 21), partly with the aim of building a basin, perhaps for a fishery. African sigillata is an excellent mean for dating the material used in the levelling process (fig. 3, 1): the residue-forms, spread over the 2nd and 3rd centuries A.D., make up about 35% of the material recovered, while the form system of the end of the 4th and early 5th centuries (f. 50, 58, 61A, 61B, 67, 80-81) is distributed fairly evenly, leading to the conclusion that together with rubbles which had perhaps already been accumulating for some time, dumps in current use were also exploited. The sigillata index allows a good evaluation of amphorae too (fig. 4, 1): beside 2nd and 3rd century remains, African

(Keay XXV and LXII) and, to a lesser extent, Iberian amphorae (Almago 50 and 51) produced between the 4th and first half of the 5th centuries, are prominent.

The extensive presence of amphorae linked to two of the routes on the high seas, one from Spain and the other from Africa, which could meet on the Tyrrhenian coast at portus Cosanus, provides of course expected confirmation also of the commercial aim typical of this port in Late Antiquity. The presence of truly 'locally' manufactured material is statistically almost imperceptible and even the singular class of pottery decorated with "rotellatura" over a thin, low quality orange glaze – which has been fancifully compared to Byzantine and Omayyad Syrian-Palestinian products (Uscatescu 1996) – can in any case be attributed to manufacturers on the Tyrrhenian circuit, as findings at Porto Torres and Rome have demonstrated (Ciampoltrini and Rendini 1988, 528, fig. 9).

In about mid 5th century further levelling using rubble (fig. 2: 19-20; 7-8) signals the ongoing re-organisation of the occupied area to those buildings surviving to today with their roofing too. The increasing number of dumps in the area immediately surrounding the dwelling space (1, 9, 18) enables us to date the last years of use of this site to immediately after mid-century. Evidence from fine imported pottery indicates that after AD 460 the portus Cosanus is not used by stable or sizeable settlements.

Although the layers linked to the last years of occupation in this area confirm the liveliness of trade at this difficult time, they point to the beginnings of change in the system of mercantile relationships. In the assemblage of fine ceramic tableware, still almost totally provided by African manufacturers, a real "system" of shapes stands out, serving to satisfy the various requirements for presenting food at table. Forms 67, 61 B, 80-81 and to a lesser extent, 91 A-B, strikingly equivalent in the composition of the finds (fig. 3, 2) appear to point to specialised cargoes integrated, perhaps in the final days of the life of this port, by "new" forms like 73 and 76, and functional, in their simplification, to a still thriving trade.

The presence, albeit statistically irrelevant, of a sherd of LRC, f. 3C, points to an opening up towards goods from the eastern Mediterranean basin, mainly absent until then, that is more definitely indicated by the bulk of kitchen pottery and amphorae. On the whole among of amphorae findings (largely documented in Ciampoltrini and Rendini 1988, 530 ff.; Ciampoltrini and Rendini 1990, 628 ff.), the African ones strongly predominate, accompanied by those of Iberian origin as in earlier decades (fig. 4, 2); the latter, however, take third place after amphorae from the eastern Mediterranean basin, in particular from the Aegean area, while the proportion of "Empolese" wine amphora made in northern Etruria increases to almost 10%.

The success of northern Etruscan wines indicates the place acquired in the Tyrrhenian markets during Late Antiquity by the farmlands in Valdarno and along the coastline from Pisa to Volterra; this land had been re-organised thanks in part to investments in a network of villas by the great Senatorial families (Ciampoltrini 1990). However, the amphorae and tableware ceramics from the East Mediterranean, with the unquantifiable but qualitatively significant presence of "Aegean" cooking pottery (Ciampoltrini and Rendini 1990, 628) show that the trade flow from the East is no longer confined to touching the Adriatic coast of Italy but now reaches the northern Tyrrhenean Sea (Albarella, Ceglia and Roberts 1993, 200 ss.). The presence of products from the Eastern Empire which, at the Tagliata, is comparable to coeval layers in Rome and other sites on the Tyrrhenian Sea (Albarella, Ceglia and Roberts 1993, 200 ss.) may have been boosted by particularly strong links (perhaps military) established between the two parts of the Empire in order to challenge the threat from the Vandals on the Mediterranean chessboard.

The changed political situation, resulting in a dramatic sense of insecurity, has heavy consequences on the port system too. As we have already observed, layers at Tagliata and Torre Saline are exhausted immediately after the mid-5th century, when the presence of buried hoards and treasures confirm the threatening situation. Port areas near the beach are abandoned in favour of better protected positions, i.e. the Cosa acropolis described at length in its desolation by Rutilius; the high ground at Bengodi and old Talamone; the area of the portus Telamonis (Ciampoltrini and Rendini 1988, 523 ss.; Celuzza and Fentress 1995). The protected settlement at Giglio Porto which go untouched during early 5th century incursions, as Rutilius enthusiastically observes, continue to exist although to a minor degree, as the presence of tombs inside the villa area indicates (Rendini 1998b).

It is this very re-occupation of sites destined to assist maritime routes that confirms the continuity in trade emerging from underwater finds, in particular on Giglio Island, between the 5th and 6th centuries. The wreck at the Scole with its cargo of African amphorae (medium-sized Late Roman cylindrical containers) accords perfectly with material continuously emerging from the Giglio Porto port dump, with a variety of African, Iberian, eastern Mediterranean and Italic amphorae from the 5th and 6th centuries. This shows how the port was an important point of reference for a still lively trade along the Tyrrhenian coast (first notices in Rendini 1991). The type samples – table and kitchen pottery, amphorae – recovered from a settlement in the immediate hinterland behind Talamonaccio confirms that commercial circuits under Theodoricus and during the years of the Graeco-Gothic wars were not confined to just skimming through the network of safe landing places but were able to penetrate at least as far as the immediate hinterland (Ciampoltrini and Rendini 1989).

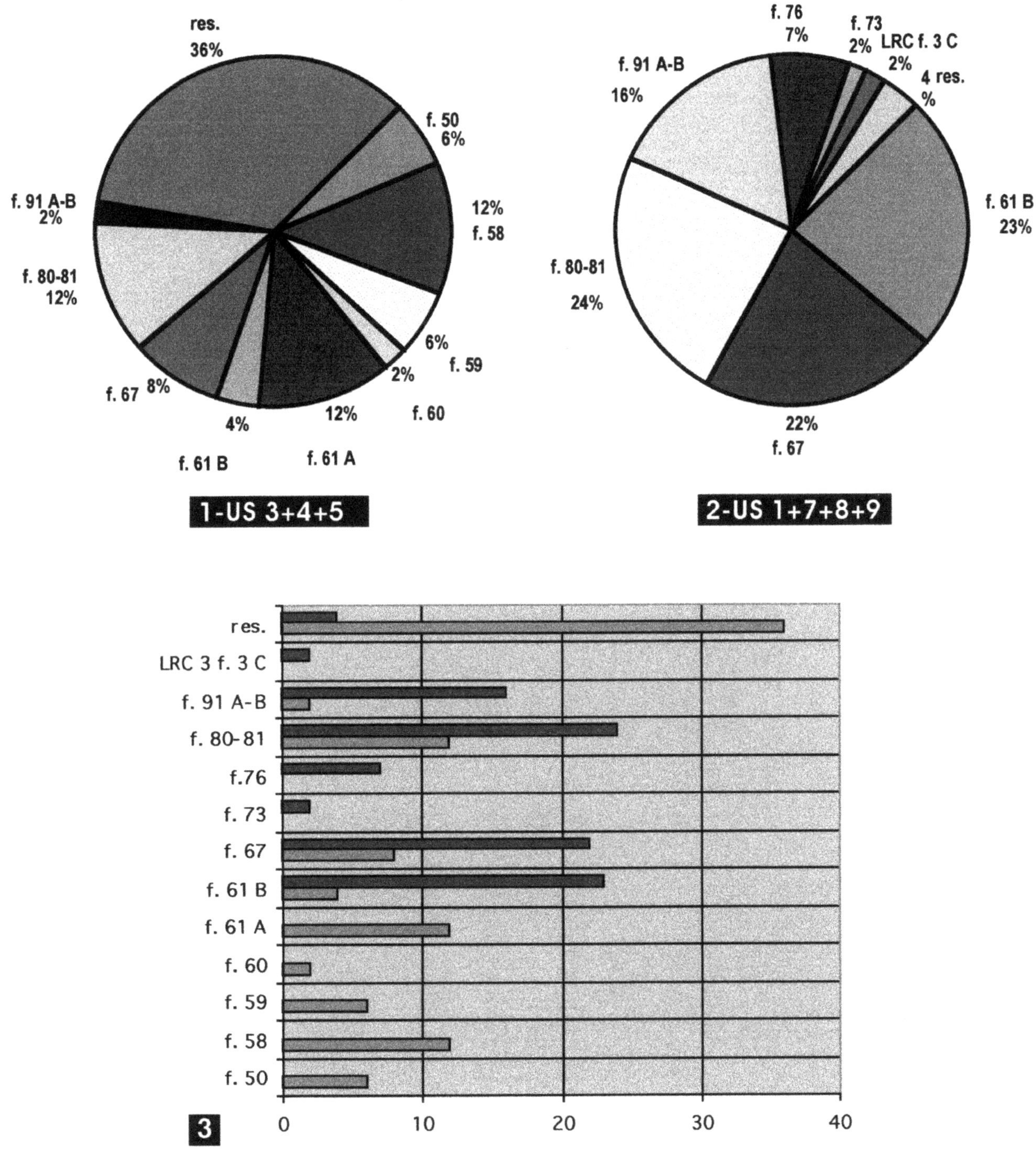

FIGURE 3. THE SIGILLATA DISTRIBUTION IN THE LATE ROMAN LAYERS OF TORRE TAGLIATA.

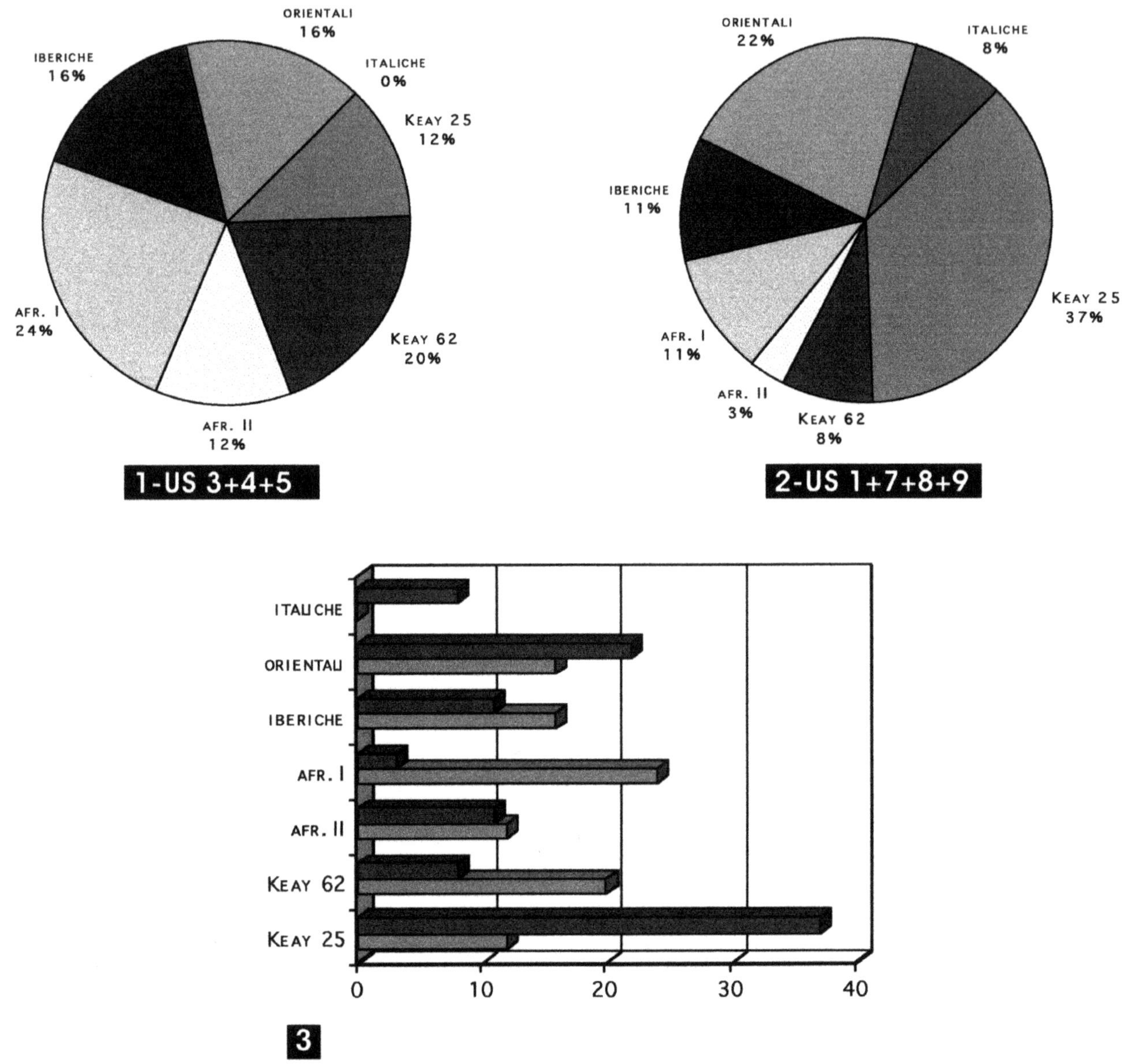

FIGURE 4. THE AMPHORAE DISTRIBUTION IN THE LATE ROMAN LAYERS OF TORRE TAGLIATA.

Giglio Porto must still have been in use even during the time of the Longobard conquest in coastal Maremma, a link in the chain of protected positions connecting the various districts of Byzantine Italy, especially on the route from Rome to Byzantine Liguria. Material from the later layers in the Saraceno area and recovered from the port dump suggests that it was only the Longobard conquest of Liguria (making this maritime corridor superfluous) that led to the abandonment – well into the 7th century – of this last vestige of the Roman system of ports (Rendini 1998b).

References

Albarella U., Ceglia V. and Roberts P. 1993, *S. Giacomo degli Schiavoni (Molise): an early fifth century AD deposit of pottery and animal bones from Central Adriatic Italy*, "Papers of the British School at Rome", 61, 1993, 157-230

Cavallo D., Ciampoltrini G. and Shepherd E.J. 1992, *La pesca nell'agro di Cosa in età romana: prospettive di ricerca e nuove acquisizioni*, in Atti V Rassegna di Archeologia Subacquea, Giardini Naxos 19-21 ottobre 1990, Messina, 103-113

Cavazzuti L. 1998, *I porti romani dell'isola di Giannutri, in Città e monumenti nell'Italia antica* (=Atlante Tematico di Topografia Antica, 7), 119-140

Celuzza M. and Fentress E., 1995, *La Toscana centro-meridionale: i casi di Cosa-Ansedonia e Roselle*, in R. Francovich e G. Noyé edd., La storia dell'Alto

Medioevo italiano (VI-X secolo) alla luce dell'archeologia, Firenze, 601-614

Ciampoltrini G. 1985, *Una statua ritratto d'età imperiale dalla foce dell'Albegna*, "Prospettiva", 43, 47-47, 47-51

Ciampoltrini G. 1990, *Mosaici tardoantichi dell'Etruria settentrionale*, "Studi Classici e Orientali", 40, 369-381

Ciampoltrini G. 1991a, *La necropoli di Cosa. Ricerche e recuperi 1985-1991*, "Bollettino di Archeologia", 7, 59-73

Ciampoltrini G. 1991b, *Ricerche sui monumenti d'età traianea e adrianea nel suburbio orientale di Cosa*, "Bollettino di Archeologia", 11-12, 67-87

Ciampoltrini G. 1993, *Il diverticolo dall'Aurelia al portus Telamonis: un contributo per la tecnica stradale nell'Etruria costiera*, in Strade romane. Percorsi e infrastrutture (=Atlante Tematico di Topografia Antica, 2), 179-182

Ciampoltrini G. 1994, *Mosaici del II secolo d.C. nell'Etruria centrale marittima*, "Prospettiva", 75-76, 2-13

Ciampoltrini G. 1994-5, *Note per l'epigrafia di Populonia*, "Rassegna di Archeologia", 12, 591-604

Ciampoltrini G. 1995, *Il vecchio, il mare, la nave. Una proposta per il fregio con thiasos marino da Telamone*, "Parola del Passato", 50, 67-77

Ciampoltrini G. 1997, *Albinia fluvius habet positionem. Scavi 1983-1987 nell'approdo alla foce dell'Albegna*, "Rassegna di Archeologia", 14, 254-296

Ciampoltrini G. 1998, *Domitiana positio: la villa di Santa Liberata*, in G. Poggesi e P. Rendini (edd.), Memorie sommerse. Archeologia subacquea in Toscana, Pitigliano, 195-205

Ciampoltrini G. and Rendini P. 1988, *L'agro cosano fra tarda antichità e alto Medioevo: segnalazioni e contributi*, "Archeologia Medievale", 15, 519-534

Ciampoltrini G. and Rendini P. 1989, *Un insediamento tardoantico nella valle dell'Osa*, "Archeologia Medievale", 15, 513-522

Ciampoltrini G. and Rendini P. 1990, *L'insediamento nella villa marittima di Torre Tagliata (Orbetello, GR). Scavi 1988-89*, "Archeologia Medievale", 17, 625-632

Ciampoltrini G. and Rendini P. 1992, *Porti e traffici nel Tirreno settentrionale fra IV e III secolo a.C. Contributi da Telamone e dall'isola del Giglio*, "Annali della Scuola Normale Superiore di Pisa", 22, 1992, 985-1004

Ciampoltrini G. and Rendini P. 1996, *Pavimenti in signinum e scutulatum dall'Etruria centro-settentrionale. Recenti acquisizioni,* in Atti del III Colloquio AISCOM, Bordighera 6-10 dicembre 1995, Bordighera, 573-590

Ciampoltrini G. and Rendini P. 1998, *Un dolio di P. Ro[cius -] Pom. Nuovi ritrovamenti dall'arcipelago toscano*, in Atti del Convegno Nazionale di Archeologia Subacquea, Anzio 30-31 maggio e 1 giugno 1996, Bari, 55-61

Ciampoltrini G., Iezzi R. and Agricoli G. 1999, *Fra la Tagliata, l'Origlio, il Chiarone. Materiali per l'insediamento etrusco e romano nel litorale capalbiese*, "Rassegna di Archeologia", 16, 219-258

Dell'Amico P. and Rendini P. 1995, *Il relitto romano di Giglio Porto*, "Bollettino di Archeologia subacquea", 2-3, 157-165

Felici E. 1998, *La ricerca sui porti romani in cementizio*, in G. Volpe (ed.), Archeologia subacquea. Come opera l'archeologo sott'acqua. Storie dalle acque, Firenze, 275-340

Rendini 1991, *La tarda età romana: il relitto delle Scole (Isola del Giglio); la discarica portuale tardoantica dell'isola del Giglio*, in Celuzza M. e Rendini P. (edd.), Relitti di storia. Archeologia subacquea in Maremma, Siena, 106-116

Rendini P. 1995a, *'Lastre Campana' nell'Etruria marittima centro-settentrionale*, "Prospettiva", 79, 24-35

Rendini P. 1995b, I *mosaici della villa del Saraceno a Giglio Porto*, in Atti del II Colloquio AISCOM, Roma 5-7 dicembre 1994, Bordighera, 149-158

Rendini P. 1998a, Postfazione, in G. Poggesi and P. Rendini (edd.), *Memorie sommerse.* Archeologia subacquea in Toscana, Pitigliano, 223-229

Rendini P. 1998b, *Ceramiche del VI e VII secolo nell'area della villa di Giglio Porto (Isola del Giglio-GR)*, in L. Saguì (ed.), Ceramiche in Italia: VI-VII secolo, Atti del Convegno in onore di J.W. Hayes, Roma 11-13 maggio 1995, Roma, 639-643

Rendini P. 1999, L*a villa Domitia dell'Isola di Giannutri (Isola del Giglio, Grosseto). Tipologie di pavimenti,* in Atti del V Colloquio AISCOM, Roma 3-6 novembre 1997, Ravenna, 141-152

Uscatescu A. 1996, *Un tipo di decorazione orientale nelle ceramiche del periodo tardoantico rinvenute in Italia*, "Archeologia Medievale", 23, 625-646

The Punta Ala "B wreck": a mixed cargo of the Hadrianic Period

Sergio Bargagliotti, Franca Cibecchini and Pamela Gambogi

Abstract
A Roman wrecksite has been surveyed and partly excavated in 1998-99, on the northern side of Punta Ala (Grosseto). The cargo was scattered on a sandy bottom at a depth of three m. and comprised various goods from many production areas: amphorae of many forms and origin (at least Dressel 20, Gauloise 4 and 5, Forlimpopoli B, Dressel 2-4 and Spello amphorae), plain and decorated late Italian sigillata from Pisa, plain African Red Slip Ware, two glass cups and African cooking ware. The variety of the cargo allows us to reflect upon the links between long distance trade and local productions from northern Etruria.

The Punta Ala promontory is located on the border between the districts of Livorno and Grosseto on the Tuscan coast. Situated opposite the Island of Elba, on the point that closes the wide Gulf of Follonica, it has always been a focus for Northwest Mediterranean sea-traffic and therefore also for shipwrecks.

In ancient times, the Punta Ala area was under the influence of Vetulonia and Populonia and its importance must have been boosted by the sea commerce of both towns. This is attested by isolated discoveries, from at least the Archaic period, in the waters of the wide and sheltered Cala del Barbiere, north of the tourist harbour. Here, the modern structures for pleasure navigation have covered, for the main part, other submerged archaeological deposits, investigated by Nino Lamboglia in the early 1970s (Lamboglia and Pallares 1975-81, 172-176). The wreck excavated by Lamboglia was a 3rd century AD cargo vessel that had onboard, amongst other things, coins issued by *Severus Alexander* and the Gordians. This can be considered the first systematic research among the mass of casual recoveries made by sport divers, attracted by the fact that these shipwrecks lie in just a few metres of water.

We know of a few artefacts, from the end of the Etruscan Archaic period, that are, by the way, of some luxury and were found in a deposit of Rhodian and Samian amphorae sherds, assignable to the end of 6th – beginning of 5th centuries BC (Memorie Sommerse 1998, 95-101). These sherds are probably the remains of a cargo that was dragged into a depression in the seabed by wave motion. Later investigation in the same depression has in fact discovered fragments of a small hull, combined with black glaze pottery datable between the end of 4th and the middle of 3rd century BC, that can be linked to the same chronological horizon as many fragments of Greek-Italian amphorae (Bollettino d'Arte 1982, 46-47), found in many locations around Cala del Barbiere. This evidence provides scattered clues of the habitual use of this area that will last throughout the Hellenistic age and, without interruption into the late Republican and Imperial periods.

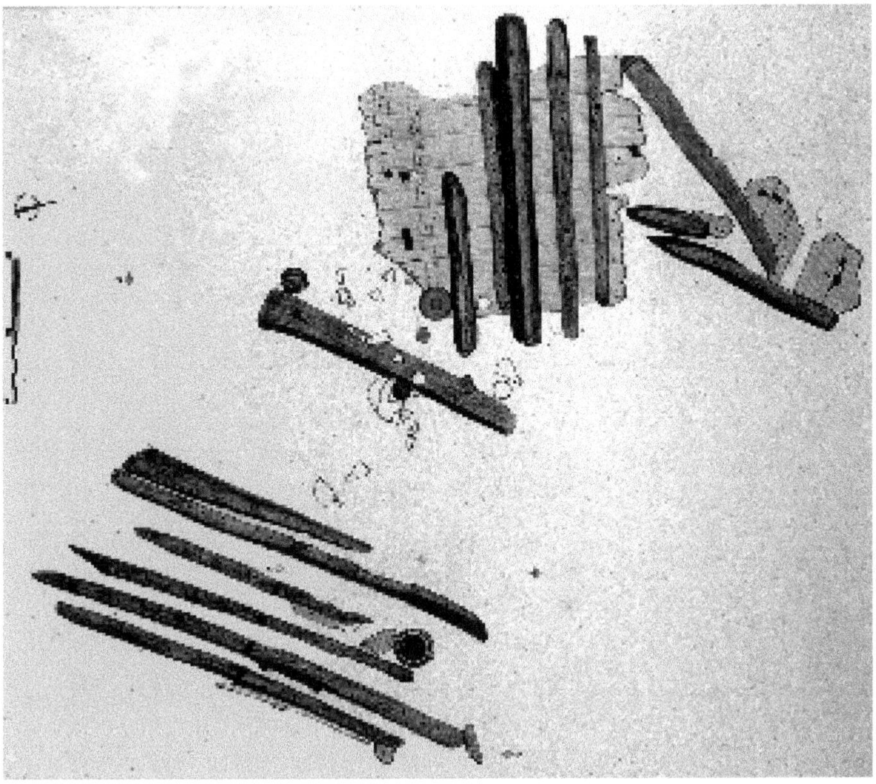

FIGURE 1: PLAN OF THE HULL OF THE PUNTA ALA B WRECK (BARGAGLIOTTI S., CIBECCHINI F.)

Dressel 1 and Dressel 2-4 amphorae, and their fragments, are scattered across the floor of the sea, while on the top of Torre Hidalgo, besides the tourist harbour, a wreck with *dolia*, whose cargo comprised two different types of large containers (an ovoid, shouldered type and a round bodied type) has recently been identified. Fine ware and coarse ware, and various types of transportation containers of the same chronology, extend from Campana A to Italian sigillata and to late African's classes. Wrecks of African amphorae are attested by types that date from the 3rd to 6th centuries AD; these sherds are found in large quantities in many locations around Cala del Barbiere, testifying to *circa* one thousand and two

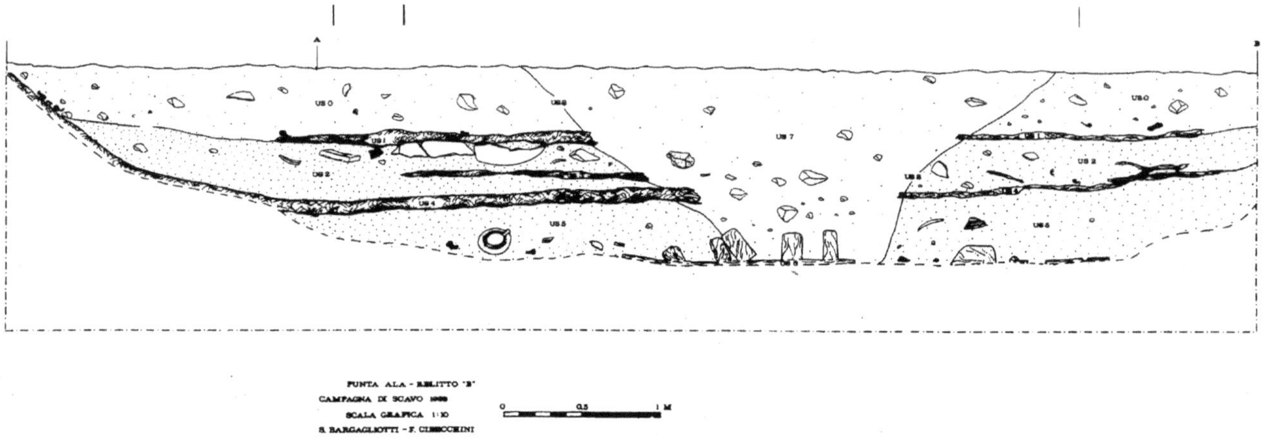

FIGURE 2: SECTION THROUGH PUNTA ALA B WRECK (BARGAGLIOTTI S., CIBECCHINI F.)

hundred years of uninterrupted trading. The intense traffic that penetrates from the Southeast Mediterranean and from the North African coasts, into the Tyrrhenian Sea to reach Rome, and the Gallic and Hispanic coasts - and to return again - would survive for a long time after the Western Empire's fall. The Tuscan islands, not far offshore from the Punta Ala coast, rich with natural resources, were an ideal station on these sea-routes.

A stratigraphic excavation of an undisturbed deposit has focused on the so-called Cala del Barbiere "B wreck", whose identification as a great cargo vessel of the imperial period (Memorie Sommerse 1998, 101-121) had already been made in the early 1990s. The three years (1998-2000) of marine excavations, led by the Soprintendenza Archeologica della Toscana, Nucleo Operativo Subacqueo, have discovered two wide sections of a large ship's hull (Bargagliotti, Cibecchini and Gambogi 2000, 4-5). The hull has been broken into many pieces and displaced through time as a result of its shallow position (4.5 m) and by continuous wave action (Figure 1). The first section (A), the larger one of the two, has a framing series (max. length 2.31 m) still in place, joined to a section of planking, in which the usual mortise and tenon technique is detectable.

The second section (B) is composed of a second series of frames (max. length 3.27 m.) that is displaced and turned upside down. The search of the seafloor for other parts of the hull, especially the keel, have not yet produced positive results.

The vessel's cargo, composed for the main part of pottery and transportation containers, appears only partially to remain in the ship's load-bearing structures, while a large amount of material has been found in the stratigraphy above the hull's remains (figure 2).[1] In this case too, the cargo's dispersal across a wide area is due to wave motion and to the collapse of the cargo vessel's structure after the shipwreck.

P.G.

The Cargo

None of the ceramic finds was in its original stowage position. With a few exceptions, the material was found in fragments. The study of the objects gives a sufficiently exhaustive picture of the mixed cargo that was carried by the ship at the moment of the shipwreck, including amphorae, tableware and maybe coarse-ware, although the systematic analysis has not yet been finished.

Fine wares

Considering all identified fine ware, a large number of examples (50) of late Italian sigillata ware has been found, a class that clearly dominates the whole assemblage (80%). This is followed at some distance by African A 1 red slip ware (14%) and by a few examples of grey imperial and thin-walled pottery with grey fabric (6%).

Late Italian sigillata

The late Italian sigillata is attested by both plain (59%: footed plates, small cups, beaker) and decorated (41%: large bowls form Dragendorff 29) examples.[2] The clay has a pinkish - orange colour, the slip varies from brown-red to orange.

Considering plain sigillata, mainly footed plates, refer, where identifiable to a known type, to the *Cons.* 3.2.2. and *Cons.* 3.3.2. (Plate I, 1-4) shapes, almost all stamped

[1] Materials from various periods (black glaze pottery, Greco-Italic amphorae, and a plate of Italian sigillata stamped by *Ateius* found in 1994 (Memorie Sommerse 1998, 106) were found in the superficial layers, transported by the wave motion and partly mixed with finds belonging to wreck 'B' cargo.

[2] For the classifications, we refer to *Conspectus formarum* (Ettlinger *et alii* 1990), and abbreviate it to *Cons.;* Medri 1992 is abbreviated as Medri followed by the number of the shape or the iconographic type.

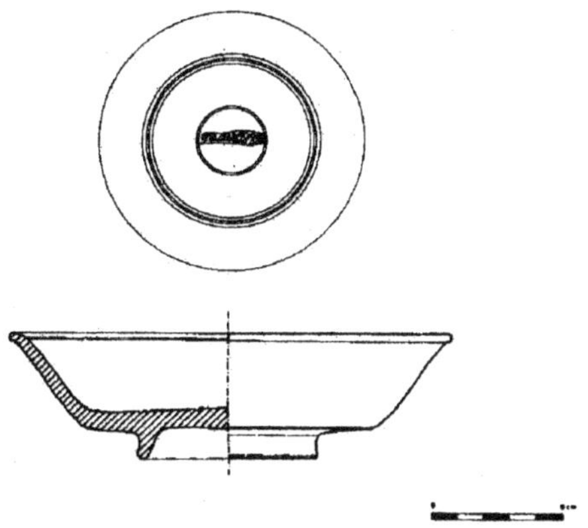

N.1

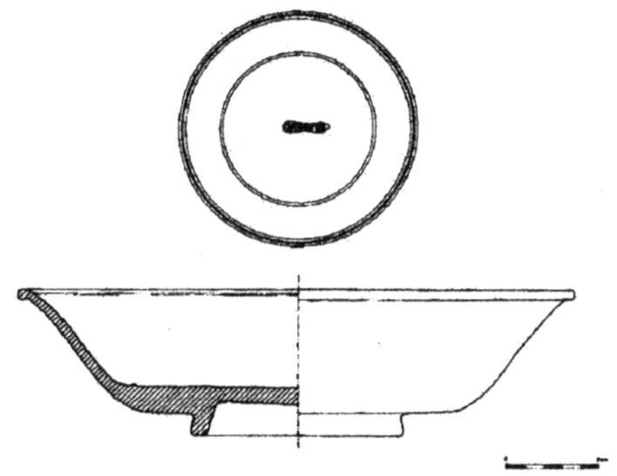

N.2

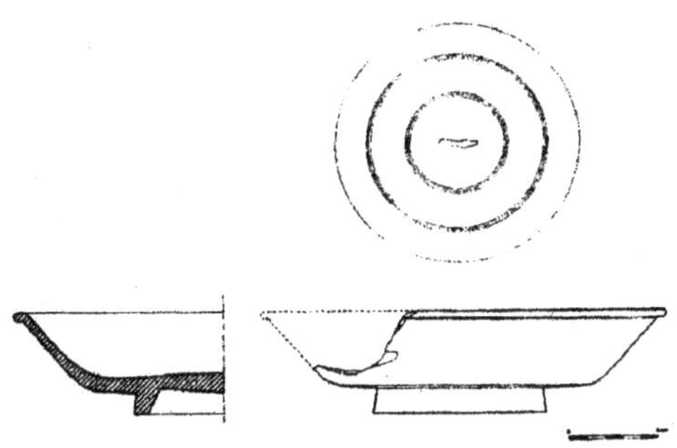

N.3

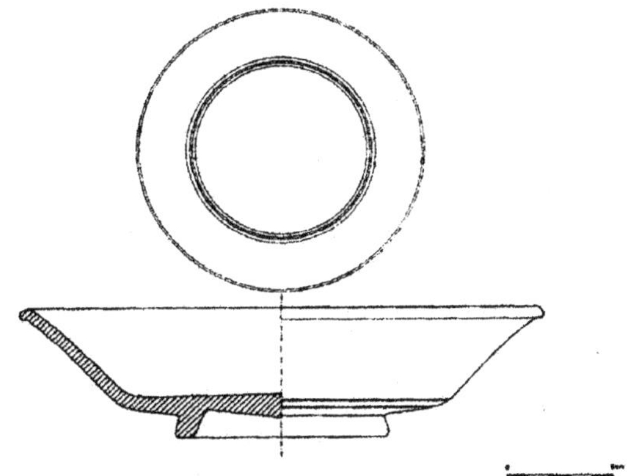

N.4

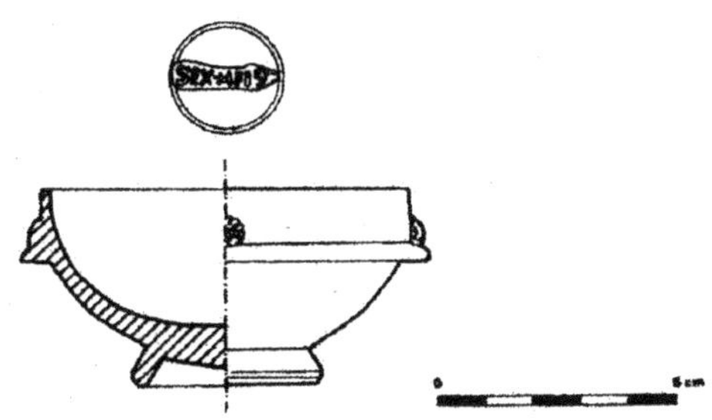

N.5

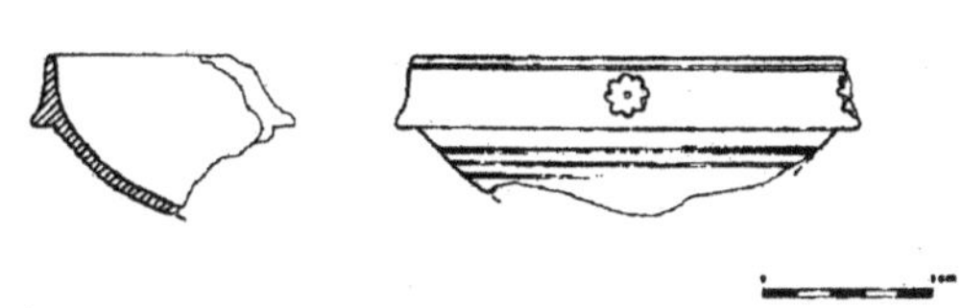

N.6

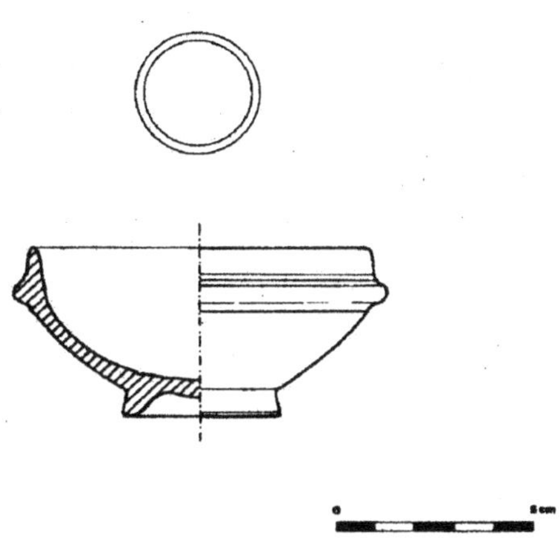

N.7

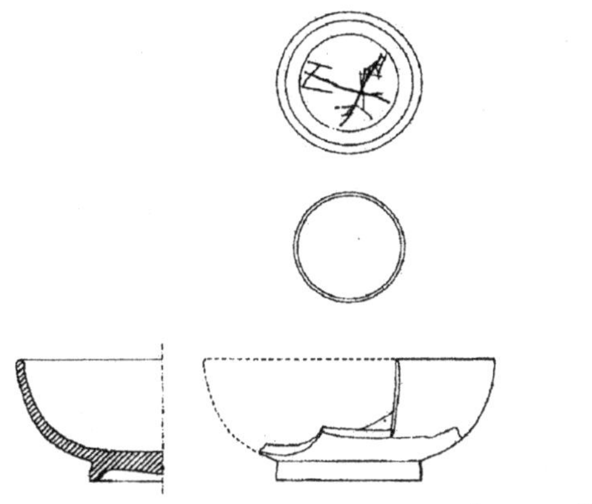

N.8

PLATE I: PLAIN LATE ITALIAN SIGILLATA (MEMORIE SOMMERSE 1998)

Potters	Plates/cups	Cons.3.2.2	Cons.34.1.3	Dragendorff 29
L. Rasinius Pisanus CVArr. 1558	LRPI in *Planta Pedis*			(RASI)N PISAN(US) in *Lunula*
C . P () P() *CVArr. 1191*		2 C C P in *Planta Pedis*		
Sex. Murrius Festus *CVArr. 1054*	SEX M F in *Lunula*; 2 SEX M F in *Planta Pedis*			
Sex. Murrius Pisanus *CVArr. 1059*			SEX M P; SEX M PIS in *Planta Pedis*	
Sex. Murrius Cladus *CVArr. 1053*	SEX M-CL in *Planta Pedis*			
L. Nonius Flor *CVArr. 1137*				2 NONI FLOR in *Lunula*
CNLUCCEIPYRR		CNLUCCEIPYR R in *Planta Pedis*		

TABLE 1: STAMPS ON LATE ITALIAN SIGILLATA

on the base of the interior in *planta pedis* (Plate I, 1-3; II, 9-10, Table 1). After these there are small flanged cups (*Cons.* 34.1), plain or with applied decorations (rosettes, grotesque figures), almost all stamped in *planta pedis* (Plate I, 5-7) and beakers decorated *à la barbotine*, in the form of scale, *Cons.* 50.5.1. In the end, there are one triconical cup, with applied decoration (dolphin, *Cons.* 23.2.2; Figure 3)[3] and one example of a hemispheric cup, *Cons.* 36.4. (Plate I, 8).

FIGURE 3: LATE ITALIAN SIGILLATA WITH APPLIED DECORATION (DOLPHIN).

The decorated late Italian sigillata is represented by the usual Dragendorff 29 large bowls, for the most part Medri 1.8.1.a types; 1.8.2.a; 1.8.3.a (Plate II, 11-15).[4]

Many figurative motifs are attested: dogs (Medri 2.2.8.01), trees (Medri 5.1.1.01), rosettes (Medri 5.5.3.07), tritons with shell trumpets, (Medri 1.1.6.09) joined to grotesque figures (Medri 1.3.1.01) (Plate II, 11); vine leaves (Medri 5.2.2.01) (Plate II, 15); festoons and rosettes on rope (Medri 8.6.1.04 and 5.5.2.05) (Plate II, 14); arcs with trees (Medri 9.1.1. e 5.1.1.01), leaves (Medri 9.7.1.03), rope (Medri 9.4.1.13), palm leaves (Medri 5.2.1.13), vine leaves (Medri 5.2.2.06), small palms in a lyre frame (Medri 5.6.3.03) with alternated palm leaves, small palms (Medri 5.6.2.04) and rosettes (Medri 5.5.1.35); intersecting frames (Medri 9.2.1.04), rosettes and rosettes hanging from ropes with dancing grotesque figures (Medri 1.3.1.01) (Plate II, 12); with *erotes* coachmen (Medri 1.1.3.01) and double flute players (Medri 1.3.4.01) with *erotes* coachmen; dolphins (Medri 2.3.02/2.3.03).

Only three specimens are stamped, two from *L. Nonius Flor* and one from *L. Rasinius Pisanus*, all in *lunula* (Table 1).

All the attested stamps, except for CNLUCCEIPYRR, not yet identified,[5] clearly refer to late Italian potters, whose workshops have been located in Pisa and in its *ager* (Menchelli 1994a; 1994b; 1997). The presence of the earliest of these late Italian potters, such as *L. Rasinius Pisanus, Sex Murrius Festus, C. P ( )P( )*[6] and the latest, *L. Nonius Flor*, with decorated examples (Medri 1992, 125) together with attestation of *Sex. Murrius Pisanus* in the plain production (Medri 1992, 124) lead to a date for the late Italian sigillata to the beginning of the 2nd century, instead of the end of the 1st century; this is also confirmed by their association with African red slip ware A 1.

[3] For the late Italian sigillata plain production of these forms, together with the following troncoconic cup, *Cons. 23.2.2,* with applied decoration, see Menchelli *et alii*; Gabler 1996, 54-59.

[4] For some types and identified decorations, see De Tommaso (Memorie Sommerse 1998, 111-114).

[5] Probably *Cn. Luccei Pyrri*, with hypothetical connection to the stamp LUCPYR (*CVArr., n. 898*) (Memorie Sommerse 1998, 108).

[6] The plain production of *Sex. Murrius Festus*, considered the first of the late Italian potters, seems to begin about AD 50 (Rizzo 1998, 843 with bibliography).

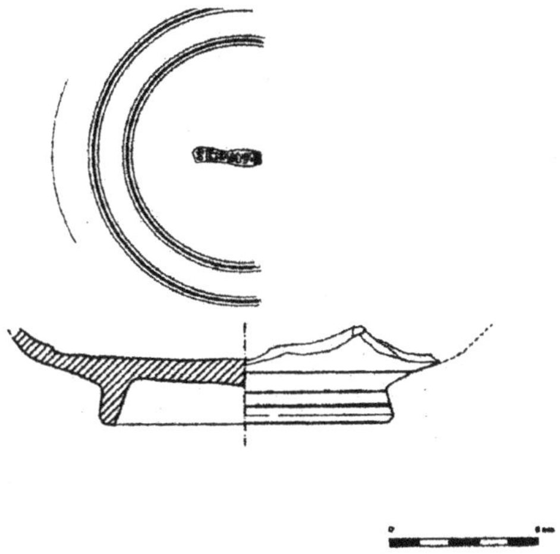

N.9

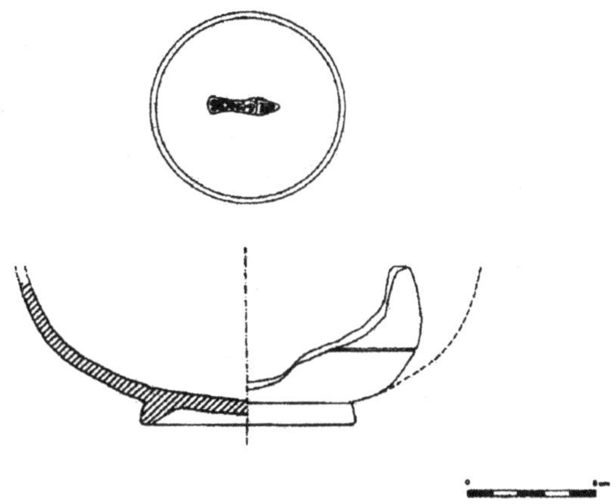

N.10

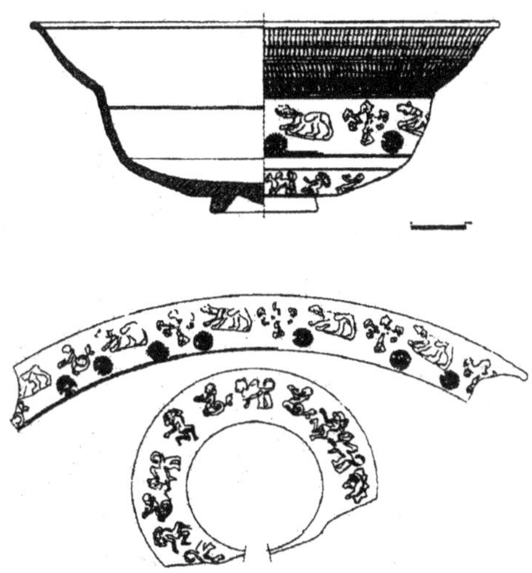

N.11

N.12

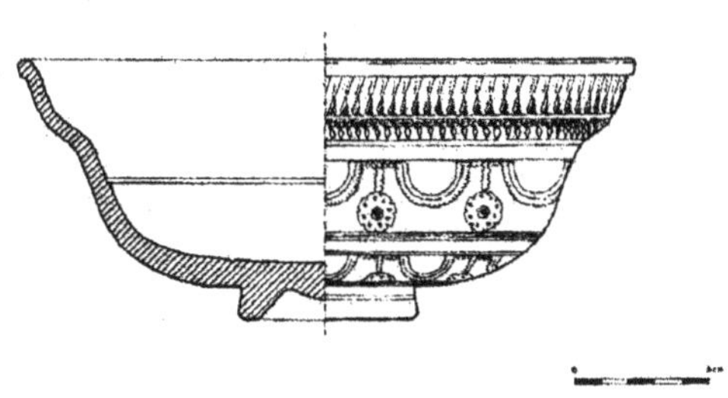

N.13

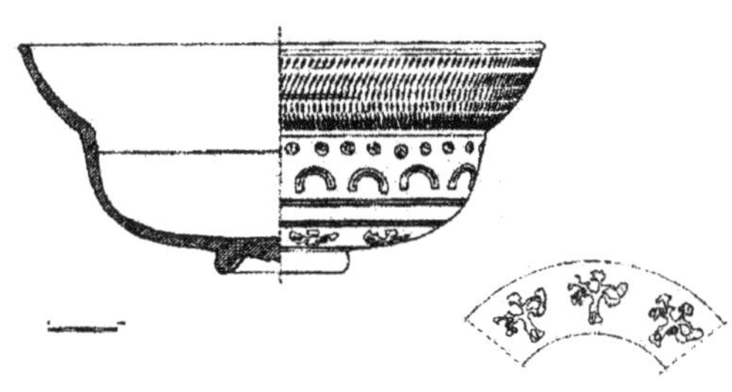

N.14

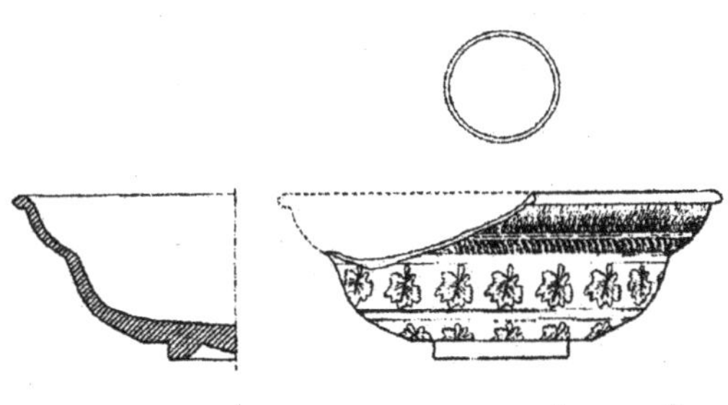

N.15

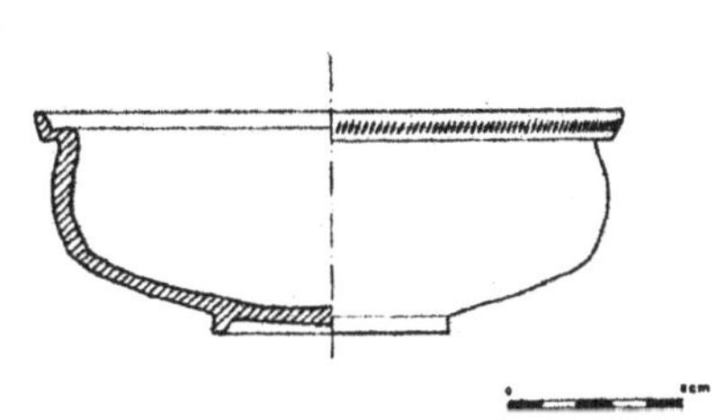

N.16

PLATE II: PLAIN (9-10) AND DECORATED LATE ITALIAN SIGILLATA (11-15); AFRICAN RED SLIP WARE (16). (MEMORIE SOMMERSE 1998)

FIGURE 4: AFRICAN RED SLIP WARE A 1.

African red slip ware A 1

The presence of African A 1 red slip ware is clearly limited - a total of nine pieces (14%): plates (shape *Atl.* I, tab. XIII, 1), cups/bowls (Lamboglia shapes 4/36 = *Atl.* I., tab. XIII.14 and Lamboglia 1a = *Atl.* I., tab. XIV.3) (Figure 4) and a soup-tureen (Lamboglia 19bis = *Atl.* I, tab. XV, 5-6) (Plate II, 16) have been identified. Except for the Lamboglia 1a cup, frequent since about AD 90, all the shapes present in the wreck relate to the first half of the 2nd century, corroborating the date previously suggested for the late Italian sigillata.

Imperial grey ware and thin-walled pottery

Probably only two examples, referring to this class[7] have been recovered. The imperial grey ware is attested with a cup, for which a comparison has not yet been found, and a small amphora (Memorie Sommerse 1998, 118-119) (Plate III, 19). For thin-walled pottery with grey fabric, just two fragments of small jugs are present.[8]

Lamps

In addition to table ware, six lamps have been recovered, two of them almost complete, all of Bailey (1980) P, group "i" type. One is decorated on its *discus* with the personification of Africa and has on the bottom the stamp AUFIFRON, workshop of *Aufidius Fronimus*, probably located in *Africa Proconsularis* (Memorie Sommerse 1998, 117). The second lamp is undecorated, with the stamp LMADIEC, workshop of *Lucius Munatus Adiectus* (Figure 5); it has been suggested that the *Lucii Munati* had two production centres (Pavolini 1993, 67), one in Central Italy and one probably in *Africa Proconsularis* (Bailey 1980, 98).

FIGURE 5: LAMP WITH THE STAMP LMADIEC, WORKSHOP OF *LUCIUS MUNATUS ADIECTUS.*

Plain and coarse ware

Unidentified plain ware (24%),[9] African cooking ware (36%) and unknown coarse ware (40%) have been grouped because they could be part of the cargo as well as the ship's own equipment. African cooking ware is present with blackened-edged plates (*Ostia* II-III, *Atl.* I., tav. CIV, 1, 3), lids (*Ostia* II, *Atl.* I., tab CIV, 1 and *Ostia* I-III, *Atl. I*, tab. CIV, 2-5 types; Palte III, 17) and cooking dishes mainly of *Ostia* III type, *Atl. I*, tab. CVII, 2-8 (Plate III, 18) including at least one Lamboglia 10a type specimen, *Atl. I*, tab. CVI, 10. All shapes attested relate to the first half of 2nd century.[10]

[7] As for imperial grey ware, see Olcese (1993, 113-116, D group, with bibliography).
[8] Production is also testified in the lower Arno valley (Menchelli 1994b, 211-212).

[9] For other types see De Tommaso (Memorie Sommerse 1998, 117-118).
[10] Plain and coarse ware of unknown origin are still being studied by the authors.

The coarse ware is attested for the most part with globular *ollae*, lids, brim edges cooking dishes, a pot with two handles (Figure 6) and a small amphora (Plate III, 21).[11]

For the plain ware, there are at least four *ollae* with flanged rim, four pitchers, two jugs (Figure 7) and a soup-tureen with two handles.

FIGURE 6: COARSE WARE, POT WITH TWO HANDLES.

FIGURE 7: PLAIN WARE, JUG.

Mortaria

Fragments of at least two mortars were found. The type is largely attested between the 1st and 2nd centuries AD (Memorie Sommerse 1998, 120-121) also in wreck contexts (Joncheray 1972).

Glass

Amongst the material recovered are two blue-green glass cups, type Isings (1957) 3a (Figure 8) and one glass bottle, type Isings (1957) 50.

F.C.

FIGURE 8: BLUE-GREEN GLASS CUP.

Transport containers

The main cargo consisted of the products contained in amphorae; none of the vessels was found unbroken. Calculated on the basis of the necks and rims, the sherds represent a minimum of forty-four amphorae. The forms are listed below, ordered according to the geographical area of production.

Gallic amphorae

Gauloise 4
This is the best represented form, with at least fifteen examples or about 33% of the total (Plate III, 23). Produced in southwest Gaul, this shape is well-known for the transportation of Gallic wine between the mid 1st and 3rd century AD (Laubenheimer 1985, 261).

Gauloise 5
This shape is attested by at least three examples, or *c.*6.6% of the total (Plate III, 24). It is similar in shape to the *Gauloise 4* and was also used for the transportation of wine. This amphora was produced in *Gallia Narbonensis* between the second half of the 1st and the first half of the 2nd century AD (Laubenhaimer 1985, 293-299). The fact that they are associated with *Gauloise 4* amphorae is a useful chronological indicator as it is mainly found in 2nd century AD contexts (Laubenheimer 1985, 392).

[11] Part of them could have been manufactured along the North Tyrrhenian coast (Menchelli 1994b, 211; Cherubini and Del Rio 1997). The lids with applied handles can be compared to types of *Albintimilium* (Olcese 1993, 242-244, n. 169 and nn. 168-172). For the small amphorae, see De Tommaso (Memorie Sommerse 1998, 120).

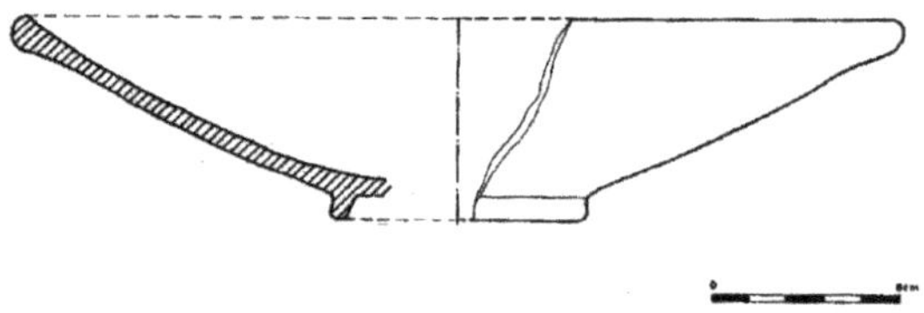

N.17

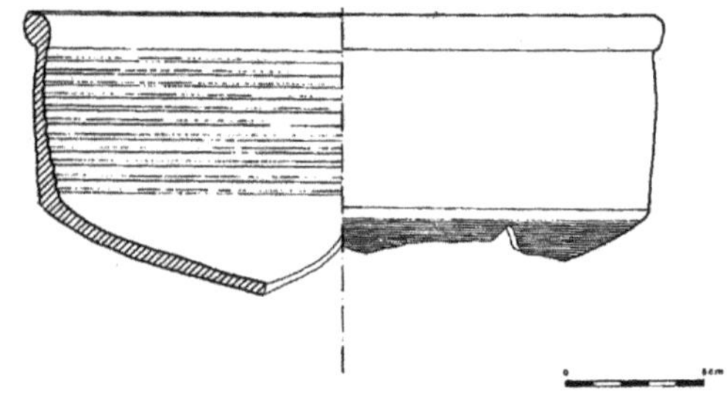

N.18

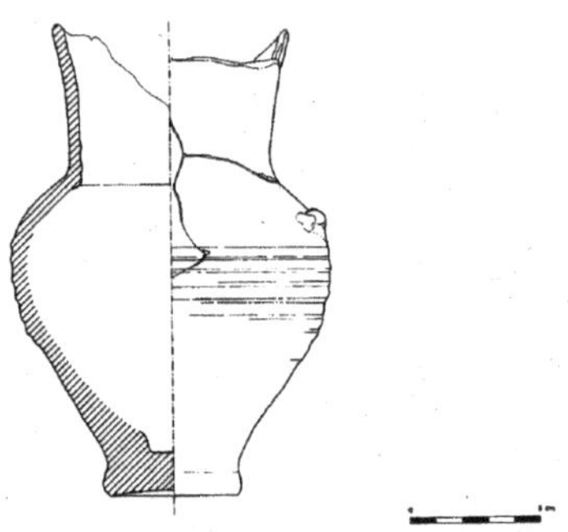

N.19

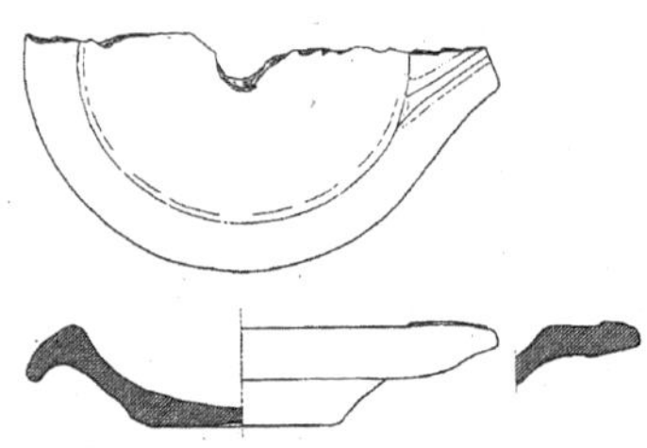

N.20

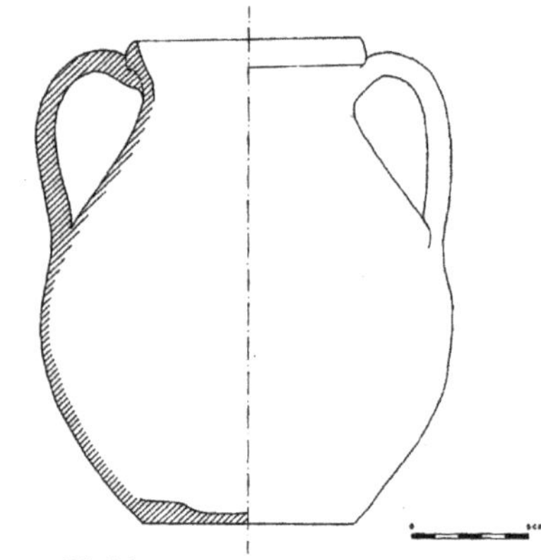

N.21

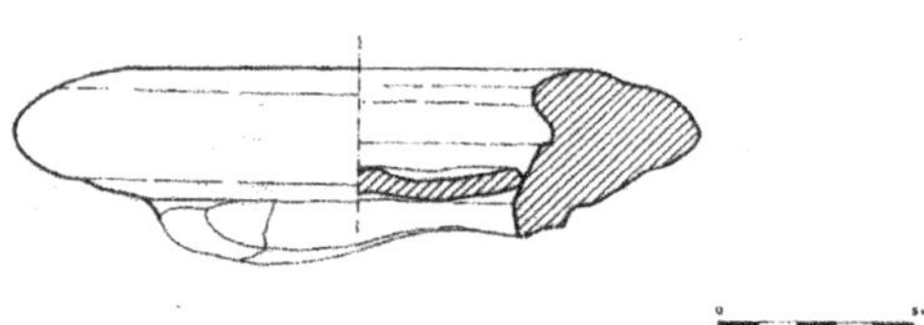

N.22

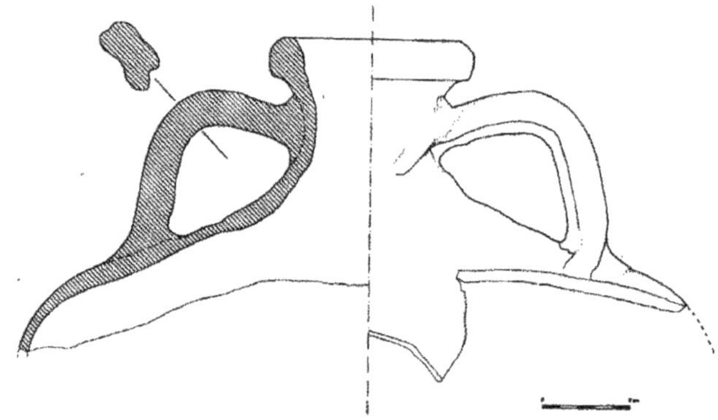

N.23

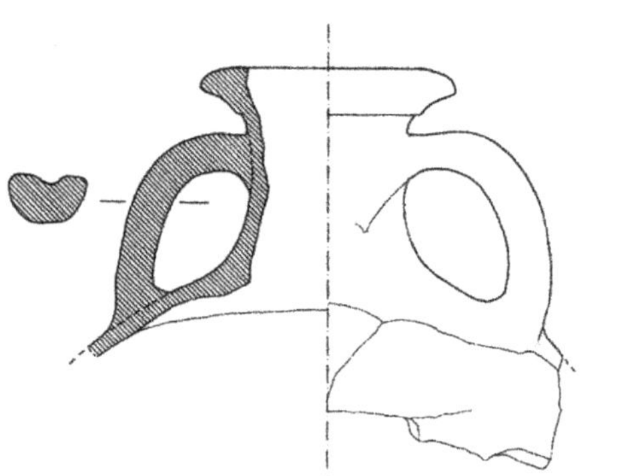

N.24

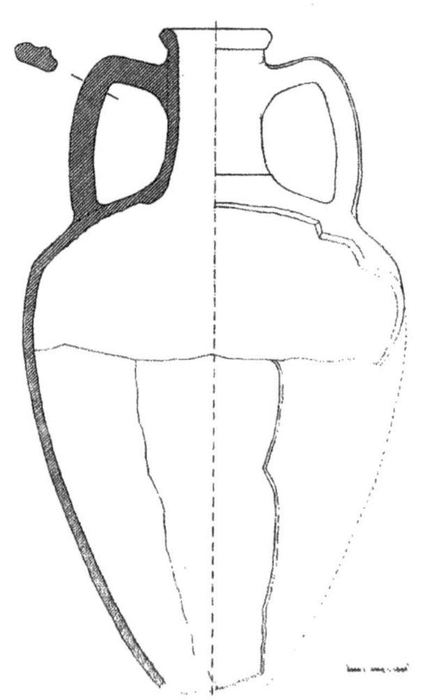

N.25

PLATE III: AFRICAN COOKING WARE (17-18); IMPERIAL GREY WARE (19); COARSE WARE (21) AND AMPHORAE DRESSEL 20 (22), GAULOISE 4 (23), GAULOISE 5 (24) AND FORLIMPOPOLI B (25).(MEMORIE SOMMERSE 1998)

Iberian amphorae

Dressel 20

With at least five examples, Dressel 20 represents 11% of the total (Plate III, 22). Produced in *Baetica*, along the Guadalquivir valley - where several kilns have been discovered - this class is the most frequently attested oil container during the first three centuries of the Empire and one of the most widespread in the Western Mediterranean. The examples from Punta Ala are similar in shape to examples datable between the end of the 1st and the first half of the 2nd century AD (Peacock and Williams 1986, 136-140). The sherds include two stamped handles: APFE in an ellipsoidal scroll and LEOI or LEPI in a scroll, partly erased and hardly readable.

Dressel 2-4

This shape, with its rounded rim and bifid handles, is represented by at least four examples, or 9% of the total. The visual characteristics of the red-brown fabric, with frequent large white inclusions, and fragment of golden mica, allow us to locate the area of production along the Catalan coast (Tchernia and Zevi 1972, 36-37; Peacock and Williams 1986, 106). These amphorae were used for the transportation of wine between the end of the 1st and the first half of the 2nd century AD.

Italian amphorae

Ostia II, 521/III, 369-370 (Spello amphora)

Generally known as "Spello" amphorae, after the Umbrian town where the first *atelier* was identified (Tchernia 1986, 253-255; Manconi 1989, 590), this form is characterized by a "spinning-top" body of reduced dimensions and by a flat base. The sherds found at Punta Ala attest the presence of at least three examples (Figure 9), that constitute 6.6% of the whole, characterized by a fabric, brown on the external surface and red-orange in the core, with tiny white shiny inclusions. Outside Umbria, these amphorae were manufactured in northern inland Etruria and along the lower and middle valley of the river Arno, particularly in the *ager Pisanus* and *Volaterranus*, from the middle of the 1st to the end of the 2nd /start of the 3rd century AD (Menchelli 1990-91, 170-171; Pasquinucci, Del Rio and Menchelli 1998, 358-359).[12]

Forlimpopoli B

Attested by two examples (Memorie Sommerse 1998, 104-106), or 4.4% of the amphorae, these containers were used for wine transportation and produced in the *Picenum*, in the *ager Volaterranus* and in the middle valley of the river Arno, between the end of the 1st century and the end of the 2nd century AD (Panella 1989, 172; Pasquinucci, Del Rio and Menchelli 1998, 358-359). They belong to the group of small containers, with "spinning-top" bodies and flat bottoms, like the so-called "Spello" amphora and can be distinguished by the thickened rim and by the pinkish fabric with white and grey inclusions. The distribution in the Tyrrhenian area is attested at Ostia (*Ostia IV*, 440), Settefinestre (Panella 1989, 172) and in southern Tuscany (Cambi 1991, 45, nn. 28-29).

FIGURE 9: SPELLO AMPHORA.

FIGURE 10: SMALL GLOBULAR AMPHORA.

[12] These amphorae substitute the Dressel 2-4 as containers of the wine produced in central Tyrrhenian Italy. They are mainly distributed on a regional scale and also on coastal trade routes — Lazio/southern Etruria and the Tuscan islands (Panella 1989, 144-146; Menchelli 1990-91,171).

Amphorae of uncertain classification and origins

Sherds of uncertain classification comprise 29.5% of the total currently under study. Among them, we can distinguish sherds of at least five examples of *Dressel 2-4* (11%), for which we cannot yet establish the area of production. It is also worth mentioning a group of sherds belonging to at least three small globular amphorae, with flanged rims. One example has been almost entirely reassembled (Figure 10) and bears the numeral XXII scratched on its shoulder.

S.B.

Conclusion

The study of the hull suggests that the ship was a medium-large *oneraria* rather than a small vessel for local coastal navigation. The finds probably represent a small percentage of the whole cargo, which has been scattered over a large area by wave action and looted by divers in the last few years.

After the analysis of the material, we can make some hypotheses about the cargo and the ports-of-call on the vessel's final voyage. *Portus Pisanus* surely represented the last stop, considering the presence of the late Italian sigillata, produced in Pisa, and of Spello amphorae, also manufactured along the Arno valley. The whole cargo could even have been loaded at a single large harbour, like Pisa, one of the most important in the northern Tyrrhenian and western Mediterranean. Otherwise, we can postulate that the ship stopped at different harbours along the route, from Spain (Dressel 20, Dressel 2-4), via South Gaul (Gauloise 4 and 5) to Pisa.

The analysis of the ceramics, principally the decorated late Italian sigillata, indicates that the ship sank around the first quarter of the second century AD.

S.B.; F.C.; P.G.

Acknowledgments

Acknowledgements: Corpo Nazionale dei Vigili del Fuoco - Sommozzatori of Tuscany; the doctors of the hyperbaric staff of Policlinico di Careggi (FI); Com.te M. Minervini (Marina di Punta Ala S.p.a.); the Yacht Club Punta Ala; the Società Immobiliare Punta Ala; the Architect P. Borghi and his wife; Livia Seravalli and Robert Witcher. A particular acknowledgment to M. Cygielman, who started the excavation of Punta Ala "B" wreck.

Bibliography

Aldini, T. 1978, *Anfore foropopiliensi*, "Archeologia Classica", 30, 86 ss.

Atl. I, Atlante delle forme ceramiche I. Ceramica fine romana nel bacino Mediterraneo (Tardo Ellenismo e Primo Impero) Enciclopedia dell'arte antica, classica e orientale, Roma, 1985.

Bailey D.M. 1980, *A Catalogues of the Lamps in the British Museum. Roman Lamps Made in Italy,* Londra.

Cambi, F. 1991, *Schede*, in *Relitti di Storia. Archeologia subacquea in Maremma*, Celuzza, M. and Rendini, P. (edd.), Siena, 45.

Cherubini L. and Del Rio A. 1997, *Ceramiche di età romana nell'Etruria Settentrionale costiera: impianti, produzioni, attrezzature,* "Rei Cretariae Romanae Fautorum Acta", 35, Abingdon, 133-141.

Conspectus - Conspectus formarum terrae sigillatae italico modo confectae. Materialen zur römisch-germanischen Keramik, 10, Bonn, 1990.

CVArr.- Oxé A. and Comfort H., *Corpus Vasorum Arretinorum*, Bonn, 1968.

De Tommaso G. 1998, *Relitto B,* in Poggesi G. and Rendini P. (ed.), *Memorie Sommerse. Archeologia subacquea in Toscana*, Pitigliano, 101-121.

Gabler D. 1996, *Terra sigillata tardo-italica in Pannonia,* "Acta Archaeologica Academiae Scientiarum Hungaricae, 48, 49-69.

Ising C. 1957, *Roman Glass from Dated Finds,* Groningen-Giacarta.

Joncheray J.P. 1972, *Contribution à l'étude de l'épave Dramont D, aà Saint-Raphaël, d'après les travaux du G.E.S.M.R.S.*, "Cahiers d'Archéologie Subaquatique", 1, 11-34.

Laubenheimer, F. 1985, *La production des amphores en Gaule Narbonnaise*, Besançon.

Manconi, D. 1989, *Anfore romane in Umbria alla sinistra del Tevere*, in *Amhores romaines et histoire economique: dix ans de recherche. Actes du colloque de Sienne* (22-24 mai 1986), Ecole Française de Rome, Roma, 590-593.

Medri M. 1992, *Terra sigillata tardo italica decorata a rilievo,* Roma.

Menchelli, S. 1990-91, *Una fornace di anfore Dressel 2-4 nell'Ager Pisanus ed alcune considerazioni sui contenitori vinari prodotti nell'Etruria settentrionale in età romana*, "Opus", IX-X, 169-184.

Menchelli S. 1994a, *Da Cn. Ateius ai vasai tardo-italici: alcune considerazioni sulla terra sigillata "pisana"*, Bollettino Storico Pisano, LXIII, . 1-29.

Menchelli S. 1994b, Le produzioni ceramiche della Bassa Valle dell'Arno, *in Olcese G. (ed.),* Ceramica romana e archeometria: lo stato degli studi, *Firenze, 205-215.*

Menchelli S. 1997, *Terra sigillata pisana: forniture militari e "libero mercato",* "Rei Cretariae Romanae Fautorum Acta", 35, Abingdon, 191-198.

Menchelli S. *et al.* 2000, Menchelli S., Capelli C., Del Rio A., Pasquinucci M., Picon M., Thirion-Merle V., *Ateliers de céramiques sigillées de l'Etrurie septentrionale maritime: données archéologiques et archéométriques*, "Rei Cretariae Romanae Fautorum Acta", 37, Lione (in press).

Ostia IV 1977, *Ostia IV: Le Terme del nuotatore: Scavo dell'ambiente XVI e dell'area XXV*, Studi Miscellanei, 23, Roma.

Olcese G. 1993, *Le ceramiche comuni di Albintimilium. Indagine archeologica e archeometrica sui materiali dell'area di via del Cardine*, Firenze.

Panella C. 1989, *Le anfore italiche del II sec. d.C., in Amhores romaines et histoire economique: dix ans de recherche. Actes du colloque de Sienne* (22-24 mai 1986), Coll. de L'Ecole Française de Rome, Roma, 139-178.

Pasquinucci M., Del Rio A. and Menchelli S. 1998, *Produzioni di vino nell'Etruria settentrionale costiera,* in *El vi a l'antiguitat. Economia, producció i comerç al Mediterrani occidental. Actes de Badalona* (6/9 mai 1998) Badalona, 357-363.

Pavolini C. 1993, *I bolli sulle lucerne fittili delle officine centro-italiche,* in Harris W.V. (ed.), The Inscribed Economy, "Journal of Roman Archaeology, Suppl. 6, 65-71.

Peacock, D.P.S. and Williams, D.F. 1986, *Amphorae and the Roman Economy*, London.

Rizzo G. 1998, *Samia etiamnunc in esculendis laudantur (Pl., N.H. XXXV, 160-161). I vasi "aretini a Roma",* "Mélanges de l'École Fraçaise de Rome,*2, 779-848.*

Tchernia, A. 1986, *Le vin de l'Italie romaine, Essai d'histoire économique d'après les amphores, Roma.*

Tchernia, A. and Zevi, F. 1972, *Amphores vinaires de Campanie et de Tarraconnaise à Ostie*, Coll. de L'Ecole Française de Rome, 10, 33-67.

Ancient riverborne transport of heavy loads

Ronald Bockius

Abstract
The typical vessels used for transports on inland waters in Roman Gaule and Germania have been flat-bottomed cargo ships ("prams") which are preserved by almost 30 finds. Most of the remains are related to the so called Romano-Celtic ship building tradition as indicated also by rounded craft either seagoing or coastal and inland found in the northern part of the Roman Empire. Some specimens of the type discussed imply technological influences from the Mediterranean. Characteristic features are sharpie-like plans and square-sections but also impressive dimensions. Ship technical investigations attempted on a selection of wrecks result in calculations of load capacities which are compared to archaeological data pointing to heavy-duty transports in the middle Rhine area.

During the last three decades of the second millennium, on the territory of the northern provinces of the Roman Empire an astonishingly large number of ancient ship finds came to light. Excavations on Roman sites near rivers and lakes of ancient Gaul and Germania revealed a special type of inland vessels, some of them of considerable dimensions. Dated by dendrochronology, C14-dating or by conventional archaeological methods, the wrecks belong to the first three centuries AD. With respect to their shape and the operational environment of those vessels indicated by the locations of the wreck sites, they are usually called "barges" or "prams". Although this terminology has been taken over from later historic, recent types of inland or harbour vessels, these names describe very well the nature of ships such as "lighter", "pontoon" and "scow". For a better understanding the term "pram" may be accepted.

One of the typical features of wrecks to be discussed here is an absolutely flat, carvel built ship bottom which runs athwartships into vertical or sloping sides; in their upper parts, the ship walls are erected by side strakes either of overlapping planking or of carvel construction (Figures 1-2). For the transition from the bottom into the walls each a single timber was used, called "île" in French, i.e. "chine-strake" in English. This element can be determined as being a profile of L-shaped or C-shaped square-sections. As similar versions are also to be found in plank-built ships from the British Bronze Age: the prehistoric background of such technical solutions is obvious. With good reason, it has been assumed that such chine-strakes transform the idea of logboats on ship constructions which are too broad to be built from a single tree-trunk. But it could be shown that the profiles pair-wise used for the transition from the ship's bottom into the sides at the lower part of the hulls were not made of single dugout being cut length-wise along the centre line. Nevertheless, the specific construction method of Roman prams signifies a continuum of prehistoric ship building procedures. If the groundplans of certain vessels are compared (Figures 1 and 3) there is more than one clue for an Iron Age background but not necessarily indigenous.

Some wrecks in good state of preservation i.e. those with more or less intact ship ends help to understand what the stem and stern looked like, which explains to us both the elevation and groundplan of the vessels: fore and aft, the flat ship bottom increases in a straight line or as a slightly rounded curve forming ramp-like ship ends ("swim-heads"), either the bow and the stern, what makes the identification of such craft as "pram" in combination with the shape of the ship-body in square-section so convincing. Focused on the latter and from the ship architects' point of view, those vessels rather belong to sharpies than to rounded plank-built ship types the more as the bows usually are blunt, too, and the stern ends - as far as found - are shaped similar to a transom. The ships found along the Rhine resemble more floating boxes whereas the specimens known from Switzerland and France partly look a little more elegant by means of the ground plan with slightly narrowing ship ends (Figure 2). And there is a further distinction between north and south: Nearly all of the prams found in the Netherlands and in Germany were built with side planks overlapping the chine-strake or - if there was more than a single side strake at each wall (Figures 1, 4 and 7) - their neighbouring plank. Contrary to that the findings from Belgium, France and Switzerland prove carvel planking of the ship sides. It has to be stressed that the largest vessels are concentrated on an area that covers the Roman province of Lower Germania but also the capital of *Germania Superior*, Mainz, as the most southern find spot of this group (Figure 5).

Discontinuing further explanations of technical details, it may be enough to summarize that the wrecks found in the zone between central Gaul and the river Rhine were constructed according to the so-called Romano-Celtic tradition (almost completely built from oak wood, the planks solely fastened to the ribs by strong iron nails, but without a close system of joints between the planking [as was typical for Mediterranean ship construction], the seams filled with some sort of caulking from moss or other vegetal material). Here, only single wrecks show traces of Mediterranean influence by sporadic use of mortise-and-tenon joints between the strakes or by copying features of sewn Greek and Roman ships in a way which obviously had not been understood by the shipwrights of those Rhineland prams (summarized by Bockius 1999; id. 2000a, 117-121 fig. 10-11.3). A wreck found at Lyon shows typical features either of Romano-Celtic and - by sequences of mortise-and-tenon joints and traces of special luting materials (pitched textiles) - classical ship building (Becker and Rieth 1995; Rieth 1998, 77-78); others as Chalon-sur-Saône and Arles

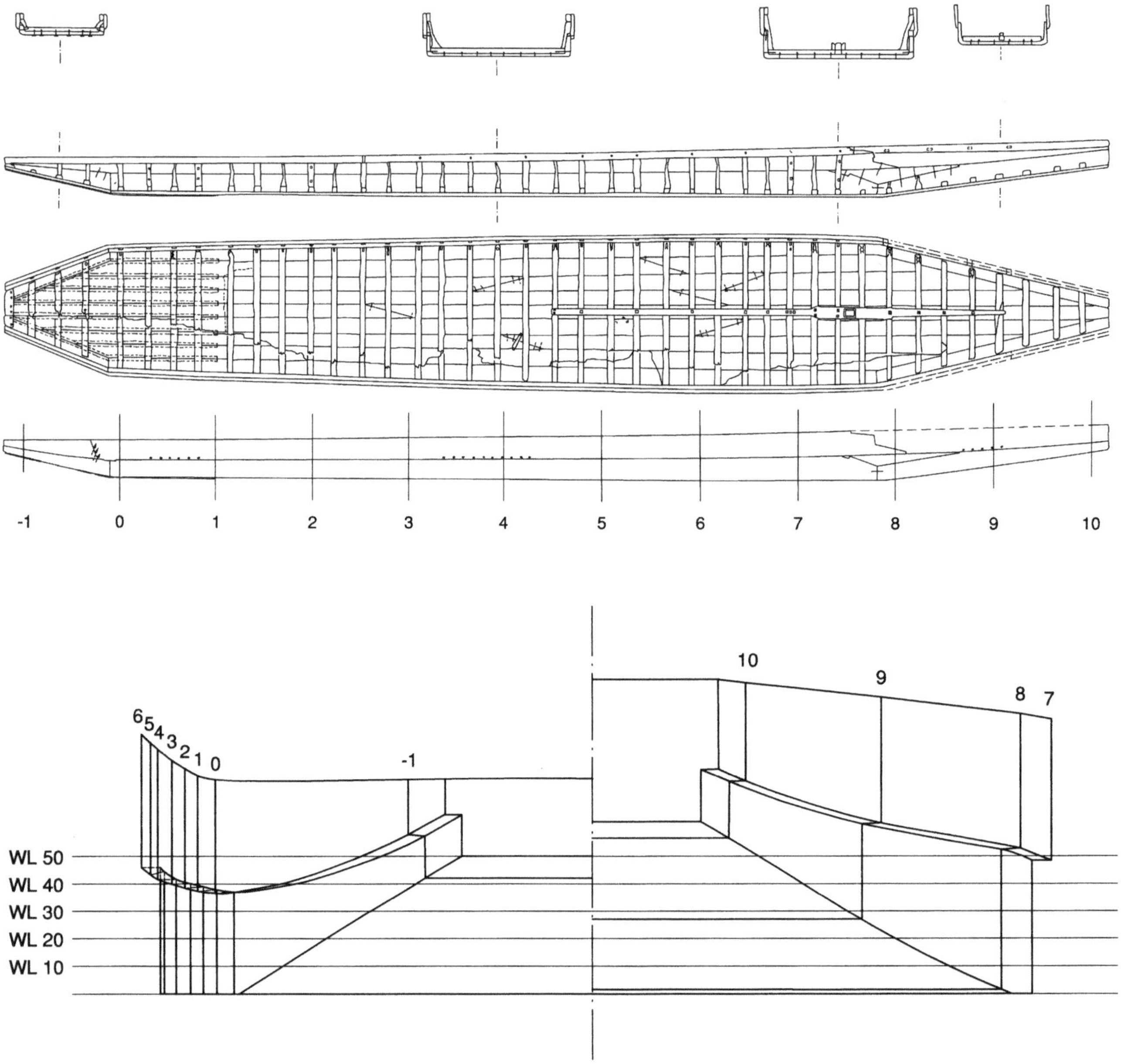

FIGURE 1. ZWAMMERDAM (NL), WRECK 2; GROUNDPLAN AND ELEVATION RECONSTRUCTED (AFTER DE JONG IN DE WEERD 1988); BODY PLAN BASED ON THE THREE-DIMENSIONAL DATA.

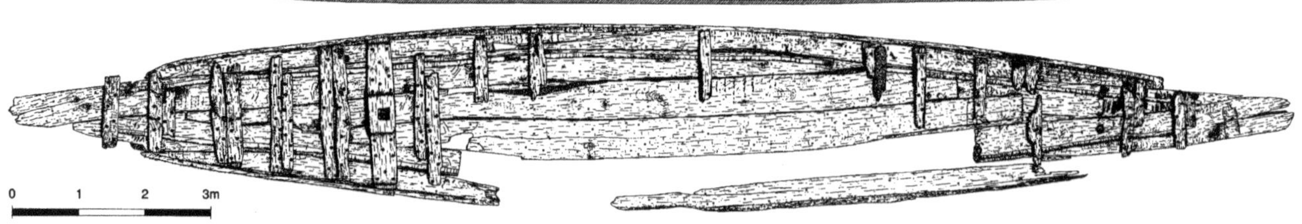

FIGURE 2. BEVAIX (CH), WRECK; GROUNDPLAN AND ELEVATION RECONSTRUCTED (AFTER ARNOLD 1992).

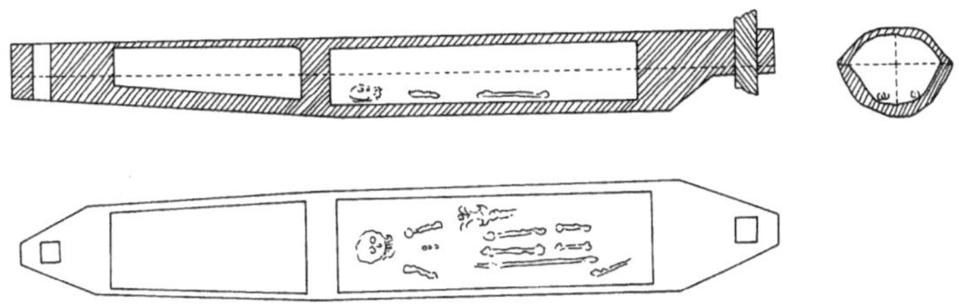

FIGURE 3. CHÂTENEY-MÂCHERON, DÉP. HAUTE-MARNE (F), IRON AGE WORRIER GRAVE, 3RD TO 2ND CENTURIES BC; SKETCH OF A WOODEN TWO-PIECE COFFIN, BOAT-SHAPED (AFTER DRIOUX 1921).

suggest the same influence (Bonnamour1999, 2; id. 2000a, 56; Longchambon 2000, 176-178 fig. 4-5; analyses of luting: Connan et al. 2000). The only pram that was completely constructed in the fashion known from a certain group of ancient Greek and Roman ships (planking made of soft-wood, internals from hard-wood; ribs connected to the shell by tree-nails, the strakes fastened to each other by sewing, the seams luted by lime tree fibres) has been found south east of the Alps in a bog near Ljubljana, Slovenia, recently dated to the late 2nd or early 1st centuries BC (Gaspari 1998, 527-528 with references). From this discovery, it is clear that prams were not concentrated on the western part of central Europe in antiquity. Further archaeological and pictorial indications imply that flat-bottomed vessels if not prams in the sense discussed above alone have been the most important class of ancient vessels used for riverborne transports in southern Gaul and probably also in Italy.

Ship depictions, e.g. the plinth relief of the Tiber statue in the Louvre, indicate rather box-like than rounded plank ships as freighters towed upstream, and similar illustrations, i.e. punted and oared craft are shown on frescoes at Pompeii.[1] So, it is not surprising to find wrecked flat-bottomed vessels (but sharp-ended contrary to the wrecks discussed) also in the Adriatic region and the adjacent sphere (Petrović 1991 [different interpretation: Bockius 2000b]; Beltrame 2000, 92-94 fig. 3 with references). It should be emphasized that neither the Mediterranean nor the central European ship illustrations (Figure 6) can be identified as prams although there is a close typological correspondence between ship finds and ship depictions which share some but not all constructional features.

Concerning Roman prams, a lot of energy was put in descriptions of ship construction and design in the past (Bockius 1999 with bibliography). The function of such inland vessels as cargo ships seems to be quite obvious. Nevertheless, the problem of load capacities of such units has scarcely been discussed and published so far (De Weerd 1988, 208f. with firm data that appear much too high; on the Bevaix ship Arnold 1992, 98-99 with convincing calculations). Some ancient prams are in a state of preservation which allows for the calculations of the ship's volumetric data and weights and can help to approximate the floating conditions, especially draught under hypothetical rates of load to estimate their capacities (Bockius 1996, 523 fig. 4; id. 2000a, 126-128 fig. 16). We do not know the original draught marks and from a nautical point of view a certain ancient freighter might not have taken over always the same quantity of goods. Therefore, it is unreasonable to suppose that distinct load-carrying capacities can be calculated for an individual ship. But it seems possible to define ranges of values that come into question for certain cargo ships, values for displacement, draught, freeboard and, not least, reserve buoyancy. Based on such data, the balance between deadweight and safety, respectively the minimum and maximum, solutions can be criticized.

From certain ancient prams, the most interesting main measurements are available because of their almost complete preservation (Figures 1-2); from others only sections of the ship body are at disposal (Figures 4 and 7). Among the former are namely the Bevaix ship, the Ljubljana pram and Zwammerdam wrecks no. 2, 4 and 6; for the latter, i.e. fragments found at Mainz, Woerden and Xanten reconstructions can be taken into consideration (Bockius 1996). As long as Zwammerdam wrecks 4 and 6, and the Xanten findings are not fully published, with plans, to help estimate their three-dimensional character we have to be satisfied with the remaining materials. Zwammerdam 2 was only disturbed to a noticeable degree on the port side of the ship so that the incomplete width of the hull can easily be found by reassembling the collapsed timbers (De Weerd 1988, 93-148 fig. 47-55); from the Bevaix wreck the side strakes above the chine-strakes were missing but the underbody and both swim-heads are fairly preserved (Arnold 1992). To the Ljubljana pram, which was found already end of the 19th century, important data on ship dimensions have recently been communicated (Gaspari 1998). Although shape and size of the ship ends remain enigmatic, weight and volumetric content of that vessel can approximately be estimated.

[1] Pictorial evidence of inland navigation in Italy is relatively rare but some impressive monuments rather depict flat-bottomed, sharpie-like vessels than round ships: e.g. P. Pomey (ed.), La Navigation dans l'Antiquité, Aix-en-Provence 1997, 130-131 above 2 figures. (Tiber statue); Pompei. Pitture e Mosaici I, 597 no. 15; VI, 687 nos. 7-8; VIII, 815 no.173 (right vessel).

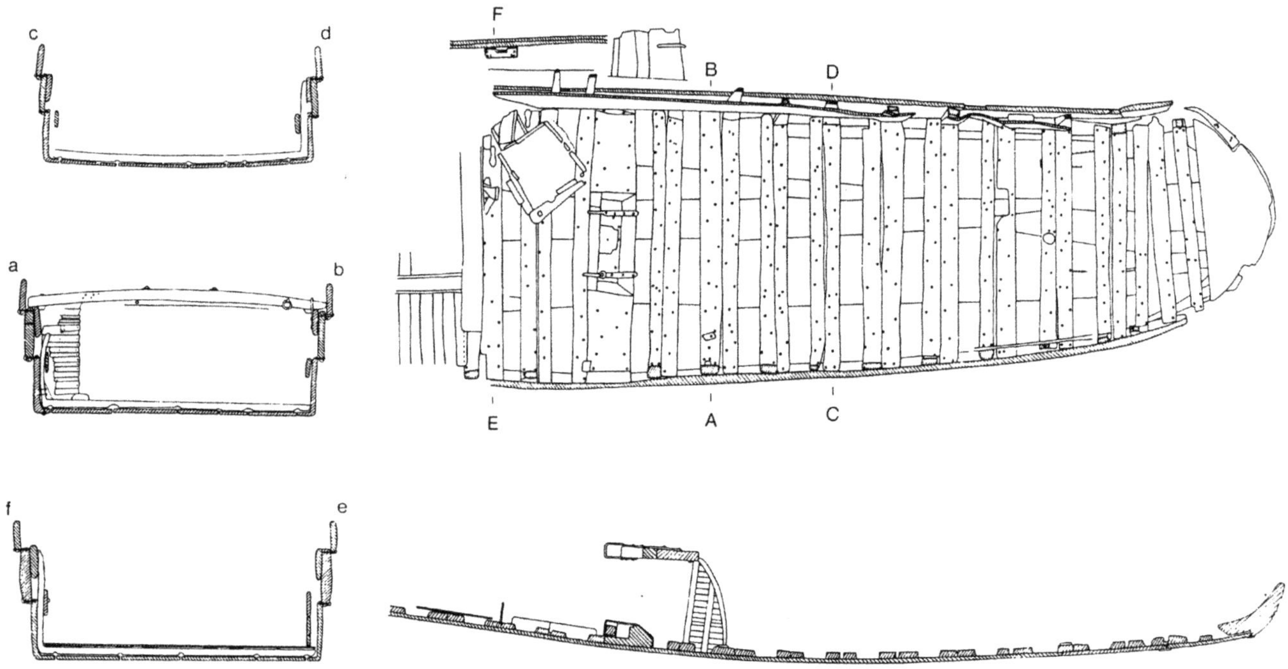

FIGURE 4. WOERDEN (NL), WRECK 1; GROUNDPLAN AND SECTIONS (AFTER BOCKIUS 1996).

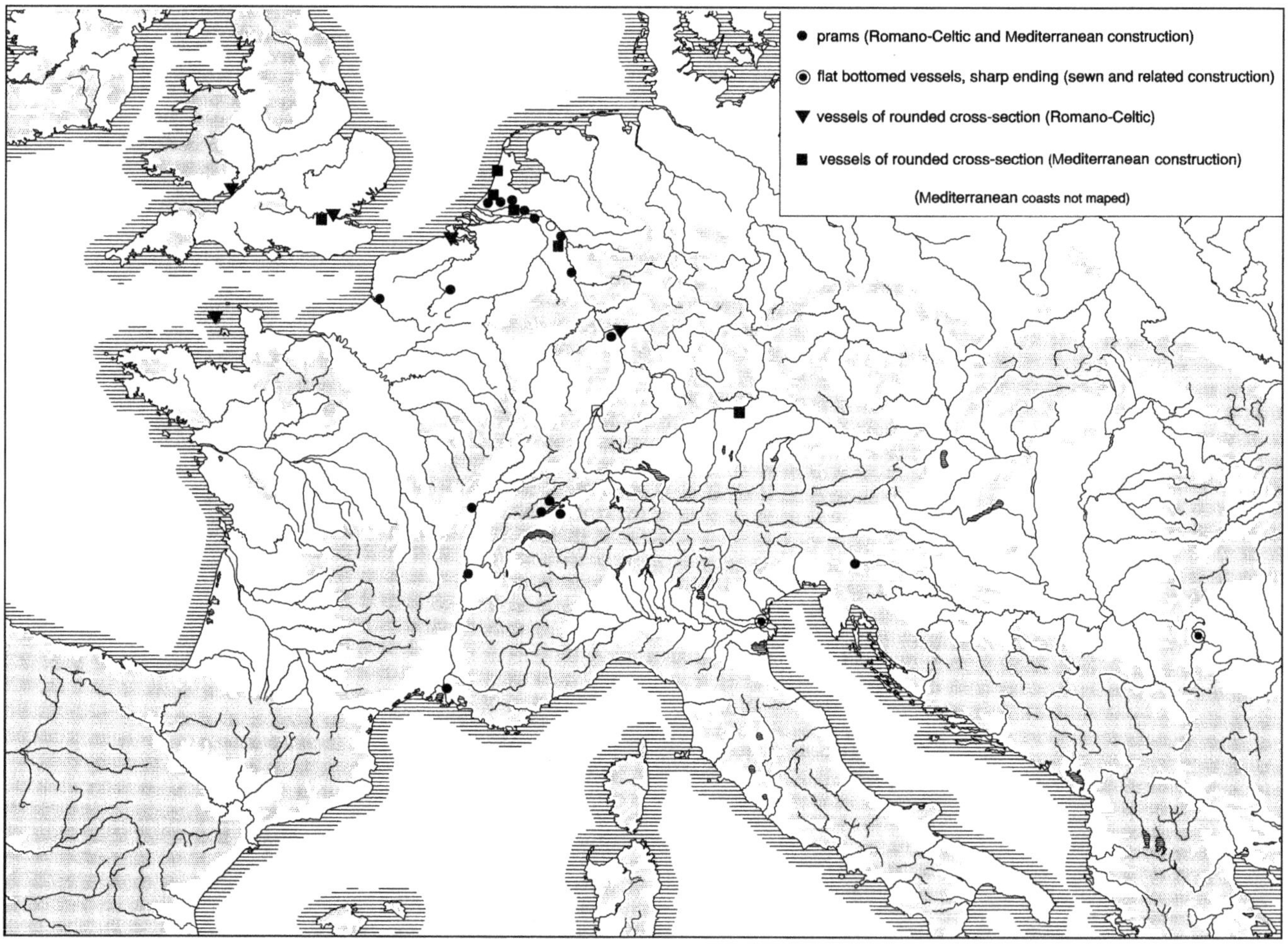

FIGURE 5. DISTRIBUTION MAP OF ANCIENT SHIP WRECKS FOUND OUTSIDE THE MEDITERRANEAN, DISTINGUISHED ACCORDING TYPES OF VESSELS, CONSTRUCTION SYSTEMS, AND CULTURAL ENVIRONMENTS (BOCKIUS 2001WITH TOPICAL LIST).

The Mainz 6 and Woerden 1 wrecks are relatively small fragments but each of them presents information to help complete the ships. Woerden 1 figures the fore part of a Roman pram with a complex device preserved for to rig a mast (also indicated by the Zwammerdam 4 and Xanten-Wardt wrecks); at one side of the fore-ship the sheer line is preserved at a height of around 1.6m. (Figure 4) and the bow construction being mainly based on a large monoxyle element left only one solution as to how to reconstruct the components (Haalebos 1996, 479-489 fig. 6 pl. 66-84; Bockius 1996). From the better preserved Mainz pram only a short section was raised, whose width and height are measurable, but indications available by the field documentation denote the approximate location of that section in the ship's groundplan by the onset of the swim-head next to the bow. Both latter wrecks provide good clues for the reconstruction of their bodies.

As may be implied from the most extensive preservation of the Bevaix and Zwammerdam (wrecks 2,4 and 6) findings (Figures 1-2), but also with respect to proportions which can be traced back from prams with complete ship ends in general (Figures 4 and 7), such craft had obviously been designed according to architectural customs. More concretely, the position of masts (and towing poles) related to the overall length (LOA) of those vessels can be limited to between a quarter and one third of LOA measured from the mast step to the stem. The ratio of length and width (here taken from LOA and maximum beam) was usually around 1 to 7. On the other hand, two different standards were current for the ratio of beam at the station of the mast and the longitudinal distance from here to the foremost end of a ship (Figure 8). If those data are calculated with the distances available from the Woerden 1 and Mainz 6 wrecks their principal dimensions can be traced back. In the latter case, either the enormous beam of around 5.5 metres and supplementary observations on the ancient measurement system pointed to an original ship length of slightly more than 40 metres whereas the Woerden 1 vessel should have been approx. 25 metres long only. As heights and sectional shapes of these units are attested by the ship remains the volumetric data and weights as well can be calculated for the purpose of further estimations. It goes without saying that such calculations, if based on reconstructed three-dimensional data, are to be taken as proposals that rise and fall with the interpretations mentioned above. But, if other versions are preferred it is rather convenient to add/subtract the volume of a certain section amidships or room above the waterline, e.g. in order to enlarge or to reduce the reconstructed LOA or ship height, and by this the values of displacement, than to calculate the whole ship body again and again.

Both the original draughts and freeboards of those ships are unknown but their displacement curves help to find approximate values because ranges between minimum and maximum can be estimated. First, their light displacement to control minimum draught of the vessels unloaded has to be calculated. As shown by the diagram (Figure 9) most of the prams concerned need water only about 10 centimetres deep, or even less, to displace their own weight. Depending on size and shape of ships, the maximum displacement ranges from around 30 tons to 170 tons, but under theoretical conditions, i.e. if the ship hulls are immersed to the lowest point of the sheer line. This state of immersion will never be intended by a responsible shipmaster because of the risk of sinking. However, the more freeboard, the more profit. In other terms: shipmasters had to find a balance between safety and economy; and, most likely, draught had also to be trimmed according to the water level available during a voyage. The historical reality has to be supposed to lie somewhere between the minimum and maximum waterlines. The more the load lines of ancient prams may have varied, the more it seems unreasonable to expect a certain value of draught. Doubtless, individual decisions of ancient shipmasters can hardly be reconstructed. But to illustrate the average capacities, approximations of reasonable load lines can at least give clues. If for each of those prams with overlapping side planks an immersion as deep as to the lower edge of the side strakes (Mainz 6; Zwammerdam 2; for Woerden 1 the second, i.e. the highest strake) is considered, and if we assume for carvel built vessels a draught of two-thirds of the minimum heights of these ships (Bevaix, if B. Arnold's reconstruction is considered [Arnold 1992]; Lubljana), both presumable load capacities and the corresponding draughts may be simulated as an approach as to how things happened. In spite of the moderate nautical circumstances it seems obvious that ancient prams could be freighted by a high quantity of cargo. Beside the smaller and (in relation to their size) heavy constructions (Bevaix; Zwammerdam 2) the hold capacity can be estimated as between four to five times the light weight of each vessel (Figure 10). In most cases the theoretical maximum displacement value is roughly twice that of the total weight added to the calculated load, leaving around 50% reserve buoyancy. Depending on conditions and circumstances one could imagine that the tonnages could be increased without risk, and also decreased if those craft sailed on especially shallow waters.

For barges or flat-bottomed vessels, draughts compared to displacements are remarkably low, particularly if the relatively slender ship bodies are borne in mind. The high cargo capacities are evidently caused by the geometry of such vessels, affording considerable buoyancy but also demanding compromises concerning speed and manoeuvring capabilities.

Based on this, ancient prams may be interpreted as inland vessels employed to carry heavy loads on longer distances. It is not surprising that in some of the wrecks characteristic materials have been found, either remains of bulk goods, such as stone and tiles, but also grain and other food (bottled in amphorae) (Bockius 1999). With regard to the approximate values of cargo capacities

FIGURE 6. FLAT-BOTTOMED SHIP WITH TYPICAL FEATURES OF INLAND NAVIGATION (OAR CREW, STEERING DEVICES AT STEM AND STERN, TOWING POLE); RELIEF ON THE REVERSE OF A TOMBSTONE DEDICATED TO THE ROMANO-CELTIC *NAUTA* *"BLUSSUS"*, FOUND 1848 AT MAINZ, DATED C. AD 40 (SEE ELLMERS 2000; PHOTOGRAPH LANDESMUSEUM MAINZ).

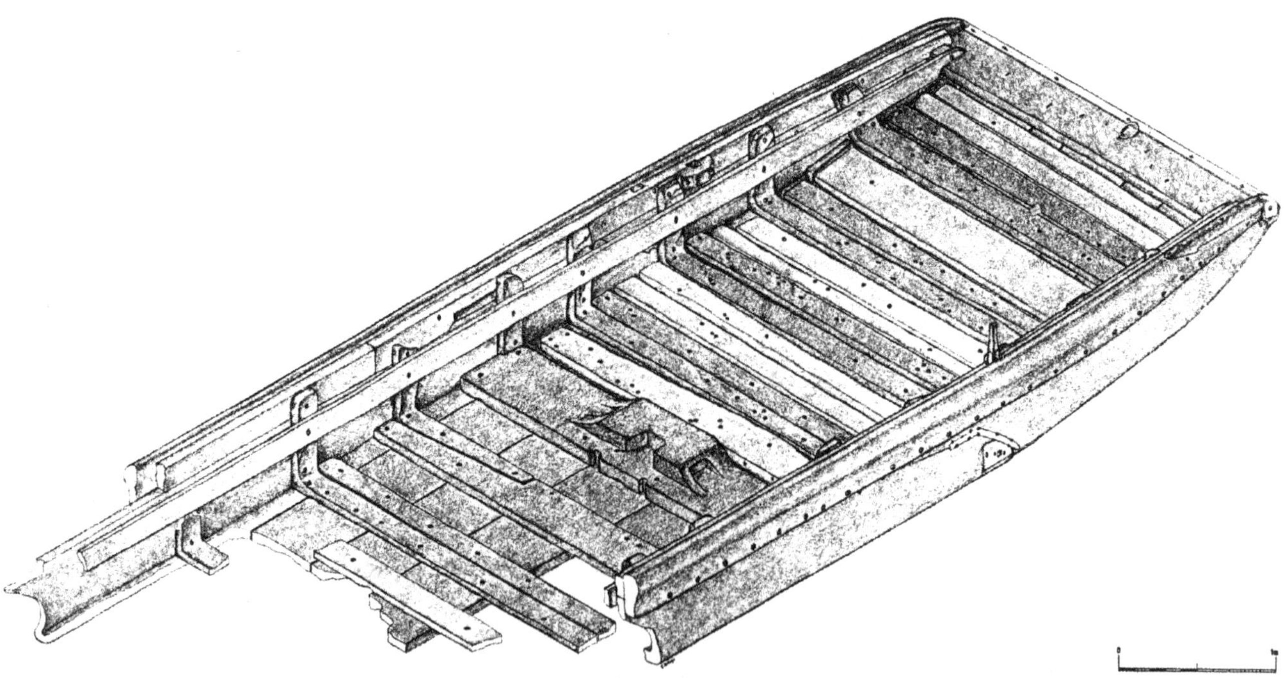

FIGURE 7. XANTEN-WARDT (D), WRECK; PERSPECTIVE VIEW OF THE FORESHIP PRESERVED; CONCERNING THE INTERNALS (E.G. MAST-STEP, FRAMES AND CEILING PLANKS COMPARE TO WOERDEN 1 AND BEVAIX SHIPS, FIGS. 2-3) (AFTER BERKEL AND OBLADEN-KAUDER 1993).

wrecks	distance to stern	distance to stem
Bevaix (CH)	70.6%	29.4%
Zwammerdam (NL) 2	76.0%	24.0%
Zwammerdam (NL) 4	c. 75.5%	c. 24.5%
Zwammerdam (NL) 6	70.5%	29.5%

wrecks	L/B
Bevaix (CH)	6.9 (for carvel construction)
Zwammerdam (NL) 2	7.1 (for overlapping side planking)
Zwammerdam (NL) 4	c.6.9 (for overlapping side planking)
Zwammerdam (NL) 6	5.7 (for overlapping side planking)

wrecks	ratio
Bevaix (CH)	2.3
Woerden (NL) 1	2.1/2.2
Xanten-Wardt (D)	c. 1.3/1.4
Zwammerdam (NL) 2	1.7
Zwammerdam (NL) 4	1.7
Zwammerdam (NL) 6	1.7

FIGURE 8. PROPORTIONS OF ROMAN PRAMS ACCORDING TO MEASURED SHIPWRECKS (DATA TO BE MENTIONED AS PARAMETRES FOR HULL RECONSTRUCTION): A) POSITION OF MAST STEPS COMPARED TO SHIP LENGTH OVER ALL (TOP TABLE).- B) LENGTH-BEAM RATIO (MIDDLE TABLE).- C) RATIO OF FORESHIP LENGTH (MEASURED FROM MAST STEP TO STEM) AND WIDTH AT THE MAST STATION (BOTTOM TABLE).

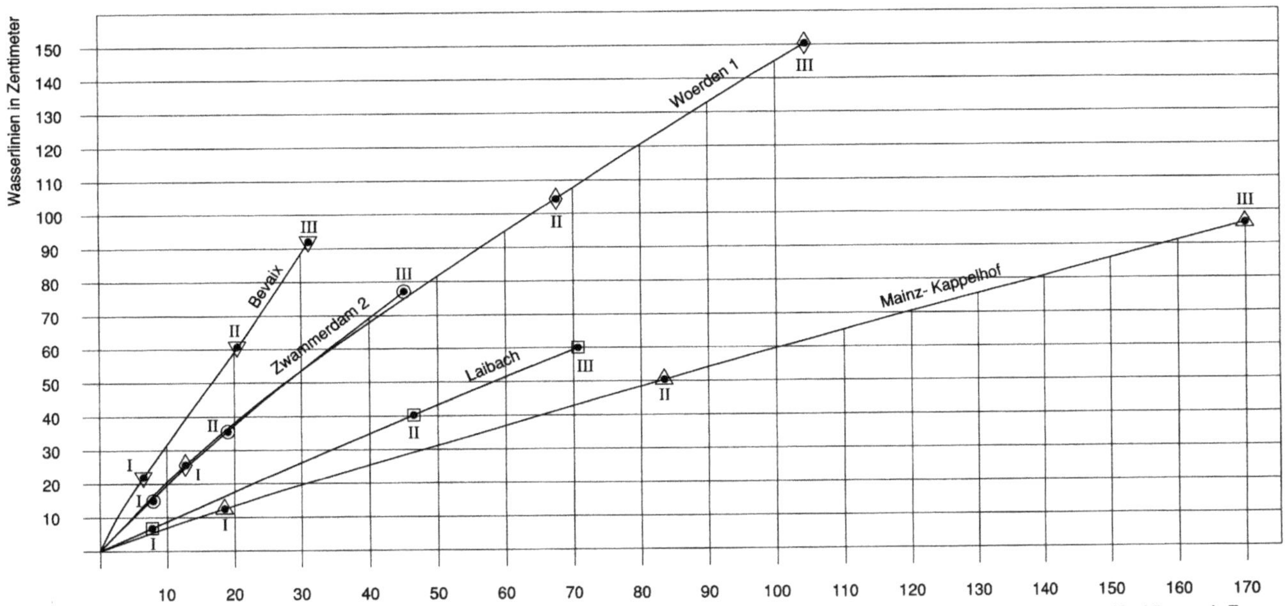

FIGURE 9. DISPLACEMENT CURVES OF ANCIENT PRAMS RELATED TO DRAUGHTS: I LIGHT WEIGHT DISPLACEMENT.- II AVERAGE CAPACITY APPROXIMATED.- III THEORETICAL MAXIMUM DISPLACEMENT ("LAIBACH" = LJUBLJANA, SLOVENIA).

it seems to be clear that such ships played an important role for logistics only in the northern part of the Roman world. Wherever wholesale provisioning was needed or extensive building activities took place near rivers and lakes it has to be assumed that use was made of riverborne transports. The former may be concluded from the distribution of wrecks which are found in large numbers along the Rhine near Roman camps and at important towns but also on sites with a military background in the hinterland (Bockius 1999; id. 2000a, 121-125 fig. 13). The significance of prams for transports of building materials can be examined by at least two examples.

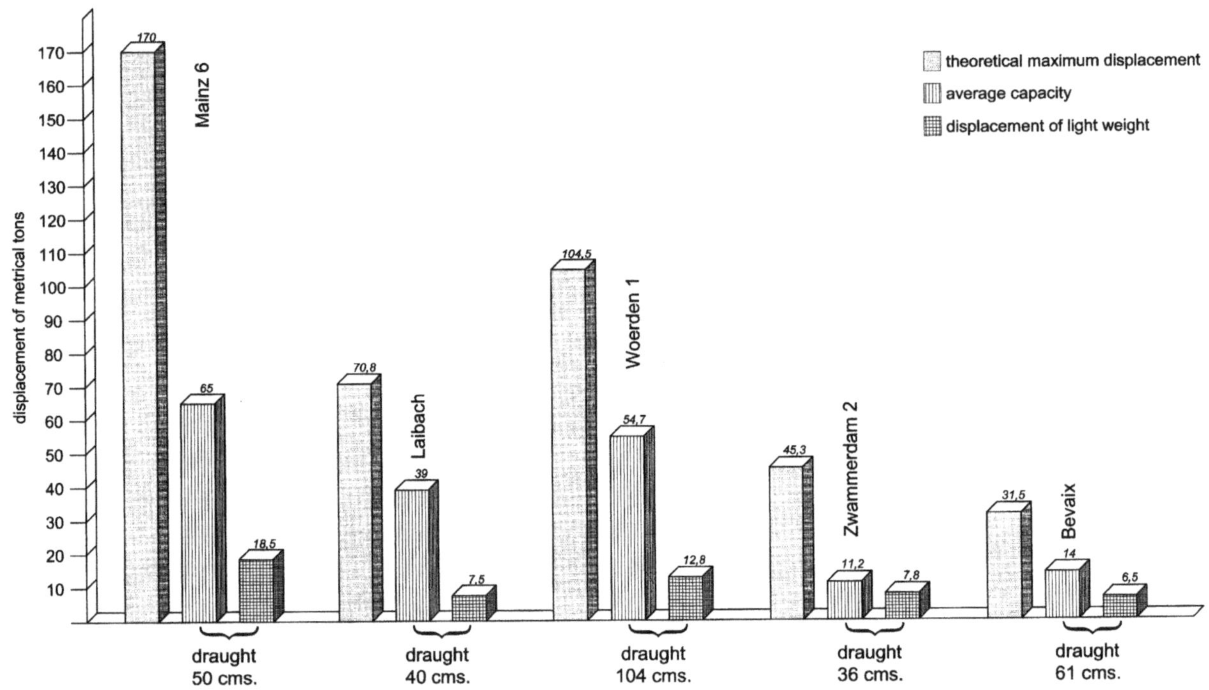

FIGURE 10. AVERAGE LOAD CAPACITIES OF ANCIENT PRAMS, BASED ON DISPLACEMENT CURVES FIGURE 8 ("LAIBACH"=LJUBLJANA, SLOVENIA).

In western Germany the Roman civilization was concentrated in the valleys of the rivers Rhine and Moselle; together with other tributaries of the Rhine, that region is part of a river system suited for inland navigation either along the Roman frontier from the south to the north, and to the hinterland in the east and the west. Here, our interest switches to the town of Trier, ancient *Augusta Treverorum*, in the Roman period an important cultural and, temporarily, political centre. From the monumental architectural remains either still preserved as upright buildings or excavated remains, the geographical origins of the stone materials are documented; in special cases it could be shown by analyses where the stones had been broken. The quarries are situated near rivers, but far more than a hundred kilometres from Trier (Figure 11). Direct road junctions did not exist and the terrain between the quarries and final destination was hilly, if not mountainous. All the most convenient, and thus economic, trade-routes are focussed on the rivers.

The Roman bridge crossing the river Moselle at Trier is preserved by its pillars, the construction being reused by the modern river crossing (Cüppers 1969). Around 6,450 cubic metres of ashlars made of a volcanic stone (basaltic lava) were hewn at a site situated 200 kilometres downstream the Moselle and River Rhine, but at a distance of less than one kilometre from the Rhine, near a Roman trade centre of mill-stones, and a river harbour called Andernach (*Antunacum*) (Mangartz 2000,12-13). From here the distance upstream to the river mouth of the Moselle is 20 kilometres, and from there a further 180 kilometres had to be navigated to reach Trier (Figure 11). If the frequency of the voyages needed to transport such masses of building material is considered, extreme solutions have to be considered: the smaller the cargo vessels, the more sails were needed, or, vice versa, the more capacity that was available in the large freighters, the fewer journeys required. All boats and ships had to be towed up both rivers, as there are no fair winds for sailing in the Moselle valley. It seems the most convincing theory that pram-type ships were used to undertake such monumental transport enterprises. Depending on the morphological density and characteristics of the material, the weight of the 6,450 cubic metres of stone needed to build the curtain pillars of the Roman bridge at Trier (Cüppers 1969, 216) would amount to 18,000 tons. Taking a medium-sized vessel, for instance the Ljubljana pram with a capacity of around 40 tons, 450 single shiploads would have been required.

Another archaeological discovery from Trier should also be taken into account when considering the Roman pram. Remains of late-Roman church buildings were found below the Romanesque cathedral and also fragments of large stone columns made of a certain type of granite occurring in the area east of the Rhine near Mainz. Here, at the so called "Felsberg" (Odenwald, Hesse), Roman quarries are well known and fragments of columns of a size comparable to that of the church finds are still visible there, and in the garden of the cathedral (Röder 1991). With regard to the reconstruction of the columns, and also corresponding with the fragments mentioned, the late-Roman monoliths were more than 12 metres high, each having a weight of about 30 tons. It goes without saying that the prefabricated stone columns must have reached Trier by water transport, especially so as there is

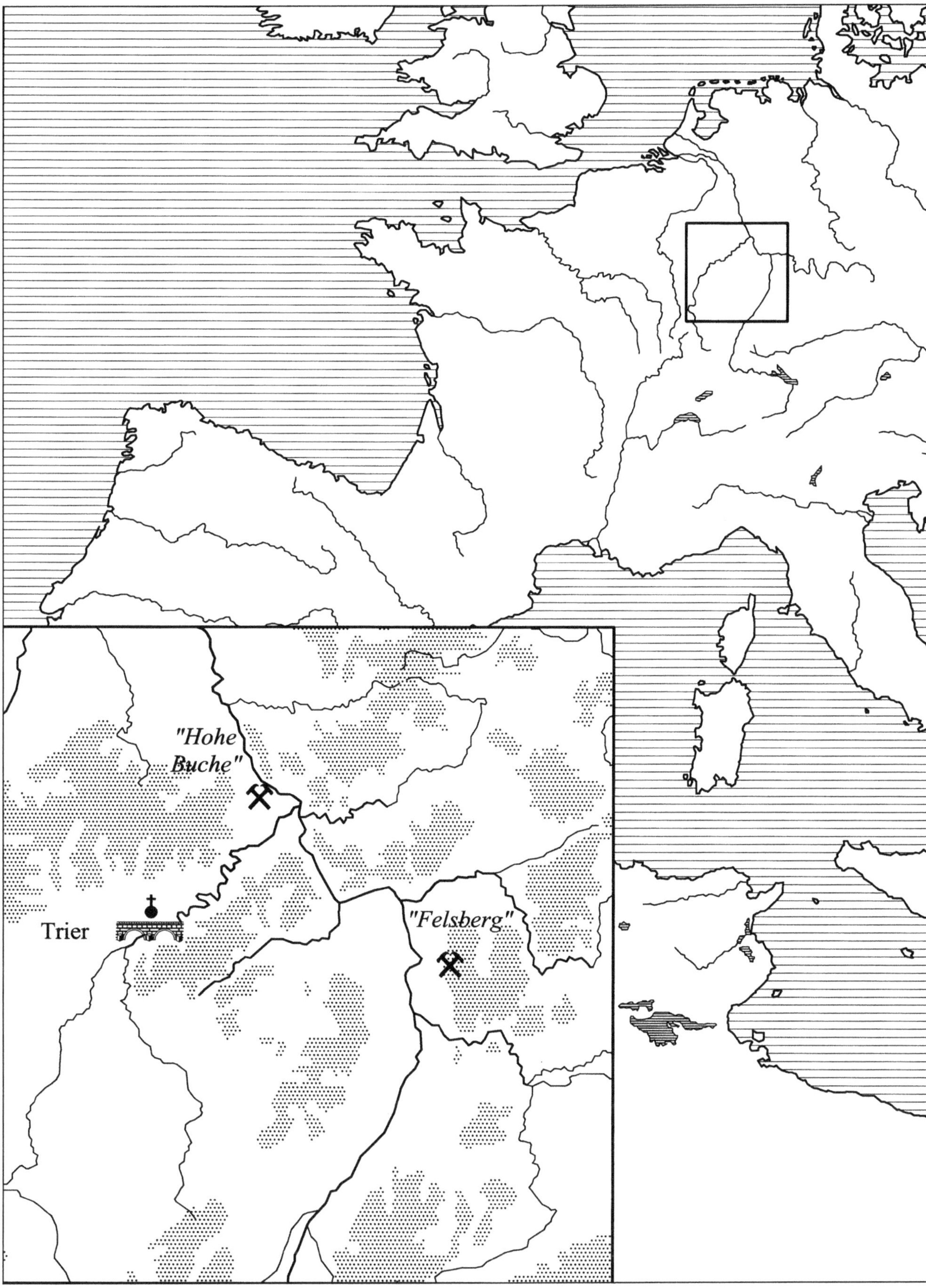

FIGURE 11. MAP OF THE RHEIN-MAIN-MOSEL AREA, WESTERN GERMANY, WITH THE RIVER SYSTEMS AND LOCATIONS OF ROMAN QUARRIES AND OF TRIER AS A CENTRE OF ROMAN BUILDING ACTIVITES.

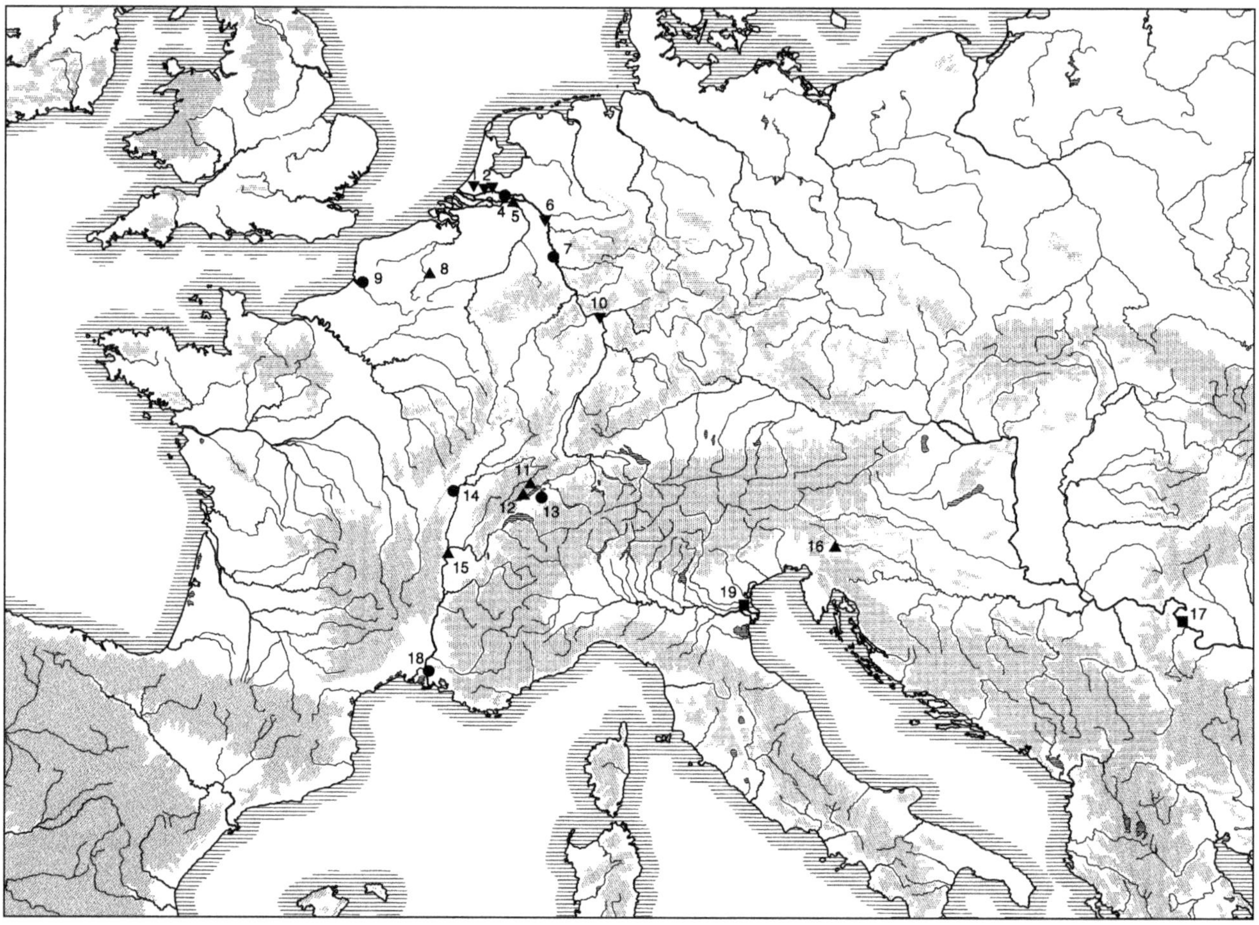

FIGURE 12. DISTRIBUTION MAP OF FLAT-BOTTOMED BOATS AND SHIPS, C. 1ST CENTURY BC TO 3RD CENTURY AD (logboats and extended dugouts not considered: ▲ carvel built prams.- ▼ prams with overlapping side planking.- ■ sharp ending vessels.- ● type unknown. List (number of finds in brackets): 1 Zwammerdam (3); 2 Woerden (2); 3 Vleuten-De Meern (2); 4 Kapel-Avezaath (1); 5 Druten (1); 6 Xanten (2); 7 Köln (1-2); 8 Pommeroeul (2); 9 Abbeville (1); 10 Mainz (2); 11 Bevaix (1); 12 Yverdon (1); 13 Avenches (3); 14 Chalon-sur-Saône (1); 15 Lyon (1); 16 Ljubljana (1); 17 Prahovo (1-2); 18 Arles (1-2); 19 Corte Cavanella (1) (after Bockius 1999; id. 2000a, 129-131 Figure 13).

a small river in the neighbourhood of the granite pits that flows into the Rhine, where cargo ships could have floated downstream on the current to the river mouth of the Moselle; from here the vessels had to be towed upstream, the same as those loaded with the ashlars for the Trier bridge (Figure 11). In order to move such a monolithic mass of stone, special ships were needed that could handle loads of 30 tons but with a draught still shallow enough to allow navigation. Concerning their capacities, prams like the Mainz 6, Woerden 1, and Ljubljana vessels discussed above, and also obviously the vessels from Xanten-Lüttingen and Zwammerdam 4, could easily have coped with the challenges of such heavy loads. One may ask whether or not these riverborne transports were too laborious and long, and whether other transport methods were preferable. The answer is provided by the wrecks themselves; the existence of those vessels is a matter of fact, and for long distances other means of transporting heavy goods are unknown.

Regarding the remarkable dimensions of the ships found in the military zone along the river Rhine, it would seem obvious that their capabilities made them ideal as large-scale transport units for the army. Dealing especially with the logistics of those troops garrisoned along the river, it is hard to believe that the legions would have overlooked such an excellent method of transportation. Moreover, the costs of building, maintaining and manning 30 to 40 metre-long craft that needed to be towed upstream - if not by the crew then by several oxen - appear much to high to assume any form of private enterprise. Almost all the prams found in the Rhineland are characterized by a specific planking system different to the construction of ships from the hinterland (Figure 12), but even for the latter, some form of military use could be suggested. The remains from Avenches, Chalon-sur-Saône and Lyon are striking on account of their early dates (1st century AD), and the contemporary presence of Roman troops in these locations is indicated by the historical record or archaeological evidence (Bockius 1999; id. 2000a, 124). Even if the hypothesis that *all* the Roman prams were sustained by the state does not hold water, then these vessels obviously played an important role in public enterprises.

Bibliography

Arnold, B. 1992, Batellerie gallo-romaine sur le lac de Neuchâtel 1, *Archéologie Neuchâteloise* 12, Saint-Blaise.

Becker, C., and Rieth, E. 1995, L`epave gallo-romaine de la place Tolozan, a Lyon: un chaland a coque monoxyle-assemblee, in: *L`arbre et la forêt. le bois dans l`antiquité,* Publication de la Bibliothèque Salomon-Reinach VII, Lyon, 77-86.

Beltrame, C. 2000, Sutiles Naves of Roman age, new evidence and technological comparisons with preroman sewn boats, in: Litwin, J. (ed.), *Down the river to the sea. Eighth International Symposium on Boat and Ship Archaeology,* Gdańsk 1997, Gdańsk, 91-96.

Berkel, H. and Obladen-Kauder, J. 1993, Das Schiff von Xanten-Wardt zwischen Bergung und Konservierung, *Archäologie im Rheinland* 1992, 56-58.

Bockius, R. 1996, Zur Rekonstruktion des römerzeitlichen Plattbodenschiffes aus Woerden, *Jahrbuch des Römisch-Germanischen Zentral-museums Mainz,* 43, 511-530.

Bockius, R. 1999, Antike Prahme. Monumentale Zeugnisse keltisch-römischer Binnenschiffahrt aus dem 2. Jh. v. Chr. bis ins 3. Jh. n. Chr., *Jahrbuch des Römisch-Germanischen Zentralmuseums Mainz,* 47, 439-493.

Bockius, R. 2000a, Antike Schwergutfrachter – Zeugnisse römischen Schiffbaus und Gütertransports, in: *Steinbruch und Bergwerk. Denkmäler Römischer Technikgeschichte zwischen Eifel und Rhein,* Vulkanpark-Forschungen 2, Mainz,110-132.

Bockius, R. 2000b, A Roman river barge (?) found in the river Danube near Prahovo, Serbia, *IX International Symposium on Boat and Ship Archaeology,* 4-8 December 2000, Venice.

Bockius, R. 2001, *Die römerzeitlichen Schiffsfunde von Oberstimm bei Ingolstadt,* Monographien des Römisch-Germanischen Zentralmuseums Mainz , vol. 50.

Bonnamour, L. 1999, Les techniques de construction navale sur la Saône du Ier au III siècle de notre ére, *Caesarodunum,* 33, 1-8.

Bonnamour, L. (ed.) 2000, *Archéologie de la Saône, 150 ans de recherches,* Paris.

Connan, J., Adam, P., Dessort, D., and Albrecht, P. 2000, Apport de la chimie moléculaire à la connaissance des enduits utilisés pour le traitement des bois et le calfatage des bateaux romains de la Saône, in: *Archéologie des fleuves et des rivières,* Paris, 40-47.

Cüppers, H. 1969, *Die Trierer Römerbrücken,* Trierer Grabungen und Forschungen 5, Mainz.

Drioux, G. 1921, Une restitution d' état civil: le poignard anthropoïde dit de Chaumont, *Bulletin de la Société Historique et Archéologique de Langres,* 8, 205-213.

De Weerd, M.D. 1988, *Schepen voor Zwammerdam,* Amsterdam.

Ellmers, D. 2000, Der Mainzer Schiffer Blussus und sein Schiff, in: *Studia Antiquaria, Festschrift für Niels Bantelmann zum 60. Geburtstag.* Universitäts-forschungen zur Prähistorischen Archäologie 63, Bonn, 99-110.

Gaspari, A. 1998, Das Frachtschiff aus Lipe im Moor von Laibach (Ljubljana), *Jahrbuch des Römisch-Germanischen Zentralmuseums Mainz,* 45, 527-550.

Haalebos, J.K. 1996, Ein römisches Getreideschiff in Woerden (NL), *Jahrbuch des Römisch-Germanischen Zentralmuseums Mainz,* 43, 475-510.

Lonchambon, C. 2000, Un bateau monoxyle-assemblé à Chalon-sur-Saône (1er siècle ap. J.-C.), in: *Archéologie des fleuves et des rivières,* Paris, 174-178.

Mangartz, F. 2000, Römerzeitlicher Abbau von Basaltlava in der Osteifel – Ein bedeutender Wirtschaftszweig der Nordwestprovinzen, in: *Steinbruch und Bergwerk. Denkmäler Römischer Technikgeschichte zwischen Eifel und Rhein,* Vulkanpark-Forschungen 2, Mainz, 6-16.

Petrović, P. 1991, Ein Donauhafen von Trajan bei dem Kastell Aquae (Moesia Superior), in: Maxfield, V.A. and Dobson, M.J. (eds.), *Roman Frontier Studies 1989, Proceedings of the XVth international congress of Roman frontier studies,* Exeter, 295-298.

Rieth, É. 1998, *Des bateaux et des fleuves. Archéologie de la batellerie du Néolithique aux Temps modernes en France,* Paris.

Röder, G. 1991, Säulen vom Felsberg für das antike Trier, *Beiträge zur Rheinkunde,* 43, 19-28.

Terra sigillata and amphorae from the Roman *Villa* at Tourega (Évora, Portugal)

Inês Vaz Pinto,[1] Catarina Viegas[2] and Luísa Ferrer Dias

Abstract
This paper presents the *sigillata* and amphorae recovered during the excavations of the Roman *Villa* at Tourega in southern Portugal, utilising the analysis of the data to identify commercial links and trade routes supplying the *villa*. Of all the *sigillata* recovered, the Italian type, the south Gaulish, the Spanish and African forms were present; but taken as a whole, there was a higher proportion of northern Spanish *sigillata*, travelling by river and road networks. The amphorae, carrying mainly fish-based products, derived from the river valleys of the Tagus and Sado in *Lusitania*. Only a small proportion of amphorae came from *Baetica* and other areas.

Introduction

This paper aims to study the *sigillata* and amphorae from a Roman *villa* in southern Portugal as presented in the session *Close encounters: sea- and riverborne trade, ports and hinterlands...*, focusing on trade, production areas and commercial routes. Even though these two types of materials, *sigillata* and amphorae, were traded for very different reasons (the former to acquire and use as table ware, and the latter bought for their contents), they are both particularly interesting in the study of the economic exchanges and commercial connections of a Roman *villa* and its region. They were both specialised commodities, produced in very specific areas, and sometimes traded over long distances.

The Roman *Villa* at Tourega was located in the Roman province of *Lusitania*, on the outskirts of the Roman city and capital, the *civitas Ebora Liberalitas Iulia* (Figure 9). According to an inscription found near the *villa*, and dated to the beginning of the 3rd century A.D., at least for a certain period the *villa* belonged to a senatorial family (Encarnação 1984, 456). Archaeological excavations undertaken from 1985 to 1996 exposed a large bath complex consisting of a building containing rooms and tanks for hot and cold baths, and a water reservoir. Although still under study, the stratigraphy, wall construction and related artefacts point to three main phases of construction (Vaz Pinto, Viegas, Ferrer Dias 1997, 73-81). The chronology, mainly based on the data presented here, is from the Tiberian period until the end of the 4th century or beginning of the 5th A.D.

The materials presented in this paper were mostly recovered from the excavation of the bath complex, although a small proportion comes from soundings in other areas of the *villa*. The large area excavated, approximately 600 square metres, suggests that the sample is valuable and deserves to be studied and interpreted, even though continuation of archaeological work in future may produce new data.

Since our approach is a commercial and economic one, morphological attributes of the samples, their excavation contexts or their chronological aspects will not be discussed as they will be published in the site monograph in the near future. As regards quantification, the minimum number of vessels (MNV) is estimated by counting the fragment type most represented for each form and for each type of ware or fabric. The main objective will be to understand the development and importance of commercial trends, mainly focusing on the ceramic production and manufacturing centres. The proportions of imports from each original centre of production at different periods will also be examined. Comparisons with materials from other sites will determine whether Tourega follows a common pattern or presents a particular site specialisation.

I - Terra sigillata

a) Characteristics of the sample

The excavations undertaken at Tourega produced about 876 fragments of *terra sigillata*, of which 193 fragments correspond to forms identified in the current typologies (Ettlinger *et al.* 1990, Dragendorff 1895, Bémont and Jacob 1986, Roca and Fernandez 1999, Hayes 1972 and 1980). The determination of different wares is based both on fabric and slip analysis undertaken with a hand magnifier (15x). The minimum number of vessels (MNV) consists of rims, body or base fragments, as long as they are a characteristic feature of a certain type. The main *sigillata* types in the western Mediterranean are present at this site. They include the Italian type, which came mainly from Arezzo but possibly from other production sites in Italy; and the South Gaulish, which derived mainly from La Graufesenque but also from Montans. In addition, the Spanish *sigillata* came mostly from Tricio (La Rioja) in the Ebro valley in northeast Spain but also from Andújar (Jaén), in the southern province of *Baetica* (today's Andalusia). African Red Slip Ware (ARS) A, C and D reached Tourega from northern Africa (Figures 1 and 7).

The *sigillata,* combined with other ceramics, is the main source of material for studying the chronology of Tourega's bath building and *villa*. In fact, the presence of Tiberian Italian-type *sigillata* (Consp. 18, 20 and 22) and an early South Gaulish form (Drag. 24/25) allows us to

[1] Departamento de História, Universidade Lusíada, Lisboa. Rua da Junqueira, 188-198. 1349-001 Lisboa.
[2] Faculdade de Letras, Universidade de Lisboa, UNIARCH. Alameda da Universidade. 1600-124 Lisboa Codex.

date the beginning of the occupation of the site to this period. The end of the occupation occurred at the end of the 4th century or beginning of the 5th century AD, since the latest forms are ARS D, Hayes 59 A and B, 61 and 67. The production of Hayes 67 spans from the middle of the 4th to the middle of the 5th century A.D., but this form is quite rare at the site and may have arrived only in the late 4th century or beginning of the 5th. Also significant is the total absence of later African forms and late Phocean ware.

	MNV	%
Italian type *sigillata*	13	7
South Gaulish *sigillata*	40	20
Spanish *sigillata*	62	32
ARS A	12	6
ARS C	34	17
ARS D	32	17
Late Spanish *sigillata*	3	2
TOTAL	193	100

FIGURE 1. DISTRIBUTION OF DIFFERENT *SIGILLATA* TYPES AT TOUREGA

Italian type *sigillata* forms 7% of Tourega's total *sigillata* yield. The earliest form is Consp. 12 (Haltern service I), dated from the middle to the end of the Augustan period (Figure 2), and the most abundant is Consp. 20.4, common in the Mediterranean area and dated up to the Tiberian period. Two of the examples at Tourega had applied decoration, although it is not possible to distinguish the motifs. Also present are the plates Consp. 18 (Haltern service II), the cups Consp. 22 which indicate imports in the Tiberian period and Consp. 37 of a slightly later date (Ettlinger *et al.* 1990, 82-90). The only decorated piece probably belongs to a chalice. The potter's stamp SEX/ANNI (*Sextus Annius*), from Arezzo, usually dated from 10 B.C. to A.D. 10. (Oxé and Comfort 1968, 27-30, n. 88), appears in a rectangular frame. Several examples have already been found in Spain (Béltran 1990, 68) and three in Portugal, two of them in Alcácer do Sal (Alarcão, 1971, 424; Faria, Ferreira and Diogo 1987, 66, 1) and one in Santarém (Viegas forthcoming).

South Gaulish *sigillata* (20%) is mainly represented by La Graufesenque production centre (Figure 2). Despite the great variety of forms produced, only the most common are present in Tourega: the dishes Drag. 15/17 and 18/31, and the cups Drag. 24/25 and 27. The rarity of decorated forms (also attested in other places in Portugal, for instance in Conímbriga (Delgado, Mayet, Alarcão 1975) is confirmed by the find of only one piece of a bowl (Drag. 30) usually dated from the Claudian-Flavian period. One unreadable stamp belongs to this production. Only two rims of a coarser buff fabric with a brown slip came from the Montans production centre. Therefore, Tourega follows the same pattern as other sites in the Iberian Peninsula during the Claudian-Vespasian period in which the La Graufesenque *officinae* were the leading exporter to the Peninsula. It is accepted that the Gaulish products became very rare under the Flavians and were slowly substituted by Spanish *sigillata*, whose production began in the middle of the 1st century to be a serious competitor in the Iberian markets.

Spanish *sigillata* is the most abundant type at Tourega (32%) and the productions from Tricio (La Rioja) are the commonest (about 80%), although the Andújar (Jaén) examples are also present. The most common forms of plain *sigillata* from Tricio (La Rioja) at Tourega are the cup (Drag. 27) and the dish (Drag. 15/17), probably used

Italian type *sigillata* (Arezzo and other origins)		
	MNV	%
Consp. 12	1	8
Consp. 18	2	15
Consp. 20	4	30
Consp. 22	3	23
Consp. 37.5	1	8
Decorated	1	8
Stamp.	1	8
Total	13	100

South Gaulish *sigillata*		
La Graufesenque		
	MNV	%
Drag. 15/17	5	13
Drag. 18/31	14	34
Drag. 24/25	8	19
Drag. 27	7	17
Drag. 35 (?)	1	3
Ritt. 8 (?)	1	3
Decorated	1	3
Stamp	1	3
Montans		
Lud Tb	2	5
Total	40	100

Spanish *sigillata*		
Tritium Magalum		
	MNV	%
Drag. 15/17	12	19
Drag. 24/25	1	2
Drag. 27	12	19
Drag. 35/36	1	2
Drag. 39	3	5
Hisp. 2	1	2
Decorated	21	33
Stamps	2	3
Andújar		
Drag. 15/17	4	6
Drag. 27	1	2
Hisp. 2	1	2
Decorated	2	3
Stamp	1	2
Total	62	100

FIGURE 2. DISTRIBUTION OF FORMS OF ITALIAN TYPE, SOUTH GAULISH AND SPANISH *SIGILLATA*

together. The dish (Drag. 39), with barbotine-decorated handles is represented by three pieces, and forms Drag. 24/25 and Drag. 35 are represented by one example each. The dishes (Drag. 15/17) with moulded walls closely imitating the South Gaulish form are not present, suggesting that the earliest production of this ware, present for instance in Conímbriga, did not reach the *villa* at Tourega. The decorated forms Drag. 29, Drag. 29/37 and Drag. 37 are abundant, but the garland decorations, known to be early in Spanish production, have not been found. The most common decoration are the metopes, dated from the middle to the end of the 1st century A.D., and the concentric circles usually combined with the typical Spanish floral motifs, dated from the second century A.D. Three stamps came from Tricio (La Rioja): C.LOD attributed to CLODIVS; SELI (...) attributed to SELIESI.FE; and (...).TI.TI.LV.PI., probably the work of TITVS and LVPIANVS, both known from La Rioja area (Saènz and Saènz 1999, 98, 109, 124, 128). The Spanish *sigillata* from Andújar is not as common and the only forms present are the dish Drag. 15/17, *Hispanica* 2 and the decorated bowl Drag. 37. No readable stamp was found from this production.

African Red Slip wares (ARS) represent 40% of the *sigillata* found at Tourega (Figure 5). ARS A is rather rare (6%) but it includes two early forms, Hayes 4 A and Hayes 6, imitations of South Gaulish wares, and dated from the Flavian period to the middle of the 2nd century A.D. The most abundant form in Tourega is, as usual, Hayes 14/17, dated from the middle of the second until the middle of the third century A.D. (Hayes 1972, 39-43). ARS C is more common (17%) and the forms found at the site are again some of the more typical: form Hayes 45, 50 and 52 with applied decoration. The large plate Hayes 50 is the most abundant at Tourega and occurs in the variants A and B, this last one being the latest and coarser variant dated to the end of the 4th century A.D. Type Hayes 49, dated from the end of the 3rd to the beginning of the 4th century A.D., is also present proving that it was not just the most common types which arrived at Tourega.

The proportion of ARS D (17%) is almost the same as ARS C, and its most frequent form is the dish Hayes 59, dated from the 4th to the beginning of the 5th century A.D. Also present, although in small quantities, are forms Hayes 58 and 61 with similar dates. The latest import is form Hayes 67, which in its later variants, may occur until the middle of the 5th century A.D. (Hayes 1972, 116), as it was referred to earlier.

Contemporary to the imports of ARS D, Late Spanish *sigillata* was also imported from the Douro and Ebro valleys (Figure 3). This *sigillata* type is rare at Tourega (2%) and its forms closely imitate some of their contemporary forms in ARS D.

b) Comparison to other *Lusitanian* *villae*

It is possible to compare the pattern of imports of Tourega's *terra sigillata* with the one from the *villa* at São Cucufate (Alarcão, Étienne, Mayet 1990, 248-251), located in the territory of *Pax Iulia*, the *civitas* south of *Ebora Liberalitas Iulia*. Although the quantity of *sigillata* present at São Cucufate (3415 rims) is much more plentiful than the one from Tourega, there are some interesting comparisons to be drawn. The higher proportion of Italian type and South Gaulish *sigillata* at Tourega is an indication of a slightly earlier occupation at this site. Spanish *sigillata* is the most important type in both sites, but the proportions from the production centres of Tricio (La Rioja) and Andújar (Jaén) in the *Baetica* province, are quite different. While at São Cucufate they are equally represented, at Tourega there is a preponderance of *sigillata* coming from Tricio (about 80%). It is also clear that the imports of African wares in São Cucufate (62%) are proportionally more frequent than at Tourega (40%).

The *villa* of Alto da Cidreira (Cascais), near the Atlantic coast, shows a completely different pattern of imports being "a good example of strong maritime commercial ties and the almost exclusion of overland commerce" as is pointed out by Nolen (1988, 61). In fact, at that site,

			MNV	%
ARS	**A**	Hayes 4 A	1	8
		Hayes 6	3	25
		Hayes 14/17	8	67
		Total	12	100

ARS	**C**	Hayes 45	6	18
		Hayes 49	2	6
		Hayes 50	21	61
		Hayes 52	5	15
		Total	34	100

			MNV	%
ARS	**D**	Hayes 58	5	16
		Hayes 59	12	37
		Hayes 61	7	21
		Hayes 67	4	13
		Decorated	4	13
		Total	32	100

Late Spanish *sigillata*	**Douro and Ebro valleys**	Bowls	3	100
		Total	3	100

FIGURE 3. DISTRIBUTION OF FORMS OF AFRICAN RED SLIP WARES (A, C AND D FABRICS) AND LATE SPANISH *SIGILLATA*.

Spanish *sigillata* is present in small proportions and the Andújar (Jaén) productions are more important than those from Tricio (La Rioja). The ARS assemblage is more abundant than that of the early imperial types, ARS A being specially numerous and represented by six different forms. ARS C and D are also present as well as Phocaean and late Gaulish "*T.S. grise*" (*Ibid.* 1988), which do not occur at Tourega.

In the *villa* of Povos (Vila Franca de Xira) on the banks of the river Tagus we have a total lack of Italian type *sigillata*, and the South Gaulish *sigillata* is rare and came only from the La Graufesenque (Ferrer Dias 1998, 15-24). Contrary to what happens in Alto da Cidreira, Spanish *sigillata* from Tricio (La Rioja) is twice that of Andújar.

Compared to Montinho das Laranjeiras (Alcoutim) on the banks of the river Guadiana, there again no Italian type *sigillata* was found and the South Gaulish is almost absent (Coutinho 1997). As in Alto da Cidreira and again opposed to Tourega, the Andújar (Jaén) products are much more abundant than those from Tricio (La Rioja). In Montinho das Laranjeiras ARS A is extremely frequent which is not the case in Tourega. Both types C and D are present in almost the same forms as in Tourega but in that site the imports seem to continue until the middle of the 5th century A.D.

II - Amphorae

a) Characteristics of the sample

The amphora sample is composed of 167 different rims, handles and bases that represent a minimum number of 79 vessels. Usually rims are the most abundant type of fragment and correspond to the number of vessels, but in some cases, handles of different forms or different fabrics also represent one vessel. The variety of forms is listed in Figure 4 and examples of each one are reproduced in Figure 8. Vessels of uncertain form or origin may represent Lusitanian production sites still unknown and less typical Baetican, Gaulish and African products. The determination of production sources is based on fabric analysis undertaken with a hand magnifier (15x) and compared to reference collections and published materials. Petrographic studies in progress, but not yet completed, may still clarify the origin of pieces now unclassified.

According to the interpretation of amphora contents developed by researchers over the years, almost all the amphora forms found at Tourega were containers for fish-based products (Beltrán IIB, Dressel 14, Almagro 51c, Almagro 50 and Almagro 51a-b), and only amphora Dressel 2/4 was a wine container, and Dressel 20 an olive oil container (Peacock and Williams 1986; Sciallano and

Form	*Lusitania* (Tagus-Sado)	*Baetica*	Uncertain	Total
Dressel 2/4	-	-	1	1
Dressel 20	-	1	-	1
Beltrán IIB	-	1	-	1
Dressel 14	13	1	4	18
Almagro 50	4	-	-	4
Almagro 51c	31	2	2	35
Almagro 51a-b	2	-	-	2
Uncertain	5	1	11	17
Total	55	6	18	79
%	69,6%	7,6%	22,8%	100%

FIGURE 4. MINIMUM NUMBER OF AMPHORA VESSELS BY FORM AND ORIGIN.

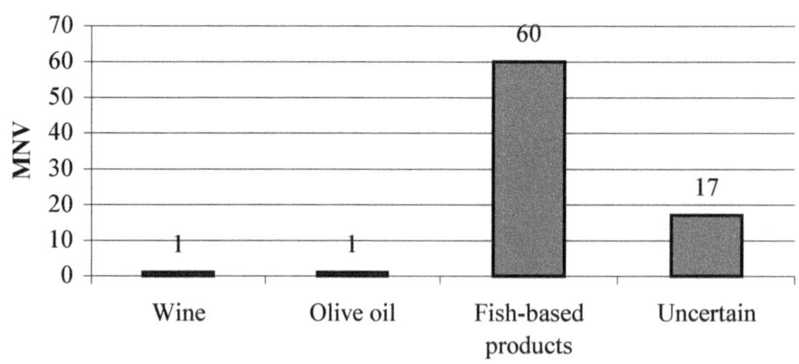

FIGURE 5 - CONTENTS OF AMPHORAE AT TOUREGA

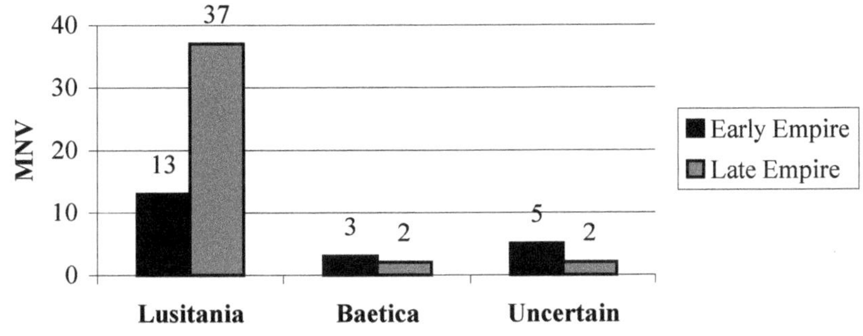

FIGURE 6 - SOURCES OF AMPHORAE FROM TOUREGA IN THE EARLY AND LATE EMPIRE.

Sibella 1994). If variant A of Almagro 51c, the so-called Lusitana 3, proves to be a wine amphora according to its resemblance to wine containers like Dressel 30 and Gauloise 4 (Diogo 1987, 184; Alarcão and Mayet 1990, 189), the decision not to distinguish the variant forms in this study does not affect the overall proportions since that type is very rare at Tourega.

The graph on Figure 5 illustrates the proportion of contents of the identified amphorae. It highlights the overwhelming importance of fish-based products (75.9%, or 96.8% of the identified amphorae) of the imports to this *villa*, and suggests the importance of this foodstuff in the diet, as it was noticed at the São Cucufate *villa* (Alarcão *et al.* 1990, 254). The rarity of wine (1.3%) and olive oil (1.3%) amphorae suggests local production of these two important dietary necessities.

The table in Figure 4 shows that the most important origin of amphorae found at Tourega are from the river valleys of the Tagus and Sado in south-central Portugal (Figure 10), which are contiguous areas of similar geological formation, and whose products are very difficult to distinguish among each other, either by fabric or form (Mayet, Schmitt, Tavares da Silva 1996). This is the only identified Lusitanian production area represented at Tourega. The other well identified source of amphorae found at this *villa* is *Baetica*, in southern Spain, famous for its olive oil produced in the valley of Guadalquivir (Figure 10) and exported all around the Mediterranean. This province was also well known for its fish-based products from the bay of Gades (Figure 10) as well as for wine. The Tagus and Sado valleys account for about 70% of the vessels, consisting mostly of forms Dressel 14 and Almagro 51c, while *Baetica* only supplies about 7.5%, and the remaining 23% are of uncertain origin.

Based on the production period attributed to each form by the development of research in this field (Peacock and Williams 1986; Sciallano and Sibella 1994), two main periods of production can be determined, i.e. the 1st-2nd centuries or Early Empire, and the 3rd-5th centuries or Late Empire. As clearly shown in Figure 6, there is an evolution in the origin of imports. The comparison of production sources in these two periods shows that the Tagus and Sado valleys were consistently the main supplier of amphorae to Tourega. Moreover, the relative proportion between this area and *Baetica* is much lower in the Early Empire (61.9%) than in the Late Empire (90.2%). In fact, Baetican containers represent 14.3% of the imports in the Early Empire but only 4.9% in the Late Empire.

b) Comparison to other Lusitanian *villae*

The comparison of Tourega's amphorae to those of other Lusitanian *villae*, i.e. São Cucufate (Vidigueira) (Alarcão *et al.* 1990 251-255; Mayet, Schmitt, Tavares da Silva 1996, 167-192; Mayet and Schmitt 1997, 71-109), Quinta das Longas (Elvas) (Almeida and Carvalho 1998: 137-163), Povos (Vila Franca de Xira) (Banha 1991-1992, 49-90), *Villa Cardílio* (Torres Novas) (Diogo and Monteiro 1999, 201-214) and Vilares de Alfundão (Ferreira do Alentejo) (Norton *et al.* 1993-1994, 181-190) may show to what extent Tourega presents the same patterns of consumption or differs from them.

Imported wine from outside *Lusitania* comes to these *villae* in small quantities, never exceeding 5% of the amphorae found, from Italy (*Villa Cardílio* and Povos), *Baetica* (São Cucufate, *Villa Cardílio* and Povos) and Gaul (Povos). At Tourega, there is one vessel possibly from *Tarraconensis* (Figure 8, n. 23), but wine represents only 1.3% of the amphorae found.

Amphorae Dressel 20 and Dressel 23, used to transport olive oil from *Baetica*, date to the period from the 1st to the 5th century. They are represented in small proportions in all the *villae* considered, but more abundant in the Early Empire (Tourega, Quinta das Longas, São Cucufate, *Villa Cardílio* and Povos), and less numerous in the Late Empire (*Villa Cardílio* and Povos). Tourega follows the general pattern confirming that imports of olive oil were regarded as a luxury item. With the exception of Alfundão, where no olive oil vessel was found, Tourega presents the lowest proportion (1.3%) and Povos the highest (10.9%) of Baetican olive oil amphorae.

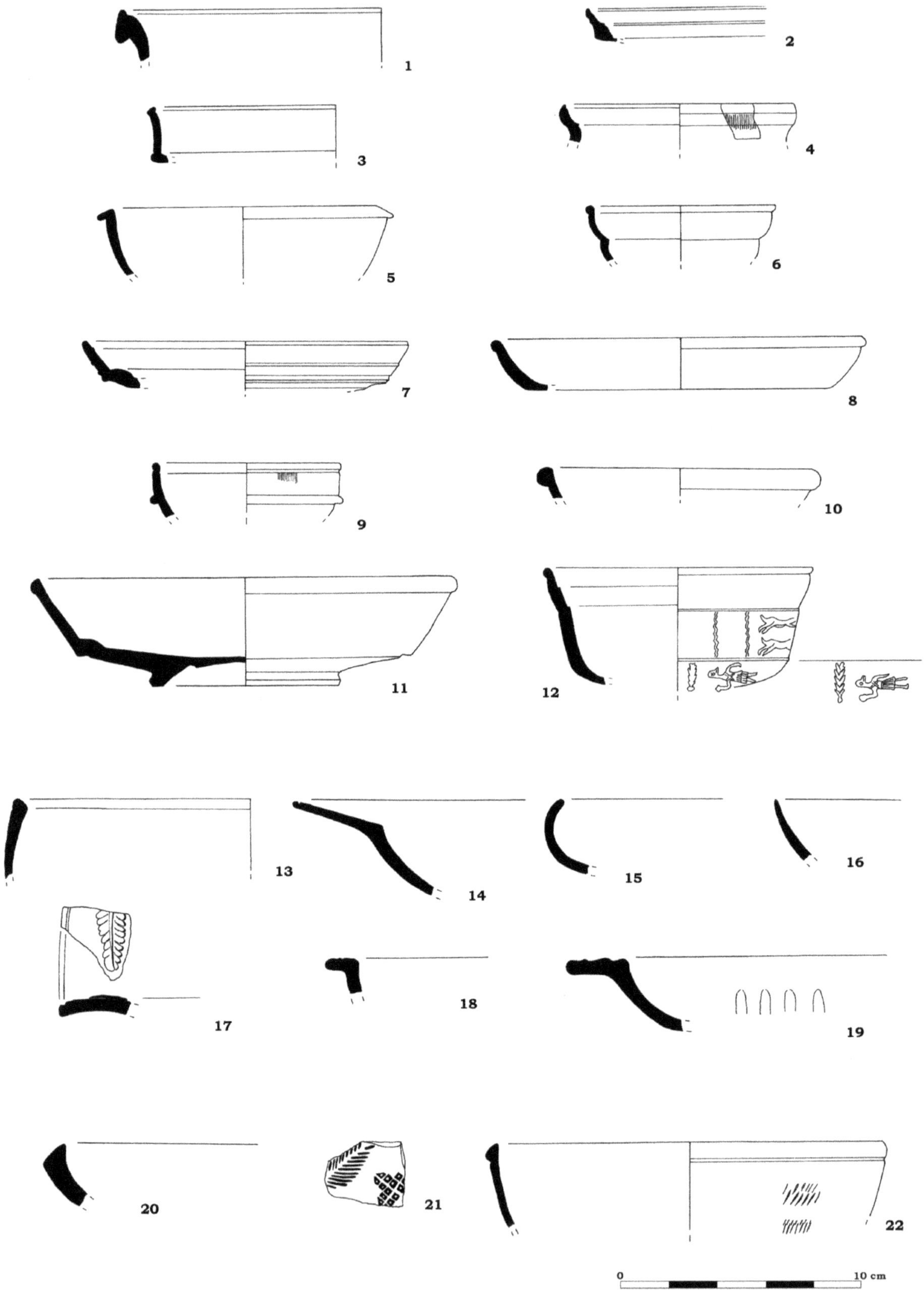

FIGURE 7. ITALIAN TYPE *SIGILLATA*: 1 - CONSP. 12; 2 - CONSP. 18; 3 - CONSP. 20; 4 - CONSP. 22; 5 - CONSP. 37.5; SOUTH GAULISH *SIGILLATA*: 6 - DRAG. 27; 7 - DRAG. 15/17; 8 - DRAG. 18/31; 9 - DRAG. 24/25; SPANISH *SIGILLATA*: 10 - DRAG. 35; 11 - DRAG. 15/17; 12 - DRAG. 29; ARS A: 13 - HAYES 14/17; ARS C: 14 - HAYES 45; 15 - HAYES 49; 16 - HAYES 50; 17 - HAYES 52; ARS D: 18 - HAYES 58; 19 - HAYES 59A; 20 - HAYES 61A; 21 - ARS D STYLE A (II); 22 - LATE SPANISH *SIGILLATA*.

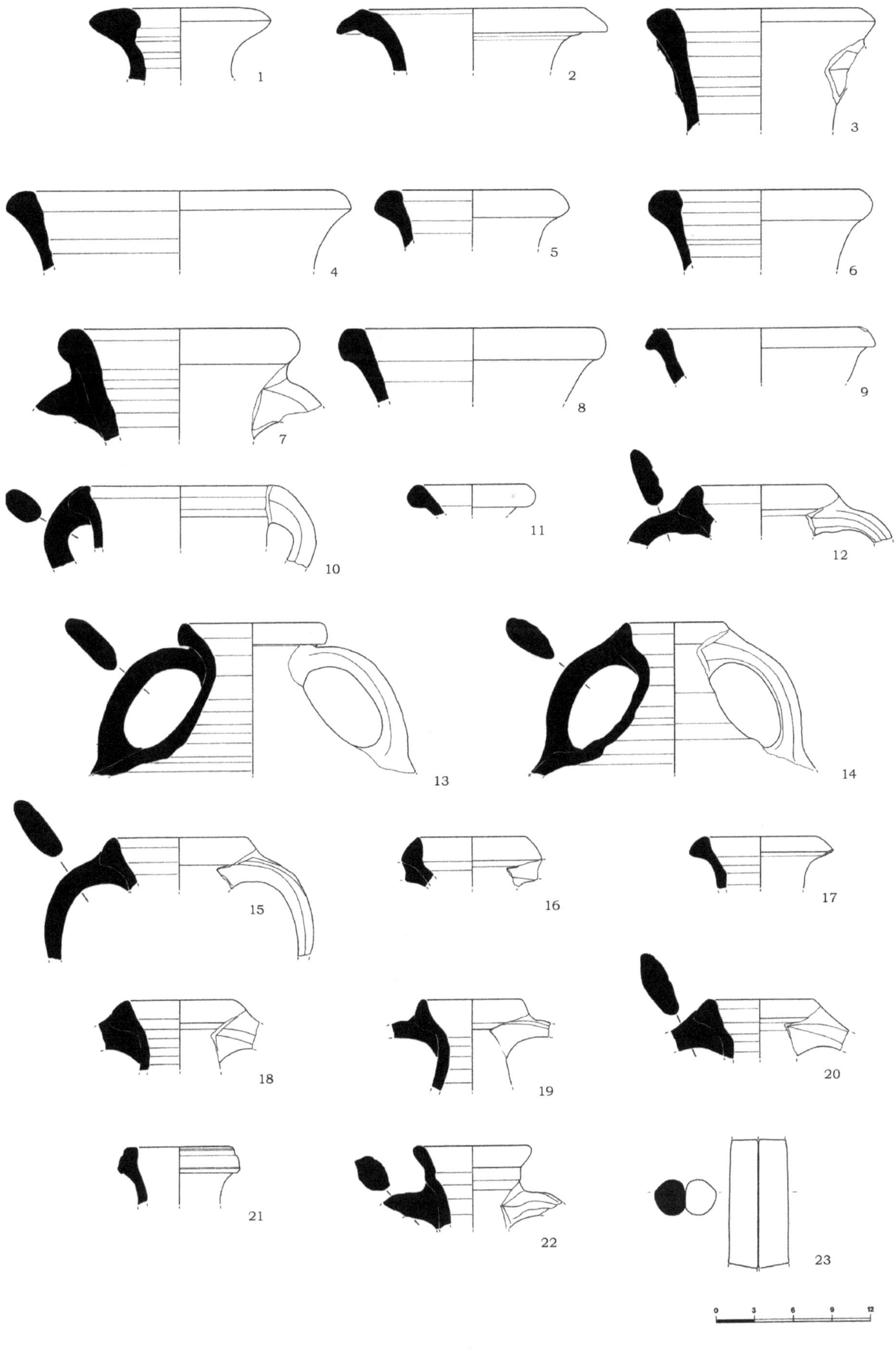

FIGURE 8. BAETICAN AMPHORAE: 1 - DRESSEL 20; 2 - BELTRÁN IIB; LUSITANIAN AMPHORAE: 3-8 - DRESSEL 14; 9 -10 - ALMAGRO 50; 11-21 - ALMAGRO 51C; 22 - ALMAGRO 51A-B; UNCERTAIN: 23 - DRESSEL 2-4.

Fish-based products represent the overwhelming majority of amphorae found in these *villae*, with the possible exception of *Villa Cardílio*, where the abundance of Almagro 51c variant A or Lusitana 3 may indicate local wine production. Fish-based products come from *Baetica* in the Early Empire in amphorae Dressel 7-11, Beltrán I, Beltrán II and Dressel 14a, and usually in rather small proportions. In Tourega there are only one Beltrán IIB and one Dressel 14 from *Baetica.* Only in São Cucufate is Dressel 7-11 the most abundant fish-based amphorae in the second half of the 1st century. These products come in much greater quantities from the valleys of the Tagus and the Sado in the form Dressel 14b, definitely dominating the Lusitanian market after the first century. Therefore, in the Early Empire these *villae* follow different patterns, not necessarily directly related to their geographical location. While at São Cucufate one third of imports of fish-based products comes from *Baetica*, in Alfundão (20 km away), that proportion must have been much lower since only one vessel was found compared to forty-five Lusitanian amphorae. *Villa Cardílio* follows São Cucufate, having five Beltrán I and II amphorae against fourteen Dressel 14b. Povos does not have any Early Empire fish-based product amphora from *Baetica*, and Quinta das Longas has one against four Lusitanian, but due to the small sample (24 identified fragments), no definitive conclusions can be drawn.

In the Late Empire, fish-based products came from *Baetica* in much lower proportions in amphorae Almagro 51c found at Tourega, *Villa Cardílio* and possibly Povos. Some productions of Almagro 50 discovered at São Cucufate, Alfundão, *Villa Cardílio* and Povos are generally considered to be from the Algarve although its production centre has not yet been found (Peacock and Williams 1986, 131; Fabião and Carvalho 1990, 52-53). The same may be said for a Beltrán 72 found at *Villa Cardílio*, which may be from that region or from *Baetica*, which would increase the quantity of Baetican imports in this period. Fish-based products may also come in very small proportions from Northern Africa (Tunisia) in amphorae Africana II A (*Villa Cardílio*) and possibly Keay XXXVII (Povos). However, the overwhelming majority comes from the valleys of the Tagus and Sado, 94.9% at Tourega, 100% at Quinta das Longas, 93.8% at São Cucufate, and 84% at Alfundão. We will set aside Povos, whose amphorae Almagro 51c and Almagro 50 do not have a well defined origin, and *Villa Cardílio* which is a different case because of the abundance of Lusitana 3, interpreted as a wine amphora. The main site specialisation at Tourega seems to be the low proportion of Baetican imports in the Early Empire, and particularly in the second half of the 1st century A.D. The absence of the southern Almagro 50 in the Late Empire, especially when compared to São Cucufate, another inland *villa*, is also significant. Other sites like Povos and *Villa Cardílio* that received this kind of amphora are close to the river Tagus that facilitated river transport. Although this low proportion of Baetican and southern imports in Tourega would have to be confirmed in other sites of the region and in the city of *Ebora Liberalitas Iulia*, it may reflect the lack of proximity to navigable rivers and a dependency on land routes. Meanwhile, São Cucufate, and its capital *Pax Iulia*, would take advantage of the proximity of the river Guadiana which would facilitate the transport of goods from the eastern Algarve up to the southern Alentejo.

III - Evidence and importance of commercial trends

In the ancient world, the economic advantage of maritime and river transport compared to land routes is well known. Evidence from shipwrecks shows that fine wares and amphorae coming from Italy and southern Gaul were transported through the Mediterranean all the way to Hispania. *Sigillata* and amphorae from those areas and different regions of *Baetica* and northern Africa were exported to the Atlantic coast of *Lusitania* according to the abundance of finds in coastal sites like Balsa (Nolen 1994), Pessegueiro (Tavares da Silva and Soares 1993) and Tróia (Etienne, Makaroun, Mayet 1994) (Figure 9). Mixed cargoes, with products from different provinces, were the most common, probably traded and loaded in Gades. Although amphorae would be the main goods carried on the ships, fine wares were complementary to the main commerce of provisions. On the other hand, Spanish *sigillata* from Tricio (La Rioja), in northern Spain, was conveyed by inland routes, both river and land ones. Likewise, to reach the inland areas of *Lusitania*, goods were preferably carried by river from the main sea harbours, and roads were only used when riverine routes were no longer possible. Certainly, an active commercial route would run from the eastern Algarve up the Guadiana River towards the capital of the province, Emerita Augusta, supplying the cities along the way, and avoiding navigation of the severe Atlantic. On the Atlantic coast, the Tagus and Sado estuaries, as well as the river Mira one, were also important distribution points for riverbourne commerce towards the interior of the province.

According to their geographical location, Tourega and *Ebora Liberalitas Iulia* would have to rely heavily on land routes possibly originating from a point off the river Sado, while São Cucufate and Pax Iulia would greatly have benefited from their proximity to the Guadiana River, and also to the tributary of the Sado River. This would explain why Tourega's imported ceramics follow rather the continental model than the maritime one (Etienne, Makaroun and Mayet 1994, 29). In fact, Tourega's Spanish *sigillata* originates to a certain extent more from Tricio (La Rioja) (80%) than from *Baetica* (10%). Meanwhile, at São Cucufate those proportions are 50% for each, and in an island harbour like Pessegueiro the production of Tricio only represents 28% (Tavares da Silva and Soares 1994, 90). This may also be related to the relative proximity of Tourega to *Augusta Emerita*, an important redistributing market for this product (Mayet 1990, 210-211). In fact, Tourega also benefited from its location certainly very close to the road from *Emerita*

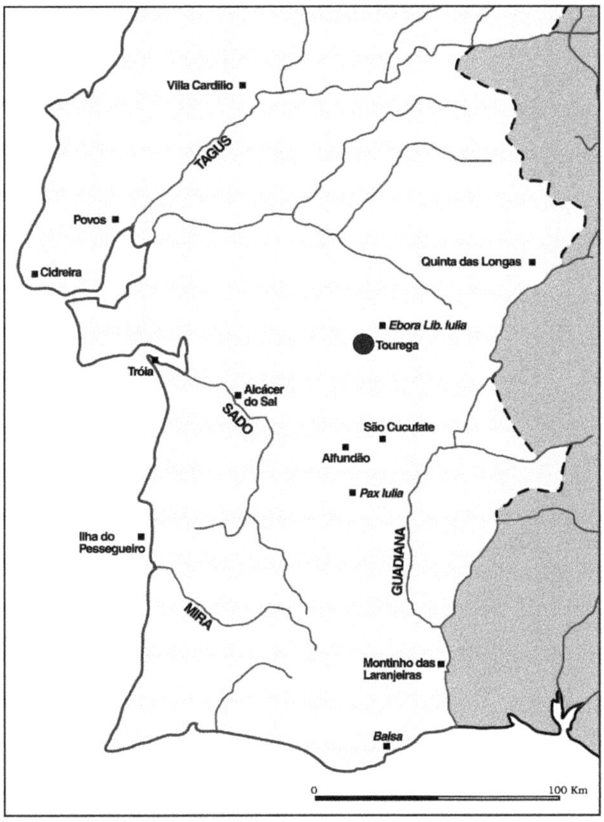

FIGURE 9. LOCATION OF TOUREGA (ÉVORA) AND OTHER SITES MENTIONED IN THE TEXT.

Augusta to *Olisipo* (Lisbon) through *Ebora* and *Salacia* (Alcácer do Sal) (Alarcão 1988, 98). African Red Slip type A, competing with Spanish *sigillata* in the markets, but coming by sea, only represents 7% at Tourega, but 16.53% at São Cucufate and 24% at Pessegueiro. In the same way, Baetican amphorae are rather rare at Tourega (7.6%) and far more common at São Cucufate (20.3%). African Red Slip types C and D, other products circulated by sea, are common in all Lusitanian sites where they do not have a serious continental competitor at the time they circulate. Nevertheless, the proportion of ARS C and D at Tourega (18% and 17%) is lower than at São Cucufate (20.57% and 23.71%). In this period, the sites along the Guadiana (São Cucufate and Alfundão) as well as those along the Tagus (Povos e *Villa Cardílio*) receive amphorae from the Algarve, although in smaller quantities, while there are none in Tourega or Quinta das Longas.

While African *sigillata* dominates the Hispanic markets in the Late Empire, African amphorae are not abundant and it is the Lusitanian products that dominate the foodstuff commerce, particularly in relation to the fish-based products that abundantly reached the inland *villae.* This is easily explained by the dynamics and quality of Lusitanian products, exported to the main areas of the Empire, and follows the tendency for importing from the nearest productive region (Fabião 1998, 181). But this also shows that the circulation of fine wares and amphorae were independent, even when produced in the

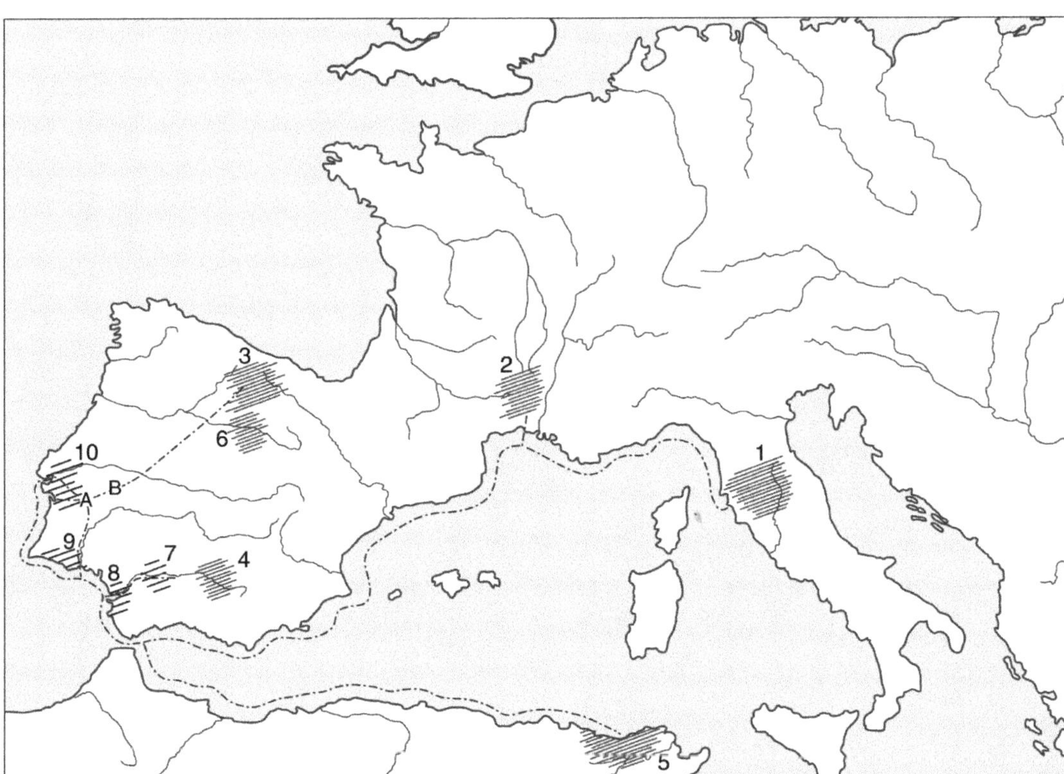

FIGURE 10. A - TOUREGA; B - *EMERITA AUGUSTA*; 1 - AREZZO; 2 - LA GRAUFESENQUE/MONTANS; 3 - TRICIO: 4 - ANDÚJAR; 5 - CARTHAGE; 6 - DOURO VALLEY; 7 - GUADALQUIVIR; 8 - GADES BAY; 9 - ALGARVE; 10 - TAGUS/SADO VALLEYS.

same regions, being subject to trade and loading in intermediary harbours, and responding to the changing demands of populations according to different patterns at various times.

Tourega's fine wares and amphorae are evidence for long-distance trade, following the trends of each period. A tendency for a lower proportion of maritime transport products is explained by its inland location, in the surroundings of a *civitas* capital rather distant from river routes.

Acknowledgements

We thank Françoise Mayet for helping with the ceramics classification; Rui Almeida for clarifying some questions on the amphorae and for drawing the amphorae presented and the maps; and Priscilla and John Lange for the revision of the English text.

Bibliography

Alarcão, A. 1971, *Terra sigillata itálica em Portugal*, in *Actas do II Congresso Nacional de Arqueologia*, Coimbra, 421-432.

Alarcão A, and Mayet F. (eds.) 1990, *Ânforas Lusitanas. Tipologia, Produção, Comércio*, Actas das Jornadas de Estudo realizadas em Conímbriga em 13 e 14 de Outubro de 1988, Museu Monográfico de Conímbriga, E. de Boccard.

Alarcão J. 1988, *O domínio romano em Portugal*, Mem Martins, Publicações Europa-América.

Alarcão J., Étienne R., Mayet F. 1990, *Les villas romaines de São Cucufate (Portugal)*, Paris, E. De Boccard.

Almagro M. 1955, *Las Necrópolis de Ampúrias*, II, Barcelona.

Almeida M. J., and Carvalho A. 1998, *Ânforas da villa romana da Quinta das Longas (S. Vicente e Ventosa, Elvas): resultados de 1990-1998*, "Revista Portuguesa de Arqueologia", volume 1, número 2, Lisboa, 137-163.

Banha C. 1991-1992, *As ânforas da Villa romana de Povos*, "Cira: Boletim Cultural", 5, Vila Franca de Xira, 49-90.

Bémont C. and Jacob J.P. (dir.) 1986, *La terre sigillée galo-romaine. Lieux de production du Haut Empire: Implantations, produits, relations*. Documents d'Archéologie Française nº 6, Paris, Édit. de la Maison des Sciences de l'Homme.

Beltán Lloris M. 1990, *Guía de la Cerámica Romana*, Zaragoza: Libros Pórtico

Beltrán Lloris M. 1970, *Las ánforas romanas en España*, Zaragoza.

Coutinho H.M.R. 1997, *Terra sigillata Clara do Montinho das Laranjeiras (Alcoutim) 1990 e 1991*, Alcoutim, Câmara Municipal de Alcoutim.

Delgado, M., Mayet, F. and Alarcão, A. 1975, *Les sigillées*. Fouilles de Conimbriga, IV. Paris: De Boccard.

Diogo A.M.D. 1987, *Quadro tipológico das ânforas de fabrico lusitano*, "O Arqueólogo Português", Série IV, 5, 179-191.

Diogo D., and Monteiro N. 1999, *Ânforas Romanas de "Villa Cardílio", Torres Novas*, "Conimbriga", 38, 201-214.

Dragendorff, H. 1895, *Terra sigillata*, "Bonner Jahrbucher", 96, 18-155.

Dressel H. 1899, *Corpus Inscriptionum Latinarum, XV, 2: Inscriptiones Urbis Romae Latinae. Instrumentum domesticum. Partis posterioris fasciculus I*, Berlin.

Encarnação J. 1984, *Inscrições Romanas do Conventus Pacensis. Subsídios para o estudo da romanização*, Coimbra, Instituto de Arqueologia da Faculdade de Letras.

Etienne R., Makaroun Y., and Mayet F. 1994, *Un Grand Complexe industriel à Tróia (Portugal)*, E. de Boccard, Paris.

Ettlinger, E., Hedinger, B., Hoffman, B., Kenrick, P.M., Pucci, G., Roth-Rubi, K., Schneider, G., Schnurbein, S. von, Wells, C.M., and Zabehlicky-Scheffenegger, S. 1990, *Conspectus formarum terrae sigillatae Italico modo confectae*, Materialen zur römisch-germanischen Keramik, 10, R. Habelt, Bonn.

Fabião C. 1993-1994, *O azeite da Baetica na Lusitania*, "Conimbriga", 32-33, 219-245.

Fabião C. 1998, *O vinho na Lusitânia: reflexões em torno de um problema arqueológico*, "Revista Portuguesa de Arqueologia", volume 1, número 1, Lisboa, 169-198.

Faria, J., Ferreira M. and Diogo, A.M.D. 1987, *Marcas da terra sigillata de Alcácer do Sal*, "Conimbriga" XXVI, 61-76.

Ferrer Dias L. 1998, *Terra sigillata da villa romana de Povos (Vila Franca de Xira). Estudo preliminar*, "CIRA", Vila Franca de Xira: Câmara Municipal de Vila Franca de Xira.

Hayes J.W. 1972, *Late Roman Pottery*. London, British School at Rome.

Hayes J. W. 1980, *Late Roman Pottery*. Supplement. London , British School at Rome.

Keay S. J., 1984, *Late Roman Amphorae in the Western Mediterranean: a typology and economic study. The Catalan evidence*, Oxford, BAR Int. Series, 196.

Mayet F. 1990, *Mérida: capitale économique?*, in *Les villes de Lusitanie romaine. Hiérarchies et territoires*, Paris, Éditions du C.N.R.S..

Mayet F. and Schmitt A. 1997, *Les Amphores de São Cucufate (Beja)*, in J. Alarcão and R. Étienne (eds.), *Itinéraires Lusitaniens*, Paris, E. de Boccard, 71-109.

Mayet F., Schmitt A., Tavares da Silva C. 1996, *Les Amphores du Sado (Portugal). Prospection des fours et analyse du matériel*, Paris, E. de Boccard.

Nolen J. U. S., 1988, *A villa romana do Alto da Cidreira (Cascais). Os materiais*, "Conimbriga", 27, 61-140.

Nolen J.U.S., 1994, *Cerâmica e Vidros de Torre de Ares, Balsa*, (*s.l.*), Instituto Português de Museus, Museu Nacional de Arqueologia.

Norton J., Cardoso J. L., Tavares da Silva C., and Canilho M. H. 1993-1994, *Ânforas da Villa romana de Vilares de Alfundão (Ferreira do Alentejo)*, "Conimbriga", XXXII-XXXIII, 181-190.

Oxé A., and Comfort H. 1968, *Corpus Vasorum Arretinorum. A Catalogue of the signatures, shapes and chronology of Italian sigillata*, Bonn.

Peacock, D.P.S., Williams, D.F. 1986, *Amphorae and the Roman economy: an introductory guide*, London, Longman archaeology series, Longman.

Roca M., and Fernàndez (eds.) 1999, *Terra sigillata Hispánica, Centros de fabricación y producciones altoimperiales*, Jaén, Málaga.

Saènz and Saènz, 1999, *Estado de la question de los alfares riojanos: la terra sigillata Hispanica Alto Imperial*, in *Terra sigillata Hispánica , Centros de fabricación y producciones altoimperiales*, (Roca and Fernàndez, eds.) Jaén, Málaga, 61-136.

Sciallano M., Sibella, P. 1994, *Amphores. Comment les identifier?*, Aix-en-Provence, Edisud.

Tavares da Silva C., and Soares J. 1993, *Ilha do Pessegueiro. Porto Romano da Costa Alentejana*, Lisboa, Instituto da Conservação da Natureza..

Vaz Pinto I, and Viegas C. 1994, *Les Thermes de la Villa Romaine de Tourega*, "Les Dossiers de l'Archéologie", November.

Vaz Pinto I., Viegas C., Ferrer Dias L., 1997, *A Villa Romana da Tourega: umas termas em ambiente rural,* in *Paisagens Arqueológicas a Oeste de Évora*, Évora, Câmara Municipal de Évora.

Viegas, C., forthcoming, *Cerâmica, economia e comércio: a terra sigillata da Alcáçova de Santarém.*

Viegas C., and Vaz Pinto I., forthcoming, *As termas da villa romana da Tourega (Évora, Portugal)*, in *Actas do Colóquio Termas Romanas en el Occidente del Império*, Gijón, December of 1999.

A fluvial harbour of the Roman period at Valentia (Hispania Tarraconensis)

Joseph Burriel Alberich, Albert Ribera i Lacomba, Marisa Serrano Marco

Abstract
The recent excavations of the northern area of the Roman town of *Valentia*, which in the ancient times was situated 2 km from the sea, brought to light a part of the neighbourhood of a port that was located next to the old river Turia bed. Some installations were identified that belonged to a small river harbour of the Early Imperial era and a large *horreum* nearby.
Other scattered archaeological remains, and knowledge of the sedimentary evolution of the swampy environment, suggest that there were other sites and routes along the river and through Lake Albufera lake, which closer to the ancient city than nowadays.

The Roman town of *Valentia* was established on a promontory located in the middle of the final section of the alluvial plain of the River Turia (Carmona, 1990a). In early times the occupational area of this town, which is today 3 km from the sea as opposed to 2 km then: *Valentia Colonia III p. a. mari remota, flumen Turium....* (Pliny, *Naturalis Historia* III, 20). Twenty-two centuries ago, the topography of the whole area was quite different. The main difference to bear in mind is that Lake Albufera would have been larger than it is today. We cannot therefore exclude the possibility that it would have reached the limits of the first city. It is possible that the lake continued into the swamps, which are still located to the north of Valencia and which meet those of the area of Sagunt and Almenara 30 km more to the north.

The environment that surrounded the Roman town was totally different to that of today. This ancient location would have had some inconveniences, but at the same time would also have offered a defensive capacity, and, especially, would have been able to offer communications with the sea-routes. Such an environment has been documented in the Roman foundations of the 2nd century B.C. in *Aquileia* in north Italy (Strazulla, 1989), or *Narbo Marius* in the south of *Gallia* (Gayraud, 1981).

An essential element in the formation of this site was the River Turia, which maintained the levels of the different surrounding lakes and whose sedimentary deposits continuously changed the environment. The acceleration of the rhythm of these depository processes can be followed from the time of the foundation of *Valentia* and the subsequent agricultural and forest exploitation with the introduction of the Roman economic system. The first sedimentological evidence of heavy overflows were detected in earlier periods (Carmona, Ribera and Lerma 1985) and are known from the written sources that start from the Medieval period and continue to the present day (Almela 1957).

The Roman town of *Valentia* was founded on an alluvial terrace, elevated over the immediate surroundings. This small promontory was elongated in form, 300 to 400 m in length, with its large axis in a N-S direction and covering a surface of approximately 10 to 12 hectares. Initially this promontory might have been an island although the possibility of a peninsular form cannot be discarded. At present, the area occupied by the ancient town and its surroundings still preserves some of the original topographical elements, which, together with a series of archaeological data, permit the identification of basic physical features of the Roman period. The north, east, and south-western sides open up to a low altitude terrain. To the northeast the topography is slightly more elevated while similar characteristics are observed to the southeast. The location of two major communication roads, the Via Augusta, which crosses the city in a N-S direction, and the road to the west towards the hinterland, as well as the necropolis (Ribera 1996) and public buildings on the periphery - the circus and the aqueduct - are all located outside the lower areas (Jiménez and Ribera 2000). The aqueduct, with a W-E orientation, runs parallel to the road towards the hinterland and both the road and the aqueduct border a wide depression extending to the southwest of the Roman town.

The area of the Roman port is located in the western half of the northern front, on the right bank of the Turia's old watercourse. Most probably two further fluvial courses existed in ancient times, located to the south. One of them, where a possible bridge pole was identified (Ribera 1998b, 278), was filled in Roman times, while the other, which delimited the Islamic city-wall (Badía and Pascual 1990), was covered in the 14th century.

Various but isolated Roman finds have been recovered along the fluvial course of the Turia. Among the most evident finds are the ones from the Tendentes area, close to the Botanical Gardens and to the west of the city. There, between 1934 and 1935, various Roman Republican coins and a Dr. 1 amphora neck were recovered, associated with low stone walls. A voluminous sand layer covered all the finds (Sentandreu 1966).

Various written references are known concerning the navigability of the Turia and the transport of merchandise

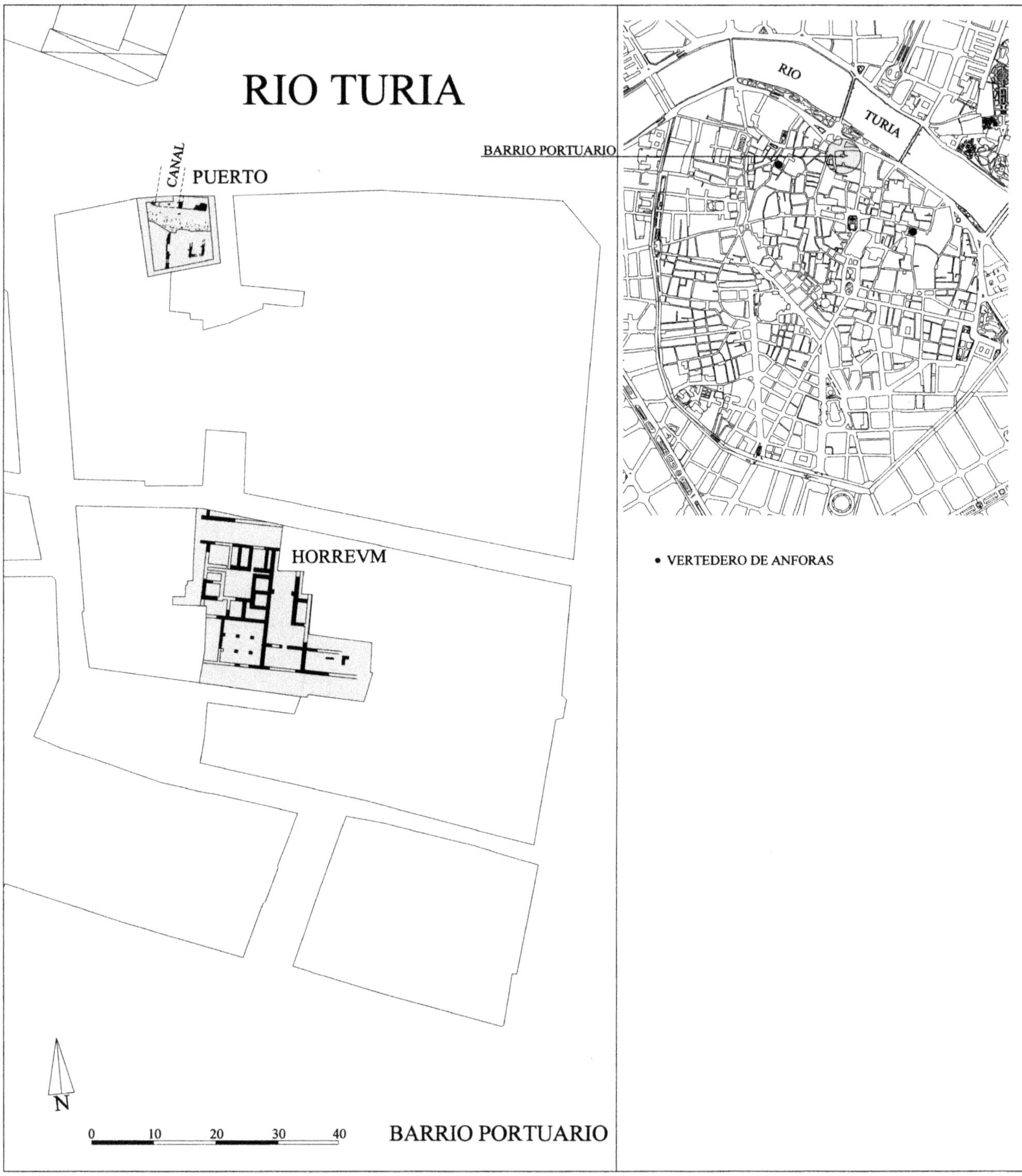

FIGURE 1. THE VALENTIA HARBOUR QUARTER LOCATION.

through the fluvial course during Medieval times. In the Roman period the Turia's course would have been deeper. The river would also carry a bigger volume of water since canals, water mills and dams, were absent and were only constructed in later periods. Therefore, direct communication with the sea was feasible, keeping in mind that only 2 km separated the town from the sea. However the river's depth would not have been excessive, thus smaller boats could carry out the fluvial communication and serve larger *oneraria* ships out to sea (Fernández 1984, 104-105). Underwater surveys have located two areas of possible exchange between larger maritime vessels and smaller fluvial boats. One is located to the north of the river mouth, opposite the neighbourhood of Malvarrosa. This location was already used at an early stage, at the beginning of 5th century B.C. and frequently from the second half of the 2nd century B.C. onwards, coinciding with the foundation of the city (Fernández, Gómez and Ribera 1989). The other landing area is located to the south of the river, opposite El Saler, where activities were initiated only after the town's foundation (Fernández 1984, Ribera and Fernández 1985).

There are no ancient references to the existence of a harbour or maritime dock. The occupation of the present port surroundings started after the 13th century when El Grau was created, which had for centuries been a loading place with wooden moles. For the Islamic period there exists information on some kind of berthing area on the coast, which could simply have been a place where ships where dragged in the dry sand. All the above information is not precise and therefore it is difficult to determine the exact location of the small maritime port, or the two Muslim fortresses ("rabidas") situated at the mouth of rivers to guarantee protection, which are known from medieval documentation contemporary to the Christian conquest (Boira and Serra 1994). The presence of these "rabidas" would argue in favour of a navigable river (Turia) since the major function of these buildings, well known all along the littoral, was to guard against naval incursions and to impede their advance through fluvial courses (Franco 1993).

As already mentioned, Lake Albufera lake extended over a much larger area than today. It is probable that the canals connecting the lagoon with the sea also served as accesses to the town or as a refuge area under adverse conditions at sea; such functions are known from the Islamic period (Azuar 1988).

The Roman Republican period

There are various options concerning the location of the Roman port of *Valentia*, and, *a priori*, they do not exclude each other since it is very probable that various accesses to the city, with their corresponding areas of berth, landing and storage, also existed.

The archaeological evidence shows that the majority of the materials used by the first inhabitants of *Valentia* was imported, especially from the Italian Peninsula. The products of Campania, such as wine amphorae, table or even cooking pottery, predominate. The merchandise from other parts of Italy - wine or oil from Apulia and pottery from Etruria or Sicily - were found in smaller quantities. Few in number, but always present, are Rhodian wine amphorae, oil amphorae from Tripolitania, salted fish amphorae from *Gades* or some *Ebusus* amphorae of unknown content, together with other scarce Greek or Punic objects (Ribera 1998). With these finds it becomes clear that the new city was an important centre of consumption of large quantities of goods which could only reach *Valentia* through maritime and river transport.

One of the most important finds is a rubbish dump dated to the foundation period and located to the northeast of the city, at Barón de Petrés Street, outside the urban area and close to the present river course. The contents are chronologically homogeneous and the broken remains of a single disembarked shipload could have filled this big hole. Italian and Tripolitan amphorae were discovered together with pottery from Naples, Etruria and Cales. These finds must indicate a nearby unloading point, located close to the road which led directly to the eastern gate, at a distance of approximately 100 m. Following this road (most probably the *decumanus maximus*) to the west one would enter the Republican town. Only a few metres before reaching the forum there was a building with foundations; the first courses of its superstructure were constructed in the *opus quadratum* technique with large blocks of stone. The width of the building, 24.2 m, was similar to that postulated for contemporary *insulae*. The building was divided into four identical and elongated wings, the full lengths of which are unknown as they stretch beyond the excavated area. A minimum of 12 m is estimated and the width of each wing is 5.2 m. This large building has been identified as a *horreum* (Ribera 1998b, 450), a big storage construction, in comparison to similar structures known across the Mediterranean world (Rickman 1971). In our opinion, the construction of one of the largest buildings in the first phase of *Valentia* to serve as a *horreum* is in accordance with the discoveries of large amounts of imported merchandise. It is very probable that the principal sources for the town's wealth during this period were related to its role as an intermediary and commercial re-distribution centre with the indigenous population. Some of the imported merchandise, which reached *Valentia* and was stored in the city's *horreum,* would be forwarded towards the indigenous settlements in the hinterland while the rest of the goods would be distributed within the city. A possibility to keep under consideration is the use of the fluvial routes beyond *Valentia*, although the main transport routes towards the hinterland would be terrestrial. Clear evidence for the town's commercial activities are the finds of *Valentia* coins, and a number of imported goods, at the important Iberian centre of Villares de Caudete de la Fuentes, identified as the mint of Kelin and located approximately 100 km inland (Mata 1991). Therefore, it is very probable that the first *Valentia* acted as a commercial *emporium* for the wider coastal and hinterland territory, especially because of its privileged location: firstly, it was the only Italo-Roman centre within a distance of 500 km between *Carthagonova* and *Tarraco*, and, secondly, it was an easily accessible centre by sea or/and land.

This initial period, however, has left no traces of structures that could be related to obvious harbour installations. Excavations at the Conde Trenor 13-14 Street, in the northern part of the city and adjacent to the river, have revealed a small fluvial port of the Imperial period but very few traces of the previous, Republican one. Nevertheless, there is abundant evidence that the area was already frequently used from the time of

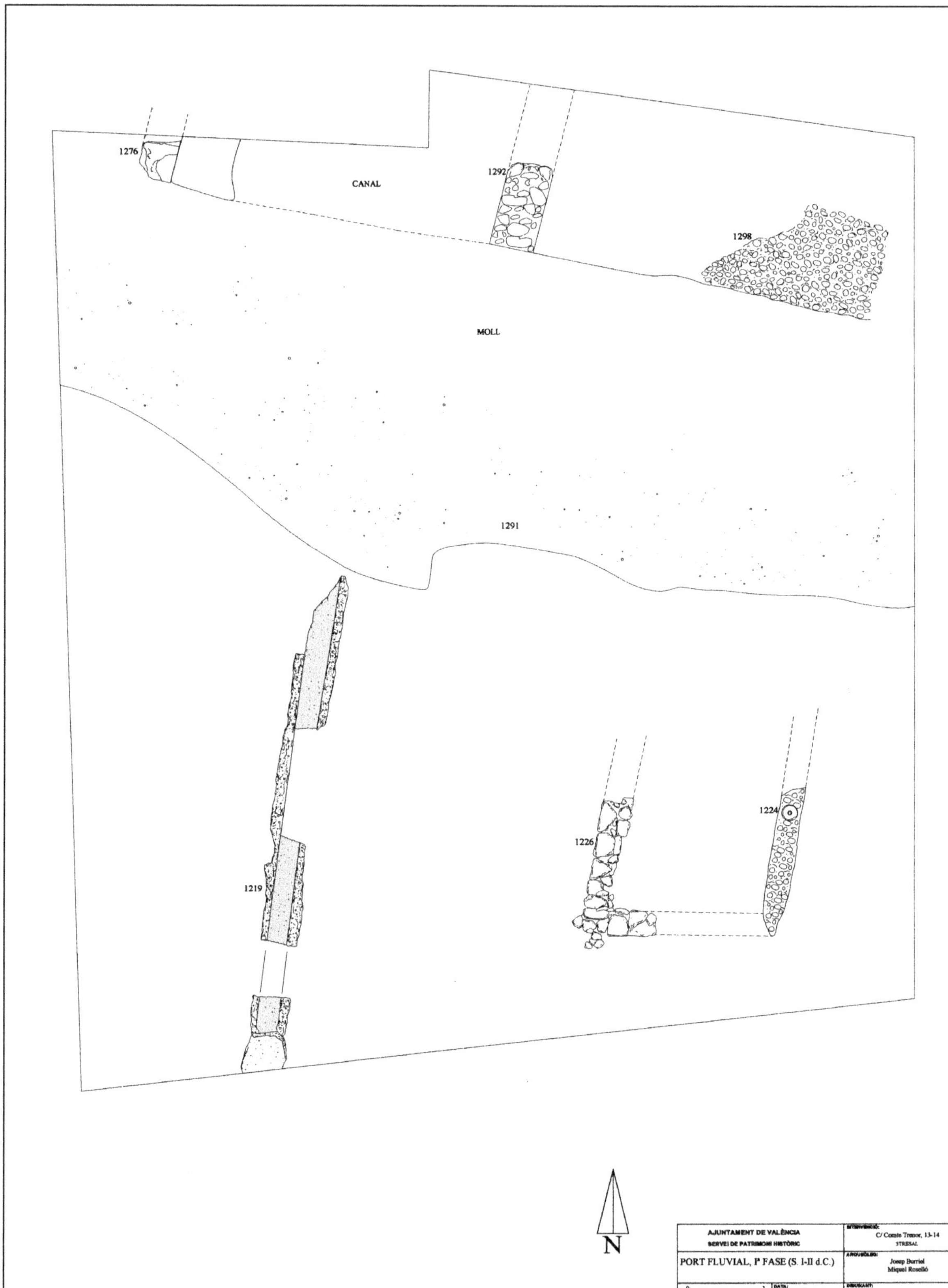

FIGURE 2. THE RIVER HARBOUR FIRST PHASE. FROM NORTH TO SOUTH: CANAL AND PAVED AREA, LOWERED AND SMOOTHED AREA AND UPPER TERRACE (DRAINS AND HOUSES)

its foundation. The presence of pits/discard areas or/and evidence of structures such as post holes or beaten earth floors, probably pertaining to huts similar to the ones discovered in other parts of the newly founded *Valentia*, should be mentioned.

Various dilapidated Republican structures and quite a lot of pottery appeared a few metres to the south, at Cisneros Square (Serrano 2000a). It was in this place that a building, of uncertain ground plan, was constructed during the Imperial period (Serrano 2000b) and which could have been some type of *horreum* (see below).

In the course of the Sertorian War Pompey destroyed *Valentia* in the year 75 B.C. (Ribera and Calvo 1995). Since there are no archaeological finds post-dating the city's destruction it is postulated that the city ceased to exist for at least 50 years after the wars (Albiach *et alii* 1998).

The Imperial Period

A small deposit of large amphora fragments dated to the late second half of the 1st century B.C. constitutes one of the first testimonies for the reoccupation of the town during the Imperial period. This deposit was located in the western part of the city, at Tenerias Street, the urban periphery (Ribera 1998b, 273), but in proximity to one of the affluents of the Turia, which was filled later during the Islamic period since it formed part of the ditch related to the town's defensive walls. The amphorae were discovered between the ditch to the west and the defensive wall to the east. The deposit was, probably, a small waste-dump close to an unloading area similar to the one dated to the Republican period (see above). However, the best example of pottery attributed to the time of the town's revival was the infill of a well, certainly ritual, located in a sanctuary related to a water cult and dated to the previous period (Albiach *et al*, forthcoming). The content of the well included great quantity of pottery, a large part of which was the product of foreign lands, namely the Arrentine sigillata, the Italian and African cooking pottery and amphorae from Betica (Albiach *et al* 1998). The proportion of locally produced material was higher at that time than what was the norm for the Republican period, although a great quantity of foreign products did reach the city. This was most probably a consequence of the reactivation of the maritime and fluvial routes and accesses. Nevertheless, from this period onwards changes are seen in commercial transactions. The export of local products became progressively more important, namely the wine that was bottled and transported in amphorae produced near *Valentia* in the workshops of Catarroja (García-Gelabert and García 1997) and Paterna (unpublished).

The storage infrastructure probably maintained characteristics similar to the ones of the previous period. This conclusion is reached if we interpret the building, with the peculiar ground plan located next to the forum, as a *horreum*. This building was constructed during the Flavian period over the remains of the earlier Republican construction, which served, in part (some of the walls), for the foundation of the later, imperial one. The imperial building is under excavation, half of its total surface still waiting to be uncovered (Marín, Piá and Roselló 1999).

The modest but obvious structures excavated at Conde de Trenor 13-14 Street constitute the most interesting finds for the discussion on fluvial ports. Their state of preservation is not the best since they were greatly affected by the foundations of the later, medieval and modern buildings. However, archaeological investigations in the area have revealed the characteristic elements attributed to a small port installation next to one of the canals of the Turia - that which bordered the city to the north. The excavated area covered 126 m^2 (10 x 12 m) and presented marked level differences from north to south: the surface always being lower towards the south. Although this level difference must have been natural, it was certainly further lowered by human activity which created a stair or sorts in the northern part, 3 m wide and cut into the Republican layers, which was only preserved in their southern part. The lowering of the terrain was followed by surface levelling with clay, stone and construction debris for the installation of some kind of infrastructure. Few poorly preserved remains of the first phase of this infrastructure were dated between the end of the 1st century and the beginning of the 2nd century A.D. To the north of this area, and to a yet lower level, an artificial canal was identified, which was 4.20 m wide and driven from the artificially lowered area towards the river course, located to the north. Two solid parallel walls formed the lateral borders of the canal. The width of the walls is 0.47 m and they are preserved to a height of 1.42 m and to 2 m in length. Their construction is *opus vittatum* type with masonry and *caementicium*. These walls were begun at the bottom of the canal ditch, therefore their base reached a depth of 6 m and was located 9 m above sea level and 1.50 m underneath the circulation level on the mole. To the east of the canal an area solidly paved with large river pebbles was discovered. To the south of the stairs the whole area was higher, by approximately 100 cm, and there the remains of a small draining sewer were found; this was very deteriorated and only a little more than its base was preserved. This draining sewer with a south-north direction reached the canal directly. Next to it, 3.50 m to the east, lay scanty remains of a small isolated rectangular building, 1.75 m wide and of unknown length but certainly not exceeding 5 m, since within this distance the stairs were located. All the above-mentioned structures were contemporary and of similar orientation.

This first phase, the canal and the paved area, was covered and sealed by various backfills, in which pottery was recovered, namely *sigillata hispanica* from Rioja (Drag. 27 from the potter *Agilianus*), African Slip Ware

A

B

FIGURE 3. A. THE RIVER HARBOUR SECOND PHASE: ON THE LEFT, STAIRCASES TO THE CANAL. ON THE RIGHT, WATER-SUPPLY B. AERIAL VIEW OF THE HORREUM

A (Hayes 3b and 3C) and African cooking pottery (Hayes 23B, 196A and 197). This pottery indicates a date about the middle of the 2nd century A.D.

Within the Imperial period, after the middle of the 2nd century A.D., changes took place in the area described above, which in great part caused the demolition and covering of any constructions from the previous phase. A hydraulic structure was built entirely in the *opus caementicium* technique and over the paved area and the eastern canal wall pertaining to the previous construction phase. This structure was not well preserved; it included a canal and small cisterns. To the north a section of three stone stairs was preserved suggesting the presence of a staircase for access to the canal. The stairs were attached to the northern *opus caementicium* wall of the hydraulic structure, which is the best preserved. This new structure indicates a small-scale expansion of the river installations to the north, since the area of the earlier phase stairs remained open and unaltered. In the southern part and over the earlier phase stairs, the building was amplified towards the east causing the demolition of some walls of the earlier phase, which were now modestly paved with compacted earth. Excavations at the port of *Londinium* on the Thames have revealed elements similar to the ones discovered at the excavations of *Valentia*, namely canals draining into the river, an open, levelled surface and/or small cuttings into the river bank (Milne 1985).

The excavations at *Valentia* revealed a building probably used for storage and located at a distance of approximately 50 m from this modest port area. A large part of this building was excavated. Its length was that of a potential *insulae* since its was delimited by two *decumani*, although it is difficult to calculate its width, which in any case would be over 30 m. The majority of the walls are preserved to foundation level but a large part of the building's ground plan is clear. A central patio surrounded by small irregular rooms, some of which are directly accessible from the street, is the main feature of the building. At the eastern part of the building there is a long corridor, which most probably served for communication between the various compartments. Three *dolia* were located on the floor on the south end of the corridor (the south-western corner) and next to the façade.

The access to this building would be from the southerly *decumanus*. From the central patio one could enter at least nine small rectangular rooms, of variable dimensions but never larger than 4 m in length. Of the walls, mainly the foundations are preserved which were constructed of medium size limestone blocks. In the few places where the superstructure of the walls is preserved the construction is of the *opus caementicium* type or of variable masonry, namely *opus africanum* or *opus vittatum*. The rare paved areas preserved showed that their construction was very modest, mainly beaten earth overlain by a thin lime layer (Serrano 2000b). A large room was excavated to the southeast of the corridor; it measured 7 to 4 m in length and probably formed part of the same building. The most important finds inside this large room were a mosaic and fragments of wall-painting among which a female head was depicted and identified as Venus, a deity closely related to commercial activities and structures (Jiménez 2000).

The whole area occupied by the large building with the corridor and the large room to the southeast has been subject to different interpretations. It was postulated that the large room to the southeast formed part of another building, supposedly a *horreum*. According to this interpretation the wide corridor to the north of the excavated area would be a *decumanus* (Serrano 2000b), the northernmost of all *decumani* known. However it is also postulated that the large room, the only one that has shown evidence for decoration on walls and floor, could have been connected with the storage building since there is only a wall separating them. Moreover, the supposed northernmost *decumanus* presents various anomalous aspects that make its identification as a public street doubtful. One of these aspects is its width, 4.5 m, which seems rather narrow, although at *Valentia* another *decumanus* with the same dimensions is known - the one discovered in the "Banys de l'Almirall" excavations to the southeast of the city (Ribera *et alii* 1991). However, this small street had a small drainage canal that ran underneath the circulation level, a common feature in Roman road networks. This feature is lacking from the supposed *decumanus* at Cisneros Square, where the only element for water drainage is a small depression in the surface. Furthermore, there are no remains of a portico, which did appear in the case of the southern *decumanus* in the "Banys de l'Almirall" excavations. This *decumanus* was also paved with large flagstones placed beneath the usual sewer while the supposed street to the north was constructed with a thick layer of compressed gravel.

During the first excavation campaign at Cisneros Square in 1986 the deeper levels were not excavated. Consequently, only a few remains of the above-mentioned building were recognized and which were interpreted as a *domus* (Albiach and Soriano 1991). However, when the excavations were completed in the area it became clear that the building belonged to a different category of construction and relating to economic activities (Serrano 2000b). Based on further study of the information derived from the excavations, we propose that the building was part of a larger *horreum*. The activities carried out in this building would be related to the small harbour described above. If we keep in mind that the peculiar northern *decumanus* most probably was one of the large corridors, which are frequently part of the High Empire *horrea* (Rickman 1971), then we may refer to a large *horreum*. With all probability, two sections excavated to the north of the corridor also formed part of this same *horreum*. Consequently the northern edge of the building would have been located several metres to the north, opening directly on the fluvial port or the town walls, supposing that during the Imperial period there were city walls around *Valentia*, assuming it was not still the earlier enclosure of the Republican period.

To summarise, we think that, thanks to fresh data from recent excavations at Conde de Trenor Street (1997) and Cisneros Square (1998), this northern zone of *Valentia* was probably used for commercial activities and the storage of merchandise. Therefore Valentia possessed the minimum infrastructure necessary to communicate with the open sea through fluvial accesses. In the general context of the period under consideration this would have been advantageous as this kind of transport was the most efficient and cheapest, and reached its maximum development and peek organizational level during the Roman Imperial period (Chic 1993). It is worth mentioning here the case of *Caesaraugusta*, where at the northern part of the town the remains of a large port and commercial area at the riverbank of River Ebro were revealed (Aguarod 2000).

Conclusions

The use of the fluvial installations of Conde Trenor Street ceased by the end of the 3rd century A.D., in consonance with what occurred during this period to the rest of the city (Ribera 2000). Although there are no remains of construction activities during the late Roman period there is some evidence that people used the area, namely the ditch or pit filled with material dated to the end of the 4th century A.D. (Burriel and Rosselló 2000). Afterwards, and until the 11th century, there is no evidence of human activity in the area. At Cisneros Square and over the *horreum* appeared the remains of a destruction level dated to the 3rd century A.D. A reconstruction phase of the 4th century A.D. was revealed which offered an extraordinary find, a glass kiln (Albiach and Soriano 1989). There are no building remains of the Visogoth period (5th - 7th centuries) in the northern part of the city, which was included in the urban area during Roman times. However, there is evidence for the frequent use of the area for economic purposes. Many silos existed, which were finally used as waste-dumps, and various large ditches utilized for the same purpose (Ribera and Roselló 2000). Part of the material recovered attests that imported merchandise, especially from North Africa and the Byzantine East, regularly reached the city until the beginning of the 7th century A.D. Therefore, it is postulated that some port installation was maintained and used in late Antiquity (Pascual *et al* 1997).

Bibliography

Aguarod, C., 2000, Zaragoza y la recuperación de la antigua Caesaraugusta: el foro, el puerto fluvial, las termas públicas, el teatro y las murallas, *1er Congreso Internacional Ciudad, arqueología y desarrollo. La musealización de los yacimientos arqueológicos*, 165-174.

Albiach, R. y Soriano, R., 1989, Un horno de vidrio romano en Valentia. *XIX Congreso Nacional de Arqueología (Castellon 1987)*, 725-734.

Albiach, R. y Soriano, R. 1991, Estudio de una domus romana de Valentia y los niveles que la amortizan. *Saguntum - Papeles del Laboratorio de Arqueología de Valencia* 24, 75-95.

Albiach, R. *et al.* Albiach, R., Marín, C., Pascual, G., Pià, J., Ribera, A., Rosselló, M. y Sanchis, A.. 1998, La cerámica de época de Augusto procedente del relleno de un pozo de Valentia (Hispania Tarraconensis), *Actes du Congrès d'Istres de la Societé Française d'Étude de la Céramique Antique en Gaule*, 139-166.

Albiach, R. *et al.* Albiach, R., Espí, I., Marín, C. y Ribera, A. en prensa, *Culto a las aguas en la ciudad romana de Valentia, Acque minero-medicinali, terme curative e culti alle acque nel mondo romano*, (Terme Euganee 1999).

Almela i Vives, F. 1957, *Las riadas del Turia (1321-1949)*, Publicaciones del Archivo Municipal. Valencia.

Azuar, R. 1988, La época islámica. *Historia del Pueblo Valenciano, Diario Levante*, 161-180.

Badia, A. y Pascual, J. 1991, *Las murallas árabes de Valencia.* Quaderns de Difusió Arqueològica 2. València.

Boira, J.V. y Serra, A. 1994, *El Grau de València. La construcció d'un espai urbà.* Col·lecció Politècnica 54, Valencia.

Burriel, J. y Rosselló, M. 2000, Un vertedero bajoimperial en la C/ Conde de Trénor, 13-14 (Valencia). Estudio de sus materiales, *Saguntum-Papeles del Laboratorio de Arqueología de Valencia* 32, 9-30.

Carmona, P. 1990, *La formació de la plana alluvial de València. Geomorfologia, hidrologia i geoarqueologia de l'espai litoral del Túria.* Estudis Universitaris, Sèrie Major 5, ed. Alfons el Magnanim. València.

Carmona, P. 1990b, Fluctuaciones recientes de la linea de costa en el area valenciana. Nuevos datos, *I Reunión Nacional de Geomorfologia*, 319-328. Teruel.

Carmona, P. 1991, El puerto romano de Sagunt. Geomorfologia y cambios recientes en la línea de costa, *Saguntum* y el mar, *Generalitat Valenciana*, 54-56, València.

Carmona, P., Ribera, A. y Lerma, V. 1985, Geoarqueología en la ciudad de Valencia. *Congreso Nacional de Arqueología* XVII, 859-873.

Chic, G., 1993, La navegación fluvial en época romana. *Revista de Arqueología* 142, Madrid, 28-39.

Fernández, A. 1984, Las ánforas romanas de *Valentia* y de su entorno marítimo, *Serie Arqueológica Municipal* 3, València

Fernández, A., Gómez, c. y Ribera, A. 1989, Anforas griegas, etruscas y fenicias del yacimiento submarino de Cabanyal-Malvarrosa (Valencia), *Congreso Nacional de Arqueología* XIX, 607-618.

Franco, F. 1993, Ràpites i Al-Monastir(s) al nord i llevant de la Peninsula d'Al-Andalus, *La Ràpita islàmica: Història institucional i altres estudis regionals*, Sant Carles de la Ràpita, 191-200.

García-Gelabert, M.P. y García, M. 1997, El asentamiento romano de Catarroja. Aproximación a su estudio, *Espacio, Tiempo y Forma, Serie II, Hª Antigua* 10, 351-374.

Gayraud, M. 1981, *Narbonne Antique, des origines à la fin du IIIè siècle*. Supplément 8 de Revue Archeologique du Narbonnaise. París.

Jiménez, J.L. 2000, Los hallazgos de pintura mural romana, *L'arqueologia fa ciutat: les excavacions de la Plaça de Cisneros*, 31-34.

Jiménez, J.L. y Ribera, A. 2000, La fundación de la ciudad. Urbanismo y arquitectura de la Valencia romana y visigoda, Historia de la Ciudad. *Recorrido histórico por la arquitectura y el urbanismo de la ciudad de Valencia*, 9-37.

Marín, C., Pià, J. y Rosselló, M., 1999. *El foro romano de Valentia.* Quaderns de Difusió Arqueològica 5. Valencia.

Mata, C. 1991, Los Villares (Caudete de las Fuentes, Valencia). *Origen y evolución de la Cultura Ibérica, Trabajos Varios del Servicio de Investigación Prehistórica* 88, València.

Milne, G., 1985, *The port of Roman London*, Batsford, Londres.

Pascual, P., *et al.* Ribera, A, Rosselló, M. y Marot, T., 1997, València i el seu territori: contexts ceràmics de la fi de la romanitat a la fi del califat (270-1031), Contextos ceràmics d'època romana tardana i de l'alta edat mitjana (segles IV-X), *Arqueo Mediterrània* 2, 179-202.

Ribera, A. 1996, La topografía de los cementerios romanos de Valentia, *Saetabi* 46, 85-99.

Ribera, A. 1998a, The discovery of a monumental circus at Valentia (Hispania Tarraconensis), *Journal of Roman Archaeology* 11, 318-337.

Ribera, A. 1998b, *La fundació de València. La ciutat a l'època romanorepublicana (segles II-I a. de C.)*, Estudios Universitarios 71, Valencia.

Ribera, A. 2000, Valentia siglos IV y V: el final de una ciudad romana, *Grandes Temas Arqueológicos 2, Los origenes del cristianismo en Valencia y su entorno*, 19-32.

Ribera, A. y Calvo. M., 1995, La primera evidencia arqueológica de la destrucción de Valentia por Pompeyo, *Journal Roman Archaeology* 8, 19-40.

Ribera, A. y Rosselló, M., 2000, La ciudad de Valencia en época visigoda, *Los inicios del cristianismo en Valencia y su entorno. Grandes Temas Arqueológicos 2, Ajuntamente de Valencia*, 151-164. Valencia.

Ribera, A. *et al.* Escrivà V., Chulià, R. y Rivas, L., 1991, La intervenció arqueològica, *Palau de l'Almirall, Generalitat Valenciana*, 173-192, València.

Ribera, A. y Fernández, A. 1985, Prospecciones arqueológicas submarinas en la zona del Saler (Valencia), *VI Congreso Internacional de Arqueología Submarina*, 83-91.

Rickman, G. 1971, *Roman granaries and store buildings*, Cambridge University Press, Londres.

Sentandreu, C. 1966, Hallazgos arqueológicos en el cauce del río Turia (Valencia), *Archivo de Prehistoria Levantina* IX, 177-185.

Serrano, M.L. 2000a, Excavaciones en Valencia: contexto arqueológico del vaso "El ciclo de la vida", *Archivo Español de Arqueología* 73, 80-85.

Serrano, M.L. 2000b, Hallazgos arqueológicos de la plaza de Cisneros nº 6 de Valencia, *L'arqueologia fa ciutat: les excavacions de la Plaça de Cisneros*, 9-22.

Strazzulla, M.J. 1989, In paludibus moenia constituta: problemi urbanistici di Aquileia in età repubblicana alla luce della documentazione archeologica e delle fonti scritte, Aquileia repubblicana e imperiale, *Antichità Altoadriatiche* XXXV, 187-228.

Access to international trade in Middle Saxon England: a case of urban over-emphasis?

John Naylor

Abstract

The paper discusses the possibility that direct access to networks of international trade may have been more widespread than is generally considered, and that previous models have focused too strongly on urban sites. Utilising data from metal-detection and excavation in eastern England, the paper shows that the sites with greatest numbers of coin finds are virtually all located within c.15km of the coast, which is taken as the calculated limit for return travel to market in a day. The concluding discussion argues that although there is an urban over-emphasis in many models of the early medieval economy, the results presented here suggest real regional variations, and that the nature of the productive site is still a matter for debate.

Introduction

The archaeological study of trade in pre-Viking England, c.650-850, has been dominated by research focusing on the re-emergence of urbanism (e.g. Hodges, 1989a). Large-scale excavations at coastal sites in the east and south of the country have uncovered extensive evidence of international contacts, much with the Rhineland and northern France. The bulk of this is confined to just four sites: York, London, Ipswich, and Southampton. Equivalent contemporary sites have also been found elsewhere in north-west Europe including Dorestad (Netherlands), Ribe (Denmark), and Quentovic (northern France). This archaeological evidence has indicated that during the later seventh and early eighth century, a number of large settlements were founded to take advantage of increasing levels of long-distance trade. There is evidence of permanent non-agrarian populations mostly involved in craft-working activities, living in planned settlements, with laid out streets and boundary ditches (Hodges 1989a, 52). Such places would require provisioning from surrounding rural communities, and have been seen as indicative of more widespread economic change, with the production of surplus, and increasing specialization a necessary contemporary development (Blinkhorn 1999).

As a result of the general bias towards these large emporia, there is a need for archaeologists and historians to assess the extent to which smaller trading settlements may have been ignored. Fifteen years ago, Astill (1985, 228) urged archaeologists to explore smaller, inland sites, which may have been focused toward regional/ inter-regional trade, but it is only very recently that research has attempted to assess the seventh to ninth century economy of Anglo-Saxon England on this more regional basis (e.g. Anderton 1999; Naylor, forthcoming a; Ulmschneider 2000). Such work has advanced our understanding of the mechanisms of both regional and long-distance trade, and the interpretation of many 'productive sites'[1] as regional market places is important.

[1] A 'productive site' is a phrase coined by numismatists and metal-detectorists to describe a site, generally an open rural area, where metal-detecting has uncovered high numbers of coinage and metalwork (Bosner 1997, 39). Increasingly, the term is also being applied to excavated sites with similar assemblages of metal objects, including, for example, the sites at Brandon (Suffolk), and Whitby Abbey (Yorkshire).

In the main, most papers have utilised the large numbers of metal detected artefacts discovered and reported over the last 20 years to show the widespread distributions of coinage and metalwork across much of eastern England. Alongside the evidence from excavation and fieldwalking, this has shown that the early medieval economy was somewhat more complex than was previously considered, e.g. by Hodges (1989a), with rural sites now seen as actively participating in trade alongside the urban emporia.

Additionally, there are a relatively high number of excavated inland sites across eastern England where imported materials have been found, ranging from lava querns from the Mayen region in the Rhineland, to northern French and Rhenish pottery, as well as foreign coinage, vessel glass, and other goods. With reference to the urban-centred theories of (Hodges 1989a) and the newer work mentioned above, it is important to ask how these rural sites obtained such imported goods. There are a number of possibilities: were they received as one side of a reciprocal goods exchange, with all goods entering the country through the nearest urban emporium, such as Ipswich or York; did they enter through the emporium, and trickle down into the rural areas through a distribution network involving the inland 'productive sites'; were they traded for directly with foreign merchants either at an emporium, periodic beach markets, or inland markets; or were a combination of these, and other, processes at work, with a general regional variation dependant upon local political and economic conditions?

Theoretical approach

The problem of assessing the nature of access to international trade is not an easy one, as the list of questions above highlights. However, by approaching the problem theoretically, it may be possible to discuss whether the population of middle Saxon eastern England could have gained direct access to imported goods.

Firstly, it is important to produce a theoretical working limit for travel to market in a single day. In his important study of the later medieval economy, Britnell (1993, 82-83) addressed the problems of transporting bulky produce, such as foods, to market in the twelfth and thirteenth centuries. These, he argued, could only be transported over relatively short distances because of the high costs involved. For example, in a legal treatise of the 1250s, the limit was set at six and two-thirds miles (10.7km) as any further would not allow the seller to travel to market and return within a day (*ibid.*). Other examples include the transport of wheat and barley over ten miles (16.1km) from Kennet (Cambridgeshire) to Bury St. Edmunds (Suffolk) in the 1270s. Britnell (1993, 83) also noted that distances much further than this are rare due to prohibitive costs. Additionally, Wilkinson (1994, 502), in his investigation of the state in early Bronze Age Mesopotamia, calculated that travel of 10-15km at c.4km per hour would be the average limit for a day's return journey (five hours total travel time). From this, the distance of approximately 15km would seem to be a useful working limit for a return journey by non-mechanised transport, and will be applied here, albeit recognising that differing terrain will allow for variation in this limit.

The second consideration of importance regards assessing how *direct* access to international trade can be traced, as opposed to simply procuring imported materials through a re-distributive network. To do this, analysis must be carried out using a material which is archaeologically visible, and can also be considered an index of trade rather than being a traded item itself. Of the materials available, such as Continental pottery, imported stone, and vessel glass, the best *indicator* of trade is probably coinage.

Finds of middle Saxon coinage have been made over much of England, especially in the eastern regions, and numbers of single finds have increased dramatically over the last 20 years due to high levels of metal detecting, and subsequent reporting of finds. Numismatists have used these finds to examine the Anglo-Saxon economy with great success, and their application to tracing patterns of trade is common (e.g. Metcalf 1998; Naylor forthcoming a). It should be noted that only single finds have been used in this study, and no grave finds or hoards are included as these latter groups would have been deliberately deposited, rather than accidentally lost.

Access to long-distance trade in middle Saxon eastern England

The analysis in this paper will be based around aspects of my doctoral research, focusing on three regions in eastern England (Figure 1): Kent, Suffolk and an area north of the Humber encompassing East Riding of Yorkshire, and parts North and West Yorkshire, which will be referred to simply as Yorkshire. Any appropriate additional information will utilised where possible.

The widespread nature of single finds of middle to late Saxon coinage, dated c.650-900, can be seen in Figure 2 a-c, with finds across much of each region. Throughout this period there is a general correlation with rivers, and Roman roads, as well as coastal locations. It should, however, be noted that in both Kent and Suffolk, many of the finds can be dated to the first half of the eighth century when the varied sceatta issues were in circulation, before the introduction of the broad flan penny in the later eighth century, which are found in far fewer numbers. Distribution in Yorkshire is similar, but the nature of finds is slightly different, with peaks in circulation of coinage during the third quarter of the eighth century, with the issues of king Eadberht (737-c.758), and with the stycas of the early-mid ninth century (Naylor, in prep). Such extensive distributions of coinage have been used to argue for wide economic monetization during the middle Saxon period, and that this monetization must have affected a large proportion of the population (e.g. Metcalf 1998; Naylor forthcoming a).

However, if the general distribution is now replaced with one showing only the most highly productive sites (Figure 3 a-c), in this case those with greater than ten finds of middle Saxon coins, an interesting pattern emerges. Figure 3a shows the distribution of the six productive sites in Kent. There is a clear concentration towards the coast of east Kent, especially the region around Reculver, Richborough and Canterbury, described previously by Metcalf (1984, 203) as the 'East Kent triangle', where large numbers of coins have been found since the eighteenth century. The other two sites in east Kent are Eastry, approximately 5km to the south of Richborough, and 'near Canterbury', whose exact location has not been released for fear of illegal metal-detecting. The only remaining site is near to Hollingbourne on/near to the North Downs Way, where 31 seventh to ninth century finds have been made (Bosner 1997, 41). This site, although high on the North Downs, is only c.15km to the coast (direct), or c.20km if travelling west along the North Downs Way, and then north at the junction with the Roman road to Rochester, a monastic site through the middle Saxon period, which gained the rights to mint coinage for a period in the ninth century (Pagan 1986, 47-48).

The distribution of the more productive sites in Suffolk (Figure 3b) is less clear: there are only five sites which have so far produced over ten single coin finds, four, including Ipswich, in the south-east of the county, and a single site, Lakenheath, in north-west Suffolk. The south-east concentration shows three sites, Ipswich, Barham, and Coddenham in close proximity, and Burrow Hill, Butley a little further away on the coast. Barham and Coddenham are only 2km apart, and both are less than 10km from Ipswich, the emporia which covered over 50Ha during this period and has produced extensive evidence of international trade and manufacture, including the Ipswich Ware pottery industry (Wade 1993, 147-148). All four sites were well within the 15km limit to navigable water. Burrow Hill, Butley was located on a probable island during this period (Fenwick 1984, 35) and could easily have caught traffic moving along the east coast. It is, however, more difficult to determine potential function or access to foreign trade for Barham

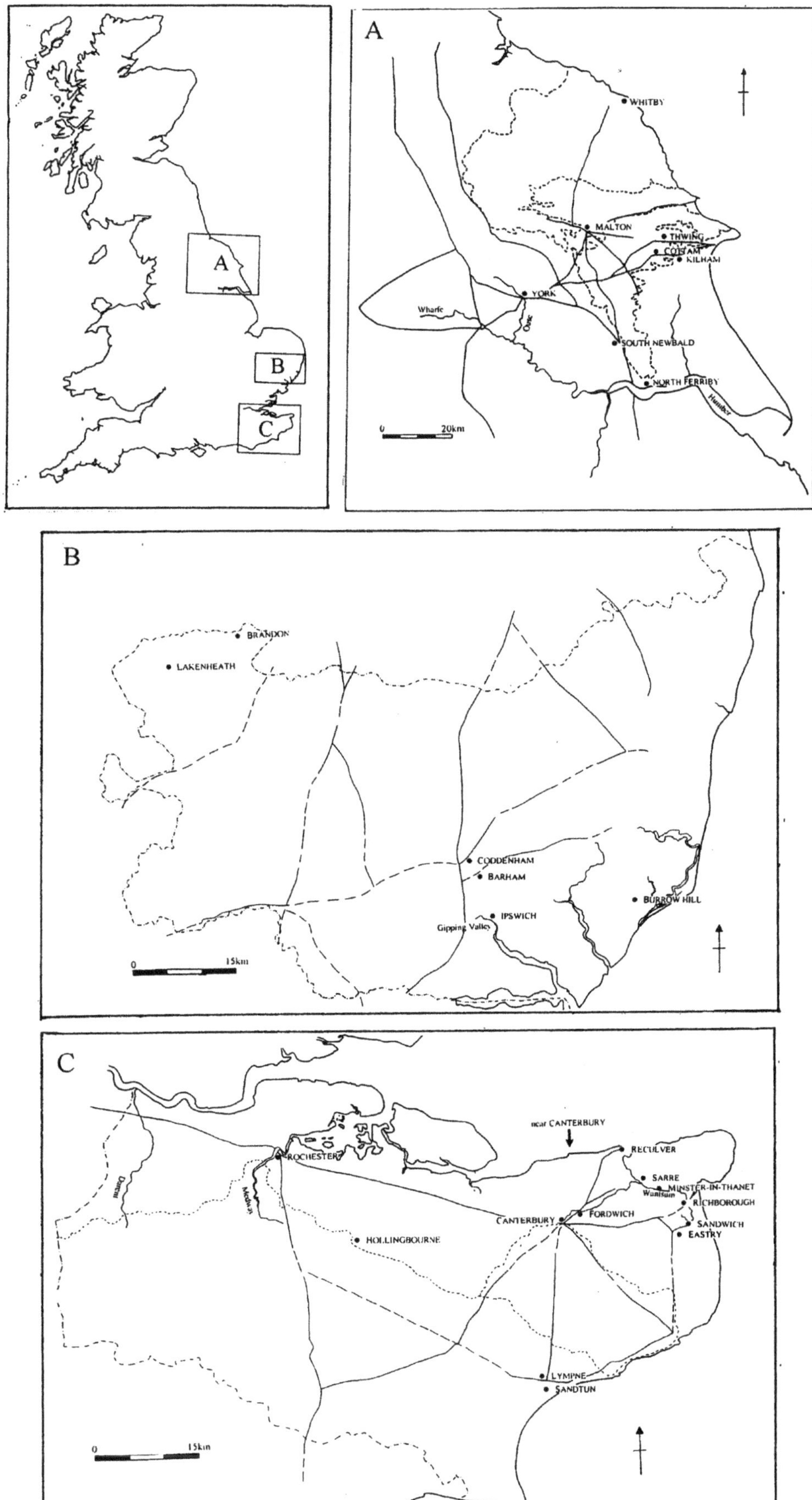

FIGURE 1. LOCATION OF THE STUDY AREAS IN EASTERN ENGLAND, AND PLACES MENTIONED IN THE TEXT.

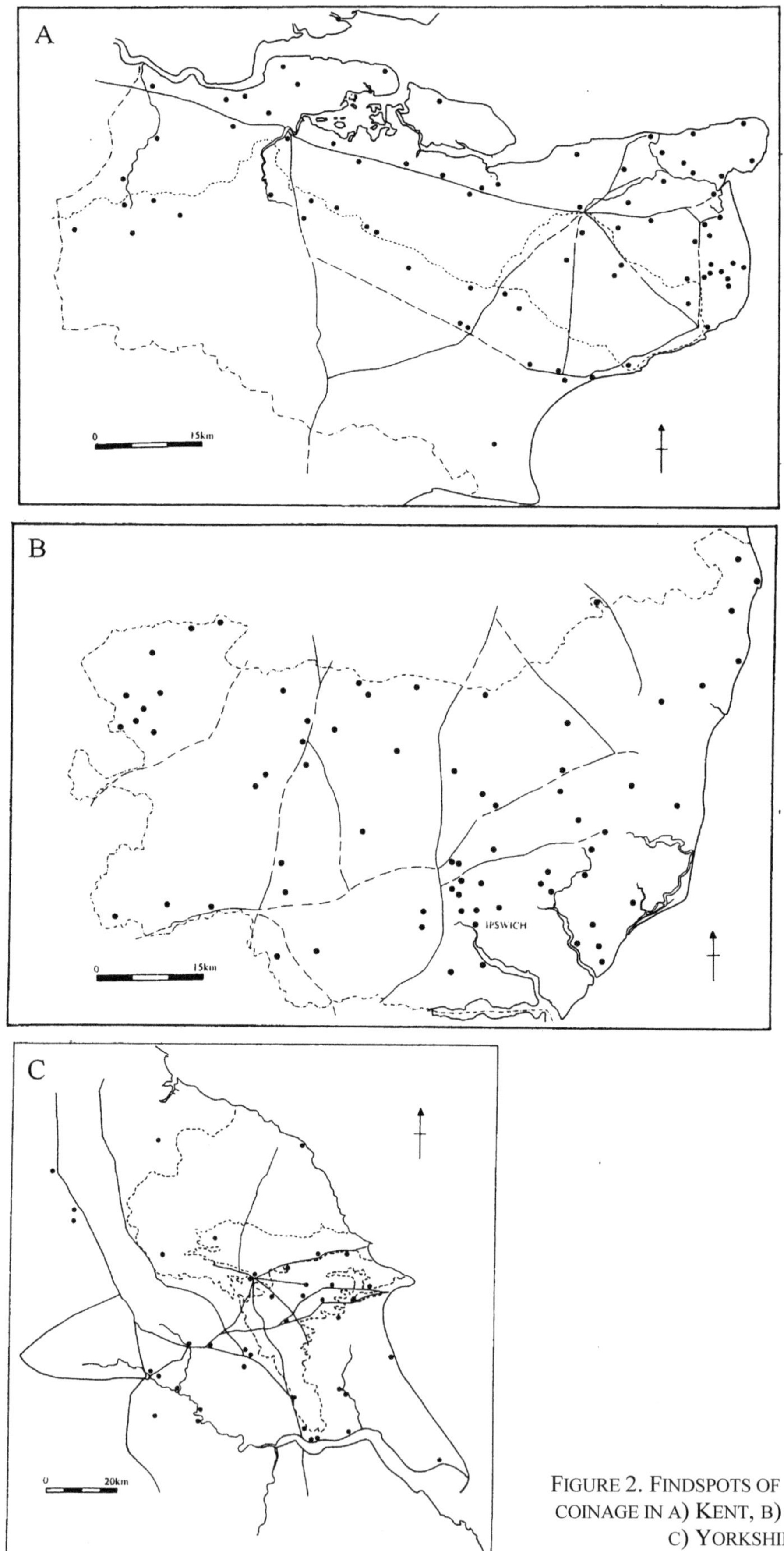

FIGURE 2. FINDSPOTS OF MIDDLE SAXON COINAGE IN A) KENT, B) SUFFOLK, AND C) YORKSHIRE.

and Coddenham. As both sites are within a day's return travel to Ipswich, it is impossible to determine, on current evidence, whether these two sites were trading directly for materials and goods which they required; if they were settlements whose inhabitants traded in Ipswich; or if they acted as centres of re-distribution for goods imported to Ipswich, possibly part of second tier of sites suggested by Astill (1985. 228). Certainly, their closeness to Ipswich, and proximity to the Roman road running east-west does point towards a regionally important sites. Newman (1999, 45) argued as much, suggesting that Barham and Ipswich may have had 'different but complementary roles', citing Barham as of importance to at least the local economy, and Hodges (1989b, 99) also thought it may have been the location of a market, probably used on a seasonal basis, as excavation in the 1980s had produced no evidence of occupation. The remaining site, Lakenheath, is well inland, about 60km from Ipswich or the coast, and is the most productive of a cluster of find-spots in the north-west of Suffolk. None appear to be closely associated with Roman roads, navigable rivers or prehistoric trackways. It is possible that these finds may be the result of a network of regional trade. One of these site, only 7km north-east of Lakenheath is the excavated elite, possibly monastic, settlement at Brandon where imported material including pottery, lava querns and vessel glass have been discovered (Carr *et al* 1988, 375).

In Yorkshire (Figure 3c), five of a total of nine productive sites are within 15km of the coast, with a sixth, Cottam, is only a little outside this, at c.17km. The city of York, located on the Rivers Ouse and Foss which is navigable from the Humber estuary and the North Sea, is one of the remaining three, and this was the seat of the northern archbishopric, and also the major international trading settlement at Fishergate. Such a site, although outside the calculated theoretical limit, can perhaps be seen as an exception as it was obviously of a different nature to other settlements in northern England at the time. The remaining two sites are both near Malton, but there exact location is currently secret.

In addition, it may be useful to examine aspects of the coinage assemblage in each region in more detail, and specifically the incidences of foreign coins. In Kent (Figure 4a), 31 sites with foreign coinage are known, including all six sites with over ten coins. The distribution of these coins is more widespread than for the other areas, and roughly follows the patterns seen for all coin finds, if perhaps slightly more restricted to transportation routes (Figure 2a). In Suffolk (Figure 4b), 18 sites include foreign coinage, all of the most productive, with the exception of Burrow Hill, Butley are represented, and the general distribution is along the coast, with a concentration in south-east Suffolk along the Gipping Valley, north-west from Ipswich. In Yorkshire, such finds have been made on 19 sites (Figure 4c), including all of the most productive sites (Figure 3c), and with a single exception, the remainder are restricted to sites within c.15km of the coast, riverine locations, and sites on the main road from the Humber estuary to York.

Overall, the numismatic evidence has shown that, in each region, the majority of the sites with the largest coinage assemblages are positioned under 15km from the coast. The application of this figure has proven interesting as it does imply that these sites would be well located to gain direct access to networks of sea-borne long-distance trade, as a return journey to, or from, the coast could be undertaken within a day. The additional presence of foreign coins at these sites, as well as number of other places along the east coast, would support the idea that the contact with international trade was not restricted to a small number of urban centres. It should be noted that the majority of these foreign coins are Continental Intermediate phase sceattas of the early eighth century, and later foreign coins are a rarity, most likely due to a concerted re-minting of non-local coins (Metcalf 1988, 237).

However, having emphasised the similarities between each of the regions, it is also important that their differences are discussed, as this may provide useful evidence regarding the internal economy of areas across eastern England. Certainly, in Suffolk, it appears that the large emporium at Ipswich may have dominated the region's international trade. The excavated evidence is unequivocal as to the range and level of Ipswich's trading contacts with Continental Europe from the late seventh century onwards, and alongside this there is the well known pottery industry, supplying Ipswich Ware to the whole of East Anglia and beyond (Wade 1993, 147-148). The distribution of coin finds in the immediate hinterland of Ipswich, and especially the numismatically rich sites at Barham and Coddenham, is interesting, and may be indicative of the scale of commerce at Ipswich in comparison to the rest of southern East Anglia.

Such a situation contrasts with both Kent and Yorkshire. In these regions, it seems, the economy may have been organized in a different way with a number of sites around each area able to gain direct access to the networks of international trade. In Kent, as described above, large numbers of seventh to ninth century coinage have been found at Canterbury, Eastry, Hollingbourne, near Canterbury, Reculver, and Richborough. Additionally, there are a number of charters granting the remission of tolls on trade for ships from the monasteries at Minster-in-Thanet, Rochester, and Reculver at Fordwich, and Sarre (Kelly 1992, 4-6). Hodges (1989b, 92-4) also mentions toll remissions at Sandwich and Minster-in-Thanet. Archaeological evidence has been forthcoming on the southern coast of Kent, at the edge of Romney Marsh. A small settlement with international connections has been excavated near West Hythe, at a place identified as *Sandtun*, which is mentioned in eighth and ninth century charters in relation to the Minster at Lympne (Gardiner, forthcoming). Finds from the site include general craft-working evidence and domestic

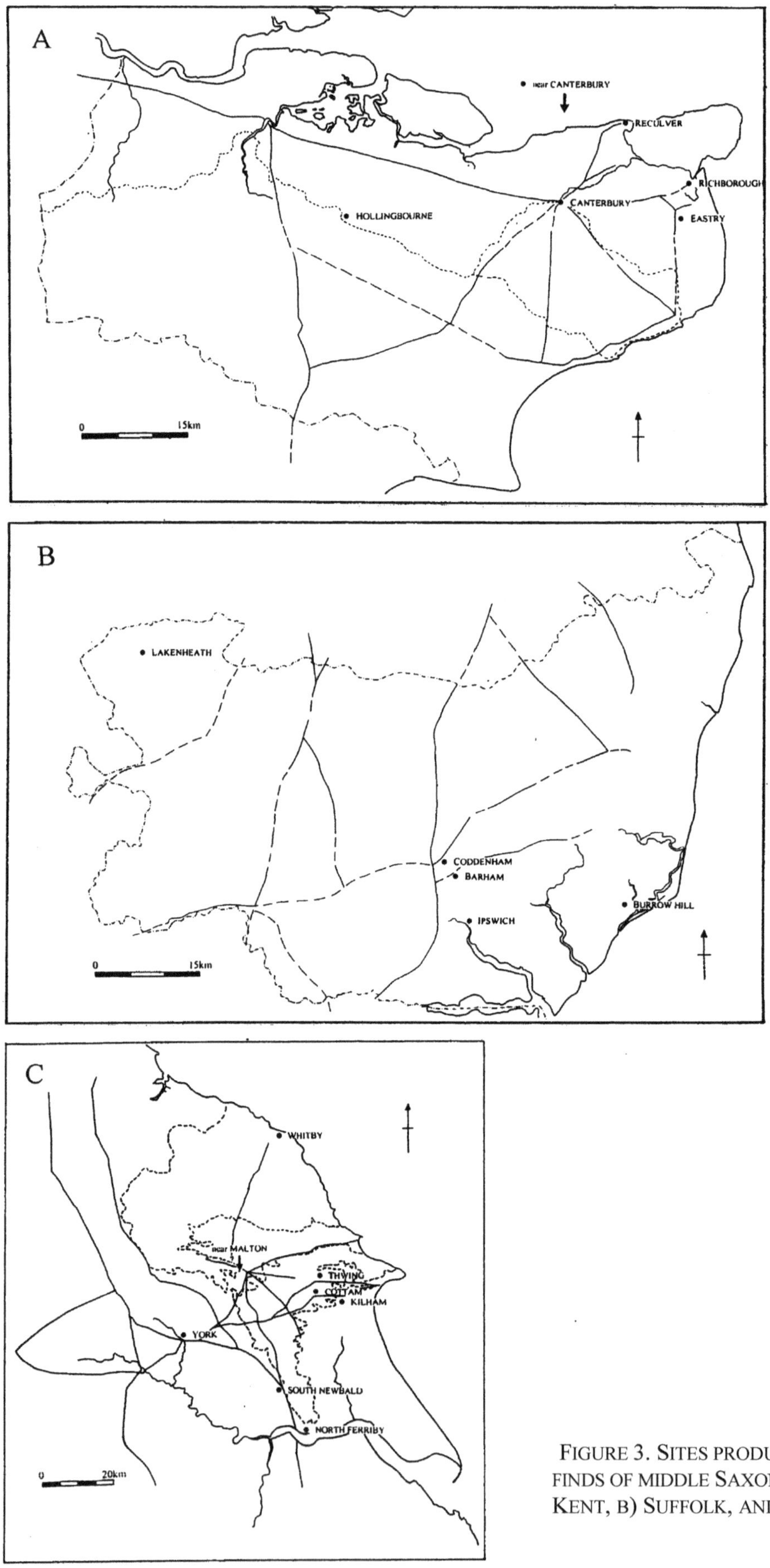

FIGURE 3. SITES PRODUCING OVER TEN FINDS OF MIDDLE SAXON COINAGE, IN A) KENT, B) SUFFOLK, AND C) YORKSHIRE.

finds, plus some coinage, and a ceramic assemblage containing a high proportion of imported pottery, mostly from northern France. Gardiner (*ibid.*) interprets the settlement as a seasonal fishing and salt-making community, also acting as a small port for cross-Channel traffic. Therefore, it would appear clear that there were a number of trading sites in the east of Kent, around the Isle of Thanet, and Canterbury, with the addition of at least one other on the south coast.

Superficially, Yorkshire would appear similar to Suffolk in that, at York, the excavations at Fishergate produced evidence characteristic of an emporium, including a large assemblage of imported ceramics, and a wide range of craftworking (Kemp 1996). However, when the coinage from the site is compared to an average pattern of coin loss produced for Yorkshire as a whole, it would appear that by the middle of the eighth century, it has peaked, and begun to decline, and only picks up again in the early ninth century (Naylor, forthcoming b). Indeed, the archaeology points towards an early eighth century phase of intense activity, followed by possible abandonment for a period between the late eighth century and early ninth century, (Kemp 1996), but I would suggest this decline has its roots in the years around c.750. With this in mind, it is not surprising to find other sites in the area which may have been involved in international trade, especially given Yorkshire's long coastline. Alongside this evidence, the earliest datable middle Saxon finds from South Newbald are from the middle of the eighth century, precisely the point when numismatic evidence indicates the emporium at York began to decline. The evidence for Yorkshire certainly implies some form of re-focusing of activity towards the regional economy, but it would also appear that this includes a long-distance component (Naylor forthcoming a).

Comparatively, it would appear, on current evidence, that there is a certain amount of regional variation in eastern England with regard to potential direct access to international trade. It should be made clear, however, that not all of these numismatically rich sites need be considered the location of markets. I would suggest that only some were, such as perhaps South Newbald (Yorkshire), Whitby Abbey (Yorkshire), and Reculver (Kent), but others were most likely settlements whose coin using population either travelled to these markets, or to coastal beach markets. This should not surprise us- a high number of finds may simply indicate a population involved in monetized exchange, and, after all, we do not consider every individual find made as a potential market! However, the differentiation between the sites interpreted as markets and ordinary settlements, which, in many cases, has to be based chiefly on the large coinage and metalwork assemblages found by metal-detectorists, is fraught with difficulty.

Recently, though, the potential nature of the 'productive site' has been discussed. Leahy (2000, 72-80) compared some of the most productive sites in East Yorkshire (South Newbald, Thwing, Cottam, Whitby, and 'near York'), concluding that South Newbald and Whitby Abbey showed marked differences to the others, and produced a good argument for the possibility of a Minster at the former. Also, taking account of their locations on routes of communication, or transportation, and the high number of finds, especially of coinage, he considered that both Whitby and South Newbald had a market component. The likely involvement of Whitby Abbey in networks of international trade has long been accepted, given the finds of imported pottery, and large numbers of coins, and the conclusion for South Newbald is one that I have also made (Naylor, forthcoming a). The possible nature of the other sites in East Yorkshire, though, remains uncertain. In this case it may be instructive to examine the patterns of coin loss at each site, and compare them to a calculated regional mean, as I have done elsewhere (Naylor, in prep). This has shown that continuous coin loss similar to the regional background is only seen at very few sites: York/ Fishergate, Kilham, near Malton site 1, South Newbald, and Whitby. Three of the other four productive sites in Yorkshire show no correlation with the calculated regional average, and the other (North Ferriby) has produced no finds later than c.750. From this, it has been argued that those sites showing a continuous average coin loss were more likely to be the sites where monetized exchange regularly took place, than sites whose coin loss was irregular, although it must be recognized that this does not rule out such exchange at the other sites from time to time. (*ibid.*).

In Kent, analysis of patterns of coin loss has also produced some interesting results, with four of the six productive sites, Canterbury, near Canterbury, Hollingbourne, and Reculver following the calculated regional pattern (*ibid.*). There is also a period of prolonged coin loss at Richborough, from c.750-c.855, but it does not closely resemble the Kent as a whole. If the theory applied to Yorkshire is again applied here, it would imply that two-thirds of the most productive sites in Kent were potential market places, with the additional possibility of one at Richborough, a site ideally positioned at the eastern end of the Wantsum Channel to take advantage of traffic moving through the channel on their way to Fordwich, or even London.

Therefore, having identified that a number of sites in eastern England could easily gain direct access to networks of international trade, and tentatively identifying a proportion of these as actual market sites, a final discussion must be made regarding the implications these results have for our current models for middle Saxon markets and access to international trade.

As briefly discussed at the beginning of this paper, the dominant theories of the last 20 years have centred around the re-birth of urbanism in northern Europe during the seventh, eighth, and ninth centuries and their role in international, and regional, trading (e.g. Hodges 1989a). Such ideas were based on the theory that early medieval

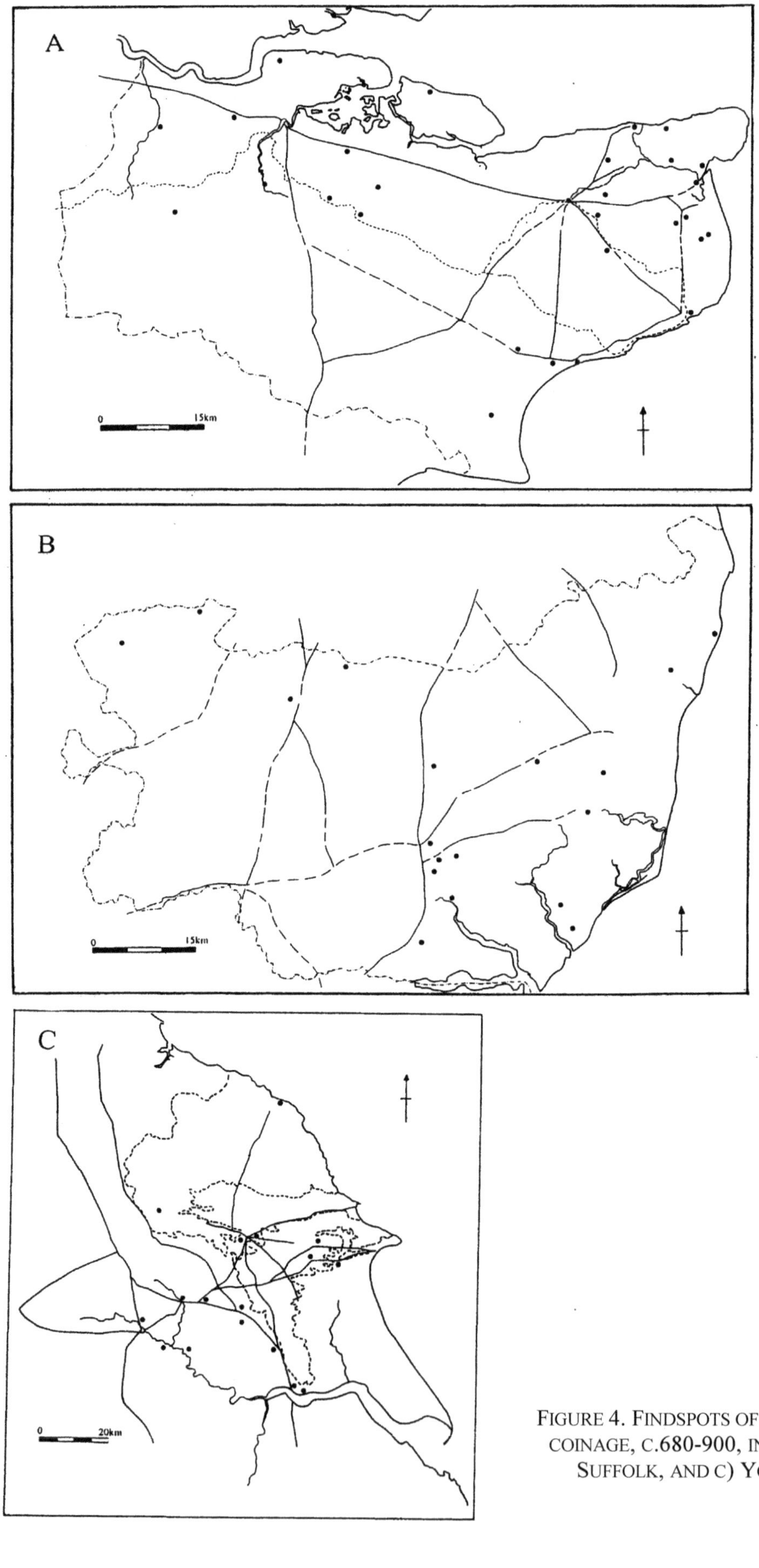

FIGURE 4. FINDSPOTS OF CONTINENTAL COINAGE, C.680-900, IN A) KENT, B) SUFFOLK, AND C) YORKSHIRE.

trade may have been founded on the needs of royalty to procure prestige goods with which to buy alliances and maintain power, and as this increased during the later seventh century, the urban emporia were created as a means of tightly controlling that trade (*ibid.*). However, with increasing archaeological evidence from the emporia suggesting that their populations were as involved in production as international trade, new models have been proposed. Hodges (2000, 76-89), although still advocating an overall monopolistic elite control, now prefers to see emporia as regional centres of production which were also trading internationally as a subsidiary activity. Hinton (1996, 100) has suggested that royal interest in the emporia may have been more directed towards the collection of tolls on trading than anything else, an exercise likely to have raised large revenues.

Such advances in our understanding of the potential economic and political functions of emporia, mean that discussions of productive sites as inland markets no longer conflicts with those regarding the urban emporia. Both Leahy (2000), on East Yorkshire (see above), and Ulmscneider's (2000) examination of productive sites in Lincolnshire, have emphasised their role in regional trade. Ulmschneider (*ibid.,* 66-72) notes their locations often in close proximity to important crossing points of rivers, boundaries, and land routes, such as Roman roads. She suggests that the wealth of these sites may be due to their exploitation of surrounding land, in the form of agriculture, and the use of natural resources, including wood and ores, and the trade in surpluses of these commodities. Newman (1999), as discussed above, has argued along similar lines suggesting that the productive sites of Suffolk complemented the role of Ipswich, perhaps helping to integrate the emporium into the regional economy.

The archaeology of production and consumption has recently been considered by Blinkhorn (1999), and he has argued that the increase in international trade during the early eighth century was accompanied by a flourishing of internal economic networks, with rural sites producing rising amounts of goods and surplus, which could be used to provision the emporia. Such change in rural areas is, he suggests, visible archaeologically. Citing a number of settlements spanning the period from the early to middle Saxon which have been excavated in eastern England, Blinkhorn (*ibid.*, 14-16) charts the changes in these sites from unenclosed, dispersed settlements, operating a broadly based subsistence economy, to sites where intensive specialized agricultural production appears to have taken place. This is important as it highlights that the foundation of the large emporia was matched by changes in at least some rural communities. Furthermore, specialist rural sites would need to trade for those things which they did not produce themselves, creating this boom in internal trade (*ibid.*, 20; Hodges 1989a, 144). Combined with the evidence from the productive sites, it would appear that the first 50 years of the eighth century represent a real change in the internal economies of eastern England.

The additional results presented in this paper do not contradict this other recent research but, I think, provide further possibilities for the role of the 'productive site'. I would agree that they are most definitely regionally important places, and my assertion that they also had the capacity to be directly involved in the networks of international trade only adds to this. Indeed, with the exception of a single site on the River Trent, all of the sites used in Ulmschneider's study of Lincolnshire (Ulmschneider 2000, 64), which have produced more than six coin finds, are within the theoretical limit of c.15km of the coast. Therefore, in the area from the Tees to the Wash, in Suffolk, and in Kent, the vast majority of the most productive sites for coinage are all located close enough to the coast for direct access to international trade. Also, in Yorkshire and Lincolnshire at least, many of these are c.5-15km inland, and as such, may have been positioned to be able to integrate the networks of regional and international trade.

Conclusion

In conclusion, I will attempt to answer the question posed in the title of this paper: has the archaeological study of the early medieval economy in Anglo-Saxon England led to an over-emphasis on urban sites, and namely the emporia? In part, I would argue that yes, urban sites been given a somewhat higher profile then they perhaps deserve. I have demonstrated in this paper that it was most likely not only the emporia which accessed international networks of trade, but also small coastal settlements, such as *Sandtun* (Kent), and inland productive sites, such as South Newbald (Yorkshire). It is here that a few caveats should, perhaps, be made. The archaeology of the emporia does show them to be somewhat different to any other settlements of the period. Although imported materials, pottery, stone, glass, for example, have been found at rural sites, such as Brandon (Suffolk), or Wharram Percy (Yorkshire) (Carr *et al* 1988; Milne and Richards 1992*)*, they still do not compare to the massive assemblage, especially of Continental pottery that has been found at Ipswich, Hamwic, London or York. Also, emporia were huge, covering many times the area of any rural settlement of the period, and, as such, must have been highly important places, the nature and function of which are still a matter of major debate (e.g. Hodges 2000; Scull 1997). It is interesting to note, in this respect, the high number of very productive sites in Yorkshire (where the York emporia may not have flourished post-c.750), Kent, and Lincolnshire, compared to Suffolk with its massive emporium. This need not suggest that the economies functioned differently. On a long coastline, such as that of Kent or Yorkshire, the regulation of trade, and its resultant tolls, may have been more efficiently undertaken through a network of smaller sites than attempting to channel everything through a single port.

Overall, the identification of the productive site, and certainly their possibilities regarding regional and international trade is proving to be important, and the potential they represent to aiding our understanding of society and economy in middle Saxon England, especially if they are investigated archaeologically, is enormous.

Acknowledgements

I would like to thank Birley Fund (University of Durham), for their contribution which enabled me to attend the EAA Sixth Annual Meeting, in Lisbon, September 2000, and Dr. Mark Gardiner for kindly allowing me access to the report for the excavations at Sandtun (Kent).

Bibliography

Anderton, M. (ed.)1999, *Anglo-Saxon Trading Centres: beyond the emporia*, Glasgow, Cruithne Press.

Astill, G. 1985, *Archaeology, economics and early Medieval Europe*, "Oxford Journal of Archaeology" 4(2), 215-231.

Blinkhorn, P. 1999, Of cabbages and kings: production, trade, and consumption in middle-Saxon England, in Anderton, M. (ed.), *Anglo-Saxon Trading Centres: beyond the emporia*, Glasgow, Cruithne Press, 4-23.

Bosner, M. 1997, *Fifteen years of coin finds from productive sites*, "The Yorkshire Numismatist" 3, 39-45.

Britnell, R. H. 1993, *The Commercialisation of English Society, 1000-1500* (2nd edition), Manchester, Manchester University Press.

Carr, R. D., Tester, A. & Murphy, P. 1988, *The Middle Saxon settlement at Staunch Meadow, Brandon*, "Antiquity" 62, 371-377.

Fenwick, V. 1984, *Insula de Burgh: excavations at Burrow Hill, Butley, Suffolk 1978-1981*, "Anglo-Saxon Studies in Archaeology and History" 3, 35-54.

Gardiner, M. forthcoming, *Continental Trade and non-urban ports in Mid-Anglo-Saxon England: excavations at Sandtun, West Hythe, Kent*, "Archaeological Journal" 158.

Hinton, D. A. 1996, *The Gold, Silver, and Other Non-ferrous Alloy Objects from Hamwic, and the Non-ferrous Metalworking Evidence*, Southampton Finds 2, Stroud, Sutton.

Hodges, R. 1989a, *Dark Age Economics: the origins of towns and trade, AD600-1000* (2nd edition.), London, Duckworth.

Hodges, R. 1989b, *The Anglo-Saxon Achievement: archaeology and the beginnings of English society*, London, Duckworth.

Hodges, R. 2000, *Trade and Towns in the Age of Charlemagne*, London, Duckworth.

Kelly, S. 1992, *Trading privileges from eight-century England*, "Early Medieval Europe" 1(1), 3-28.

Kemp, R. L. 1996, *Anglian Settlement at 46-54 Fishergate*, The Archaeology of York AY7/1, York, Council for British Archaeology.

Leahy, K. 2000, Middle Anglo-Saxon metalwork from South Newbald and the 'productive site' phenomenon in Yorkshire, in Geake, H. & Kenny, J. (eds.), *Early Deira: archaeological studies of the East Riding in the fourth to ninth centuries AD*, Oxford, Oxbow Books, 51-82.

Metcalf, D. M. 1984, Twenty-five notes on sceatta finds, in Hill, D. & Metcalf, D. M. (eds.), *Sceattas in England and on the Continent,* British Archaeological Reports, British Series 128, Oxford, 193-205.

Metcalf, D. M. 1988, Monetary expansion and recession: interpreting the distribution-patterns of seventh and eighth century coins, in Casey, J. & Reece, R. (eds.), *Coins and the Archaeologist*, London, Seaby, 230-253.

Metcalf, D. M. 1998, The Monetary Economy of Ninth Century England South of the Humber: a topographical analysis, in Blackburn, M. A. S. & D. N Dumville (eds.), *Kings. Currencies and Alliances: History and coinage of southern England in the ninth century*, Woodbridge, The Boydell Press, 167-197.

Milne, G. and Richards J. D. 1992, *Wharram, a study of settlement on the Yorkshire Wolds, volume VII: two Anglo-Saxon buildings and associated finds,* York, York University Archaeological Publications 9.

Naylor, J. D. forthcoming a, 2001, *York and its Region in the Eighth and Ninth Centuries AD: an archaeological study*, "Oxford Journal of Archaeology" 20(1).

Naylor, J. D. forthcoming b, The circulation of Anglo-Saxon coinage in Yorkshire, c.650-c.900, in Blinkhorn, P & Cumberpatch, C. (eds.), *The Chiming of Crack'd Bells*, Oxford, Oxbow.

Naylor, J. D. in prep, *Urban-hinterland relationships in eastern England, c.650-c.900.*

Newman, J. 1999, Wics, trade and the hinterlands- the Ipswich region, in Anderton, M. (ed.), *Anglo-Saxon Trading Centres: beyond the emporia*, Glasgow, Cruithne Press, 32-47.

Pagan, H. 1986, Coinage in southern England, 796-874, in Blackburn, M.A.S. (ed.). *Anglo-Saxon monetary history: essays in memory of Michael Dolley*, Leicester, Leicester University Press, 45-65.

Scull, C. 1997, Urban Centres in Pre-Viking England?, in Hines, J. (ed.), *The Anglo-Saxons from the Migration Period to the Eighth Century- an ethnographic perspective*, Woodbridge, The Boydell Press, 269-298.

Ulmschneider, K. 2000, *Settlement, economy, and the 'productive' site: Middle Anglo-Saxon Lincolnshire AD 650-780*, "Medieval Archaeology" 44, 53-79.

Wade, K. 1993, The urbanisation of East Anglia: the Ipswich perspective, in Gardiner, J. (ed.) *Flatlands and Wetlands: current themes in East Anglian archaeology*, East Anglian Archaeology 50, 144-151.

Wilkinson, T. 1994, *The Structure and Dynamics of Dry Farming States in Upper Mesopotamia*, "Current Anthropology" 35(5), 483-505.

A Modern Experiment in 16-17th Century Celestial Navigation at Sea: The Mariner's Astrolabe and Cross-staff

M. J. Beach and D. E. Atkinson

Abstract
Sixteenth Century navigators such as Bartholomew Dias and Vasco de Gama demonstrated competent blue water navigational ability using the mariner's astrolabe and cross-staff. In evaluating many antiquated arts and sciences and their associated tools, we often face the risk of under-appreciating the skill and understanding required to use the tools effectively.

For a modern experiment, the authors have manufactured a mariner's astrolabe in the likeness of the Portuguese astrolabe in Dundee, Scotland and a contemporary cross-staff. Using modern declination tables for the sun and stars, these instruments were employed in a trans-Atlantic Trade Wind crossing from San Sebastian, Canary Islands to the Caribbean in November 2000.

An understanding of how the instruments were used was researched to determine the effectiveness of the mariner's astrolabe and cross-staff for sighting the sun, moon, and stars. Subsequently, the instruments were compared to a modern sextant, a Global Positioning System (GPS), and different levels of ability between different users were tested. This presentation focuses on the construction of the instruments and the results of the experiment during the trans-Atlantic voyage.

Introduction

Navigation at sea may be understood in two ways: coastal navigation and blue-water navigation (Bauer, 1995). Coastal navigation or *pilotage* refers to navigation within sight of a landmass or through lead-line soundings (Cotter, 1968). Blue water navigation depends on celestial bodies for determining position without the benefit of any land or bottom reference. Although a brief explanation of latitude and longitude proves necessary, this paper focuses elsewhere. The following experiment analyses early instruments used to navigate in blue water environments in the sixteenth and seventeenth centuries.

Elements of Navigation

In finding position at sea, two basic elements exist: parallels of latitude and meridians of longitude. Today we understand a parallel of latitude as a circular belt around the earth parallel to the equator. Latitude is 0° at the equator increasing to 90° north and south of it. This phenomenon was understood this way as early as the sixteenth century (Bourne, 1574; Garcia, 1587). A meridian of longitude is a straight line between the North Pole and the South Pole crossing the equator at right angles, and moving east or west of a datum line. The datum or prime meridian used today runs through Greenwich, England. Hence, the meridian passing through the Royal Observatory in Greenwich represents 0° longitude[1]. Prior to this arrangement, many prime meridians had been established depending on where people lived. Therefore, a prime meridian ran through Paris for the French, through Madrid for the Spanish, and through Lisbon for the Portuguese, to name a few (Cotter, 1968).

When describing a vessel's position at sea, one uses the present latitude and longitude relative to these prime parallels of degree: the equator and Greenwich respectively. The determination of the latitude and longitude was, and still is, made by observing calculated movements of celestial bodies: the sun, moon, and stars. This proved difficult for many centuries, but through determined scientific and nautical advances along the way, the riddle of finding position at sea was answered.

For early blue water navigators, latitude proved much easier to discover than longitude. North of the equator, measuring the height of the North Star[2] will provide one's latitude with only very slight alteration (Bauer, 1995). Longitude proved much more elusive. Until the invention of John Harrison's H4 chronometer, longitude was mainly assessed by a process called dead reckoning (Waters, 1978). Dead reckoning relies on a constant knowledge of a vessels heading and speed over time. The distance covered each hour may then be logged on a chart. However, this does not effectively consider various environmental influences such as current and wind effects. Therefore, it was impossible for early navigators to know exactly what their speed over the ground actually could have been; they would only have been aware of their speed and heading through the water.[3]

A Brief History of Celestial Navigation

The initial use of celestial bodies in navigation proves difficult to date. Ancient Arab navigators employed a celestial device called a *kamal*[4]. The kamal consisted of a wood block held at no more than an arms length employing a knotted string held taut in the teeth of the user. When the block fit between the pole star and the

[1] The prime meridian in Greenwich was internationally established as 0° longitude in the nineteenth century (Cotter, 1968).
[2] Synonymous names include Polaris, Stella Maris, and the Pole Star.
[3] Magnetic variation plays a crucial role in reading a ship's compass today as well as in the 16th Century. It is not the intention of this paper to explain magnetic variation or deviation in ship's compasses.
[4] The Arabic translation of kamal means, "guide" (Bauer, 1995).

horizon, the observer could discern his latitude, relative to that of his destination (Bauer, 1995). Evidence indicates that fifteenth century sailors from the Iberian Peninsula used some form of astronomical method for navigating far from land (Waters, 1978). The indication of this knowledge hints at a rich and useful past in the art of navigation both nautical and terrestrial. The basis of their celestial education, which was grounded in general astronomy and not at first intended for navigation at sea, certainly ranges back far longer. Indeed references can be found in Homer's Odyssey (cited in Cotter, 1968). Biblical references appear to describe and date various navigating staffs known as a Jacob's Staff or *baculus Jacob* (Bryuns, 1994)[5]. Thus it may be argued that sailors like Odysseus had used astronomy in maritime navigation long ago in the Mediterranean and elsewhere.

Prior to the sixteenth century, Prince Henry the Navigator (1394-1460) had supported sea voyages of discovery down the west coast of Africa. These voyages were longer and consequently more ambitious, which necessitated the development of improved navigation at sea. The initial development seems to have been the first edition quadrant, which was used to run down latitude by use the North Star, possibly in tandem with the other known ports and their references such as the Star for Lisbon (Anderson, 1972). The early quadrant, not to be confused with the Hadley's reflecting quadrant or the Davis quadrant, was another type of instrument used in land surveying and by astronomers (Hill, 1958). The primary purpose of the quadrant was to measure angles used in measuring distances and heights or altitudes on land and not necessarily at sea. The quadrant was a wooden quarter circle equipped with two sighting vanes and a plumb line to indicate degrees. This instrument predates the astrolabe and must have been terribly frustrating in true nautical applications.

The most important development to come from the early voyages of discovery was the realization that while the North Star was suitable, it was only approximately in the direction of the earth's axis. Consequently, correction tables were introduced for the North Star, north of the equator, and the constellation of the Southern Cross for sailors south of the equator (Anderson, 1972). The other, more important progression at this time proved the invention of solar declination tables in *The Regiment of the Sun*. King John II of Portugal petitioned the solar tables through an established commission in 1484. They were tested in 1485 and served to enable mariners to measure position during the day (Cotter, 1968). Armed with these theories, navigators would press through several instrumental refinements into and ultimately beyond the pursuit of precise longitude measurements, resulting finally in the Board of Longitude's establishment in the eighteenth century (Forbes, 1974).

[5] The reference is from Englishman Thomas Hood (1590) pointing to Genesis 32:10. However, historians have been noted to accept a description dating to 1382 by Jewish philosopher and scientist Levi ben Gerson (cited in Bruyns, 1994).

Thus, the most important mathematical development in the introduction of navigational science in the sixteenth and seventeenth centuries must have been the skill of any navigator to find his position not only by the North Star, but just as efficiently with the more complicated measurement of the sun (Waters, 1958). The next development would take place in a practical and instrumental area, the development of the mariner's astrolabe.

In 1488, Bartholomew Dias, voyaging from the South Atlantic, rounded the Cape of Good Hope and recorded his vessel's position using a mariner's astrolabe and cross-staff. His observations provided the basic route for Vasco de Gama to follow ten years later coming and going to the Indies (Waters, 1978). Based on that information, we can conclude that they at least knew how to use the astrolabe *effectively*, and that in practice it was a useful instrument if used correctly. Nevertheless, the astrolabe became more obsolete after the seventeenth century in favour of presumably more accurate and arguably easier instruments such as the wooden back-staff and/or the Davis quadrant invented in the late sixteenth century. Another instrument still used in all probability for its accuracy and ease of use, was the ever improving cross-staff or fore-staff originally used at sea in Western Europe by the Portuguese by 1514 (Waters, 1976).

The Trade-Wind Crossing

To conduct an experiment into early navigation, it made sense to select a route that may have been sailed by mariners of the time. In this case, the route selected was the westbound journey from the Canary Islands, notably San Sebastian, to the Caribbean region. San Sebastian proves an interesting point of departure because Columbus topped his water tanks and attended mass there before departing for several of his exploratory voyages using the same route in the fifteenth century.

This route extends roughly 2400 nautical miles over open ocean and would therefore require a time period of several weeks to accomplish on a modern sailing vessel. The experiment took place on a 41-foot sloop rigged vessel, which would be equipped with modern means of navigation to ensure control over the reproduction instruments. In addition, a modern sextant would be used to measure modern celestial techniques.

The experiment observed the following intentions:

- Accurately reproduce a sixteenth century mariner's astrolabe.
- Accurately reproduce a contemporary cross-staff.
- Learn how to use the instruments from contemporary instructions.
- Use the instruments consistently in a trans-Atlantic crossing.
- Evaluate the effectiveness of the instruments.

- Compare the results to modern instruments and technology.
- Explore the ability of different users under the same conditions.
- Evaluate the effects of environmental, physical, and human influences on the ability to navigate on the open ocean.
- Explore the notion of navigation as an acquired art.

The Reproduction of the Navigational Devices

The construction of the *Sundancer* astrolabe

In order to make an accurate reproduction of a sixteenth century mariner's astrolabe, an existing astrolabe had to be used as a model. The oldest dated astrolabe known to exist, the Palermo astrolabe, dates to 1540 (Waters, 1966: 24). This made a perfect sample for a model in sixteenth century navigation, but this astrolabe managed to disappear after World War II[6]. The second oldest known astrolabe dates to 1555 and remains in excellent condition. Known as the Dundee astrolabe, it is most likely of Portuguese design (ibid: 25-26)[7]. The reproduction astrolabe would strive to resemble this astrolabe in every way. The specifications of the Dundee astrolabe are as follows:

Date of Manufacture: 1555
Composition: Solid smoothed brass, with some lead repair in the ring
Diameter: 222mm
Scale: 90-0-90; zenith
Distance between pinnules: 60mm
Thickness: 16mm
Weight: 2900gm
Origin of Manufacture: Portuguese
Current Location: Museums and Art Galleries Dept., Dundee, Scotland
Inscriptions: 1555, Andrew Smyton 1688, x (on alidade) Portuguese stamp of manufacture

Attempting an exact replica proved excessive for this experiment so long as the reproduction was accurate in every other way. A well-established British clockmaker with experience in brass work, Mr. Robert Bray at Sinclair Harding, Ltd., manufactured the reproduction astrolabe. Though original astrolabes were likely cast in brass, this astrolabe would be made differently and using modern equipment. The process of manufacture was as follows[8]:

1. The general specifications of the Dundee astrolabe were used for scale and a like design was created using a computer aided design (CAD) package at Sinclair Harding, Ltd.
2. A sheet of naval brass 5/8" (~16mm) thick was marked with pilot holes for the shaping.
3. A pillar drill then drilled the holes and the profile of the astrolabe was cut out on a computer numerical controlled (CNC) wire erosion machine.
4. The alidade and the pinnules were made using the same techniques.
5. The pinnules were then hard soldered in position on the alidade and drilled in line with the centre hole.

The graduation of the *Sundancer* astrolabe

In graduating the newly made *Sundancer* astrolabe, several factors were considered. Typically, there were two ways in which an astrolabe may be graduated. The Dundee astrolabe is calibrated with **90** degrees marked on either side of the mid line and **0** degrees marked at the top (**90-0-90**). This would indicate a desire on the part of the navigator to determine a zenith height. Without going into the mathematical formulae, the height of the celestial body is the goal of the measurement. Other astrolabes were graduated in the opposite manner, 0-90-0, and some were cross-graduated in both manners.[9] For our purposes here, the *Sundancer* astrolabe would be marked without numbers, so it could be used in either fashion (See figure 1).

Having no method to refer to in order to calibrate the instrument, the horizontal line was simply made in the center of the astrolabe. The universal joint at the top is made after the examination of several universal rings atop astrolabes from different periods as well as the locking mechanism on the back of the alidade.

The construction of the *Sundancer* cross-Staff

The *Sundancer* cross-staff depicts the ultimate in the evolution of the mariners cross-staff in that it has four crossbars and four separate scales for each crossbar. Until the end of the 16th Century only one side of the staff was graduated and consequently only used one crossbar (Stimson, 1977). This meant that on the whole the staff needed to be longer so as to maintain an easily readable scale. The introduction of the shorter mariners cross-staff meant that separate scales and crossbars were required to avoid inaccurate readings. By the 1580s it became normal practice to use shorter staffs with three scales and three crossbars, each representing the various stages of

[6] The Palermo astrolabe bears strong resemblance to one illustrated in another work referenced in this text: Dr. Diego Garcia de Palacio, 1587: *Instucción náutica para navigar*.

[7] The Dundee astrolabe is located at the Museums and Art Galleries Department, Dundee, Scotland.

[8] Personal communication with Robert Bray, Sinclair Harding, LTD. For more information please see: http://www.sinclairharding.co.uk

[9] For example, the Elias Allen astrolabe (1616) located at the University of St. Andrews is graduated 0-90-0. It also remains the only astrolabe of definite English origin (Wray, 1984: 7).

FIGURE 1.THE *SUNDANCER* ASTROLABE. NOTICE THE DOT OF SUNSHINE ON THE LOWER PINNULE, WHICH IS LINED UP JUST NEXT TO THE HOLE USED FOR ALIGNING THE SIGHT.

the 0 to 90 degree scale. Indeed, by the 1650's all four sides of the staff were graduated and the Dutch navigator Abraham de Graaf first described this development (Bruyns, 1994).

The construction of the *Sundancer* cross-staff was based on the descriptions of the mariners cross-staff given by historical and contemporary sources (Garcia, 1587; Bruyns, 1994; Stimson, 1977)[10]. The staff employed four crossbars or vanes in conjunction with the method described by de Graaf indicated above. Two cross-staffs were constructed and are both identical in their component parts.

The staff was constructed from a square dowel 32 inches (80cm) in length and roughly ¾ inch (1.875cm) in width. Four crossbars were constructed these being 20 inches (50cm), 10 inches (25cm), 5 inches (12.5cm), and 2.5 inches (6.25cm). The varying lengths enabled a more accurate reading given the varying altitude of the object being sighted, these being 60 to 90 degrees (20 inch), 20 to 60 degrees (10 inch), 10 to 30 degrees (5 inch) and 5 to 16 degrees (2.5 inch). Each crossbar was 4 ¾ inch (10.45 cm) wide and ½ inch (1.1 cm) in thickness. All component parts were constructed from Scots Pine[11] and treated with a protective wood stain (See figure 2).

The graduation of the *Sundancer* cross-staff

There are two principal techniques that can be used to graduate the staff, these being the geometric method and the mathematical or trigonometric method. Both methods

[10] Another reference used was the website by Richard A. Paselk, Humboldt State University: http://www.humboldt.edu/~rap1/EarlySciInstSite/Instruments/X-Staff/X-staff.html

[11] Cross-staffs were constructed from a variety of materials including ebony, ivory, boxwood, pear wood and brass for decorative fixtures (Bruyns, 1994). The *Sundancer* cross-staff was constructed using scots pine due to the scarcity and expense of the aforementioned materials.

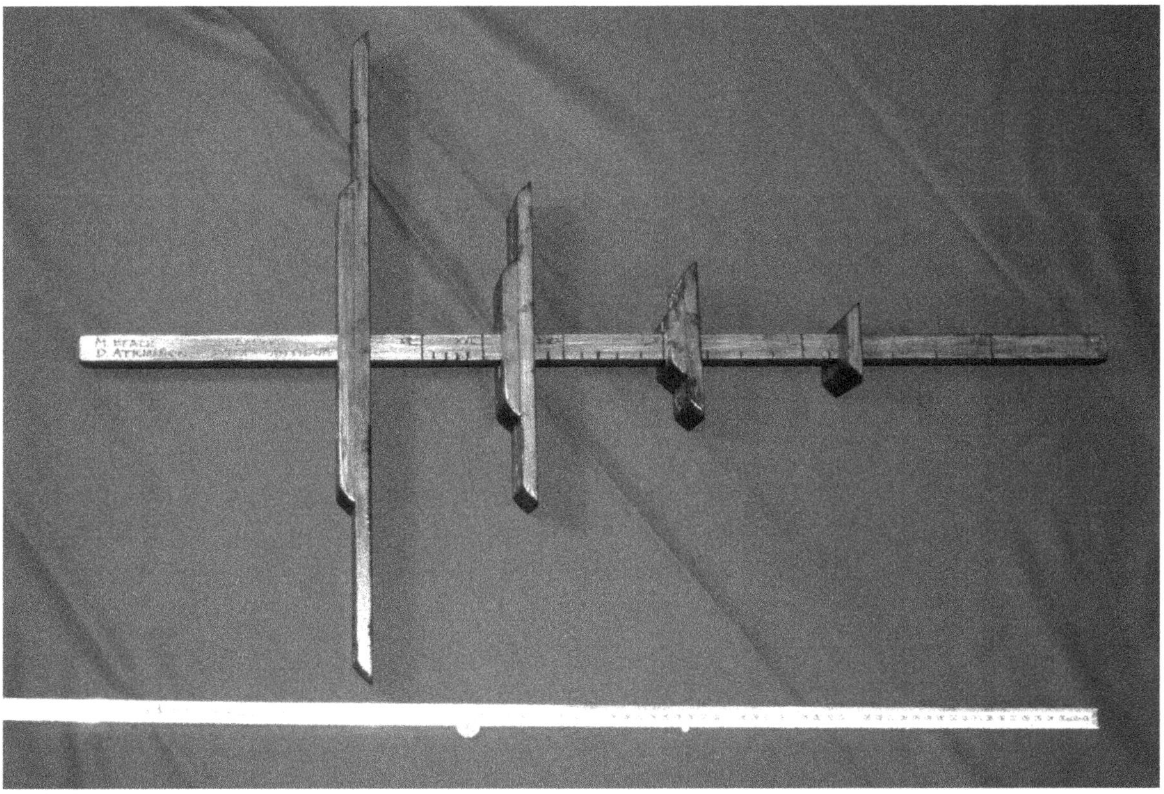

FIGURE 2. THE COMPLETED *SUNDANCER* CROSS-STAFF. ALL FOUR CROSS BARS OR VANES ARE FEATURED IN THIS PICTURE, THOUGH ONLY ONE IS USED AT A TIME.

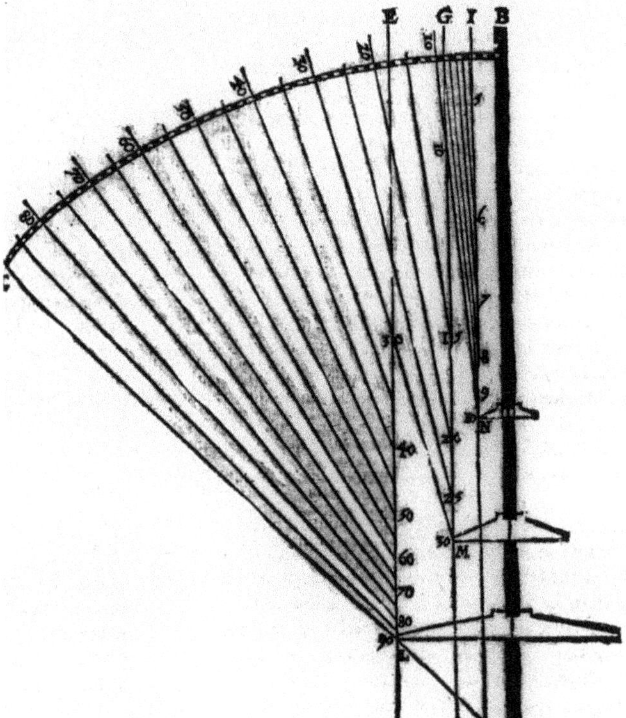

FIGURE 3. A CONTEMPORARY 16TH CENTURY DIAGRAM FOR GRADUATING A CROSS-STAFF USING THE GEOMETRIC METHOD. (CITED FROM BRUYNS, 1994)

allow the accurate graduation of the staff allowing degrees of angle to be measured when sighting an object. A third method can be employed after the graduation of the first scale and this simply involves the copying of the scale from one staff to another. Although both methods were included in navigation manuals right into the 18th century, the mathematical method was preferred, being more reliable and less prone to lapses of accuracy. Despite this, it was decided to graduate the *Sundancer* cross-staff using the geometrical method. The method used by the authors was based on historical descriptions such as those given by L.J Waghenaer in 1584 and P. Goos in 1662 (cited in Bruyns, 1994). (See figure 3)

In order to construct the scales using the geometrical method, a construction diagram had to be made. This consisted of a flat board or card and was rectangular in shape. The long side of the card became the 'baseline' for the staff that was equal in length and the short side became the length equal to the half distance of the longest crossbar or vane. The bottom left corner of the card represented the eye end of the staff and acted as the centre of concentric circles of which the radius equalled half the length of the intended crossbars. From this point an arch of 45 degrees was established from the baseline. The established arch was then divided into 90 equal parts equating to angles of ½ degrees. For every ½ degree, straight lines were drawn from the centre and then lines equal to the half-length of each vane were drawn in a line parallel to the baseline. The blank staff was then placed on these parallels and where each ½ degree intersected the surface of the staff a mark was made with a knife. In most cases the length of the vanes were established prior to the marking of the parallel lines on the board, as this negated differences in the length of the vanes at the end of the process (See figure 4). The *Sundancer* cross-staff was graduated using the method outlined above. The scale was marked using pencil and then chiseled using a ¼ inch carpenter's chisel. Attention was given to the optimum width of each individual scale so as to minimize discrepancies in the accuracy of the scale, but also to create a large enough scale to allow for easy translation. The staff was then tested making an observation of the North Star from St Andrews in Fife, Scotland. The test observation gave a precise reading of 56.25 degrees of latitude.

Learning to use the instruments

Learning to use the instruments from contemporary sources was a key element to making the experiment work. The primary texts referenced for this purpose were William Bourne (1574) and Dr. Diego García de Palacio (1587).

In the introduction to William Bourne's *A Regiment for the Sea* (1574), the point is made that understanding mathematics and reading books was not commonplace in sixteenth century Britain. Navigational and mathematical sciences and instruments were essentially reserved for military engineers. A simple sailor was not educated well enough to read and comprehend contemporary books dealing with navigation or the calculating of other mathematical angles such as artillery fire. Therefore, English sailors took comfort in the lead line and memorized landmarks rather than with charts or navigational instruments to measure celestial heights (Bourne, 1574). William Bourne's book then became the first legitimate attempt to demystify the science of mathematics for the average English sailor or gunner with whom he would have had contact. While describing himself (c. 1573) he wrote:

FIGURE 4. THE SCALE AND MARKING OF THE *SUNDANCER* CROSS-STAFF USING THE GEOMETRIC METHOD. NOTICE THE FOUR PARALLEL LINES TO THE RULER FOR EACH CROSSBAR.

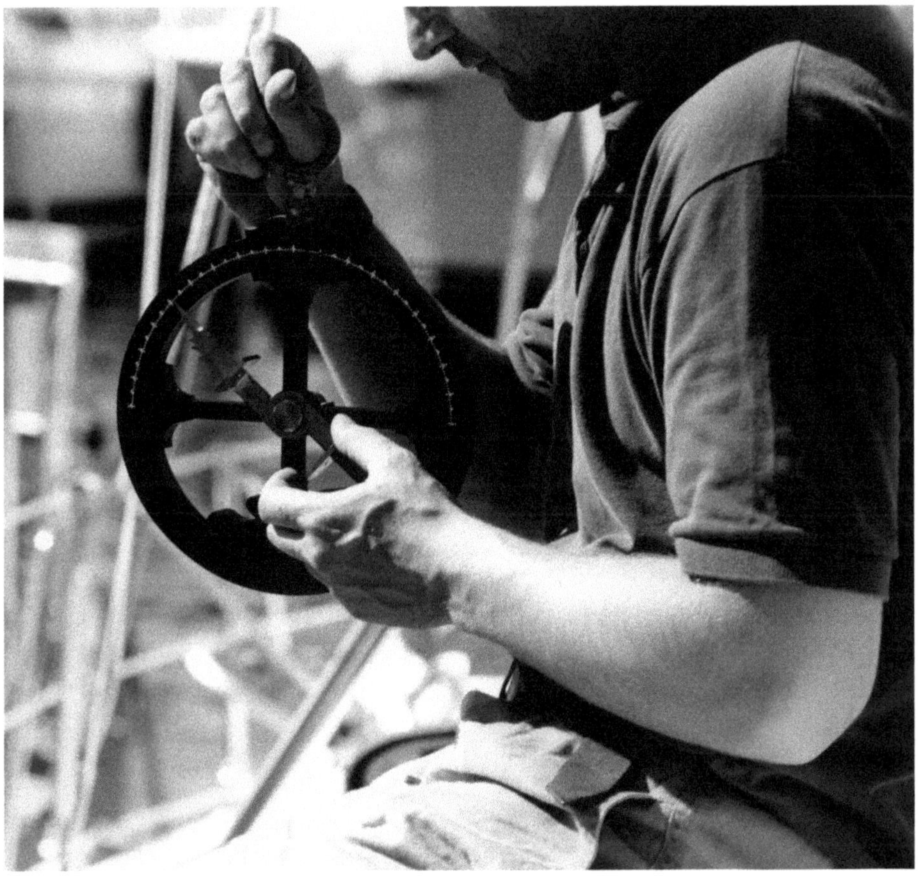

FIGURE 5. THE CO-AUTHOR USES THE ASTROLABE AT SEA TO TAKE A MERIDIAN SOLAR SIGHTING.

'To ye gentell reder: I praye you hold me excused, I being altogether ignorante, lacking the capacitye bothe of knowledge and experience have taken upon me…to open any scyence' (Bourne, 1574: xiii).

He was a simple, practical man who took it upon himself to teach the sailors and local townspeople what they could not learn otherwise. He was at times forced to rely on instruments and references from other countries, which were accelerating their own navigational pursuits. Since navigational ability was one that relied on other skills such as mathematics and astronomy, good navigators could be hard to come by. Many examples of how to use the astrolabe effectively appear in the text and he uses the graduation of 0-90-0.

Chapter 4 of Diego García's work is entitled: *The demonstration of the astrolabe for taking the altitude of the sun, and of its use.* This section dedicates itself to describing exactly how to use the astrolabe on a ship. The instructions are as follows:

1. Stand at the base of the main mast, where ship movement will be least.
2. Face the sun directly.
3. Hold the astrolabe by its ring from the second finger of the right hand.
4. Raise the index arm (alidade) of the astrolabe to align the sun until the sun comes through the leaf-sights (pinnules).
5. With the astrolabe thus suspended, one will be able to read the degrees of latitude (Garcia, 1587:39)(See Figure 5).[12]

A series of five rules, with examples and a section filled with questions and explanations follows this instruction until giving way to a section on using the cross-staff. For the cross-staff Garcia instructs:

1. Take up your staff or wand (cross-staff) and rattles (crossbars).
2. Put the extreme end of the staff at the corner of the eye.
3. Draw the rattle out and in until the lower part of the rattle comes to and corresponds to the horizon.
4. Being thus, the upper part of the rattle will be joined with the sun or star, and if it does not reach it, one will extend the said rattle so that the lower part is at the horizon and the upper part is at the sun or star.

[12] Although the instructions in García's work call for suspending the astrolabe with the second finger of the right hand, we found that in practice it proved more effective and easier to manipulate using the thumb.

5. The degrees at the inward face of the vane indicated on the staff will give one the degrees from the horizon to the sun or star.
6. After this, one may calculate the position (García, 1587: 54) (See figure 6).

FIGURE 6. THE CO-AUTHOR USES THE CROSS-STAFF TO TAKE A MERIDIAN SOLAR SIGHTING.

Primarily using these texts, methods of employment contemporary with the instruments was researched. The only substantial difference would include the tables of declination being used. Every year, new declination tables are produced by official organizations such as the British Admiralty. During the sixteenth century, they also would have had tables made with much more elementary knowledge of the celestial bodies, but they would have been fairly decent. German almanacs, for example, were commonly employed. Columbus used one such German almanac as early as 1504 to predict a lunar eclipse on the north coast of Jamaica (Smith, 1996: 40). For this experiment, we would simply use modern declination tables in the Nautical Almanac 2000.

Methodology

The most common method of obtaining position during the day proves sighting the sun as it makes a meridian passage or high noon. At this point in any given latitude, the sun will reach its highest altitude (Bauer, 1995). This is achieved by taking measurements well before the expected high noon. Taking observations with an instrument, a navigator notices an increasing altitude in the sun followed by a constant height and finally a decrease. With solar declination tables, one may then calculate the latitude from the highest altitude attained on the given day. This process is called sighting the meridian passage of the sun (Bauer, 1995).[13]

The most common method of obtaining position during the night in the northern hemisphere proves sighting the North Star. As noted previously, the height of the North Star should closely indicate the latitude with very little, if any, adjustment. Additionally, several easily sighted stars and planets were noted to sight as well as the moon. In addition to solar tables, the Nautical Almanac includes lunar, planetary, and star declination tables. The same instruments are used for nocturnal sightings under the same instructions as the daylight sightings.

The instruments used to take this observation on this voyage were:

- The *Sundancer* astrolabe
- The *Sundancer* cross-staff
- A modern sextant[14]

In addition to the instruments, the position was subsequently logged using a global positioning system (GPS). Therefore, at the conclusion of a sighting, four positions would be recorded: three for each instrument and one for the GPS. The GPS would serve as our control.

In using modern declination tables and chronometers, it is possible to determine longitude as well as latitude. However, during the sixteenth century before the invention of the chronometer, longitude would have been ascertained using dead reckoning. On this experiment, we would be able to make full position determinations, but would also make use of dead reckoning to illustrate how accurate this may or may not have been.
A rigid daily methodology was established to insure control over the sightings with the different instruments. To this end, the daily procedure required each author to undertake the following:

- Sight the sun on its meridian passage with each of the three manual instruments.
- Sight the astrolabe on two scales: 0-90-0 and 90-0-90
- Record the sightings independently.
- Calculate position for each sighting with each instrument.
- Record the position of each instrument on the chart.
- Take note of the weather conditions (e.g. cloud

[13] As noted earlier, it is not the intention of this paper to discuss mathematical details of calculating positioning. For more information on this process see Bauer (1995) or any endorsed instructional book on celestial navigation.
[14] The sextant used for this experiment was a 1999 vintage Celestaire ASTRA IIIb, with an index error of 1.0 degree.

coverage, wind-speed and direction, precipitation)

- Take note of the sea conditions (e.g. wave height, stability of vessel relative to waves)
- Record any other notable observations.[15]

In keeping a detailed record of the above regimen, it was hoped that insights would be developed into not only the instruments themselves, but general early blue water navigation as well.

Results

In undertaking a journey such as the Atlantic trade wind crossing, it is important to understand that many underlying influences play upon the blue water navigator. The effectiveness of the individual and the accuracy of his instruments represent only a portion of the criteria that affect the realization of the overall goal, quite simply to be able to determine where you are and where you want to go. In this experiment it became perfectly apparent that the results were a mélange of many important variables and these can be categorized into three main groups:

1. *Natural Phenomena*; weather, sea state, clarity of object to be sighted.

2. *Physical Phenomena*; accuracy of instruments used, calibration (instrumental), type of vessel, stability, type of sailing.

3. *Human Phenomena*; competence of user, accuracy of sightings by user, type and time of observations, calculations.

The above criteria form the basis for the discussion on the results below. The results have been split into three main sections representing the different stages of the crossing:

1. The period prior to entering the North East trade winds
2. The mid Atlantic phase
3. Approaches to the Caribbean

The experiment was conducted during a trans-Atlantic crossing lasting 20 days. Of these 20 days only two were unsuitable for any navigational observations. On the whole the weather was quite favourable. Before examining the results it is perhaps pertinent to point out that the correct time of year for the east to west passage across the Atlantic is in November. Consequently, the dominant point of sail is downwind. It is not inconceivable to suggest that early blue water navigators would have been privy to this knowledge thereby utilizing the favourable weather for square rigged vessels and subsequently the more effective use of navigational instruments. In this experiment it became clear that the astrolabe must be regarded as an instrument used in conjunction with the cross-staff and not as a forerunner. The following results are given in relation to the position recorded by the GPS.

The period prior to entering the North East trade winds (22 to 28 November)

During the initial period, the weather and sea conditions were highly favourable in general. Gentle to moderate swells (2-3m) coupled with light winds (8-12 kts.) and clear skies enabled optimum conditions for observations. Inconsistency in the results of both the astrolabe and the cross-staff proved interesting. Throughout this period, the average discrepancy from the latitude position of the GPS was 77.2 nautical miles (nm) for the cross-staff and 54.4 nm for the astrolabe. This suggested that despite the favourable environmental conditions, the unfamiliarity of the users with the instruments and the situation meant that accurate and competent observations were not always achieved. What is significant however is that in a number of cases the difference in the results of sightings between the cross-staff and astrolabe was minimal but the overall difference compared to the GPS was high. For example, on 27 November the difference between the instruments was only 4 nm, but 64 nm and 60 nm respectively from the GPS position. The results obtained with the astrolabe during daylight sightings were also seen to be marginally better than those of the cross-staff during this period. This can be partly explained by the more favourable conditions, but it may also suggest that the astrolabe is not necessarily a difficult instrument to use, especially in the hands of the novice. Nocturnal sightings made on the same day were attempted with all three instruments. Although the astrolabe proved ineffective at night, the cross-staff was as efficient as the sextant. Despite clear skies and gentle swell, the absence of the moon resulted in an obscure horizon. As a result, the cross-staff proved slightly more efficient than the sextant. This phenomenon was also noted by Stimson (1977: 19). What became clear during this period is that despite favourable conditions, the readings from the instruments were on the whole sporadic. The human and physical influences played a key role in this area.

The Mid-Atlantic Phase (29 November to 05 December)

After experiencing slightly overcast conditions initially, the weather became generally fair. The sea state during this period, however, tended towards bigger waves (2-3m), larger swells (8-10m), and a subsequently less stable vessel. Despite this change, improved accuracy in the sightings indicated that an increase in user proficiency took place. Another influencing factor at this time proved the point of sail. As the trade winds settled in, the deployment of an efficient downwind rig provided a more stable platform for taking observations. On the first day of this period, 29 November, the noon observation with the cross-staff matched the GPS position nearly exactly.

[15] As the trip progressed, it became easier to use the instruments for reasons of adaptability and individual aptitude. More on this appears in the discussion section.

The astrolabe was a mere 14 nm off. Another change that took place under human elements was user confidence. Despite gradually intensifying sea conditions, the accuracy of the observations fluctuated. On a particularly challenging day, 02 December, results were no closer than 100 nm for the astrolabe yet only 45 nm for the cross-staff. It became tempting to theorize that in the presence of advanced swell, the usefulness of the astrolabe decreased while the cross-staff and sextant proved more accurate. However, results show that the instruments were more closely matched than first thought. This indicated that the cross-staff was simply less frustrating to use than the astrolabe during this time. It was also noted that the crossbars used on the cross-staff during the noon sightings did not differ a great deal on account of our latitude in general (16-26°N). On account of the increased awkwardness of the larger vane, it was suggested that the sole employment of that crossbar gave a potentially less precise reading than the next smaller one. The average deviation for the cross-staff was 34.3 nm and the astrolabe was 42.4 nm. Compared to the average discrepancies in the first period there is a notable increase in accuracy, which is indicative of increased user ability.

Approaches to the Caribbean (06 to 12 December)

Sea conditions varied greatly as we made our approach towards land. On 06 December, winds were from the East Southeast (ESE) at 5-10 kts accompanied by a gentle swell (1-2m). By comparison, 10 December brought winds in excess of 30kts ESE, swells up to 5 meters, and intermittent squall activity. The results were accordingly diverse. On two separate days, it was impossible to take accurate sightings due to overcast skies that blocked the sun entirely. The average readings between the astrolabe and cross-staff were consistently close and closer than before. Once again it was suggested that increased user ability played a key role in this outcome. A misreading of the scale on the cross-staff hinted at the massive potential of human error. This led to the realization that one user was consistently more accurate than the other over the duration of the whole trip. On 08 December, an experiment in dead reckoning over a 24-hour period revealed a 21-mile deviation. As noted earlier, night sightings were effective with the cross-staff and sextant. Although it was barely possible to sight a bright moon with the astrolabe, it was apparent that no one could have ever intended to navigate successfully at night using such a device. Therefore, it was suggested that the instruments must have been intended to work in tandem. The average deviation between the instruments and the GPS for this period proved the most accurate. The deviation for the astrolabe was 35.14 nm and 44.4 nm for the cross-staff. The closeness between the two instruments proves striking.

The following tables indicate average deviations in nautical miles for meridian solar sightings between the cross-staff and the mariner's astrolabe relative to the GPS.

The period prior to entering the North East trade winds

Date	Cross-staff	Astrolabe 0-90-0
24 Nov.	80	53
25 Nov.	60	120
26 Nov.	120	15
27 Nov.	60	64
28 Nov.	66	20
AVERAGE	**77.2 nm**	**54.4 nm**

The Mid-Atlantic Phase

Date	Cross-staff	Astrolabe 0-90-0
29 Nov.	0	14
30 Nov.	26.5	26
01 Dec.	23	12
02 Dec.	77	60
03 Dec.	45	100
AVERAGE	**34.3 nm**	**42.4 nm**

Approaches to the Caribbean

Date	Cross-staff	Astrolabe 0-90-0
04 Dec.	55	14
05 Dec.	40	40
06 Dec.	21	20
07 Dec.	55	44
08 Dec.	86	66
09 Dec.	48	48
11 Dec.	06	14
AVERAGE	**44.4 nm**	**35.14 nm**

These results reveal a number of interesting points. Averages often became exaggerated by one day of poor sightings. This is directly relative to the solar visibility and the sea state. Keeping good balance on a heaving vessel, while not impossible for an experienced sailor/navigator by any means, does occasionally have impacts on the clarity of a reading. It is important to note that the errant sightings are not exponentially bad and improve immediately with the settling of environmental conditions. Finally, the success of each instrument improves from the beginning to the end, notably the astrolabe. This powerfully implies that navigating is a skill or specialized trade that is honed over time, not nearly as dependant upon the instruments as upon the navigators themselves. The employed declination tables and mathematical methods would also prove more crucial than the instruments themselves.

Discussion

In 1576, Viceroy Enríquez indicated to Phillip II of Spain that most of the good navigators (pilots) had died and that it was impossible to find competent new ones with any experience (Schurz, 1985: 209). Other contemporary reports indicated that positions of authority aboard ships were given to relatives or servants in order to make space (ibid: 166). This would also have created more personal room to carry trade goods as higher ranked officers were allowed to carry more belongings. Viceroy Valesco referred to the "ancient custom" used by his predecessors of appointing all their officers. Though all positions offered to such under-qualified officers would have suffered greatly, the position of pilot, not excluded here, would have probably suffered the most. Not only did the welfare of the whole ship depend on the navigator's job, but also the speed of the journey and the safety of the vessel were greatly challenged. This practice eventually led to severe disputes and was discontinued (ibid: 167).[16]

Considering the results from this recent experiment, it became empirically apparent that celestial navigation with any instrument is an art. As an art, it must be honed through learning, experience, and familiarity. The tables above clearly show the observations improved dramatically. For instance, in the case of the cross-staff the average deviation improved by 42.9 nm. The astrolabe improved from a deviation of 54.4 nm to 35.14nm, which is a correction of 19.26 nm. Notions that the cross-staff was favourable to the astrolabe and possibly an improvement are certainly not based on these results. In our own case, we felt the cross-staff was more user-friendly, but that is not supported in the findings. It did prove less frustrating in heaving seas than the astrolabe and perhaps that is why the general impression that it is preferable exists. To an inexperienced navigator with an astrolabe and a cross-staff to choose from, the cross-staff would appear easier to use. We include ourselves in that category, much as an appointed or inexperienced contemporary navigator would have been. Based on the tables above, the astrolabe certainly shows more inclination towards becoming more refined and closer to 0nm deviation than the cross-staff. The only real difference being that the astrolabe was totally ineffective at night.[17]

Natural Phenomena

In an Atlantic voyage away from large landmasses, sea conditions are simply different. In some cases this is a good thing, because larger swells often impose less of a threat as they sometimes move more slowly and spread out more than coastal swells. As a result, a ship often sails up one wave and down into a trough making for a rather pleasant ride in comparison to short choppy seas. As we approached the islands of the Caribbean for instance, we experienced a change in sea state relative to the mid-Atlantic condition. This relates into physical phenomena as well. The point of sail relative to these waves greatly alters the ride. Therefore, an experienced sailor and navigator would cope with conditions on varying seas infinitely better than one with little practical experience. The impact on navigation would certainly be apparent.

The most complicating of natural phenomena proves the weather or clarity of the skies. As we experienced on several days, if an object is not visible and you consequently fail to sight it, then you have no updated knowledge of your position. This applies to all forms of sighting (solar, lunar, star) with any manual instrument (astrolabe, cross-staff, sextant). Precipitation played no significant role in sighting our position.

Physical Phenomena

The first element of physical phenomena must be the instruments themselves. Firstly, one must question whether or not the instruments are accurate, and if they need calibration. A modern sextant is very rarely in exact alignment (Bauer, 1995). Therefore, it must be inspected and an index error assessed. When taking a sight, the index error is then applied to correct the sight. This proves much easier and safer than attempting to calibrate the sextant while sailing, even if the index error is as high a 5 degrees or more.[18] Therefore, it would be foolhardy to expect an astrolabe or cross-staff made according to sixteenth century standards to have no degree of index error. While a specific index error was never assigned to the *Sundancer* astrolabe and cross-staff, certainly this could be done through familiarity and further experimentation. It is the opinion of these authors that a proficient contemporary navigator would have been aware of some corrective error, though no written text supports this. Nor is it a surprise that no written materials exist since this would not have been a universal adjustment; rather, it would have been one element of a navigator's complex or artistic ability to navigate.

The point of sail that a vessel is on greatly helps determine stability. Sailing with the trade winds, our ship sailed on a downwind rig most of the time. A square-rigged vessel sails best in this situation or slightly off-wind (broad reach). On a modern vessel, this may create some increased roll. Our ship was a winged-keel as opposed to a deep keel sailboat, which accentuated the roll further. As various other sails were employed, stability changed from time to time.[19] We found that as the tip progressed, the rolling and pitching of the vessel became less and less of a navigational factor. This supports the notion that experience in navigation at sea is second to none.

[16] One account tells of a Spanish shipwreck in which most of the passengers survived. Upon reaching a near shore, they promptly hanged the navigator for landing them in their predicament (Schurz, 1985).

[17] As noted above in the results, we attempted several lunar sightings with the astrolabe, which were an experiment in tolerance and yielded no positive results.

[18] A degree of latitude is equal to 60 nm. Therefore an index error of 5 degrees (300nm) would indeed prove terribly significant.

[19] The most effective point of sail for our best stability was our off-wind rig employing our largest sail: the chute.

Human Phenomena

The most compelling facet of human phenomena in navigation at sea proves the competence of each individual user. Consistently noticeable differences in readings took place on this trip between the two authors. For example, author one dependably supplied a low reading, while author two tended to produce a higher result. Bearing in mind that an error of 1 degree means sixty 60nm, this could translate into success or failure. In our cases the readings became closer throughout the journey. This indicates that the learning curve for each author was inevitably taking place, just not in the same way. Another element of human phenomena appeared as author one bore a preference for the astrolabe over the cross-staff and therefore applied more patience towards its employment. This is neither right nor wrong, but it does show how human elements play a big role in manual navigation.

The time and type of observations played a key role. By sighting the meridian passage of the sun everyday it was possible, we were able to establish a pattern of results. Therefore, in knowing which way we headed, our speed, and our last position, it was possible to sense when readings were going to be off before making any calculations at all. This also proves a function of human awareness, inherent in some and not in others. One must also then take into the account the fastidiousness with which the sightings and the subsequent mathematical calculations were treated. It proves very easy to make minute errors in such calculations. For this reason, *inter alia*, certain people will simply make better navigators than others.

Summary

In an experiment of any kind, one seeks to answer a question or satisfy a curiosity. The findings often produce insight into a far greater range of questioning. In this case, the curiosity was the effectiveness of sixteenth century navigational instruments at sea as they might have been used. The mariner's astrolabe was reproduced with modern machinery in a clock-makers workshop, and the cross-staff was fashioned more crudely in a university workshop by the authors using hand tools. In the end, one thing became very apparent: the instruments themselves could never be to blame for the success or failure of an ocean crossing. The objective of an astrolabe, a cross-staff, a back-staff, a quadrant, and a sextant to name a few, has always been the same. They all seek to create an angle by which to measure the height of a celestial body no matter if it is the sun, moon, stars or planets. By making this 30-60-90 degree triangle one can work out the height of the body in question. The mariner's astrolabe and the cross-staff were quite adequate for this purpose, especially used in tandem. What happened to this information next was the most challenging, in this experiment as well as for early navigators.

We used the process of dead reckoning on occasion over extended periods to test the legitimacy of such navigation at sea. In the most compelling instance, careful readings produced a simple deviation of 15 miles over a 24-hour period. In making a crossing of this type, the real concern is latitude, more so than longitude. After all, one knows the destination lies Westward; you only need to know how far from the equator you want to be when you get there. Latitude proved the easiest sight to obtain with the right declination tables for the sun and using the North Star. This would always have been the case.

Having said as much as possible about the many different influences that play upon the blue water navigator, the conclusion proves simply that navigation is a learned and acquired art. Abilities to deal with the various external influences (e.g. natural, physical, and human) mark the difference between good and bad navigation. The type of instrument employed, while certainly very different in terms of precision and convenience, is far from the most influencing factor.

Acknowledgements

This experiment would not have been possible without the generosity of Raymond Holliday. Mr. Holliday not only permitted the use of his vessel, but also was responsible for introducing M. J. Beach to Bob Bray of Sinclair Harding, Ltd. who manufactured the astrolabe. Exceptional thanks must be extended to Mr. Bray, who donated countless hours of his time and resources to making the *SUNDANCER* astrolabe as authentic as possible. Dr. Robert Prescott, director of the Scottish Institute of Maritime Studies (SIMS), University of St. Andrews offered advice on background resources, editing, and extended workspace for the photographing of the instruments as well as for their construction. Mr. Steve Liscoe of the Archaeological Diving Unit (ADU) assisted greatly in the fabrication of the cross-staff, cutting wood and loaning tools. We must also thank Dr. Colin Martin for his contributions in editing. Other thanks are presented to Nadia David.

A final thankful sentiment must be offered to mother nature for delivering the persistent trade winds and to a special lady, without whom we never could have completed this experiment: *S/V SUNDANCER*.

Bibliography

Anderson, R. 1972 *The Mariner's Astrolabe*. Edinburgh.

Bauer, B. 1995 *The Sextant Handbook: adjustment, repair, use and history*. Maine.

Bourne, W. 1574 *A regiment for the Sea*. Hakluyt Society reprint, 1963. Cambridge.

Bruyns, W. 1994 *The Cross-Staff: History and Development of a Navigational Instrument*. Zutphen.

Cotter, C. 1983 *A History of the Navigator's Sextant.* Glasgow.

Cotter, C. 1968 *A History of Nautical Astronomy*. London.

Forbes, E. 1974 *The Birth of Navigational Science*. Maritime Monographs and Reports **10**

García de Palacio, Diego. *Instucción náutica para navigar*. Mexico City:

Pedro Ocharte, 1587. Translated by J. Bankston, Bisbee, Arizona, 1986.

H.M. Nautical Almanac Office and United States Naval Observatory. *The Nautical Almanac 2000*.

Hill, H. and Paget-Tomlinson, E. 1958 *Instruments of Navigation*. London.

Schurz, W. 1985 *The Manila Galleon*. New York.

Smith. R. 1996 The Voyages of Columbus: The Search For His Ships. i*n* Bass, G. (ed.) *Ships and Shipwrecks of the Americas*, 33-44. London.

Stimson, A. and Daniel, C. 1977 *The Cross Staff, Historical Development and Modern Use*. London.

Waters, D. 1978 *Science and Techniques of Navigation in the Renaissance*, Maritime Monographs & Reports **19**

Waters, D. 1976 *The Planispheric Astrolabe*. Greenwich.

Waters, D. 1966 *The Sea- or Mariner's Astrolabe*. Coimbra.

Waters, D. 1958 *The Art of Navigation in England in Elizabethan and Early Stuart Times*. London.

Wray, E. 1984 *Historical Scientific Instruments*. St. Andrews.

Preliminary assessment of the daily life on board an Iberian ship from the beginning of the 17th century (Terceira, Açores)

Catarina Garcia

Abstract
The archipelago of the Azores falls at a convenient spot for a stopover, not only for vessels travelling between Europe and the Americas but also for those plying between Europe and Asia. Therefore the large number of wrecks discovered in recent years is not surprising. The construction of a breakwater in Agra on Terceira called for the excavation of several wrecks lying in the bay. The wreck Agra D is discussed in this paper. It dates from the beginning of the 17th century. Inside its hull several artefacts were discovered, providing information about daily life on board and the ship's cargo.

Introduction

During the western European maritime expansion of the 15th through to the 17th centuries, the Azores became an obligatory stop for ships in transit to and from Europe. Its privileged location on the North Atlantic, amidst prime trade winds, enabled a sustained connection between old Europe, the African coast, the Far East and the New World. This base made the opening of markets in Guinea and Mina possible, allowing for a profitable trade which financed the systematic exploration of the African coast. During the 16th century, after the discovery of India and the Americas, the Azores began to play a key role in the Portuguese and Spanish trade routes, consolidating the Iberian Empires. The archipelago was also used in the maritime expeditions of other European countries as an obligatory stop (Memmes 1998, 721).

As early as the 16th century, the Azores were the object of the expanding ambitions of the northern Europeans, who looked upon this port of call as a means of reaching over sea territories and as an important way of obtaining more valuable and exotic cargos. The dynamic of the transatlantic trade and the problems of privateering and piracy brought greater importance to the 16th and 17th centuries. In fact, the regularity of the homebound stop from the Indian and American sea routes, usually the island Terceira, promoted trade, smuggling and war.

The Azores played an important role base for the Western voyages of discovery. Later considered the door to the Portuguese and Spanish Americas (Martins 1989, 1498), the bay of Angra do Heroísmo was the repair and supply centre of the returning ships from Mexico, Central America, the African coast and India. The most important

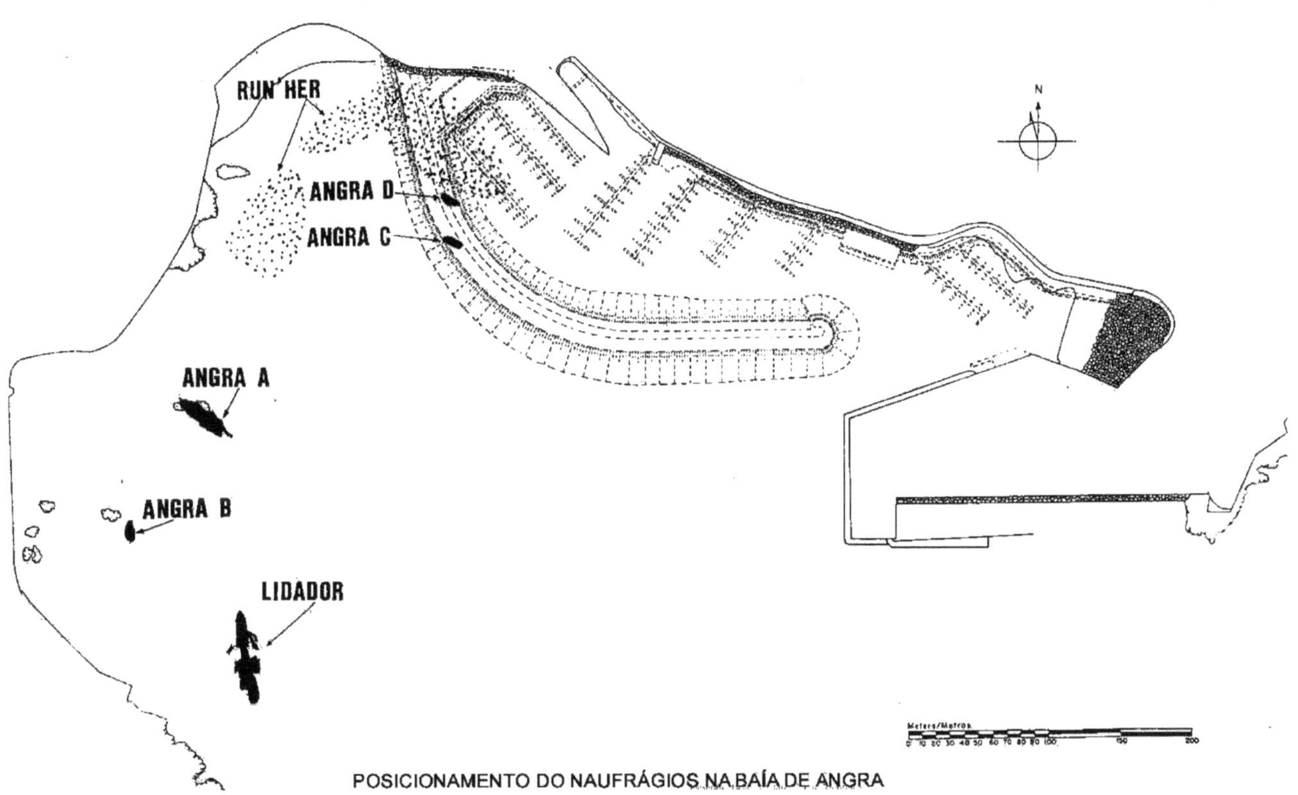

FIGURE 1. SHIPWRECKS FOUND IN ANGRA BAY. DRAWING – KEVIN CRISMAN AND PAULO MONTEIRO

events in the city centred around the arrival the arrival of the fleets, which usually arrived twice a year and stayed in the harbour of Angra do Heroísmo for periods of up to three months.

The bay, having good anchorage conditions for incoming ships, offered a sheltered harbour from all quadrants, except the southern winds, treacherous winds which give rise to unexpected storms.

Better known as "carpenter wind", these storms caught the ships by surprise, causing many to sink. From the available records, it is known that more than 80 ships sunk in this bay from the 16th century until the present (Figure 1).

In 1996, a marina construction project in the bay of Angra do Heroísmo was initiated, and it became necessary to identify archaeological sites in the construction zone.

A sub-bottom profiler succeeded in identifying the nature of the harbour sediment, but was not effective in locating shipwrecks. Next, a survey using metal detectors was carried out in order to mark possible metal masses with which shipwrecks might be associated. The search zone was divided into strips, then covered by the metal detector; the echoes found were then marked. Later, those echoes were excavated with a water dredge. It was with this method that the remains of two ships, later *called Angra C* and *Angra D* were found.

In December 1996, *Angra C* was the first site found. The hull was found under 1m of sediment, at a depth of 7m, by the echo from the remains of a large copper cauldron. Angra D was located at the end of the survey, in the last days of February 1997, because of an enormous metallic mass. The shipwreck of *Run'Her* was found on top of *Angra D* at about 7m of depth, less than 8m from *Angra C* and about 50m from the city's edge. *Run'Her* belonged to the North American Navy, destined for the Civil War as a blockade runner, which sank on November 5th 1864 due to a error in seamanship. Visible next to this structure were a few timbers covered with sand and extending 10m parallel to the structure of the *Run'Her* (Figure 2).

After the detection of the archaeological remains, found in exact alignment to the future breakwater of the marina, the excavation was requisite. The project of the excavation began thirteen months later, and interrupted prematurely started marina work. The excavation had a three month deadline that was later extend to four. A team of 16 people worked non-stop in order to excavate and remove the artefacts and ship timbers from both sites to a safe place. The timbers of these two hulls are currently located at the bottom of the bay, at about 11m depth, outside the breakwater artefacts are being stored in fresh water tanks awaiting conservation.

The Wreck Stratigraphy

The entire stratigraphy of Angra D can be represented by a sample section; the majority of artefacts were found under and between the ballast stones. Angra D has a

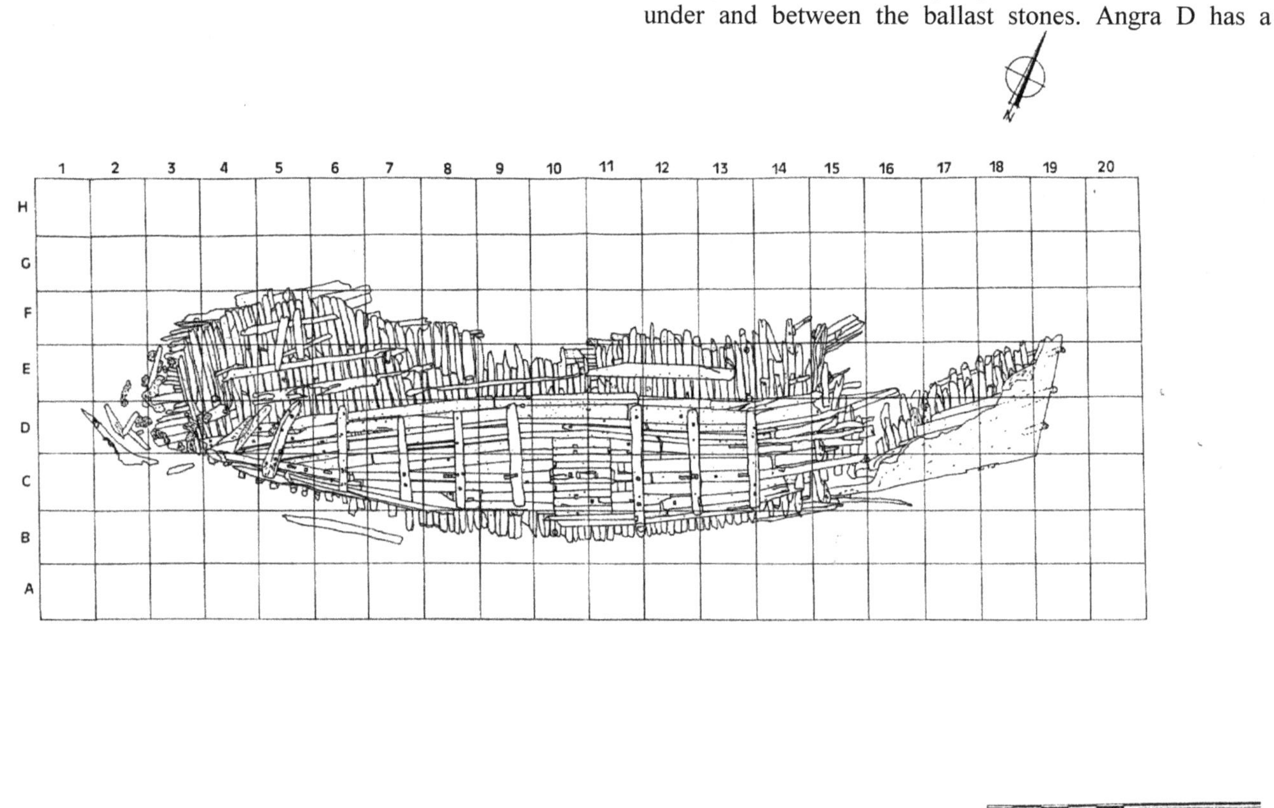

FIGURE 2. PLAN OF *ANGRA D* – DRAWING: CATARINA GARCIA AND ERIK PHANEUF

length of 35m by 9m, situated SW-NE, and was almost completely covered by an 80cm layer of ballast stones; only partial edges of the ship's structure were visible. The first 10cm stratigraphic division between piece 4 and piece 5 (two riders) displayed ceramic fragments, lead bullets, and wood fragments amongst sand and small rocks. In the next 10cm layer, one with no ballast, artefacts and organic material were evident. This thin and rather compact layer was comprised of various materials: organic matter, from which about 90% were remains of wood (between 3cm and over 10cm diameter), insect remains (mainly cockroach eggs with adult insect remains) and bone fragments. The next 30cm contained ballast (20 to 30cm in diameter) mixed with bits of rope and cordage, and some ceramics. In the final level (no deeper than 3cm), there was a thin layer of fine mud covering the internal lining, where some insects were also visible.

Due to the excavation deadline, it was not possible to dig troughs around the hull; thus the artefact settlement pattern outside the hull is unknown. Concerning the material dispersal, there was a grater concentration in squares D4, C10, D8, D11, C18, C16 e D19. D4 corresponds to the bow of the ship, C10, D8 and D11 to the area of the mast step and C19, C16 and D19 to the area of the sternpost.

In the bow, the artefacts settled primarily under the ballast and between the timbers of the ship's structure. Here they consisted of organic materials such as willow, bits of corn cobs and ceramics. Next to hull on piece 61, a bowl 30cm in diameter was recovered. The bowl was in good condition and contained organic matter (insects, corn ears, various seeds and fish bones). Also beside piece 61 were the remains of a mat containing fish bones and a few mouse bones. The largest collection of artefacts was recovered next to piece 1 of the hull, in square D4. Here, the materials were deposited among thick layers of mud, between the timbers of the midship frame. The mud characterizes this area of the hull as the deepest; and having protection from the ballast the artefacts here were well-preserved. Beside piece 72 on D5 what is probably a fragment of a rosary was recovered; it was detected while the hull was being disassembled, in the slime around the frames.

Around the mast step artefacts under the ballast consisted of ceramics, bones, organic matter, seeds, corks, barrel staves, musket bullets, and rope and cordage. These materials were well preserved, especially the bones. A wooden bucket was also recovered here; containing organic matter, it was on its side between rider n.°7 and the mast step, in the slime and ballast. There was a large quantity of bones found near the pump well; they were deposited among the remains of the mast step of the surviving mast, adjacent to several ceramic fragments. The largest proportion of staves and barrels bottoms were located in this area. Some of the quicksilver found in *Angra D* was also found here, concentrated in the pump well.

In the area of the sternpost ceramics were prevalent, namely fragments of olive jars, along with lead strips from the ship's caulking. To starboard the sternpost was in one piece, so the excavation in this area consisted of opening a trench around the sternpost. This freed the stern section for later removal in one piece. The vast majority of the materials appeared progressively around and under the sternpost. On the southern side of hull, the settlement occurred between layers of sand, while on the northern side, materials were deposited in the ballast, in an area where the hull was broken and leaning towards the North.

From the excavation of *Angra D* 786 elements were recorded; some of these were individual pieces and others corresponded to sets of artefacts designated by allotments. Currently much of the artefactual evidence has not been registered, and it is not possible to know exactly how many individual items exist. In this report, some of the more meaningful and representative of the artefact assemblage will be discussed. These artefacts illustrate various aspects of life aboard this ship and the nature of its cargo. It is possible to draw some conclusions about some of these artefacts their function or date, but the majority of these cases, study is in a preliminary phase.

The remains have been divided into different categories; artefacts of the hull, personal possessions, religious items, cargo, those related to food and its preparation, and pests and livestock aboard ship.

Hull Artefacts

In this category, there are several fragments of rope and cordage with different diameters, representing a meaningful sample. As well, a double block ANGD/98-217 (a kind of running rigging which was located outside the hull) was found in the bow area of the ship. Bricks were also found, particularly ANGD/98-220, that may be associated with the kitchen section of the ship. The same type of brick was found in the excavation of *Mauritius* (L'Hour et al. 1989, 181), and they were identified parts of the galley oven.

A bone whistle was found, ANGD/98-673, having a circular shape at the blowing end that becomes more oval in the body. It has grooves along the length from the buccal to the opposite end. Approximately 6.5 cm long, this whistle has a finishing on the end opposite to the blowing area which, due to its grooves, might have attached to another piece. It may have played a key role in shipboard relations (Figure 3).

A complete bucket, ANGD/98-139 was recovered in the area of the mast step, still attached to its transport rope. The bucket is formed by eleven lateral pieces and three bottom pieces. On its sides are traces of concretions, showing the use of metal belts for stability. Boards with hexagonal finishing adjacent to the transport rope, are longer than the other functions, this type of bucket with a long rope was often used to collect sea water for ship.

FIGURE 3. A BONE WHISTLE. PHOTO: CATARINA GARCIA

Personal Possessions

In this category there are several well preserved artefacts that provide clues to life on board this ship in future studies. They are artefacts related to clothing, personal hygiene and adornment. The clothing consists of soles of different shoes as illustrated by samples ANGD/98-166, ANGD/98-481, ANGD/98-797.1, ANGD/98-797.2 and ANGD/98-797.3 are examples of those differences. ANGD/98-797.1, from a small, delicate shoe is narrower than the shape of ANGD/98-797.3, with is notably bigger and has a wider shape, although only part of the heel has been preserved. With ANGD/98-797.2 its shape and dimensions indicate that it may be a fragment from a large boot, but only the front section of the sole was preserved. The leather has not been submitted for analysis, so the leather type is still unknown.

A few pipe fragments were found in *Angra D*. One of them, ANGD/98-436 corresponds to a buccal, and displays wear patterns that may have been caused by erosion and friction against the sediment. No signs of decorations have been found, as only 5 cm of the piece remain.

Along with shoe soles, three bronze buttons have been recovered, ANGD/98-298, ANGD/98-461 and ANGD/98-226. The button ANGD/98-226 has a decoration in the shape of a flower, while ANGD/98-298 and ANGD/98-461 have only the holes through which they would have been sewn to clothing. The small pieces ANGD/98-636.1 and ANGD/98-636.2 are also bronze and, like some pieces found in the excavation of the *Mary Rose*, may have been finials of a shoe-lace (Rule 1982, 199).

A bronze thimble and bronze pins were also found. The thimble ANGD/98-596.1, recovered in square D17, has a round head (about 3 cm in diameter by 3 cm in height). Although it shows some wear and tear, having a hole on one side it is fairly well preserved (Figure 4).

The bronze pins ANGD/98-577 and ANGD/98-706 have spiral heads in two different sizes (3 cm and 5 cm) and are similar to the ones found in the excavation in the northern part of *Mullion Cove*, in a merchant ship of the 17th century (McBride et al. 1974, 135).

FIGURE 4. A BRONZE TIMBLE: PHOTO: CATARINA GARCIA

Used to maintain personal hygiene aboard ship, three wooden combs were found: ANGD/98-666.1, ANGD/98-666.2 and ANGD/98-685. They are of similar dimensions (about 4.5 cm wide) and have thicker teeth on one side than the other (Figure 5).

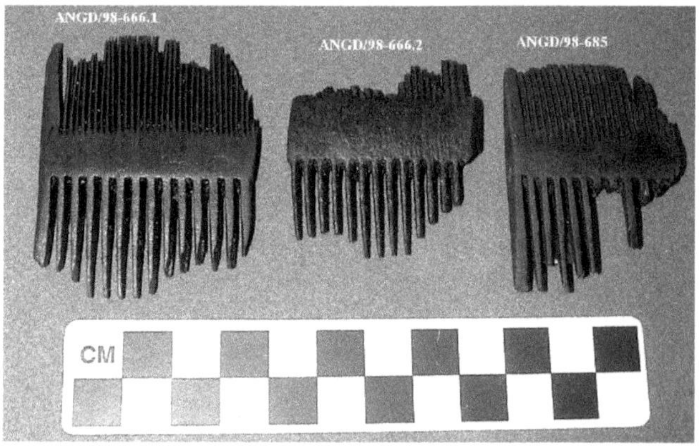

FIGURE 5. THREE WOODEN COMBS. PHOTO CATARINA GARCIA

Beads were recovered, ANGD/98-490 and ANGD/98-426, which could have been necklace beads or rosary beads. ANGD/98-426 is made of bone and has a flat, circular shape with 2.5 cm in diameter and a central hole. ANGD/98-490 is ivory with a spherical shape about 1cm in diameter and a well drilled and defined hole in the centre.

Artefacts related to religion

A piece in sculptured resin has been recovered (ANGD/98-538) with the shape of a human figure. It is a rough figure wearing long garments down to its feet, and may be a religious image. The head is no longer attached to the body, and with such features the gender has not been determined.

A fragment of a rosary (ANGD/98-756) was recovered as the hull was being disassembled. The bronze chain structure still holds seven wooden beads; one of them is concretionary. One of the beads is larger than the others, marking the passage from the *Lord's Prayer* to the *Hail Marys*. In the excavation of the ship *San Diego* a whole rosary made of ivory and gold was found that is very similar in shape to this one (Desroches et al. 1984, 170) (Figure 6).

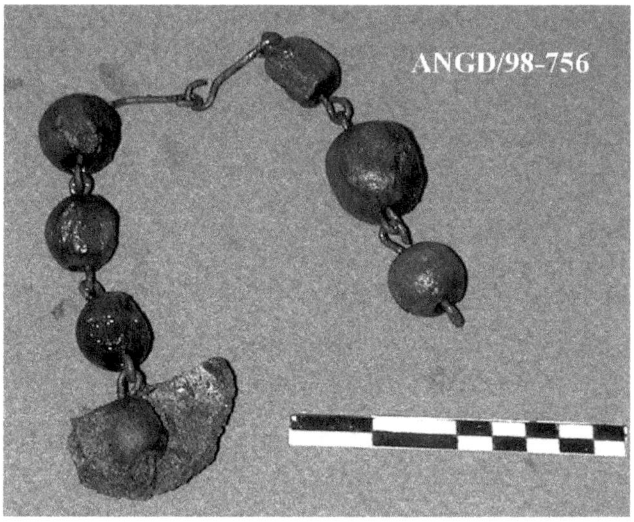

FIGURE 6. FRAGMENT OF ROSARY. PHOTO: CATARINA GARCIA

Miscellaneous artefacts

This category includes some of the unidentified artefacts. The ivory piece ANGD/98-297 (12 cm long) has a conical shape, with an opening on the wider end. Its decoration covers 1 cm near the opening and consists of grooves that envelop the piece along with diagonal grooves (Figure 7).

FIGURE 7. CONTAINER FOR NEEDLES. PHOTO: CATARINA GARCIA

At the open end, there are bits of concretion which may indicate that this piece is the remains of a lid. This piece may have been used as a container for needles, as the interior space is very finely turned. ANGD/98-297 may parallel an object found in the excavation *Amsterdam,* a Dutch Indiaman ship from mid-17th century, where a wooden object with lid having similar dimensions to that from *Angra D* is referred to as a needle-case (Marsden 1974, 94). An object similar in shape and function was also found in the excavation of *Kennemerland* (Preice et al. 1977, 319).

ANGD/98-767 is made of bronze and may have been a cleat, but it is not clear in which context. It is a ring whose ends are linked to another circular piece. ANGD/98-372, about 8 cm long, has at one of the ends a ring which finishes in a progressively thinning screw thread. The bronze piece ANGD/98-707, around 10 cm long, is a piece of bronze without a defined shape, and has not been ascribed to a particular function. Finally, the wooden piece ANGD/98-215, hollow and conic in shape has a preserved 7 cm length. It has not been possible to attribute a particular function to this piece: it may well be only a seed.

Cargo

From the cargo, many fragments of ceramics, corks, staves and barrel bottoms and some quicksilver have been collected. Of the large quantity of ceramics, the vast majority corresponds to olive jars. The fragments are from necks and numerous bellies of these olive jars. The shape of the neck pieces ANGD/98-102 and ANGD/98-170, it may be possible to assign their typology and date. These two pieces have a thick ring-like edge, directly linked to an enlarged body with an egg-shaped tendency, and are covered by a whitish engobe with a grey paste in the nucleus and a reddish one in the extremities. In ANGD/98-102 there is a visible inscription, *HIS,* which is associated to the *Company of Jesus*. Samples of the contents from the piece ANGD/98-170 were collected that have not yet been identified. In comparison to some typologies and dates attributed to this type of containers, there are similarities between these jar necks and those found in the excavations of the *Harry Cox Wreck* (Marken 1994, 61), *Atocha* (Marken 1994, 74), *La Trinidad Valencera* (Martin 1979, 279), *San Martin* and *Rosario* (Smith et al. 1995, 97), all ships that operated at the end of the 16th century or the beginning of the 17th century (Figure 8; 9).

Several corks have been found with varying diameters and thickness, probably belonging to olive jars with different openings and functions. One cork has been recovered with its lead seal still clinging to it, ANGD/98-348; this one probably belonged to a glass bottle. However, neither a glass bottle nor its fragments have been found during the excavation of this hull.

Several staves and barrel bottoms have been found. The study of these pieces is still in a preliminary phase; however, one of the staves shows what could be an inscription, not yet duly studied, and which may provide some clues as to the nature of the ship. Related to the barrels, are remains of the barrel straps and several recovered wedges that were probably used to close the drain holes.

Among the artefacts classified as containers, there is a whole bow. ANGD/98-334, was found next to piece 63 of the hull still containing insects, fish bones, and corn ears. Next to the bowl was found a large mat with a deposit of fish bones.

Quicksilver has also been collected and it is believed that it belonged to the cargo at some point in the ship's life, as it is scattered through the wood of the hull in small quantities.

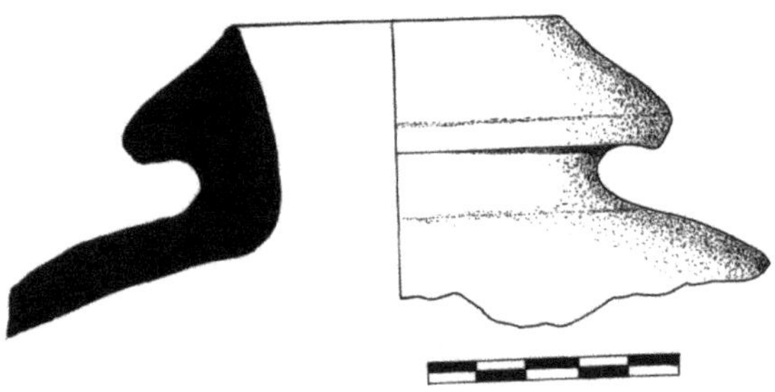

ANGD798-671.1

FIGURE 8. NECK PIECES OF *OLIVE JARS.* DRAWING: CATARINA GARCIA

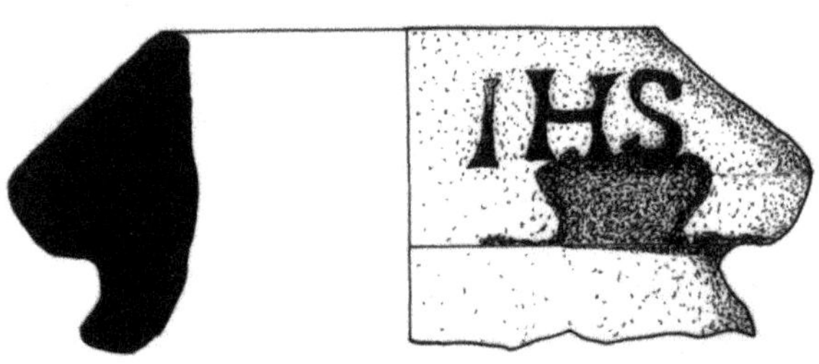

ANGD/98-494

FIGURE 9. NECK PIECES OF *OLIVE JARS.* DRAWING: CATARINA GARCIA

Shipboard Diet

Animal bones, both whole and fragmented, have been found, next to the mast step. They are from goats and pigs, and some of these bones have cut marks. Sample for DNA testing have been sent to the University of the Azores for identification. As well, samples of fish bones are being analysed at the Department of Oceanography of the University of the Azores.

Dried fruits, hazelnuts, unknown nuts, plums, grape seeds have been collected, along with abundant peach and olive pit. From the layers of mud some fragments of corn cobs have also been recovered.

Food Preparation

Some utensils and dishes used in the preparation and consumption of food aboard ship have survived. A wooden spoon has been recovered, ANGD/98-633, well preserved and measuring about 7 cm long by 4 cm wide in the slightly concave bowl; a handle of about 1.5 cm in length is left. Among the ceramics that would have been commonly used aboard the ship, there are fragments of *Majolica,* ANGD/98-219, a white paste with cobalt blue glazing decorated with a light strokes in a darker shade of blue. It appears to be a small dish, similar to some dishes recovered from the ship *La Trinidad Valencera* (Marin 1979, 295).

In analysing the porcelain sherds from Angra D, the only fragment with an identifiable external mark is a bottom fragment from a small bowl, ANGD/98-682.1. That mark dates from the final period of the Ming Dynasty (AD 1522-1644) and is considered a "folk kilns" product (Figure 10).

FIGURE 10. FRAGMENT OF A PORCELAIN SMALL BOWL. PHOTO: CATARINA GARCIA

Two whole porringers have been recovered, ANGD/98-494 and ANGD/98-671.1, having a light brown paste with a straight roundish edge. They are both bowls where fingermarks can be seen on the external walls (Martin 1979, 172), keel with an obtuse angle and ring-shaped foot in stanniferous glazing, probably blackened due to the proximity of iron concretions (Martin 1979, 284). There are similarities between these porringers and those from *Columbia Plain Escudilhas* of the Spanish Fleet of 1588, *Atocha* (Marken et al. 1994, 171), 1622 and *La Trinidad Valencera* (Martin 1979, 173). This may help date *Angra D* as these bowl typologies point to the end of the 16th century or the beginning of 17th (fig 11; 12).

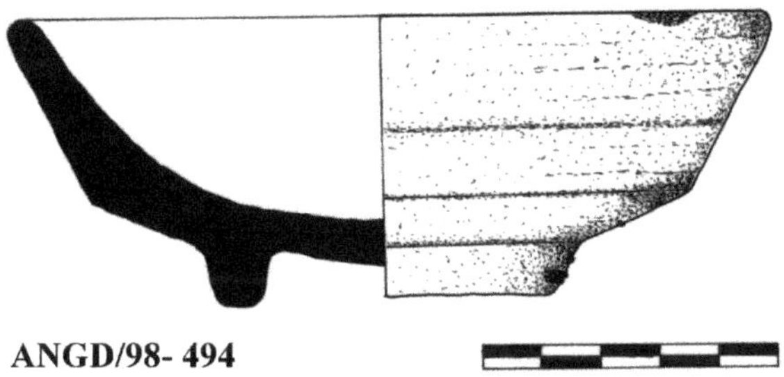

ANGD/98- 494

FIGURE 11. COMPLETE PORRINGER – *ESCUDILHA*. DRAWING: CATARINA GARCIA

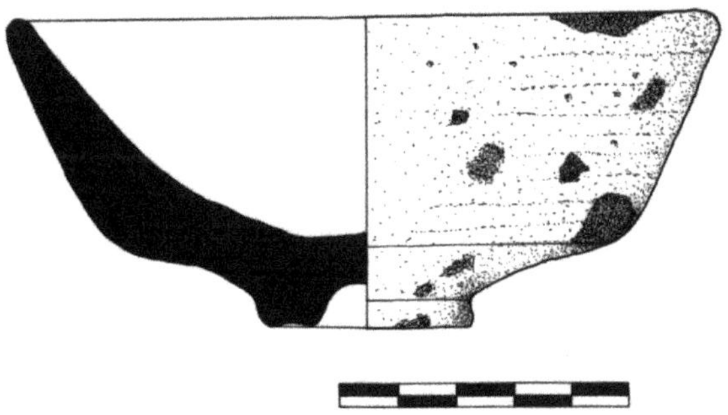

ANGD/98 - 671

FIGURE 12. COMPLETE PORRINGER – *ESCUDILHA*. DRAWING: CATARINA GARCIA

Remains of pests and animals on board

Mouse bones, some, of whole skeletons, were found near areas with fish bones and areas with unidentified insects and cockroaches. A sample of insects from bucket ANGD/98-139 has been sent for analysis. The mouse bones have also been sent for analysis. These analyses are expected to yield species identifications which could indicate the origin of these creatures, and a port of call for the ship in question.

Bibliography

Desroches, J.-P. and Goddio, F. 1984, *El San Diego. Un Tesoro bajo el mar*. Madrid, Compañía Española de Petróleos, S. A. CEPSA.

L'Hour, M., Long, L. and Rieth, E. 1989, *Le Mauritius, la mémoire engloutie*. Grenoble, Casterman.

Marken, M. W. 1994, *Pottery from Spanish Shipwrecks 1500-1800*. Gainesville, University Press of Florida.

Marsden, P. 1974, The wreck of the Dutch East Indiaman Amsterdam near Hastings, 1749. An interim report. *International Journal of Nautical Archaeology* 1, 90.

Martin, C. J. 1979, Spanish Armada Pottery. *International Journal of Nautical Archaeology* 8, 279 – 302.

Martins, F. E. O. 1989, Os Açores nas Rotas das Américas e da Prata. In: *Os Açores e as dinâmicas do Atlântico do descobrimento à II Guerra Mundial*. Angra do Heroísmo, Instituto Histórico da Ilha Terceira, 1498.

McBride P., Larn, R. and Davis, R. 1974, A mid-17th century merchant ship found near Mullion Cove, Cornwall. An interim report. *International Journal of Nautical Archaeology* 1, 135.

Meneses, A. de Freitas 1998, Angra na Rota da Índia: funções, cobiças e tempos. In: *A Carreira da Índia e as rotas dos estreitos* – Actas. Angra do Heroísmo, 721 – 740.

Preice, R. and Muckelroy, K 1977, The Kennemerland site. The third and fourth seasons 1974 and 1976. An interim report. *International Journal of Nautical Archaeology*, 6, 187 – 218.

Rule, M. 1982, *The Mary Rose. The excavating and raising of Henry VIII's Flagship.* London, Conway Maritime Press, London.

Smith, R. C., Spirek, J., Bratten and J. Ireton, S. D. 1995, *The Emanuel Point Ship. Archaeological Investigations 1992 – 1995*. Florida Department of State. Division of Historical Resources. Bureau of Archaeological Research.

Whale-oil casks and Atlantic trade networks, circa 1565

Brad Loewen

Abstract
Casks are often encountered in ship archaeology and these "modern amphorae" contain much clues for reconstructing functions and itineraries. For example, the itinerary of 16th-century whale-oil casks found at Red Bay, Labrador, included previous halts in Brittany, Bordeaux and the Basque Country. These ports of call also relate to steps in a chaîne opératoire and a division of labour extending across the Atlantic. Archival research into the 16th-century coopers' community at Bordeaux reveals the central role of these artisans in port activities and Atlantic commerce.

Casks are an increasingly important object-type in maritime archaeology. They are often encountered in large numbers on modern shipwreck sites and recent methods of studying archaeological wood are able to bring large amounts of information out these ubiquitous containers. Early interest in casks focussed on cooperage as a craft, since tool marks and other visual evidence often allowed the sequence of manual fabrication tasks to be reconstructed with great completeness (Ross 1980). The goal was to relate the archaeological evidence to the technological history of cooperage as found in historical descriptions of the trade (Diderot 1763, Fougeroux de Bondaroy 1763, Paulin-Désormeaux et al 1874, Renard 1921, Brunet 1948) or to ethnographic descriptions of 20th-century hand cooperage (Kilby 1971, Taransaud 1976). Other researchers set typological goals and sought to link the various cask types to archival evidence of regional cask sizes, names and contents (Shackelford 1988, Hulst 1987). These approaches, in coming to grips with the wealth of information contained in archaeological casks, set field and laboratory standards for recording information and identified a large body of published and archival material related to historical cooperage.

However, these approaches also had limitations. In treating cooperage as a craft and taking a somewhat simplistic view of artisanal production, they failed to see that coopers were in fact central to the organisation of large Atlantic ports and behaved in sophisticated ways that Gallinato (1992: 286-289) has characterized as a *gros artisanat*. With their daily links to merchant outfitters, ship captains and timber dealers, coopers naturally practiced their trade in a capitalistic and industrial manner. By the 16th century, they obtained credit, bought materials and hired journeymen to build hundreds of dozens of casks in large workshops situated near the ports (Loewen 1999b). Contrary to the image of the hand craftsmanship portrayed in the *Encyclopédies* of the 18th century, cooperage was quick to employ an extensive division of labour and machines. By the 1680s, naval cooperages in Rochefort were partially mechanized (Loewen 1999a) and machinery was used extensively in private Dutch and French workshops by the 1740s and 1750s (Hulst 1987).

Port coopers were also the stevedores of the late medieval and early modern era, loading and unloading ships with their own lighters, tackle and carts, and often called upon by city officials to gauge the tonnage of ships during charter negotiations and disputes (De Lespinasse 1886: 12). Coopers and cooperage guilds enforced municipal weights and measures and were prominent as guards and officers in urban militias (Loewen 1999b: 223). In the 16th century, these strong-armed, straight-forward individuals, skilled at directing operations and equally at ease on land and on water, regularly hired on for fishing and whaling voyages to the New World, especially as young men in need of cash to buy their own workshop or to pay off a dowry debt. They served as officers during the crossing and organised packing and loading activities at the shore stations or on the fishing banks of the "New Found Lands". They were especially numerous in time of war, as in 1554 and again in 1562-63 when French and Spanish fishing crews fought over prime fishing harbours and roads (Loewen 1999b: 223).

Since the 14th century, journeymen coopers formed a mobile brotherhood, making friendships at sea and sometimes settling down far from their native soil (Sosson 1966). Their skills were easily transferable from one port to another and thus it is not surprising that archaeological casks display little regional variety in manual cooperage techniques. In studying the casks which form the core of the maritime cooper's trade, it is necessary to look beyond their technological and local framework, so as to detect those signs of mobility and trade networks that shed light on the complexity of the New World fishery and on the role of specific ports as transfer points in an integrated Atlantic landscape (Westerdahl 1980).

The 16th-century Labrador whale fishery

During the 16th century, Atlantic ports from Aveiro to Bristol were gripped by the New World fishing fever, which transformed local maritime economies and ways of life. The first fishing voyages were recorded at the beginning of the century (Bernard 1968: 805-826) and, by the 1530s and 1540s, Basque and French fishermen dominated this activity. By mid-century, Rouen, La Rochelle and Bordeaux outfitted more than 150 vessels to Newfoundland each year. Most of the cod-fishing vessels were not large, ranging from 50 to 120 tons and only exceptionally up to 400 tons (Turgeon 1998: 590-591). Coopers did not play an important part in cod-fishing voyages, except to look after the ship's water and wine supply and pack small amounts of cod oil. However, they were very active in the whale fishery, which developed in the 1530s in southern Newfoundland. Whale meat packed in casks was its principal product during these early years but, from about 1542 or 1543, French and Spanish Basques began extracting oil from blubber at shore stations in the Strait of Belle Isle. During its peak in the 1560s and 1570s, the whale hunt brought as many as 20 or more large whaling ships and 1,000 men to half a dozen havens on the south Labrador coast, in a 120-day season extending from August through November (Loewen 1999b: 100-103). Before 1560, most whaling expeditions were financed and equipped in Bordeaux and involved French Basque ships and crews. After the treaty of Cateau-Cambrésis in 1559, the advantage shifted to the Spanish Basques based in San Sebastian, due in part to state shipbuilding subsidies instituted in 1563 by the dynamic Cristobal de Barros who directed the Basque and Galician navy from that year to 1590 (Casado Soto 1988: 87-93). In Newfoundland, heavy Spanish Basque whalers soon controlled the Strait of Belle Isle and ruled the fishing grounds, to the displeasure of their English and French competitors.

After the harpooners, the coopers were the most important tradesmen on these voyages. Their work was quantified by the number of casks that a ship expected to bring back to Europe. A captain would hire one cooper for every 50 tons of ship's burthen, or 200 casks. A 250-ton ship that held 1,000 *barriques* of oil would bring five coopers and a large, 400-ton ship would bring eight (Loewen 1999b: 153-161). While the average of 1.67 *barriques* per cooper per day might seem like an unimpressive pace, the coopers' work included the making of 24 wooden hoops for each cask, setting up the staves were brought to Labrador "shaken down" in bundles, replacing broken pieces, filling the casks and lading them securely on board ship. Work in the whaling cooperage was divided according to the experience of the artisans. A crew of five would include a head cooper who supervised the operations and an apprentice who was assigned less skilful tasks. Hoop-making and setting up the *barriques* were parallel operations carried out simultaneously, while the intermittent work of filling and bunging up casks depended on the harpooners' success in bringing whales to the shore station. During calm periods at the ovens, coopers towed the casks behind a shallop to the ship, hoisted them aboard and stowed them below decks (Proulx 1993).

Since the Middle Ages, whale oil found a small market as a lighting fuel on ships, in wealthy homes and in religious establishments. On the Basque coast, it was also mixed with pitch and tar as a caulking material for ship's hulls. Fine Castillean soaps had a whale-oil base. However, the market that drove the 16th-century whaling boom was the textile industry of England, Normandy and Flanders. Wool, after it had been washed and dyed, had to be re-oiled before it could be spun and woven. Olive oil was preferred for finer fabrics, while linseed oil and whale oil were used for medium and inexpensive textiles (Savary de Bruslon 1742: columns 263-264). While the Norman and Flemish markets peaked in the 1560s, English imports of Basque oil rose from less than 200 tons in 1566 to about 2,000 tons in 1577. During the same 12-year period, total Basque production rose from 4,200 to about 6,000 tons per year, equal to the part sold in England. The rapid rise in oil imports led to the feeling among English merchants that their purchases were financing Spanish naval power in Newfoundland. When England suddenly placed an embargo on Spanish oil in February 1579, just as the season's oil was on route from San Sebastian to the Channel ports, Basque outfitters were dealt a heavy financial blow from which they never fully recovered. The following year, Dutch and English corsairs began attacking Spain's heavy, state-subsidized ships, and Madrid was obliged to redirect many large Basque ships to the West Indies (Loewen 1999b: 116-118).

In keeping with its strategic character, the history of 16th-century Basque whaling boom often reflected admiralty decisions in the major Atlantic capitals of the day. From an archaeological standpoint, however, the whale fishery was characterized by an international organisation and a reliance on a vast, Atlantic network of trade and finance. The artifact that gives us access to the whale fishery as a whole is the cask, which accompanied the oil to its final destination and then returned to the Basque coast in spring for a new voyage to Labrador. Bordeaux and the Basque coast were the keys to this annual cycle and to the maritime landscape in which the whale oil circulated.

The Red Bay barriques

In 1565, as Spanish Basque whaling was gaining in vigour, the 250-ton whaler *San Juan* wrecked in the south Labrador harbour of *Buitres*, today's Red Bay. It sank with a full load of whale oil, of which about 200 *barriques* could not be recovered at the time and were excavated in 1978-1985 (Grenier 1988). Of these, 43 could be fully or almost entirely reconstructed.

The casks had a capacity ranging from 194 to 237 litres, although 85% fell in a narrower range of 212 to 231 litres (Loewen 1999b: 63). They contained from 17 to 21 oak staves (*Quercus* type *robur*), while each head contained 5 parallel pieces plus a transversal reinforcement that was held in place with pegs. In length, the casks averaged 87 cm and, in diameter at the bilge, about 66 cm. The average head diameter was 58 cm. Each *barrique* was bound with 22 to 24 closely spaced alder (*Alnus* spp.) hoops that were lashed with willow bindings (*Salix* spp.). The central part of the cask was not covered by hoops. A bung hole appeared in the middle of one stave, and an air hole was bored in one head, next to the bung stave. All the willow hoop bindings, which covered 30 to 40 cm of the hoops, were centred on the bung stave (Ross 1979). In classic maritime fashion, the casks were stowed so that the bung stave and the hoop bindings were oriented upwards, and the head pieces were vertical.

Our analysis of the casks focussed on evidence that could be linked to specific ports or regions on the Atlantic coast, with the goal of reconstructing the artifacts' "itinerary" throughout the different stages of their lives as whale oil containers. Each call along this itinerary added to our perception of a cohesive maritime landscape, as Westerdahl (1980) has theorized it, in which no single port or region was able to furnish all the necessary materials, skills or capital needed for whale hunt, but all were integrated into a "decentred", international space.

Britanny

Firstly, the tool of dendrochronology was used to discover the geographical origin of the wood. This method uses the patterns of growth found in tree rings to date archaeological wood samples but, since these patterns are regional in character, the wood's origin is discovered at the same time. In one way, staves are ideally suited to this kind of study. Since they are split radially from the parent log, all the tree rings are oriented at right angles to the stave's width, providing a maximum number of rings for study. On the other hand, according to historical cooperage practice, the final sapwood rings were removed from staves, and this prevents us from discovering the exact year in which the tree was felled. This inconvenience can be partially obviated when a small number of sapwood rings can be identified along the edge of the stave. The date of the oldest sapwood ring helps to estimate the tree's felling date since mature oaks have a typical number of sapwood rings. In Britanny and southern England, this number is 36 ±18 rings (Guibal 1995), while on the Basque coast, the number appears to be less, at 11 ± 9 rings according to one limited study (Loewen 1997).

Precise geographical data is contained in the tree-ring sequences themselves, as growth patterns are region-specific. The Red Bay casks showed some level of correspondence with references from a long band extending from east-central France to southern Britanny. However, the level of correspondence increased from east to west, with the highest degree of similarity occurring with reference sequences from the lower Loire and Vilaine valleys (Guibal 1995). The analysis, carried out by Frédéric Guibal, concluded that the staves came from this area of south-eastern Britanny.

The earliest records of stave exports from southern Britanny date to the mid-16th century (Tanguy 1956a: 35-36 and 1956b: 194-195). They reveal that stave wood was an important local product that was sent as far afield as the Basque coast and the England but, particularly, to Bordeaux (Heutz de Lemps 1975: 420-425). Staves could be either simply split or finished with a cooper's adze (*doloire*). On the Loire, they were sent downstream to Nantes or to a smaller port at the mouth of the river, depending on the size of ship that took them aboard. In the 16th century, ships larger than 50 tons did not generally reach Nantes because of the low water levels in the river. As well, at certain times of the year when floodwaters swelled the Loire, no mariners dared fight the current. The downstream ports of Couëran and Pellerin, as well as Bourgneuf-en-Retz on the coast, were more popular trans-shipment points for staves than Nantes, even though the majority of stave contracts were signed here (Loewen 1999b: 72).

Bordeaux

The second port of call in the Red Bay casks' itinerary appears to have been Bordeaux, where the staves were converted into casks which were subsequently broken down into "shooks" and shipped to the Basque country. Bordeaux was identified following an analysis of the system of measure used to build the casks, based on the historical relationship between specific systems of measure and a locality such as a city or a region. In the case of the Red Bay whale oil casks, dating to 1565, two possible regional systems of measure existed, on the basis of Basque records of the whale fishery: the French Bordeaux standard and the Spanish Gipuzkoa standard. Up to the 1560s, the Bordeaux standard was used in the Basque fishery. It was progressively supplanted by the Gipuzkoa standard in the 1560s, as San Sebastian replaced Bordeaux as the chief outfitting centre for whaling voyages.

Bordeaux cask metrology was already established by the 13th century and remained stable until the 19th century when it was adapted to the metric system. For the retail wine trade, which imposed a high degree of accuracy and control, a *barrique* had to contain at least 100 *pots*, or 226.5 litres, to be considered legal. However, according to an older tradition, a range of 29 to 30 *veltes*, or 220.7 to 228.3 litres, was tolerated. On the other hand, the Spanish Basque *barrica* of whale oil was evaluated by weight at 400 *libras*, or 196.8 kg (Hocquet 1995: 73-74, Balzola 1917: table 6). This weight, at whale oil's density of 0.9 compared to water, resulted in a minimal capacity of 213.2 litres per *barrica*.

Because of their significant difference in size, the Bordeaux and Gipuzkoa standards could be differentiated archaeologically among the Red Bay casks. It was found that all new, unrepaired casks had a minimum capacity of 100 *pots* (226.5 litres). In contrast, all casks that fell below 100 *pots* had also been repaired or rebuilt in ways that reduced their capacity, although they capacity generally remained above 400 *libras* (213.2 litres). It seems plausible therefore that the new casks had been built according to the Bordeaux system of measure.

This reading of the archaeological remains corresponds with references in the notarial archives of Gipuzkoa indicating that, as late as 1565, whale oil was sold in the Basque port of Orio in casks of the "measure and contenance of Bordeaux" ("*de la medida e boja de Burdeos*", 20 April 1565, AHPG, III, 1793: 20r), or "of the regulation size of the gauge and measure of Bordeaux" ("*del grandor hordinario de la jauja y medido de Burdeos*", 2 May 1565, AHPG, III, 1791: 33r). Exports of whale-oil casks appear in the Bordeaux notarial archives. In a charter party from the same year, local casks, shaken down for transport ("*barriques defettes*"), were sent by coastal freighter to the Basque coast, "for use in the Newfoundland fishery" (21 April 1565, ADG, 3E 3042: 52v-53r). The historian Selma Barkham has noted that Spanish Basques used the Bordeaux standard as early as 1553 (Barkham 1988: 30, note 23). After 1566, however, we find no further mention of this practice in the archival record.

The Basque coast

The third stop in the Red Bay casks' itinerary, the Spanish Basque coast, was reconstructed through another metrological analysis of archaeological remains. In this case, it was the wrecked ship itself, in which the *barriques* were found, that yielded this geographical information. Basque shipbuilding metrology in the late Middle Ages and early modern period was based on a unit of measure, the *codo de ribera* of 57.5 cm, that was found only on the Basque coast. It was somewhat longer than the neighbouring Castillean *codo* (55.7 cm) and diverged considerably from the French *pied du roi* (32.5 cm).

Basque shipbuilders were conscious of the unusual character of their traditional unit of measure for, in construction contracts, sales of planking and in legal documents involving the tonnage of ships, the *codo de ribera* was often specified. In one 1571 legal case it was even defined as "two thirds of a Castillean *vara* plus one *dedo*" (ACG, Ejecutivos Uria, legajo 1, corregido 1: 78r). In other words, it was considered as two Castillean feet or one Castillean *codo*, plus 1/16 of a Castillean foot. In the 18th century, we find a simpler, but identical, definition as 33/32 of a Castillean *codo* (Villareal de Berriz 1736: 112-113, Proulx 1993).

The origin of this idiosyncratic shipbuilding measure, also used by Spanish royal astronomers, engineers and surveyors (Villareal de Berriz 1736: 112), remains unknown. However we do know that its use was confined to a very limited band along the French and Spanish Basque coasts (*cf.* Bayonne, 3 June 1585: ADG, 3E 3918: 331r-331v). A 1559 contract for the sale of ship's planking, in the Biscayan port of Lekeitio, specified that the timber should be gauged according to the coastal *codo* and not the *codo* used on the inland plain ("*en la Tierra Llana de Bizcaya*") at the neighbouring town of Ea, just a few kilometres upstream (AHPG, I, 2577: 22v). The *codo de ribera*'s geographical distribution coincides with the coastal strip, 2 leagues or 11 km wide, in which naval timber producers were eligible for royal subsidies, according to a 16th-century privilege that may be traced back as far as the 12th century (Loewen 1999b: 65-69). This privilege seems to have instituted the *codo de ribera* as the traditional shipbuilding measure of the Basque coast.

In the shipwreck that contained the Red Bay *barriques*, the *codo de ribera*'s use could be detected at literally dozens of points in the hull, thanks in large part to the archaeological strategy of dismantling the hull underwater, and recording and studying its architecture in laboratory conditions (Grenier 1988). The most convincing evidence of its use was found in the design of the master frame, whose breadth at six critical points corresponded to even *codos de ribera*. These breadths were at (1) the flat floor, (2) the "turn of the bilge" that was marked on the frame and (3) the ceiling's edge, as well at the "touches" of the circular arcs of different radii used in the master frame's design - (4) between the bilge arc and the futtock arc, (5) between the futtock arc and the breadth arc and, finally (6), between the breadth arc and the straight tangent line known as the "tumblehome" (Loewen 2001). Because the distances measured were relatively long, ranging from about 1 metre to over 7 metres, it was possible to conclude that the Basque *codo de ribera* was indeed the unit of measure employed by the ship's builders.

This solely archaeological approach to discovering the geographical path of the casks, once added to the wealth of contextual information linking the wreck to the Spanish Basque whale hunt and to the loss of the *San Juan*, extended the *barriques*' itinerary from Bordeaux to the Basque coast. Their fabrication process completed, the casks were placed in the hands of Basque captains and outfitters and began a different phase of their career.

Labrador and the Channel ports

The annual use-cycle of whale oil casks included a voyage to Labrador, followed by a round trip to the Channel ports where the principal whale oil markets were located. These two voyages were carefully timed so that the empty casks could be returned to San Sebastian and its deep-water port of Pasajes by June, just in time for the whalers' next departure for Labrador. An interesting time-space relation can thus be detected, for the spatial limits of the maritime landscape formed by the whale-oil casks' itinerary corresponded to the area that could be navigated in one year. In the 16th century, the financial year of Atlantic merchants ran from Easter to Easter. Basque outfitters hurried their oil to the markets of Antwerp or Rouen in February and March so that they could be paid out before the end of the year, and could organize the following expedition to Labrador (Smith 1992, Fletcher 1992).

Somewhat surprisingly, Spanish and French Basques followed different routes to the New World. French

Basques, leaving from the port of Saint-Jean-de-Luz, followed the coast northward to Bordeaux or La Rochelle where they took on supplies and men, before heading westward *par droite route* to Newfoundland. Spanish Basques, leaving from the port of Pasajes, followed the coast westward, stopping at small ports to pick up sailors. Cristobal de Barros described their trans-Atlantic route in 1571:

> When they leave this coast, they recognize, from about 15 leagues at sea, the cape de Peñas which is in Asturia, 2 leagues from Gijon. From here, they head west-north-west until they reach 52 and a half degrees where lies the Grand Bay (Strait of Belle Isle), without touching any coast or island, for the whole route is an abyss of 800 leagues (Barkham 1988: 58).

In October, returning cod-fishermen brought news of the whale hunt's progress, and sometimes as well the first casks of whale oil. The main fleet returned around Christmas Day and the month of January was spent unloading the ships, paying off sailors, coopers and harpooners and reloading the casks on smaller coastal freighters for the trip northward. The trans-shipment was not limited to Pasajes and Saint-Jean-de-Luz but also took place in smaller deep-water ports along the Spanish Basque coast, where the heavy whalers could ride at low tide. Smaller ships were preferred for the voyage northward, since the ports of Rouen and Antwerp, like Nantes, were inaccessible to vessels of over 50 tons. In both ports, large ships had to unload their cargos onto lighters for the last leg of the voyage. This 50-ton limit, while not absolute, nonetheless appears with astonishing clarity in the archival record. It allowed for a type of one-decked ship called a *barque*, usually hailing from Britanny, the Saintonge coast of France or the Basque Country, to dominate coastal shipping. Only English and Dutch freighters surpassed the informal 50-ton limit, often attaining up to 80 tons.

The return traffic in empty casks was a constant of Atlantic coastal navigation in the 16th century, whether for the whale oil trade or for wine, cider and other on-board necessities. In 1566, one Bordeaux shipping agent picked up 2,000 empty *barriques* on the quay at Morlaix, in northern Britanny (ADG, 3E 5407: 783v-784v and 1298r-v). Ironically, the captain of the ill-fated *San Juan*, in the years following his wreck in Labrador, hauled load after load of empty wine casks from San Sebastian to Seville (ADB, 39, 360v, 365v, 368r, 409r). These cargos held only the oaken staves and head pieces, for the hoops were discarded and made anew every year. The same maritime regions that furnished the majority of the coastal freighters - Britanny and Saintonge - were also the greatest exporters of wooden hoops and hoop bindings (Loewen 1999b: 155-167).

Outfitting in Bordeaux and Pasajes-San Sebastian

In the two stages in a whale-oil cask's life cycle, its manufacture and its use, two ports emerge as complementary but competing centres - Bordeaux and San Sebastian. The 1560s were a period of transition, as the balance shifted in favour of the Spanish whalers, and the year 1565 when the Red Bay casks were lost was perhaps the penultimate year when the influence of Bordeaux cooperage was still clearly visible. In 1567, we see a sharp and irreversible reduction in the number of Bordeaux coopers hired onto Basque whalers, and the contracts for whaling supplies diminish dramatically.

Bordeaux never sent significant numbers of whaling ships to Labrador, relying instead on Basque ships and sailors to whom the city's merchant community supplied capital as well as materials produced in the Gironde hinterland and in other coastal regions as far afield as southern Britanny. French Basque ships and sailors were the Bordeaux merchants' principal clients (Turgeon 1986). San Sebastian, on the other hand, was a shipbuilding centre and large numbers of sailors were recruited here and in the small ports along the Basque coast. The merchants of San Sebastian relied on outside capital to finance their expeditions and purchased many of their supplies abroad, as the mountainous Basque coast did not provide adequate amounts of foodstuffs and equipment for the whalers' needs. In the 1560s and 1570s, San Sebastian captains and outfitters turned to the wool merchants of Burgos for additional financial support and, especially for maritime insurance (Barkham 1980-1981). The two outfitting centres, both based on Basque navigation, were pushed into further rivalry by the ongoing enmity of France and Spain in the middle of the 16th century.

Bordeaux's attraction as an outfitting centre was exemplified by the visits of two San Sebastian whaling captains in the spring of 1565, identified in the Bordeaux archives as Anthoine de Lajus and Jean de Chemendy. The latter arrived at the end of March and proceeded to hire four port coopers for a voyage to *Terreneufve* in June. The coopers were all young men who also worked as stevedores for one of five or six cooperages in the port parish of Saint-Rémy that specialised in handling casks as well as building them. Of the 300 or so active coopers in the city about 60 worked in the maritime branch of the trade. Since the early 1550s, a tradition of working in the Newfoundland fisheries as young men existed among the port coopers. Some sailed as many as four or five times before settling down in Bordeaux to buy a house and a workshop. The four hired by Chemendy on 29 March and 11 April agreed to sail to San Sebastian where they would await their departure (ADG, 3E 3042: 12v-13r and 3E 5406: 64r-65r). The Basque captain also proceeded to purchase 218 empty casks, three *barriques* of candles and another of oats, along with other materials including several tons of wine. Two coastal freighters were needed to transport all the men and provisions to San Sebastian.

The four coopers and the captain sailed from Bordeaux on 12 April on the *Marie* of Capbreton, along with a full load of wine (ADG, 3E 3042: 112v-13r), while the *Marie* of Cônac followed on 21 April with the empty casks, 12 tons of wine, the candles and the oats (ADG, 3E 3042: 52v-53r).

All of Chemendy's interactions were brokered by a French Basque named Roger Dalguelarraudo, who was an important link between Basque captains and Bordeaux outfitters. Dalguelarraudo himself was specialized in roofing tiles, which were used as ballast on outgoing voyages and to cover the buildings at the Labrador whaling stations. He also translated for Basques, Spaniards and French, and frequently guaranteed salaries and other financial transactions. As an agent for a Ciboure company owned by the Daguerette family, he also negotiated state contracts for the upkeep of port infrastructures (ADG, 3E 6020, s.f., 14 July 1568). His career as an agent illustrates the extent of trade between the Basque coast and Bordeaux.

The second whaling captain, Anthoine de Lajus, was in Bordeaux from 28 March to 2 April 1565. He called on a prominent fishing outfitter and financier, François de Poncastel, to arrange for a credit letter for 260 *livres*. With this loan, he purchased 12 tons of wine, 40 quintals of rope, and 20 tons of herring from Poncastel's company. He also hired two port coopers, friends and relatives of the four hired by Chemendy, for his upcoming voyage to Labrador. Lajus then chartered a small ship, the *Jehanne* of Marenne, to convey the materials to San Sebastian where Pontcastel's agent, a La Rochelle native called François Barreau, was to receive them (ADG 3E 5406: 9r-10v, 27r-v, 28v-30r).

These examples highlight the flourishing trade of outfitting materials from Bordeaux to San Sebastian, which saw beans, wheat, wine, rope, clothing, ship's biscuit, casks and other materials flow southward in exchange for interest payments and oil sales. In the first half of the century, Bordeaux supplied mostly raw materials such as wheat and hemp while, in the 1560s, most of the provisions were fully manufactured by Bordeaux merchants. Large amounts of herring, cod and salt were purchased in Britanny by the Bordeaux merchants and resold to the Basque mariners. We may estimate the sales of these provisions at 2,000 tons in 1565. By way of comparison, the total tonnage of the Basque cod and whale fishing fleet may be estimated between 7,000 and 8,000 tons. The fleet of coastal freighters, made up of *barques* of less than 35 tons on the average, was insufficient for this intense trade and many Basque fishing captains were obliged to load supplies at Bordeaux on their way to Newfoundland (Loewen 1999b: 84-85). The interrelation of the two ports, Bordeaux and San Sebastian, thus appears as a central feature of the mid-16th century Newfoundland fishery.

Conclusion

The archaeological casks from Red Bay, lost in 1565, bring our attention to a peculiar aspect of the trans-Atlantic whale fishery. While this fishery is often, and rightly so, said to be "Basque", this is only one part of a much more complex picture. The Basque coast was unable to furnish all the elements needed for a trans-Atlantic venture. Indeed, no other single region can be said to do so. The entire Atlantic coast was engaged in the New World trade, with some regions supplying specific materials and others supplying men, ships or capital. Rivalry among the participating regions nonetheless gradually propelled some into a position of dominance, but their advantages could be lost a generation later. In following the itinerary of the Red Bay casks, which leads us to all the major regions and ports involved in the whale-oil trade, these interrelationships are given a concrete structure based on a use-cycle of one year (Westerdahl 1980, Smith 1992, Fletcher 1992). The maritime landscape that is sketched by this itinerary is thus given a finite geographical frontier, based on the distances that could be sailed during the same one-year period. Here was a defining characteristic of the North Atlantic, which may be contrasted, for example, to the two-year cycle of navigation from Seville to the West Indies, requiring a much greater financial capacity and largely excluding small "investors" such as the fishing captains who drove the trans-Atlantic fishery (Chaunu 1977). Rather than bringing out the influence of one port, the study of the Red Bay casks brings out the "decentred" aspect of the trans-Atlantic fishery, both in terms of regional organisation and of human investment.

Archival collections

Archives départementales de Gironde, Bordeaux (ADG).
Archivo de la Diputación de Burgos, Burgos (ADB).
Archivo histórico de los protocolos de Guipúzcoa, Oñati (AHPG).
Archivo de la Real Chancillería, Valladolid (ARC).

Bibliography of cited works

Balzola, P. de 1917, *Tablas de Correspondencia de todas las Pesas y Medidas de Guipúzcoa y las principales des extranjero con las del sistema métrico ... publicadas en 1853*, San Sebastian, Imprenta de la Provincia.

Barkham, M. 1981, *Report on Spanish Basque Shipbuilding, c. 1550 to 1600*, Ottawa, Parks Canada.

Barkham, S. 1980-1981, Burgos insurance for Basque ships: maritime policies from Spain, 1547-1592, *Archivaria*, 11, 87-99.

Barkham (Huxley), S. 1988, Los Vascos y las pescerías transatlánticas, 1517-1713, in E. Ayerbe, ed. and S. Barkham, coord., *Itsasoa 3. Los Vascos en el marco Atlántico Norte. Siglos XVI y XVII*, San Sebastián, ETOR, 26-164.

Bernard, J. 1968, *Navires et Gens de mer à Bordeaux, 1400-1500*, 3 vols., Paris, SEVPEN.

Bradley, C. s.d., *Preliminary analysis of the staved container remains recovered from the 1981 underwater excavations at Red Bay,* Ottawa, Parks Canada, microfiche 260.

Brunet, R. 1948, *Manuel de tonnellerie,* Paris, J.-B. Baillière.

Brutails, J.-A. 1912, *Recherches sur l'équivalence des anciennes mesures de la Gironde*, Bordeaux.

Casado Soto, J.L. 1988, *Los Barcos Españoles del Siglo XVI y la Gran Armada de 1588*, Madrid, San Martin.

Chaunu, P. 1977, *Séville et l'Amérique aux XVIe et XVIIe siècles*, Paris, Flammarion.

De Lespinasse, 1886, *Les métiers et corporations de la ville de Paris*, vol. 1: *Ordonnances générales XIVe-XVIIIe siècle*, Paris.

Diderot, H. 1763, *Encyclopédie de Diderot et d'Alembert*, Paris.

Doursther, H 1965, *Dictionnaire universel des poids et mesures anciens et modernes, contenant des tables des monnaies de tous les pays* (Bruxelles, 1840). Amsterdam, Meridian.

Fletcher, R. 1992, Time perspectivism, *Annales,* and the potential of archaeology, in A.B. Knapp, ed., *Archaeology,* Annales, *and Ethnohistory*, Cambridge, Cambridge University Press, 35-49.

Fougeroux de Bondaroy, A. 1984, L'art du tonnelier, *Descriptions des arts et métiers* (Paris, 1763), Geneva, Skatline Reprints.

Gallinato, B. 1992, *Les corporations à Bordeaux à la fin de l'ancien régime,* Talence, Presses Universitaires de Bordeaux.

Gilles, B. 1972, Prolégomènes à une histoire des techniques, *Revue d'histoire des mines et de la métallurgie*, 4, 1/2, 3-65.

Grenier, R. 1988, Basque Whalers in the New World: the Red Bay Wrecks, in G. Bass, ed., *Ships and Shipwrecks of the Americas*, London, Thames and Hudson, 69-84.

Guibal, F. 1995, *Analyse dendrochronologique des épaves de Red Bay (Labrador), contrat: 1632/90-173*, Marseille, Laboratoire de botanique historique et palynologie CNRS URA 1152.

Hocquet, J.-C. 1995, *La métrologie historique,* Paris, Presses universitaires de France.

Huetz de Lemps, C. 1975, *Géographie du commerce de Bordeaux à la fin du règne de Louis XIV*, Paris, Mouton.

Hulst, R. 1987, Casks as a Packing Material: An Archaeological Typology and a Historical Reconstruction, in J. Gawronski, ed., *Annual Report of the VOC-Ship "Amsterdam" Foundation 1986*, Amsterdam, VOC-Ship "Amsterdam" Foundation, 73-85.

Kilby, K. 1971, *The Cooper's Craft*, London: John Baker.

Loewen, B. 1997, The 15th-century Cavalaire-sur-Mer (Provence) shipwreck. A precursor to the Red Bay vessel?, paper read to the *Society for Historical Archaeology*, Corpus Christi (Texas), 8-12 janvier.

Loewen, B. 1999a, *The casks from La Belle and the Rochefort arsenal, ca. 1684*, manuscript report, Austin, Texas Historical Commission.

Loewen, B. 1999b, *Les barriques de Red Bay et l'espace atlantique septentrional, vers 1565*, doctoral dissertation, Université Laval (Québec).

Loewen, B. 2001, The structures of Atlantic shipbuilding in the 16th century. An archaeological perspective, in F. Alves, ed., *Proceedings of the International Symposium on Archaeology of Medieval and Modern Ships of Iberian-Atlantic Tradition,* Lisbon, Instituto Português de Arqueologia, 241-258.

Paulin-Désormeaux, H. Ott, W. Maigne 1874, *Nouveau manuel complet du tonnelier et du jaugeage*, Paris, Mulo (republished 1897).

Proulx, J.-P. 1993, *Les Basques et la pêche de la baleine au Labrador au XVIe siècle*, Ottawa, Parks Canada.

Proulx, J.-P. 1993, Essai sur la jauge des navires basques au XVIe siècle, in *L'aventure maritime, du golfe de Gascogne à Terre-Neuve*, Actes du 118e congrès national annuel des sociétés historiques et scientifiques, Pau, octobre 1993, Paris, Éditions du CTHS, 115-124.

Renard, A. 1921, *La tonnellerie à la portée de tous*, Paris, Malfère.

Renouard, Y. 1953, La capacité du tonneau bordelais au Moyen-Age, *Annales du Midi*, 395-403.

Renouard, Y. 1956, Recherches complémentaires sur la capacité du tonneau bordelais au Moyen-Age, *Annales du Midi*, 195-265.

Ross, L. 1980, *Sixteenth-Century Spanish Basque Coopering Technology: A Report on the Staved Containers Found on the wreck of the whaling galleon* San Juan *sunk in Red Bay (Labrador), AD 1565*, Ottawa, Parks Canada.

Savary de Bruslons, J. 1742, *Dictionnaire universel de commerce*, Geneva, Cramer et Philibert.

Shackelford, K. 1988, The Casks from Cork, *Historic Trades* I, Williamsburg, Colonial Williamsburg Foundation, 38-51.

Smith, M. 1992, Braudel's temporal rythms and chronology theory in archaeology in A.B. Knapp, ed., *Archaeology,* Annales, *and Ethnohistory*, Cambridge, Cambridge University Press, 23-34.

Sosson, J.-P. 1966, La structure sociale de la corporation médiévale: l'exemple des tonneliers de Bruges de 1350 à 1500, *Revue Belge de philologie de l'Histoire* 44, 457-478.

Tanguy, J. 1956a, *Le commerce du Port de Nantes au milieu du XVIe siècle*, Paris, Colin.

Tanguy, J. 1956b, *Le commerce nantais à la fin du XVIe siècle et au début du XVIIe*, 2 vols., doctoral dissertation, Université de Nantes.

Taransaud, J. 1976, *Le livre de la tonnellerie*, Paris, la Roue à livres.

Turgeon, L. 1986, Pour redécouvrir notre 16e siècle: les pêches à Terre-Neuve d'après les archives notariales de Bordeaux, *Revue d'Histoire de l'Amérique française*, 39, 4, 523-549.

Turgeon, L. n.d., *Inventaire informatisé des actes notariés de Bordeaux relatifs au Canada, année 1564-1565,* Ottawa, National Archives of Canada.

Turgeon, L. 1998, French fishers, fur traders and Amerindians during the 16th century: History and Archaeology, *William and Mary Quarterly*, 60, 585-610.

Villareal de Berriz, P.B. 1973, *Maquinas hydraulicas de molinos, y herrerias y govierno de los arboles y montes de Viscaya* (Madrid, Antonio Marin, 1736), San Sebastian, Sociedad Guipuzcoana de Ediciones y Publicaciones.

Westerdahl, C. 1980, The maritime cultural landscape, *International Journal of Nautical Archaeology* 9, 4, 311-329.

The Waterfront Archaeology of Early Modern St John's, Newfoundland

Peter E. Pope

Abstract

From the early 1500s migratory European crews prosecuted a shore-based migratory cod fishery at St John's, Newfoundland. Gradual settlement by West-Country fisherfolk began ca. 1620 followed by a gradual transition from fishing station to commercial port, a process marked archaeologically by the usual encroachment on the harbour. Waterfront advance is evident in maps from 1750. Archaeological excavations along Water Street have recovered traces of the early fishery. They also permit us to date the beginnings of commercial development of the harbour to about a century before we have clear cartographic evidence. Finds of jewelry and high-quality ceramics attest to the presence of relatively well-off merchant "planters" in seventeenth-century St John's.

St John's, the capital of Canada's easternmost island province of Newfoundland, sometimes claims to be the oldest city in North America. This is, of course, absurd, since by 200 our era Teotihuacán already had a population of one or two hundred thousand, about the size of St John's today. The latter was, however, one of the first places in North America to attract Europe's attention. In the early sixteenth century, European fishermen began to frequent Newfoundland. They set out each spring from the coasts of Normandy, Brittany, northern Portugal and the Basque country to catch and dry fish, during the windy summers along the coasts of what was first known as Terra dos Bacalhaos - the land of the cod (Pope 1997). They were likely using St John's, the best protected harbour on the east coast, by 1519, when it appears on a manuscript chart of the North Atlantic by Pedro and Jorge Reinel (Seary 1971, 30, 303). In 1527, an English visitor found thirteen ships fishing out of St John's: eleven Norman, one Breton and two Portuguese (Rut 1527). English West Country crews began to take a regular interest in Newfoundland in the 1560s and by the 1580s they were dominating or at least attempting to dominate the seasonal fishery at St John's and other fishing stations on the east coast of the Avalon Peninsula or English Shore, as it was later known (Hayes 1583). St John's was not permanently settled until the seventeenth century, a few years after Jamestown, Virginia, in 1607 or Quebec, in 1608 – probably sometime between the planting of the first English colony in Newfoundland at Cupids Cove in Conception Bay, in 1610, and the establishment of Sir George Calvert's colony at Ferryland, in 1621 (Figure 1). St John's, in other words, can at least claim to be one of North America's oldest ports.

So, from 1620 or so, English fishing masters were overwintering at St John's. When the Royal Navy took censuses of Newfoundland in the 1670s, St John's was a well-established community, long since the largest settlement in Newfoundland, with about 200 fisherfolk regularly over-wintering. In 1677, for example, there were 27 fishing "plantations", mostly occupied by families, with their houses and gardens, 80 storehouses and lodgings for servants, 46 fishing rooms for salting and drying cod, 45 fishing boats, and 29 fishing stages (Poole 1677, 157-166). A map of St John's in this period shows the major fishing plantations scattered along the north side of the harbour (Figure 2). The planter census understates the importance of the port, however, for it was very oriented to the migratory fishery. In the summer of 1677, there were also 38 ships with crews fishing at St John's, which meant an additional 384 boats moored at 118 additional fishing stages, on an additional 175 fishing rooms, manned by 1973 men, lodged in 88 additional servants' lodgings. The ships fishing ranged in size from the 40 ton *Samuell*, with its single boat and crew of 6, to the 200 ton *Darius*, with its 19 fishing boats and its crew of 95. By August, the 2500 or so fisherfolk catching and processing fish at St John's were joined by over 400 deep sea mariners, who crewed the 45 cargo or "sack ships" that called there in the summer of 1677 (Poole 1677, 167-170). Many were small, like the 25 ton *Adventure Sloop* of Boston, arrived with provisions *en route* to the French Newfoundland settlement of Placentia or the 40 ton *Endeavour Katch* of Dartmouth, with wine from Fayal in the Azores; some were larger, like the 150 ton *Hopewell* of Dartmouth, arrived with salt and bound for Alicante, Spain, with fish. This was not just a fishing station, it was already a busy port. Large or small, each of these ships and all of the fishing boats needed moorings, so the St John's waterfront must have been very crowded. Little wonder that, as far as the naval commodore Captain Sir William Poole was concerned, "this particular harbour of St John's makes more trouble then all the country besides" (1677, 147-148).

Economic activity was not restricted to the seasonal cod fishery. Ships from Britain, France, the Netherlands and New England exchanged goods in a kind of free port which was only gradually controlled in the second half of the seventeenth century, as merchantilist policies were more strictly enforced. The relative importance of St. John's grew with fortification and the stationing of troops in 1689. During the extended Anglo-French wars of 1689-1713 the town was razed no less than three times (1697, 1705 and 1708). This provides a convenient archaeological fire horizon, capping the first century of settlement and underlying a century in which the town began to develop as a colonial capital. The turmoil of the French wars resulted in the centralization at St. John's of some settlers from elsewhere on the Avalon Peninsula. While its role as administrative capital of the colony was still technically in doubt in this period, in fact the die was cast: Newfoundland's second-tier settlements would remain regional centres at best. Following the treaty of Utrecht in 1713, St John's gradually recovered, as the

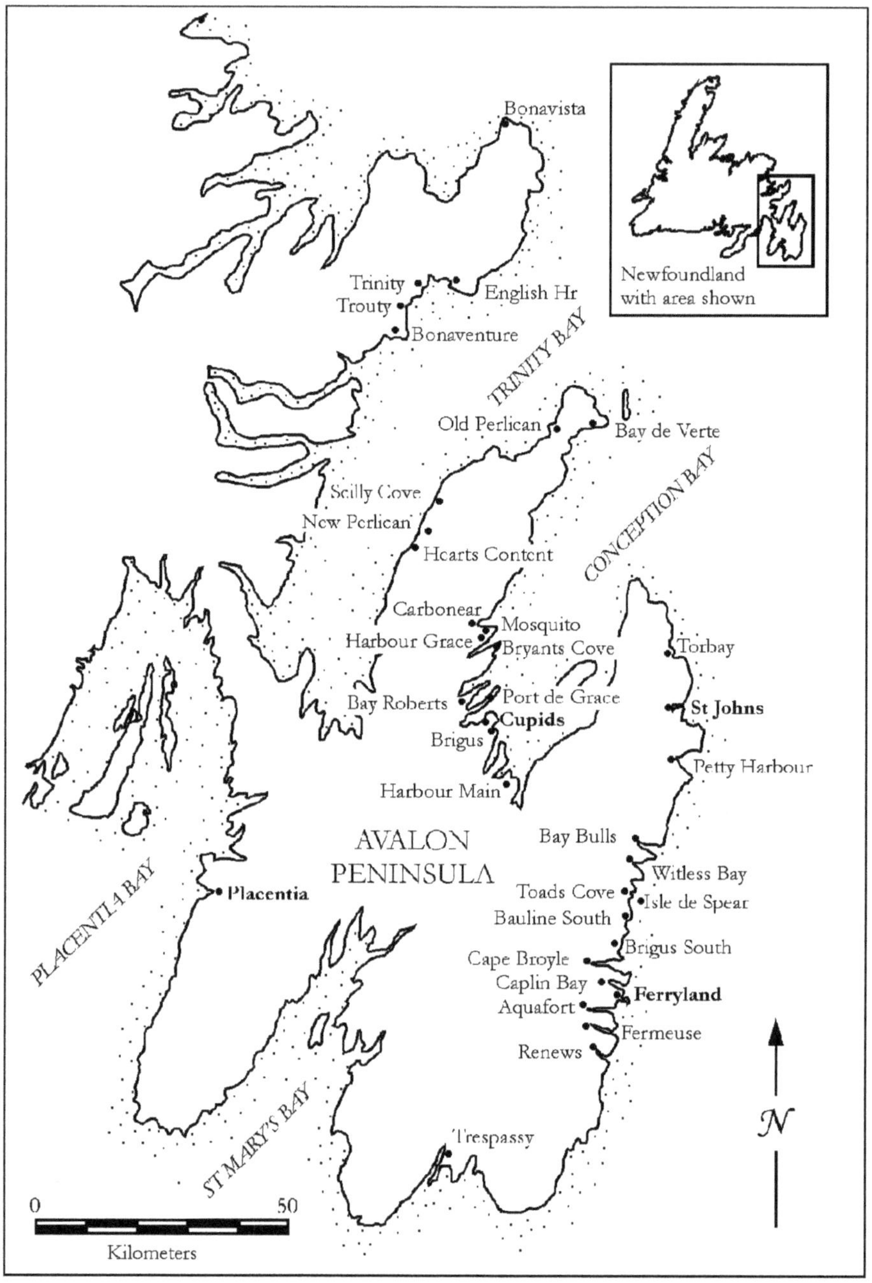

FIGURE 1. NEWFOUNDLAND'S AVALON PENINSULA, SHOWING SEVENTEENTH CENTURY SETTLEMENTS.

fishery began to flourish under the intermittent protection of a British garrison. After 1740 the island experienced accelerating immigration, many of the new arrivals coming from the impoverished hinterland of the Irish port of Waterford (Head 1976, 86-97, 250-251; Mannion 2002). This followed, perhaps, an expansion of the carrying capacity of the island, with the introduction of potato cultivation. The population of St John's grew rapidly at the turn of the nineteenth century, from about 5000 to almost 10000, by the end of the Napoleonic wars (O'Neill 1975, 51). Newfoundland was now populous enough to man its own fishing fleet and a migratory fishery was no longer competitive, at least for Britain. The nineteenth century saw St John's become the dominant central place, the "emporium of the island" it was said (Ryan 1983). Governor Gower wrote, in 1805:

> ...this Harbour is no longer a mere fishing station, built round with temporary Flakes, Stages, and Huts of trifling value, but...it is a port of extensive Commerce....importing near two thirds of the supplies for the whole Island, and furnished with extensive Store-Houses and Wharfs for trade, containing a quantity of Provisions, Stores for the Fishery, British Manufactures and West Indian Produce, as well as Fish and Oil ready for exportation, which together with the Buildings is computed to be worth more than half a million Sterling (Ryan 1983, 44).

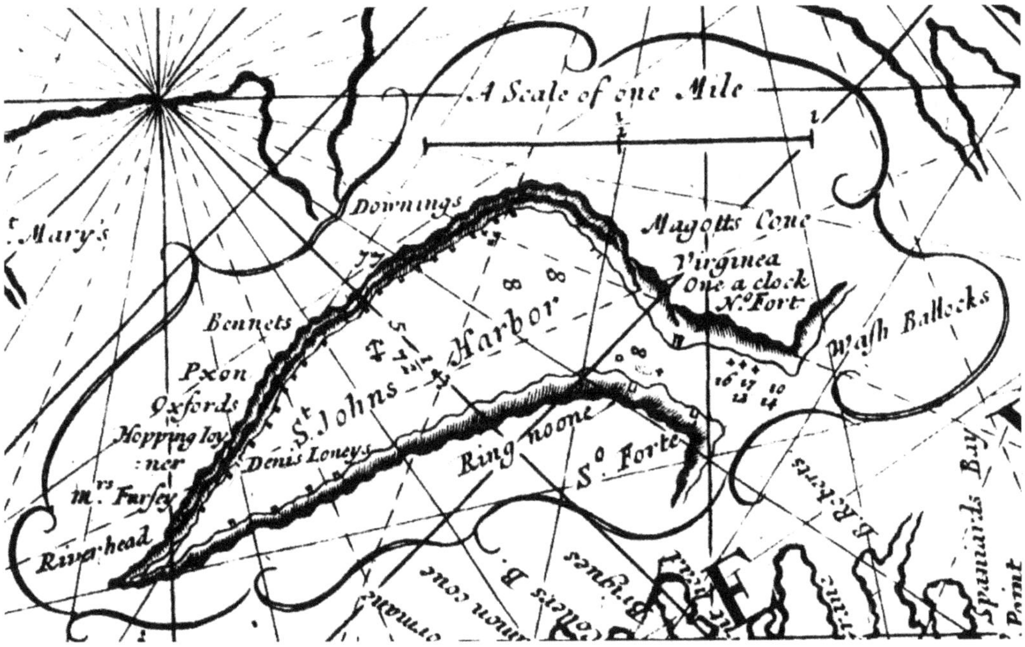

FIGURE 2. HENRY SOUTHWOOD'S MAP OF ST JOHN'S, CA 1675 (INSET IN SOUTHWOOD 1689).

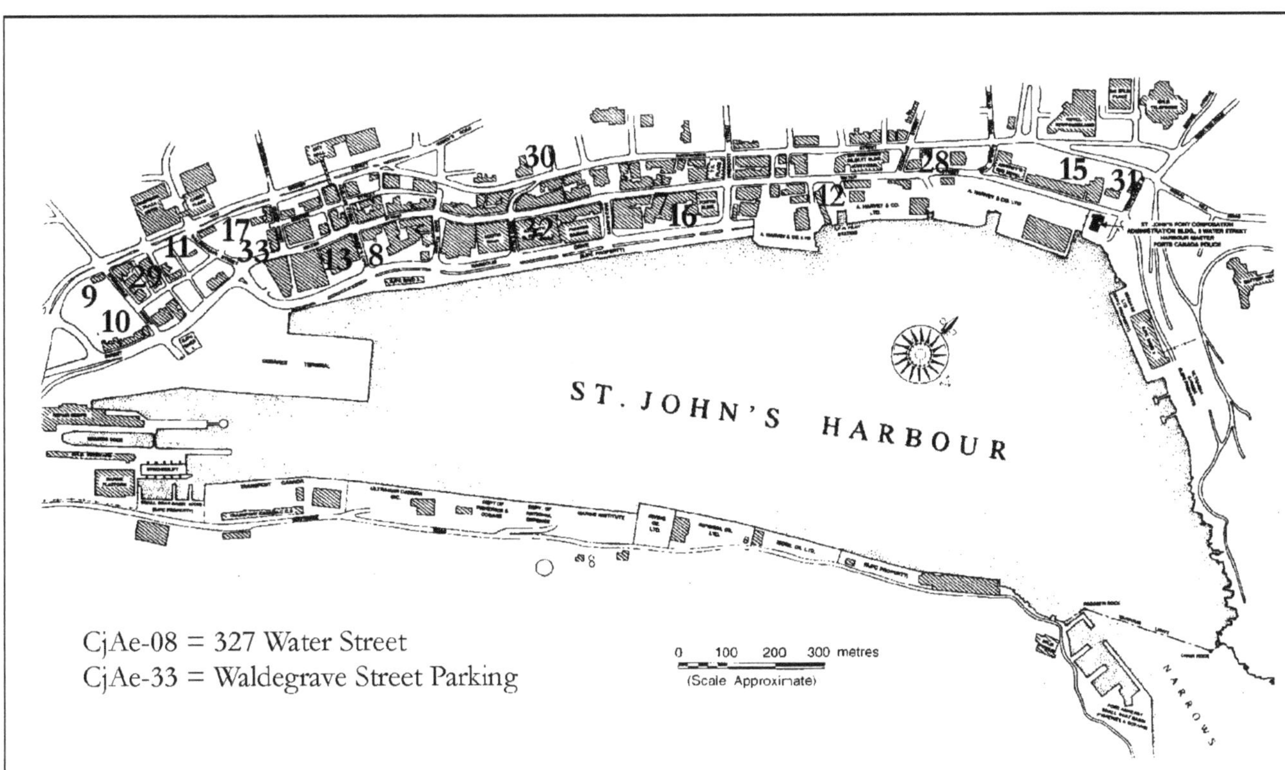

FIGURE 3. THE PORT OF ST JOHN'S TODAY, SHOWING ARCHAEOLOGICAL SITES IDENTIFIED BY THE WATERFRONT ARCHAEOLOGY PROJECT. NUMBERS IN BOLD ARE SITE BORDEN NUMBERS.

St John's has suffered a series of devastating fires, beginning with the deliberate destruction of the town by d'Iberville in the winter of 1696/97. These are useful to archaeologists, since they provide visible horizons which permit us to relate events at different sites. The fire horizons of 1696, 1705, 1708, 1780, 1816, 1817, 1846 and 1892 are often identifiable during excavations (Pope 1991, 78-87). The fire of 1892 had a decisive impact on the present-day city. Historic St John's has a late Victorian look, because the old town consists almost entirely of buildings erected in the 1890s, after the disaster of the Great Fire. This provides another archaeologically useful fire horizon, at the close of an era of commercial and industrial development, before the economic stagnation into which Newfoundland fell in the first half of the twentieth century.

From its origins in an evaluation of archaeological resources for the city, the St John's Waterfront Archaeology Project had three major aims (Pope 1991). First, this was an attempt to balance the emphasis on military sites which, with one or two exceptions, characterized most of the archaeology done in St John's to date (Tuck 1986). Second, archaeological research offered a way to better understand the thinly-documented early history of the harbour and town. Finally, harbourside excavations promised to provide the basis for an interpretation of the St John's waterfront as a single site – and one with a long material history by North American standards (Pope 1996). Between 1993 and 2000 we used heavy machinery to survey vacant lots to which we could get access and identified 16 archaeological sites in the waterfront area (Figure 3) (Pope 1995a). With the support of Memorial University of Newfoundland and the provincial Archaeology Office, we then carried out more extensive excavations at several sites, notably Waldegrave Street Parking (CjAe-33), now the site of St John's new Convention Centre, and 327 Water Street (CjAe-08), a vacant lot adjacent to the historic Murray's Premises, a nineteenth-century waterfront warehouse complex, now redeveloped as a downtown shopping precinct.

The Waldegrave Street area was originally a low-lying coastal fen, too wet in its natural state for building but useful space for the construction of fish flakes, i.e. rough wooden platforms lined with spruce boughs for drying cod fish, after they are split and salted (Figure 4). Although it seems counter-intuitive, experienced fishermen say that damp sites are the best locations for drying cod, perhaps to moderate the effects of the bright sun and brisk breezes of the typical Newfoundland summer. The Waldegrave Street site was intensively used for fish processing in the seventeenth and eighteenth centuries (Figure 5) and was filled in the early nineteenth century, as an artisans' quarter developed (Pope 1999a). The older contexts were wet, permitting good organic preservation, so that we were able to recover some of the wooden tools used in the fishery (Figure 6). These artifacts will repay close study, when conservation is complete, since the ephemeral nature of fishing stations means that preservation and recovery of such materials is rare (Faulkner 1985). The Water Street site likewise provided ample evidence of fish processing but it also yielded insight into the intensification of the use of the St John's waterfront and gave a glimpse into the lives of the merchant planters who sponsored early investment in harbour improvement (Pope 1999b).

To date, our research strategies have focused on the key transition, in the seventeenth and eighteenth centuries, from a seasonal fishing station to a colonial central place. On the waterfront, this entailed a shift away from the casual wooden structures of the fishery: notably, stages for unloading fish and flakes for drying them. As St John's became a commercial centre it needed developed work and storage areas. The simplest index of this transition would simply be the replacement of wood by stone or, eventually, concrete; but this was not normally an early transition in Newfoundland. Within living memory outport fishers relied on wooden fishing stages (Pocius 1992). Even St John's relied on wooden finger piers until the 1970s, when these were filled and converted into "Harbour Drive" and its adjacent paved commercial apron. Wooden features are not, therefore, a useful index for the migratory fishery. Stone features and serious cutting and filling, on the other hand, can be taken as evidence for the presence of resident fishers and traders, since they imply an attachment to a particular property which was impractical for migratory crews, who could never be sure of continued access to the same shore room in subsequent summers, unless they leased space from a planter.

Newfoundland's best examples of early permanent stone wharves and warehouses have survived at Ferryland, originally a sixteenth-century fishing station about 80 km south of St John's (Figure 1). Ferryland was developed, as a permanent fishing station and defensible harbour, by the colonial proprietor Sir George Calvert, Lord Baltimore, in the 1620s and later, in the 1640s and 50s, as a market and port, by Sir David Kirke (Pope 2004). The waterfront structures there have been uncovered by James Tuck and his students, who are currently exploring an extensive early seventeenth-century sea wall and quay on the Ferryland Pool (Gaulton 1997; Tuck and Gaulton 2001). The St John's waterfront, or at least the area we have been able to explore archaeologically, has not yielded similar evidence. Here the major manifestation of waterfront development uncovered to date is encroachment on the harbour.

Filling is the great commonplace of harbour development (Hobley 1981). It was promoted in St John's, as elsewhere, by several factors, notably the increasing draft of ocean-going vessels and the high value of waterfront property. The average tonnage of ships involved in the Newfoundland fishery grew from about 50 in the 1580s to something like 100 tons by the 1670s (Cell 1969, 131; Poole 1677c). As for the incentive to fill, constituted by the value of waterfront property, this was nicely summed up by the agent for a London insurance company, in 1809:

> St John's has of late years rapidly increased in population and buildings, and the properties on the water-side have become of great value. In proportion with these causes, the buildings upon them have become more numerous, and indeed a more crowded range of wharfage and stores I have yet seen in no places. Even the narrow coves reserved by government for boats have been encroached upon and every year adds to the list (O'Neill 1976, 620)

FIGURE 4. FISH FLAKES IN THE FOREGROUND OF AN ANONYMOUS *VIEW OF THE UPPER END OF THE HARBOUR FROM A LITTLE BELOW FORT WILLIAM*, NAC C-003372.

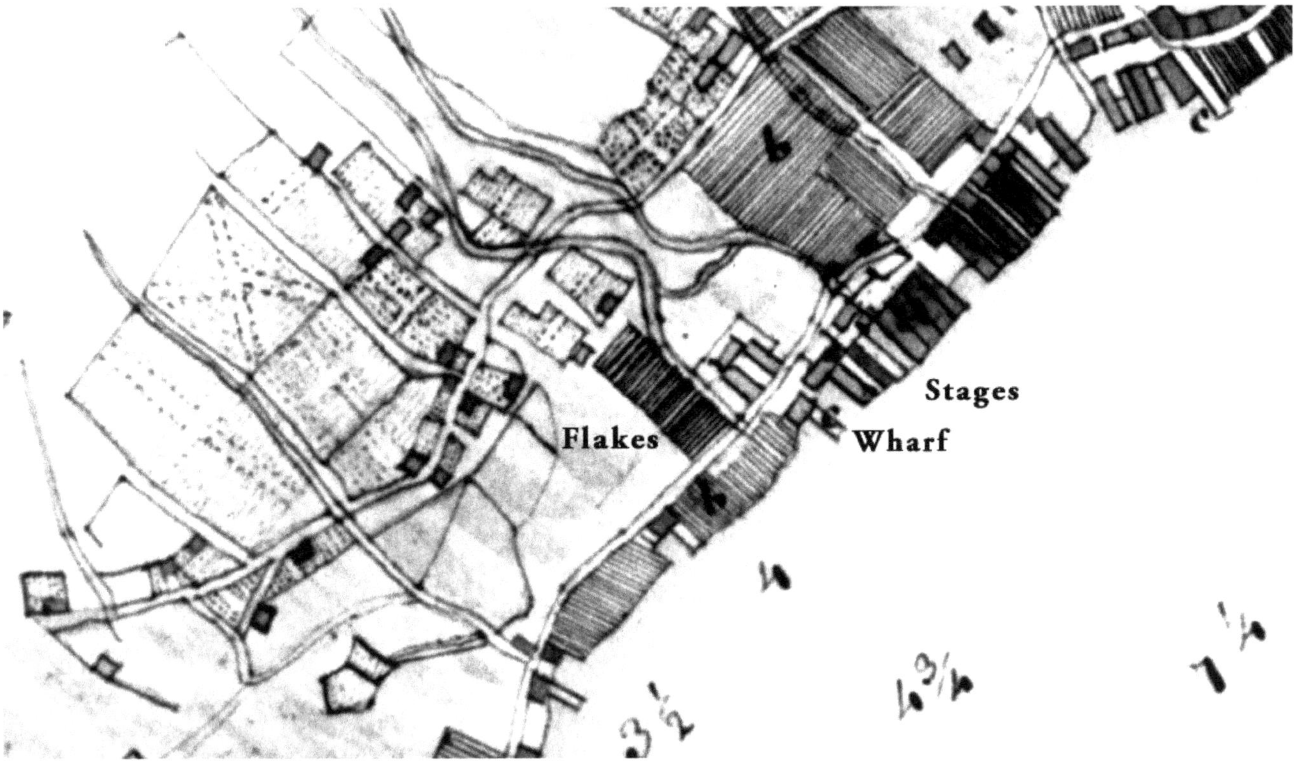

FIGURE 5. THE WALDEGRAVE STREET AND WATER STREET AREAS IN 1751 (BRAMHAN AND HYLTON, 1751). THE WALDEGRAVE STREET SITE (CJAE-33) IS AT THE FISH FLAKES MARKED. THE 327 WATER STREET SITE (CJAE-08) IS JUST INSHORE OF THE MARKED WHARF AND STAGES.

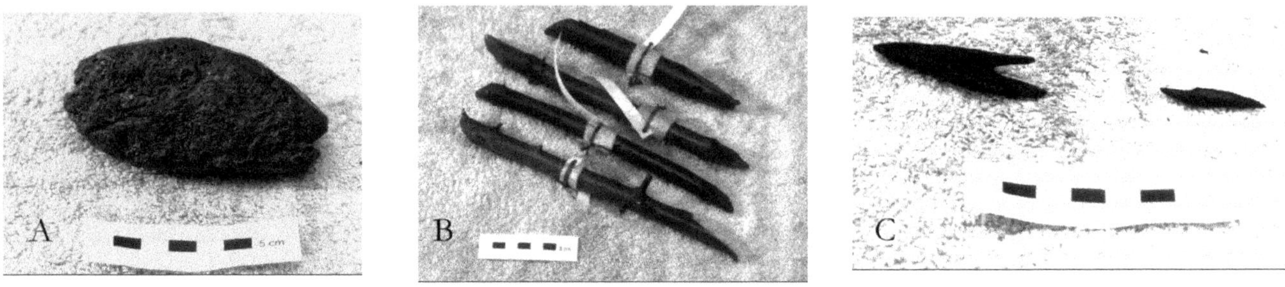

FIGURE 6. WOODEN FISH PROCESSING ARTIFACTS FROM WALDEGRAVE STREET (CJAE-33).
a. Notched softwood burl netfloat. b. Softwood sticks, up to 30 cm long, sharpened at both ends, function uncertain. c. Fragments of a wooden netting needle.

A final consideration was surely the steep coastal geography of St John's Bay. Residents had every incentive to engage in cutting, in order to create usable horizontal workspace – and where there is cutting there is, inevitably, filling.

The early cartographic record of St John's is, fortunately, exceptionally rich, for a North American town, reflecting perhaps its early importance to the imperial ambitions of Britain and France (Pope and Carter 1988). Although several earlier maps and views have survived, it is only from the mid eighteenth century that we have a map accurate enough to compare the waterfront of this period with later waterfronts (Bramham and Hylton 1751). A comparison with selected charts and maps of the succeeding centuries provides a clear history of waterfront advance. Comparison of succeeding waterfronts indicates that filling progressed rapidly in the eighteenth and nineteenth centuries, with a particularly rapid development in the first half of the nineteenth century and a rather striking retreat in the first half of the twentieth century. Can we read this puzzling pullback as an indicator of the economic difficulties Newfoundland faced in this period, first as a self-governing dominion within the British Empire, over- eager to invest in railways, banks and British war bonds and, after 1933, as an economic basket case, supported on iron rations by a colonial Commission of Government? Significantly, the waterfront began to advance again with the hyperactivity of the Second World War and, later, with Newfoundland's entry into the Canadian confederation in 1949. The most recent advance came in 1970, with the in-filling of the finger piers and the creation of modern docking facilities, suitable for the container ships, industrial trawlers, oil-rig supply vessels, and cruise liners that frequent the port today.

Predictably, every site surveyed showed evidence of deliberate filling, in one period or another. At several sites, we have unambiguous evidence for a major episode of massive filling, during cleanup following the disaster of fire or war. A melted William III shilling recovered from the destruction level which caps the seventeenth-century deposits at 327 Water Street nicely dates the older burnt fill at this site. At Duckworth Street East (CjAe-15) a metre-thick deposit of shattered stone and disturbed glacial clays obliterated the underlying "New Fort" – a civil refuge of row housing, huddled in the shadow of the British garrison at Fort William, constructed in 1706 and destroyed by French forces in 1708 (Pope 1995b). On Water Street itself, all-too-brief mechanical testing at the Ayre's Premises (CjAe-32) uncovered a thick deposit of burned rubble much of which consisted of melted or scorched creamware and refined gray stoneware – the remains, apparently, of a wholesale stock of ceramics, destroyed in the fire of 1780 (Tuck 1986; Simmonds 2000). A similar thick deposit of scorched English brown saltglaze stoneware (*e.g.* Figure 7i) recovered from the George Neal Premises (CjAe-7) marks a comparable filling event, after the fire of 1816 destroyed what seems to have been a dealer in ink and boot-blacking (Pope 1995c). Excavations at Temperance Street (CjAe-31), which intersects poetically with Water Street in the east end of St John's, uncovered almost 2 metres of fire rubble, used to re-landscape the area following the Great Fire of 1892 (Pope 1998b). Although identifying each of these intermittent episodes of massive filling was useful, in a way, in understanding the impact of reconstruction on harbour development, the larger picture of gradual waterfront advance was clearest at 327 Water Street.

The underlying aim of the project, so to speak, was to find the original waterfront, in order to understand the subsequent accretion of stages, wharves, warehouses and harbour-side aprons (Figure 5). The first reasonably good map of the port, a naval chart of 1697, was simply not accurate enough to read back the position of the waterfront at that time (Anon 1698). Besides, significant waterfront advance might have already occurred during the two preceding centuries, when the harbour of St John's was intensively used but rarely mapped. Archaeological research was clearly indicated. City workers told us that a Victorian brickwork trunk sewage line ran along an even cobble beach about 3 m under present day Water Street. That put the original waterfront somewhere just to the south of St John's downtown thoroughfare, about 100 m from the existing harbour side. In order to pinpoint the original water's edge in at least one specific place, we had to find a site where it would be possible to dig a series of tests proceeding further and further towards the water from "the lower path", as Water

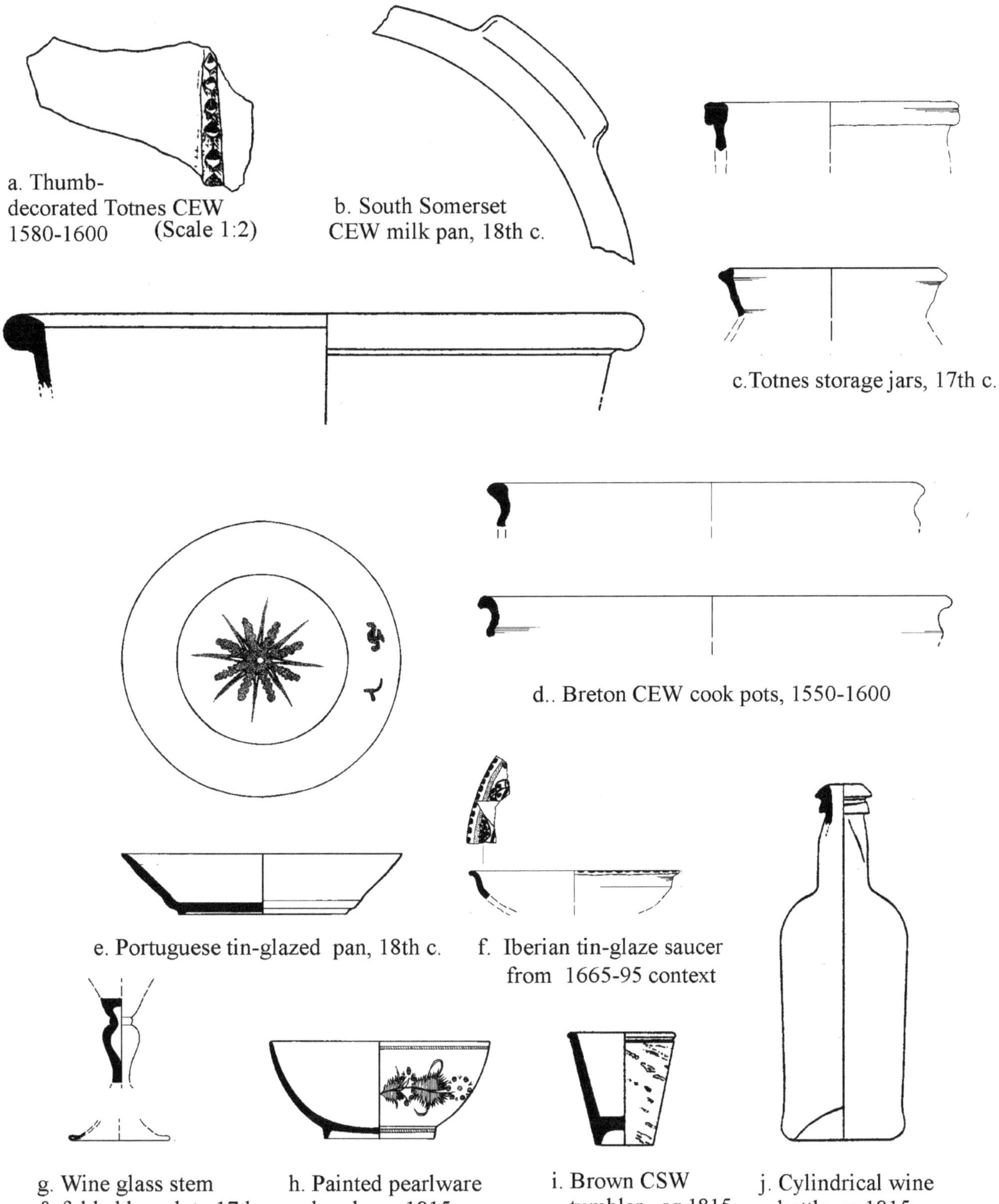

FIGURE 7. CERAMIC AND GLASS FINDS FROM THE ST. JOHN'S WATERFRONT.
Figures a - h from 327 Water Street (CjAe-08), Areas D and E; figures i and j from George Neal premises (CjAe-07).
Scale 1:4 unless noted. CEW = coarse earthenware. CSW = coarse stoneware.

Street was once called (O'Neill 1975, 416). During a series of investigations between 1993 and 2000, 327Water Street emerged as that site, despite the fact that it had suffered some completely unnecessary disturbance, during demolition activities following a late twentieth-century fire. There are only a few lots currently vacant on the harbour side of Water Street and only some of these are accessible to archaeologists, so in the end we were lucky to find one where we could piece together a more or less continuous picture of waterfront use over four or five centuries.

It was evident from our initial investigations at 327 Water Street that the site's history reached back to the sixteenth century migratory fishery. One redeposit yielded a sherd from a Totnes coarse earthenware cook pot, thumb-decorated in a distinctively early style (Figure 7a). Given the very restricted distribution of Totnes earthenwares in England itself, finds in Newfoundland are a strong indication of the presence of fishing crews from Dartmouth, just down river from Totnes (Allan and Pope 1990). St John's close commercial relationship with Dartmouth in the later seventeenth century is attested both in the fishing censuses of the 1670s and 80s and also in the relatively strong representation of this ware in contexts of this period at this site (Figure 7c) (Temple 1999, 16). Recovery of an early form gives us a sense that Dartmouth's interest was of long-standing. North Devon coarse earthenware cook pots and tall "butter pots" recovered from the site suggest links with the ports of Barnstaple and Bideford, though these may have been indirect, since this ware was widely distributed in the period (Grant 1983, 101-130). South Somerset wares are also well represented at the site, particularly in the eighteenth-century contexts (*e.g.* Figure 7b). Redeposits yielded rims of several cook pots in a distinctive gritty beige micaceous ware (Figure 7d). With the assistance of John Allan, of the Royal Albert Museum in Exeter, these were recently identified as Breton. On petrological as well as historical grounds it is likely that these were produced sometime in the sixteenth century in southeast Brittany around Vannes or Rennes (Pope 2002). Similar wares have also been found in sixteenth-century contexts at Ferryland (Tuck 1996, 28).

We also recovered quantities of the micaceous Portuguese earthenware known to northern European archaeologists as Merida (Hurst, Neal and van Beuningen 1986, 73-74). Merida bottles and pans occur regularly on Newfoundland sites of the later seventeenth century and can usually be interpreted as tokens of the triangular trade among Newfoundland, Portugal and southern England, rather than as evidence for the presence of Portuguese fishing crews in this period. Merida turned up frequently at 327 Water Street among the water-worn ceramic sherds in a pebble beach context sealed by harbour in-filling at the close of the seventeenth century (Walsh 2000: 11). This context must represent harbour activity over the two centuries between 1500 and 1700 and, in this case, the very strong representation of Merida may be material evidence of migratory Portuguese activity on the coast of Newfoundland in the sixteenth century, something which has been surprisingly difficult to find (cf. Abreu-Ferreira 1998).

The Water Street site also contained significant seventeenth-century contexts (Pope 1999b). Working through disturbed deposits we uncovered an undisturbed household midden dating between about 1665 and 1695. The dating is based on a nice assemblage of pipe bowls (Figure 8). The upper surface of this midden contained charcoal, as well as melted artifacts and most likely represents the destruction horizon of the French attack on St John's in 1696/7. Curiously enough, these strata of the second half of the seventeenth century lay directly on sterile glacial soil. This was a puzzling situation, since by 1665 St John's harbour had been in use for at least 150 years so that deposits of that period should overlie some natural soil, if not earlier cultural strata. As we approached the sterile subsoil it became clear that any such earlier strata had been cleared by deliberate cutting into the slope of the harbourfront *ca.* 1665 and this hypothesis was confirmed when we fully exposed the sterile level to find its surface unnaturally erratic, as well as being pock-marked with early post-moulds, truncated by cutting before renewed cultural deposition after 1665. Early capital investment in harbour improvement, represented by this episode of soil levelling, must have created quite a bit of fill – fill which would likely have ended up closer to the water, in order to make land. Our excavations naturally proceeded towards the water but we did not find our missing mid-century fills.

In the adjacent section of the site, we exposed water-worn bedrock and a pebble beach. Judging by the styles of wine bottle glass and ceramic sherds recovered from the beach which were still sharp or only lightly water-worn, it was not in-filled until the later 1690s. The materials cut during harbour improvements in 1665 were not, in other words, deposited here but must have been displaced somewhat along the harbour side. Early filling is more probable to the east, the site of the later Murray's Premises, than to the west, which was, well into the twentieth century, a quay known as Bishop's Cove. This late seventeenth-century filling episode involved construction of a simple ledge, created by aligning recycled wharf posts along the beach, just uphill from high water. The harbourside cutting improvements of *ca.* 1665 and the filling of the beach itself *ca.* 1695 mark the moments from which waterfront advance began, in this part of St John's harbour, at least sixty to ninety years before we have interpretable cartographic evidence for this basic aspect of harbour development. Together with the remains of a stone-line quay side of *ca.* 1830, uncovered at the site, these early events permits us to assemble a composite profile of 327 Water Street, providing the first archaeological evidence for the pace of waterfront development in early modern St John's (Figure 9).

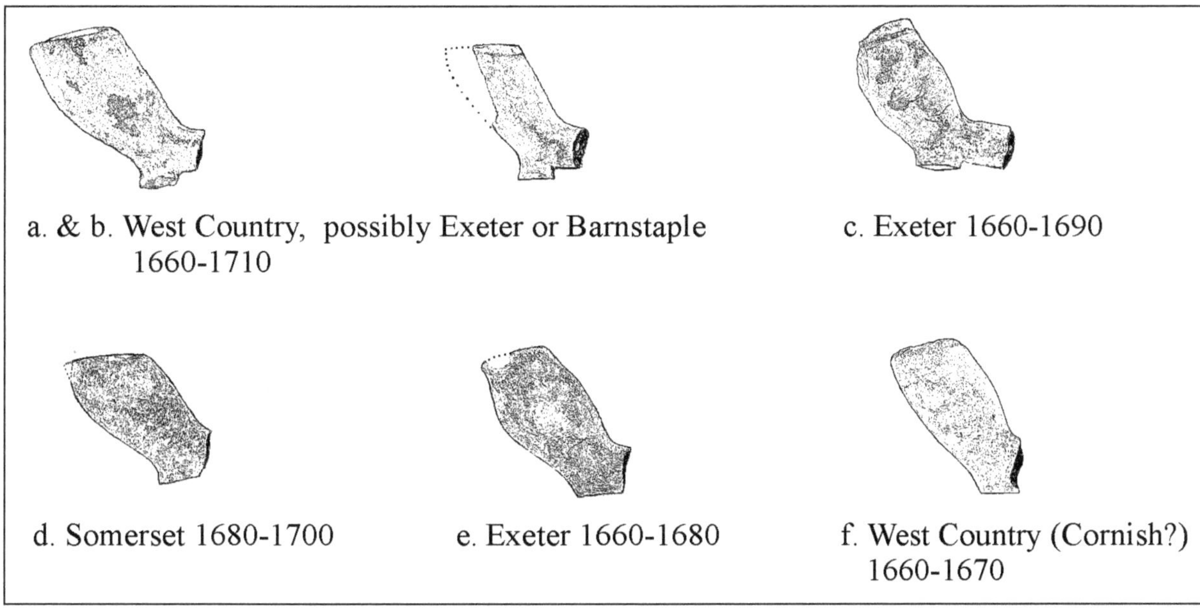

FIGURE 8. CLAY TOBACCO PIPE BOWLS FROM A CONTEXT OF 1665-1695 AT 327 WATER STREET (CJAE-08), AREA D. SCALE 1:2

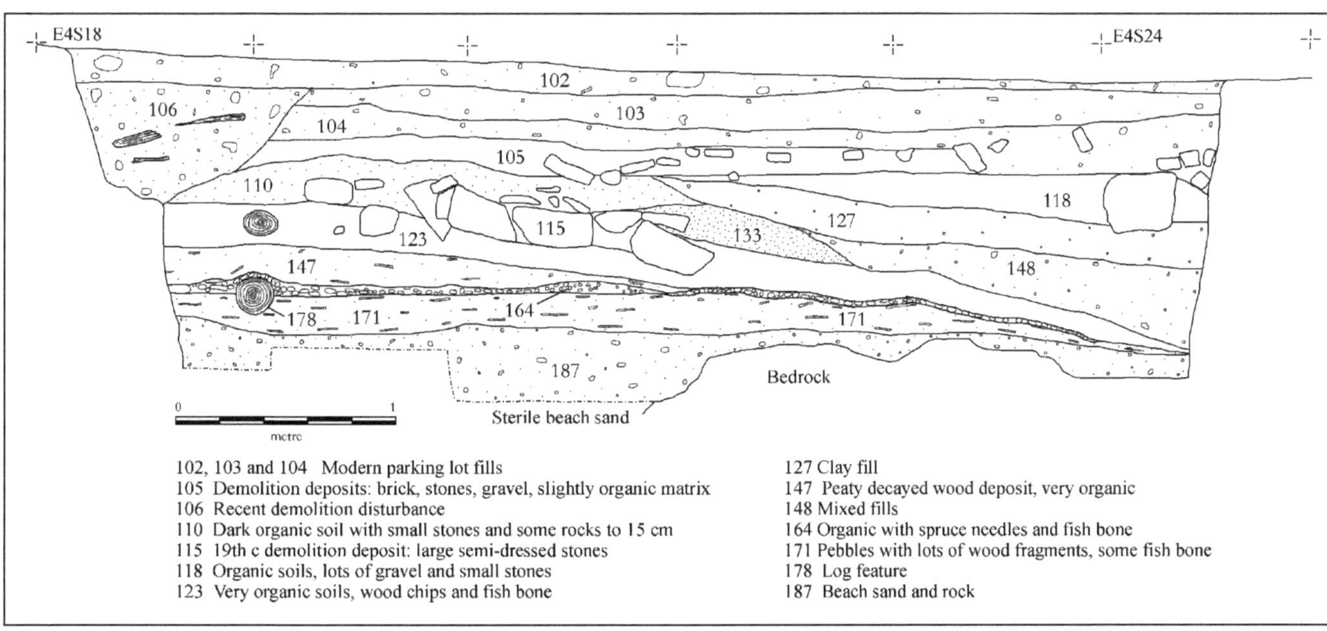

FIGURE 9. PROFILE AT 327 WATER STREET (CJAE-08), AREA E. WATER STREET IS TO THE NORTH OR LEFT IN THIS PROFILE, THE HARBOUR IS TO THE RIGHT.

The unusually high proportion of high status tin-glazed wares *(e.g.* Figure 7 f) as well as the recovery of wine glasses (Figure 7 g) and a piece of gentleman's jewellery, in the form of the gilded "point" or lace tip, suggests that our primary deposit of 1665-1695 relates, at least in part, to a reasonably well-off resident household, rather than of migratory crews (Pope 1999, Temple 1999). The relatively weak representation of bottle glass and Westerwald coarse stoneware, which typically occurs in beverage service forms, may indicate that this was not a typical planter household, almost of which operated tippling houses, but one wealthy enough either to forgo this sideline or to keep it far enough from the family domicile to separate the deposit of household and tippling house debris. Southwood's map of St John's in 1677 (Figure 2) shows a plantation in the area, belonging to

Thomas Oxford, who was one of the leading planters of the period, and this secondary deposit might well be a product of the Oxford household (Southwood 1689). The plantation partially excavated at 327 Water Street is of some historical interest, as the early social and economic history of St John's has not been adequately explored.

Later finds suggest the continued presence of substantial merchant planters close to the 327 Water Street site. Excavation of organic deposits inside the log retaining wall uncovered two separate caches of gold wire, wound with what seems to have been finer silver wire, suitable for the ornamentation of higher-status clothing. The same context, which probably dates close to 1700, also yielded a wine bottle seal with the initials "I.C." the initials of John Collins, a prominent merchant of early eighteenth-century St John's. Personally monogrammed wine bottles are an unambiguous indication of wealth and in Newfoundland contexts of the seventeenth and eighteenth centuries are closely identified with the owners of substantial fishing plantations and transatlantic merchants (Wicks 1998). Here, as elsewhere on Newfoundland's English Shore, we recovered many wine bottles. (For a late example, see Figure 7j.) These are not a useful status indicator in such contexts, since ordinary fishing folk were able to obtain wine and spirits easily and consumed both in quantities astonishing to visitors from the old country, who expected ordinary working people to content themselves with beer (Pope 1994). Other finds do give an impression that pockets of elegance continued to exist, hidden probably in the second storey residences that eighteenth and nineteenth century merchants maintained above their retail premises on Water Street. These include some very handsome examples of eighteenth-century Portuguese *faiança* and an elegant footed pearlware bowl, delicately hand-painted in the olive and brown tones fashionable *ca* 1815 (Figures 7 e and h).

Some of these finds were useful for close dating of the events which overlie the original beach. The younger overlying strata are usually clay, or occasionally sandy secondary deposits, almost always with cultural material. These fills were probably deliberately introduced in a series of what must have been frustrating attempts to create a dry work surface, at what is naturally an extremely wet site, where ground water still flows in some quantity after every rainfall. These secondary fills cap a series of dark black organic primary deposits consisting of a mixture of spruce needles, deriving no doubt from fish flakes, with cod vertebrae and cranial elements from heading and splitting fish, sometimes mixed with beach pebbles and wood debris. Only one of these organic events seemed to be a deliberate secondary deposition. This consisted of whole spruce boughs and a kilogram or so of a yellow-orange fatty deposit, almost certainly cod-liver oil. This was spilled in the late eighteenth century, perhaps when the Verwood coarse earthenware pot, from the same context, with the same fatty residue, broke. The pot will eventually make a nice museum piece. It is less obvious what to do with the cod liver oil, now the consistency of cheddar cheese, if somewhat more odiferous. Significant pollution of the site with fuel oil rules out some kinds of organic analysis but the sample remains in a freezer, awaiting the researcher with an interest in two hundred year old marine oils.

Event	Date	Mean Length from Cranial Evidence	Mean Length from Vertebral Evidence
123	1770-80	n/a	958 cm (n=27)
147	1730-50	902 cm (n=4)	1003 cm (n=119)
164	1720-1730	856 cm (n=11)	1095 cm (n=160)
171	1700-1720	891 cm (n=9)	1028 cm (n=133)

TABLE 1. LIVE LENGTH OF CODFISH, BASED ON CRANIAL AND VERTEBRAL REMAINS, 327 WATER STREET, ST JOHN'S, NEWFOUNDLAND (CJAE-08), USING REGRESSION FORMULAS (ROJO 1986, ROJO 1987).

The cod bones retrieved from the site have proved somewhat more amenable to analysis. There are three large samples, each of which is datable within a decade or so, from associated cultural deposits. Following measurements of the vertebral and cranial elements, we used a regression formula to estimate live length (Rojo 1986; Rojo 1987). Cod from all three samples appeared to be in the order of 90 to 100 cm long (Table 1). While cod this size and even twice as big certainly existed, even in the twentieth century, adjusted comparison with historically-attested dry weight of fish processed in the early seventeenth century suggests that our figure may be too large (Whitbourne 1622, 176-177). Perhaps our samples were biased by the collection methods, which relied primarily on trowel collection; although it is not obvious that these would seriously skew the collection of cranial elements, which yielded similar, if somewhat smaller, size estimates. Even discounting the absolute significance of our preliminary size estimates, two conclusions remain of interest. Each sample shows only moderate internal variation, suggesting that fishers were preferentially seeking a particular size of fish, amenable to their methods of processing and distribution. Second, there is no significant trend over time, suggesting that human predation on cod in this period was not impacting stocks to an extent which affected fishers' ability to reliably catch fish of a preferred size. Our faunal remains are significant too, in a more general sense, because they confirm that well into the nineteenth century the St John's waterfront supported continued mixed use for fish processing as well as for trade.

Our project is complete, or the field work phase of it, at least. Of course, further research on the waterfront would be worthwhile, as existing properties along Water Street come up for redevelopment. One of the significant results of excavations in the area has been to establish that early modern contexts survive under these nineteenth-century structures (Tuck 1986; Pope 1996). The Waterfront Archaeology Project enables us to say, with more precision, that the zone within 30 m of the south side of Water Street should be treated as particularly sensitive, from the point of view of heritage resource management. Our project evolved out of a sense that St John's early history had been lost, obliterated in part by the repeated devastation of St John's by fire and in part by recent redevelopment of the port. Although City Council has occasionally made pleasant noises about the need for archaeological mitigation in the downtown area, the city's track record is not impressive and, despite repeated promises, the Engineering Department regularly forgets to notify the provincial Archaeology Office of impending excavations. It is the latter, one hopes, that will be able to use the provincial Historic Resources Act to ensure that archaeologists have access to other significant waterfront sites, as the historic harbour area is redeveloped in the future. The St John's Waterfront Archaeology Project has, we hope, given provincial regulators some sense of where these are likely to be found.

Acknowledgements

The author acknowledges, with thanks, the support of Memorial University of Newfoundland, its Institute for Social and Economic Research (ISER), the Smallwood Foundation for Newfoundland Studies, the Social Sciences and Humanities Research Council of Canada through the Newfoundland Archaeological Heritage Outreach Program, and the Culture and Heritage Division, Province of Newfoundland and Labrador. The project depended on the enthusiastic assistance of students in the Waterfront Archaeology Field Schools, 1997, 1998 and 2000, as well as the public-spirited cooperation of the owner of the 327 Water Street site, Wayne Kelly. Petrological examination of the Breton ceramics was carried out by Dr. Roger Taylor, formerly of the British Geological Survey and Dr. David Williams of the English Heritage Ceramic Petrology Project. The osteological measurements were carried out under the direction of Patricia Wells, with the advice of Dr. Lisa Hodgetts, both researchers with Memorial's Archaeology Unit.

Bibliography

Abreu-Ferreira, D. 1998, Terra Nova through the Iberian looking glass: the Portuguese-Newfoundland cod fishery in the sixteenth century, *Canadian Historical Review* 79(1), 100-115.

Allan, J. P., and Pope, P.E. 1990, A new class of south-west English pottery in North America. *Post-Medieval Archaeology*, 24, 51-60.

Anon. 1698, *A draught of St. John's Harbour with the soundings*, British Library, K. Top. CXIX 103, in National Archives of Canada (NAC) NMC 65.

Bramham, J. and Hylton, E. S. 1751, *Plan of St John's Harbour in Newfoundland*. British Library, K. Top. CXIX 104, in NAC, NMC 18046.

Cell, G.T. 1969, *English enterprise in Newfoundland, 1577-1660*, Toronto, University of Toronto Press.

Faulkner, A. 1985, Archaeology of the cod fishery: Damiriscove Island. *Historical Archaeology*, 19(2), 57-86.

Gaulton, B. 1997, Seventeenth-century stone construction at Ferryland, Newfoundland (Area C), *Avalon Chronicles*, 2, 1-43.

Grant, A. 1983, *North Devon pottery: the seventeenth century*. Exeter: Exeter University Press.

Hayes, E. 1583, Narrative of Sir Humphrey Gilbert's voyage, in D. B. Quinn (ed.), 1979, *New American world: a documentary history of North America to 1612*, vol. 4, *Newfoundland from fishery to colony. Northwest Passage searches*. New York, Arno Press and Hector Bye, 23-42.

Head, C. G. 1976, *Eighteenth century Newfoundland: a geographer's perspective*, Toronto, McClelland and Stewart.

Hobley, B. 1981, The London waterfront – the exception to the rule?, in G. Milne and B. Hobley (eds.), *Waterfront Archaeology in Britain and Northern Europe*, Council for British Archaeology Research Report, no. 41, 1-9.

Hurst, J. G., Neal, D. S., and van Beuningen, H. J. E. 1986, Pottery produced and traded in north-west Europe 1350-1650, *Rotterdam Papers*, vol. 6, The Hague, Museum Boymans-van Beuningen.

Mannion, J. 2002, Irish migration and settlement in Newfoundland: the formative phase, 1697-1732, *Newfoundland Studies*, 17, in press.

O'Neill, P. 1975, *The oldest city: the story of St. John's, Newfoundland*, Don Mills, Ontario, Press Porcépic.

O'Neill, P. 1976, *A seaport legacy*, Don Mills, Ontario, Press Porcépic.

Pocius, G. L. 1992, The house that poor-jack built: architectural stages in the Newfoundland fishery, in L. McCann and C. MacMillan (eds.), *The sea and culture of Atlantic Canada,* Sackville, New Brunswick , Centre for Canadian Studies, Mount Allison University, 63-105.

Poole, W. 1677. Letter to Committee of Trade and Plantations, with enclosures, 10 September, Great Britain, Public Record Office, CO 1/41 (62), 147-172.

Pope, Peter E. 1991, *St. John's harbour area archaeological potential*, Past Present Consulting, report for Heritage Advisory Committee, City of St. John's, Newfoundland, on file Centre for Newfoundland Studies, Memorial University of Newfoundland (CNS).

Pope, Peter E. 1994 Fish into wine: the historical anthropology of the demand for alcohol in 17th-century Newfoundland, *Histoire Sociale/Social History* 27 (54), 261-278.

Pope, Peter E. 1995a, *Final report, St. John's harbour area archaeological survey, 1993*, Past Present Consulting, report for Culture and Heritage Division, Province of Newfoundland and Labrador (CHD), on file CNS.

Pope, Peter E. 1995b, *Site Report: CjAe-15, (49) Duckworth Street East, the "New Fort". St. John's Archaeological Survey, 1993*, Past Present Consulting, report for CHD, on file CNS.

Pope, Peter E. 1995c, *Site Report: CjAe-7, George Neal Premises. St. John's Archaeological Survey, 1993*, Past Present Consulting, report for CHD, on file CNS.

Pope, Peter E. 1996, Under Water Street: the early waterfront of St. John's, Newfoundland. In *Archaeological remains in situ preservation, Proceedings of the Second ICAHM International Conference, Montreal 1994, Montreal,* ICOMOS International Committee on Archaeological Heritage Management, 243-250.

Pope, Peter E. 1997, The 16th-century fishing voyage, in J. E. Candow and C. Corbin (eds.), *How deep is the ocean? historical essays on Canada's Atlantic fishery*, Sidney, Nova Scotia, Louisbourg Institute, University College of Cape Breton Press, 15-30.

Pope, Peter E. 1999a, *1998 Excavations at Waldegrave Street Parking, St John's, CjAe-33*, St John's, St John's Waterfront Archaeology Project, report for CHD, on file CNS.

Pope, Peter E. 1998b, *1997 excavations at Temperance Street, St John's, CjAe-31,* St John's Waterfront Archaeology Project, report for CHD, on file CNS.

Pope, Peter E. 2002, Early European occupations in southeast Newfoundland: archaeological perspectives on competition for fishing rooms, 1530-1680, *Archéologiques* (Montreal), in press.

Pope, Peter E. 2004, *Fish into wine: the Newfoundland plantation in the seventeenth century*, Chapel Hill, North Carolina, University of North Carolina Press, in press.

Pope, P. and Carter, J. 1988, *The shape of St. John's through time,* exhibition catalogue, St. John's, Memorial University Art Gallery.

Rojo, A. 1986, Live length and weight of cod (Gadus morhua) estimated from various skeletal elements, *North American Archaeologist* 7(4), 329-351.

Rojo, A. 1987, Excavated fish vertebrae as predictors in bioarchaeological research, *North American Archaeologist*, 8(3), 209-226.

Rut, J. 1527, Letter to Henry VIII of England, 3 August, in D. B. Quinn (ed.), *New American world: a documentary history of North America to 1612*, vol. 1, *America from concept to discovery. Early exploration of North America,* New York, Arno Press and Hector Bye, 189-190.

Ryan, S. S. 1983. Fishery to colony: a Newfoundland watershed, 1793-1815, *Acadiensis*, 12(2), 34-52.

Seary, E.R. 1971. *Place names of the Avalon Peninsula of the Island of Newfoundland*, Toronto, University of Toronto Press.

Simmonds, M. 2000. *A study of the ceramics from CjAe-32*. Undergraduate honours dissertation, Memorial University of Newfoundland.

Southwood, H. 1689. *A new chart of the trading part of Newfoundland*, in J. Thornton, *The English Pilot* vol. 4, London, William Fisher and John Thornton.

Temple, B. E. 1999, *Seventeenth- and eighteenth-century ceramics from CjAe-08, Test D, 327 Water Street, St. John's, Newfoundland.* Undergraduate honours dissertation, Memorial University of Newfoundland.

Tuck, J. A. 1986, *Salvage excavations in the City of St. John's*, in J. S. Thomson and C.

Thomson (eds.), Archaeology in Newfoundland and Labrador 1985, *Newfoundland Museum, Historic Resources Division, Annual Report*, no. 6, St. John's, 233-236.

Thomson (eds.), 1996, Archaeology at Ferryland, Newfoundland *1936-1995, Avalon Chronicles*, 1, 21-42.

Tuck, J. A., and Gaulton, B. 2001, Archaeology at Ferryland 1998-2000, *Avalon Chronicles* 6, 89-106.

Walsh, M. 2000, *An analysis of early eighteenth-century material culture from CjAe-08, test E, 327 Water Street, St. John's, Newfoundland,* undergraduate honours dissertation, Memorial University of Newfoundland.

Whitbourne, R. 1622, A discourse and discovery of New-Found-Land, in G. T. Cell (ed.), *Newfoundland discovered: English attempts at colonisation, 1610-1630*, Hakluyt Society, 2nd series, no. 160, London, 1982, 100-206.

Wicks, J. 1998, Seventeenth- and eighteenth-century bottle seals from Ferryland, Newfoundland, *Avalon Chronicles* 3, 99-108.

1817. From Trieste to Pesaro. Last voyage of the “Arduz”

Maria Cecilia Profumo

Abstract.
In 1978 an amateur SCUBA diver sighted an ancient wreck off the beach in Pesaro. Early investigation and systematic digs carried out since 1991 by the Soprintendenza Archeologica per le Marche, (Archaeological Superintendence of the Marche, Italy) have concerned the areas around the prow and stern to find the vessel’s size, technical characteristics and state of conservation. The plentiful materials collected (crockery, bottles, arms, amphorae, tools and personal objects as well as ropes, hawsers blocks etc. belonging to the hull) indicate the date as the early decades of the 19th century. Research in the archives brought to light the story of the *Arduz*, a ship flying the Ottoman flag which set sail from Trieste in November 1817 for Alexandria in Egypt, but, taken by surprise by a storm, ran aground on the beach at Pesaro. The coincidence of many facts, together with the absence in the archives of any reference to other events of this importance, makes this identification an almost absolute certainty.

It is the morning of November 27th 1817. For the last two days there has been a storm at sea and something is happening on the beach just East of Pesaro.

> The present special report is to inform your Most Reverend Excellence that this night, towards eleven, Italian time, a man of Levantine origin [Figure 1] knocked at the Fano Gate. He was thoroughly soaked in water and with some difficulty gave the Duty Corporal to understand that he was seeking refuge, having been shipwrecked with his companions on the seashore. When the Duty Corporal asked him the whereabouts of the others, he replied that they had taken shelter in a hamlet beyond the gates. The Corporal, without letting him into the guardroom and keeping his distance, had him accompanied to the hostelry called Garatoni’s where there were eleven men. The Corporal had a sentinel mount guard so that no one could leave the hostelry, and immediately informed the Adjutant who sent a picket of soldiers to the place to keep an eye on both the shipwrecked men and the hosts.[1]

The alarm is sounded and help arrives.

> Following the notification received by me at about 13.00 hours this morning that a foreign vessel had run aground on the beach opposite the Fortress of this town, I the undersigned Chancellor for Health, went together with the Secretary for Health to the place indicated where we saw the said vessel, parts of which the waves had already washed ashore, all broken up, with a quantity of the crew’s baggage and sea chests.
> However everything was guarded by the Health Guards and the troopers, in obedience to orders given earlier.
> Three people clinging to the remaining part of the vessel still in the water were imploring help. Two were lost when the part of the vessel to which they were clinging sank. The third was saved by a boat sent out to help.[2]
> So far the corpse of an Ottoman and three dead horses have been beached as well as many other objects.[3]
> Clearly, as well as humanitarian, the primary concerns, are of a sanitary nature and on the subject there was an intense exchange of correspondence between Pesaro, Ancona and Rome, which lasted until early the following year, 1818.

To avoid the danger of contagion, it was the practice in fact for ships to travel with a sanitary certificate listing the members of the crew and passengers; they were to load and unload in particular places, under supervision; coasts would be patrolled and guarded from fixed positions (watchtowers) and, if there were any suspicion, goods and passengers were to be confined in a quarantine station, which in this particular case was the Mole Vanvitelliana in Ancona.[4]

---

[1] “Col presente rapporto straordinario rendo intesa l’Eccellenza vostra Reverendissima, che in questa notte verso le ore undici Italiane si è presentato a porta Fano un essero di nazione Levantina (Figura 1), che era tutto intriso dall’acqua, quale stentamente si è fatto intendere al Caporale di guardia che aveva necessità di ricovero mentre era naufragato con altri compagni alla spiaggia del mare, ed il Caporale di guardia avendoli richiesto ove si trovavano li medesimi, rispose che si erano reffugiati in un casale fuori di porta. Il Caporale senza introdurlo al corpo di guardia e senza avvicinarsi lo fece scortare ove si trovavano li altri, che si erano ritirati nell’osteria detta di Garatoni in numero di undici. Il Caporale vi lasciò una sentinella di vista affinché nessuno si allontanasse dalla detta osteria, ed indi ne fece subito avvertito il Sig. Aiutante Maggiore di Piazza quale vi mandò in detto locale un picchetto di soldati per tenere tanto li reffugiati, quanto li padroni di casa in osservazione...” (ASP: Archivio di Stato di Pesaro, Delegazione Apostolica, Sanità, 1817, busta 23, prot. 859).

[2] “In seguito di avviso pervenutomi circa le ore 13 di questa mattina che nella spiaggia di rimpetto alla Fortezza di questa città aveva naufragato un legno Straniero, io sottoscritto Cancelliere di Sanità mi sono recato in unione del Sig. Segretario di Sanità sul luogo indicato ove si è veduto il Legno suddetto ridotto in pezzi, del quale parte era già stato gettato in spiaggia dalle onde del mare, assieme con diversi Bagagli e Bauli dell’equipaggio.
Il tutto era però custodito dalle guardie di Sanità e dalle truppe di linea in sequela delle disposizioni precedentemente date.
Sulla parte poi del Legno rimasto in acqua esistevano tre individui che imploravano soccorso, due de quali si sono perduti, essendosi sommersa una porzione di detto legno, su cui esistevano, e l’altro si è potuto ricuperare col mezzo di un Battello mandato in soccorso... “ (ASP, Del. Ap., San., 1817, b. 23, document not numbered).

[3] “ ... Finora in terra alla spiaggia vi è un cadavere di un Ottomano ed anche tre cavalli morti, oltre molti altri oggetti... “ (ASP, Del. Ap., San., 1817, b. 23, prot. 859).

[4] For the history and restoration of the Mole Vanvitelliana see *Lazzaretto* 1990.

FIGURE 1. WATERCOLOUR BY DAVID ROBERTS (1838-39) OF AN EGYPTIAN SCENE (DETAIL): NOTE THE "LEVANTINE" COSTUMES AND THE SHAPE OF THE AMPHORA CARRIED BY THE WOMAN, A SHAPE WHICH IS STILL IN USE TODAY (FROM D. ROBERTS, *VIAGGIO IN EGITTO*, FIRENZE 1994).

As well as the helpers and guests at the hostelry, who had come into accidental contact with the survivors, these measures were supposed to be applied to the passenger, whose three servants (a grave omission) were not mentioned on the sanitary certificate. However, following a brief investigation it was decided, thanks to the good sanitary and hygienic conditions of the port they had set sail from (but more probably thanks to a bribe), to waive quarantine for these individuals.[5]

Another fact that soon transpires is a fear of Levantines. From documents in the archives we know that the presence of Turkish or North African ships was signalled by messages which flew from town to town along the coast (chiefly via the already mentioned watchtowers, which enabled news to travel from Otranto to Venice in one and a half hours)[6] and they were feared with good reason. The historian Enrico Liburdi, from San Benedetto del Tronto (Ascoli Piceno, Marche), has studied in some depth episodes of piracy to the detriment of fishermen from San Benedetto who were captured and forced into slavery in Barberia early in the 19th century.[7] A famous son of Pesaro, Gioachino Rossini, composed the opera *L'Italiana in Algeri* that tells of the young Isabella who (*Cruda sorte / Cruel fate*) is shipwrecked and herself imprisoned, and her search for her sweetheart who has been captured by pirates, with Italians who, in slavery sing a chorus expressing their determination to return to their far-off native land.[8]

But what was the name of this ship whose wreck cost the lives of five people and six horses and left 28 survivors?

Our conscientious functionaries from Pesaro lost no time in commencing interrogations (Figure 2) beginning, of course, with the ship's captain.[9]

> Interrogated as to name, Surname, Subject of where, Age etc.
> Answered my name is Omer Rodos Ottoman subject 36 years old, Ship's captain by profession and as such commander of the vessel that unfortunately I lost, as you have seen. Interrogated as to where he set sail from with said vessel, what sort its is and where bound for.
> Answered I sailed with the vessel named Arduz, flying the Ottoman flag, from Trieste, from where

[5] For health regulations see for example ASP, Del. Ap., San., 1817, b. 23, prot. 848; ASP, Del. Ap., San., 1817, b. 23, prot. 15807 (several documents with this number); ASP, Del. Ap., San., 1817, b. 23, prot. 15987. For the exemption from quarantine see: ASP, Del. Ap., San., 1817, b. 23, prot. 18284; ASP, Del. Ap., San., 1817, b. 23, prot. 15913.

[6] De Nicolò 1999.

[7] Liburdi 1943, 169-186.

[8] On this subject see also De Nicolò 1989, 317-340; Anselmi 1991, 183-212; Anselmi (ed.) 1998.

[9] "... Interrogato del di lui nome, Cognome, Suditanza, Età ecc.
Rispose mi chiamo Omer Rodos suddito ottomano d'anni 36, di Professione Capitano di Bastimento e come tale comando il Legno, che per disgrazia ho perduto, come avrà visto. Interrogato d'onde sia proveniente con detto suo Legno, di che qualità sia, e per dove diretto.
Rispose sono proveniente con la nave nominata Arduz di Bandiera ottomana di Trieste, da dove sono partito la sera dei 23 andante ed era diretto per Alessandria ad Egitto. Interrogato a manifestare il numero dell'equipaggio, e carico, che portava detta nave.
Rispose sono partito da Trieste con numero ventisette Persone di equipaggio ed un Passeggiero, come risulta dalla mia fede, rilasciatami dalla Sanità di Trieste nel giorno 20 andante, e col carico di sei cavalli, e suo necessario foraggio con tre individui destinati al serviggio dei medesimi non contemplati nella fede stessa.
...
Interrogato come sia accaduto il suo naufragio (Figura 3).
Rispose Martedì scorso nel mentre che mi ritrovava di rimpetto a Rovigno per circa venti miglia venni sorpreso da vento greco tramontana, percui fui obbligato chiudere le vele, ed in tal guisa scorrere per ostro scirocco fino al giorno seguente in cui mi avviddi che il mio Legno incominciava a far acqua per i grandi scuotimenti che produceva la fiera burrasca, che mi impedì proseguire il camino, come di prender porto in Ancona giacché il Legno stesso era per metà pieno di acqua, che mi aveva sommersi i cavalli. Ciò mi fece determinare per salvare la vita mia, e dell'equipaggio di appressarmi alla spiaggia. Vi riuscii circa la mezza notte scorsa essendosi coperto di acqua il Legno fino al Boccaporto, ho potuto col mezzo della Barcaccia porre in salvo me stesso, e ventiquattro del mio equipaggio. In questo tragitto si sono perduti tre Individui, che si erano posti sopra la Lancia. Uno si era affogato nella Nave, che era uno dei inservienti per i cavalli, e due rimasero sulla nave stessa, dei quali uno si è perito, mi dicono, e l'altro è stato salvato per le providenze, e socorso, che gli è stato recato... " (ASP, Del. Ap., San., 1817, b. 23, document not numbered).

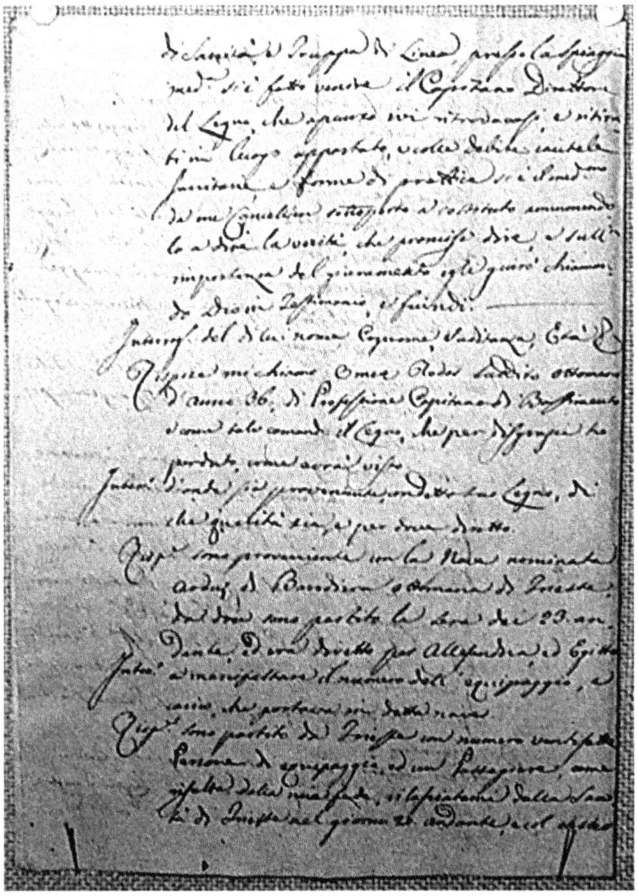

FIGURE 2. REPORT OF THE INTERROGATION OF COMMANDER OMER RODOS, OTHER MEMBERS OF THE CREW AND THE THREE SURVIVING PASSENGERS.

I departed in the evening of 23rd last, bound for Alexandria in Egypt.

(N.B. the captain here omits to mention that he set sail without paying port toll, which is apparent from documents still in Trieste).[10]

Interrogated as to number of crew on board and nature of load.

Answered I set sail from Trieste with twenty-seven crew and one passenger on board as you can see from my certificate, issued by the Trieste Health Authority on 20th last and with a load of six horses, enough forage for them and three persons for their care who are not mentioned on the certificate.

...

Interrogated as to the manner of his shipwreck [Figure 3]. Answered Last Tuesday while under sail about twenty miles off Rovigno the North Wind took me by surprise so I was obliged to furl the sails and thus drift south before the wind until the following day when I realised that my vessel was leaking because of the shuddering caused by the gales which impeded me from sailing on or from sailing into Ancona port because the boat was half filled with water which had drowned the horses. This made me decide, to save my life and that of the crew, to sail closer to the beach. By about midnight last night I had accomplished this with the ship filled with water up to the hatch, with the ship's boat I saved myself and twenty-four of my crew. During the passage three individuals who had boarded the launch were lost. One drowned on board, he was one of the horses'

FIGURE 3. "STORM AT SEA" BY F. PERUZZINI (1682-84), FROM THE CATALOGUE OF THE ANCONA EXHIBITION, JULY- NOVEMBER 1997, MILANL997.

[10] At this Archivio di Stato, in the registry of the Imperiale Regio Governo per il Litorale in Trieste, atti generali n. 1781, at no. 22619 of 29 November 1817, a communication is registered from Alessandro Basili, a representative of the Turkish authorities at the port of Trieste, concerning the departure of this ship without paying toll; unfortunately this document cannot be found. I wish to thank the Director and staff of the Trieste Archivio di Stato for their search.

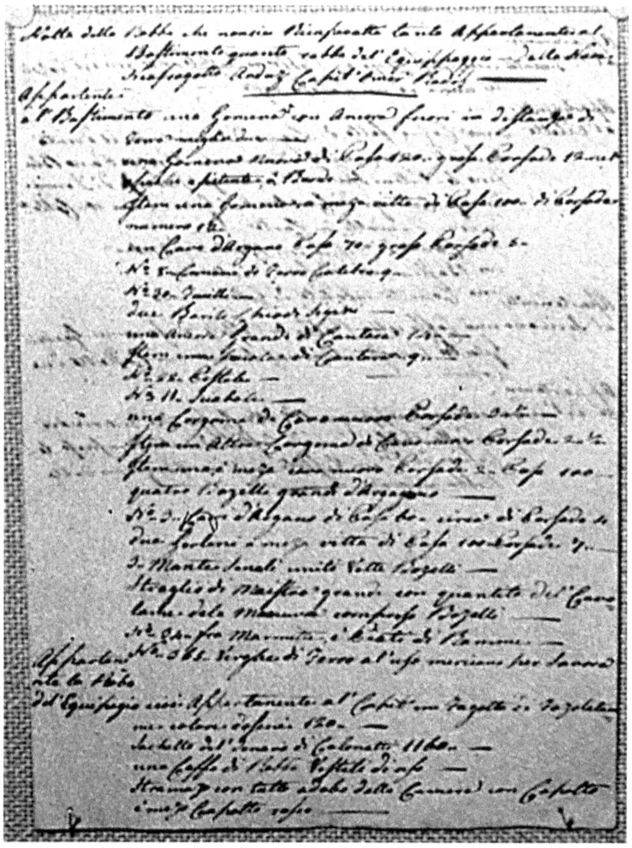

FIGURE 4. LIST OF THE GOODS LOST IN THE SHIPWRECK.

attendants, and two stayed on board, one of which they tell me perished and the other was saved by providence and the help he was given.

A further concern of the authorities is to organise pickets to guard the effects of the ship and the crew's property washed up on to the beach, as the documents quoted here (from the Archivio di Stato di Pesaro - State Archives) tell us; these objects were handed back to their owners once quarantine was over; other flotsam was recovered in the days after the shipwreck but much was lost forever (Figure 4): ropes and hawsers, cannons (Figure 5), rifles, pistols, nails, blocks, copper kettles clothing (Figure 6).[11]

Now we come to July 27th 1978: an expert amateur SCUBA diver from Pesaro, Franco Semenza, while swimming underwater a few dozen metres from the beach espies, at a depth of 4-5 metres, the remains of an ancient shipwreck visible after shifts on the seabed following the placement of an artificial reef (Figure 7).

While popular imagination baptised the wreck "a galleon" and hoped to find a fabulous treasure trove, Sub Tridente, the diving club to which the discoverer belonged, informed the Soprintendenza per i Beni Artistici e Storici and the Soprintendenza Archeologica (Superintendence for Artistic and Historic Property and the Archaeological Superintendence).[12] Archaeological investigations began while the Marine Authority took measures to protect the wreck from harm.

The first stage of investigations was carried out by Sub Tridente members; everything exposed above the bottom was drawn, photographed and recovered. After an interruption of several years, the investigation, financed by the Ministero per i Beni e le Attività Culturali (Ministry for Artistic Heritage and Cultural Activities), has continued since 1991 on an annual basis, under the direction of the present contributor and with the collaboration of several expert underwater archaeologists.[13] This has resulted in our finding that the vessel measured almost 30 metres along the keel and has enabled us to investigate its technical details (Figure 8), while examination of the materials set the date of the shipwreck at around 1820.[14]

It is worth mentioning at this point that although this wreck is a fairly recent one it is almost unique in that ships of this age, whose characteristics may be well-documented in written and iconographic sources or even in building projects, are not usually the object of archaeological investigation (Figure 9). For a similar reason studying the finds of goods and furnishings from the cargo and equipment on board meets with difficulty because, due to their date and the generally less than excellent quality, they are not of interest to archaeologists, art historians or antique dealers; consequently publications in the literature concerning comparable material are a rarity (Figure 10).

Of course, the question was also raised as to the identity of the wreck; this could be answered by a search in the archives, since it was extremely unlikely that the sinking so recently of a vessel this size would pass without written comment. Perhaps the exhibition *Barche e Marinai nelle carte d'archivio (secc. XV-XIX)* (Ships and Sailors in the Archive Papers – 15th-19th centuries), organised at the Archivio di Stato di Pesaro in December 1996 gave us the key to the answer. The final document to be presented at the exhibition was the file relative to the sinking of the Ottoman ship Arduz.[15]

[11] Cf note 5 and in particular the list in ASP, Del. Ap., San., 1817, b. 23, document not numbered, *"Notta della Robba che nonsiè Ricuperatta tanto appartenente al Bastimento quanto robba del'Equippaggio della nave naufragatta Arduz Capit. Omer Rodos* ", which is definitely the enclosure to the letter ref 17404 of 31 December 1817.

[12] Profumo 1982, 172; Profumo 1986, 40-41.

[13] AA.VV. 1994, 70-74; Profumo, Riccardi, Uguccioni (eds.) (1996); Profumo 2000, 7-11. The firms of Aquarius, Trebbi Nautica e Subacquea and Edil Giraldi have at various times worked under the direction of the present writer, as have the archaeologists Alice Freschi, Edoardo Riccardi and Stefano Medas and Sub Tridente Club.

[14] In particular, a white earthenware plate shard with a poorly impressed trade mark on the underside but nonetheless easily readable as "D.D&CO/CASTLEFORD/POTTERY", showing it to be the product of the firm of D. Dunderdale between 1803 and 1820 (Godden 1986).

[15] Curator of the exhibition was dott.ssa Maria Lucia De Nicolò and organised by this Institute and its Fano and Urbino sections and was accompanied by a publication of the same title.

FIGURE 5. IRON CANNON, RECOVERED IN 1978 AND AT PRESENT IN THE MUSEO DEL MARE, PESARO.

FIGURE 6. TERRACOTTA PIPE BOWL WITH DEVIL'S HEAD.

FIGURE 7. PLACE WHERE THE WRECK WAS FOUND.

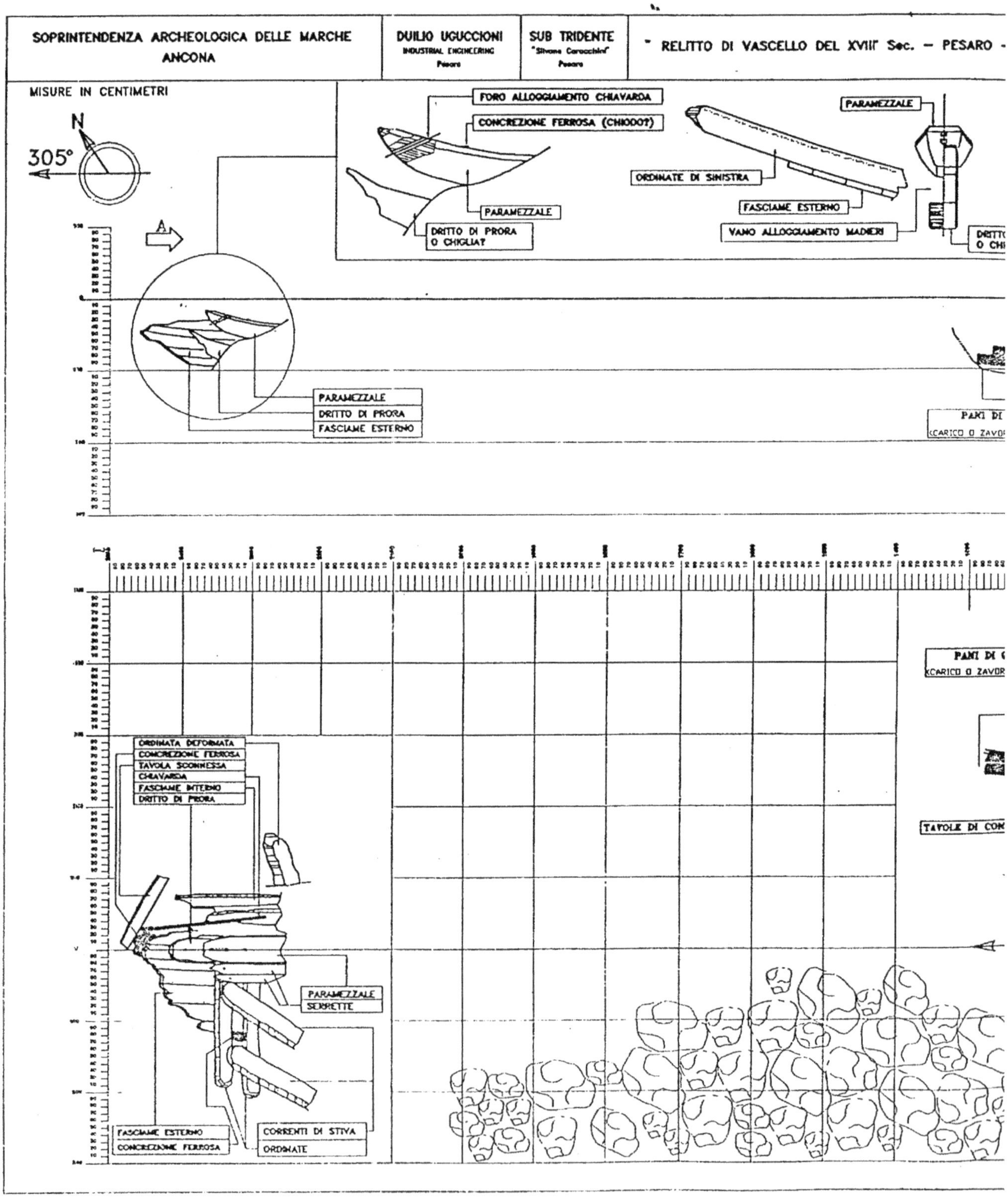

FIGURE 8. THE STATE OF THE WRECK IN 1995.

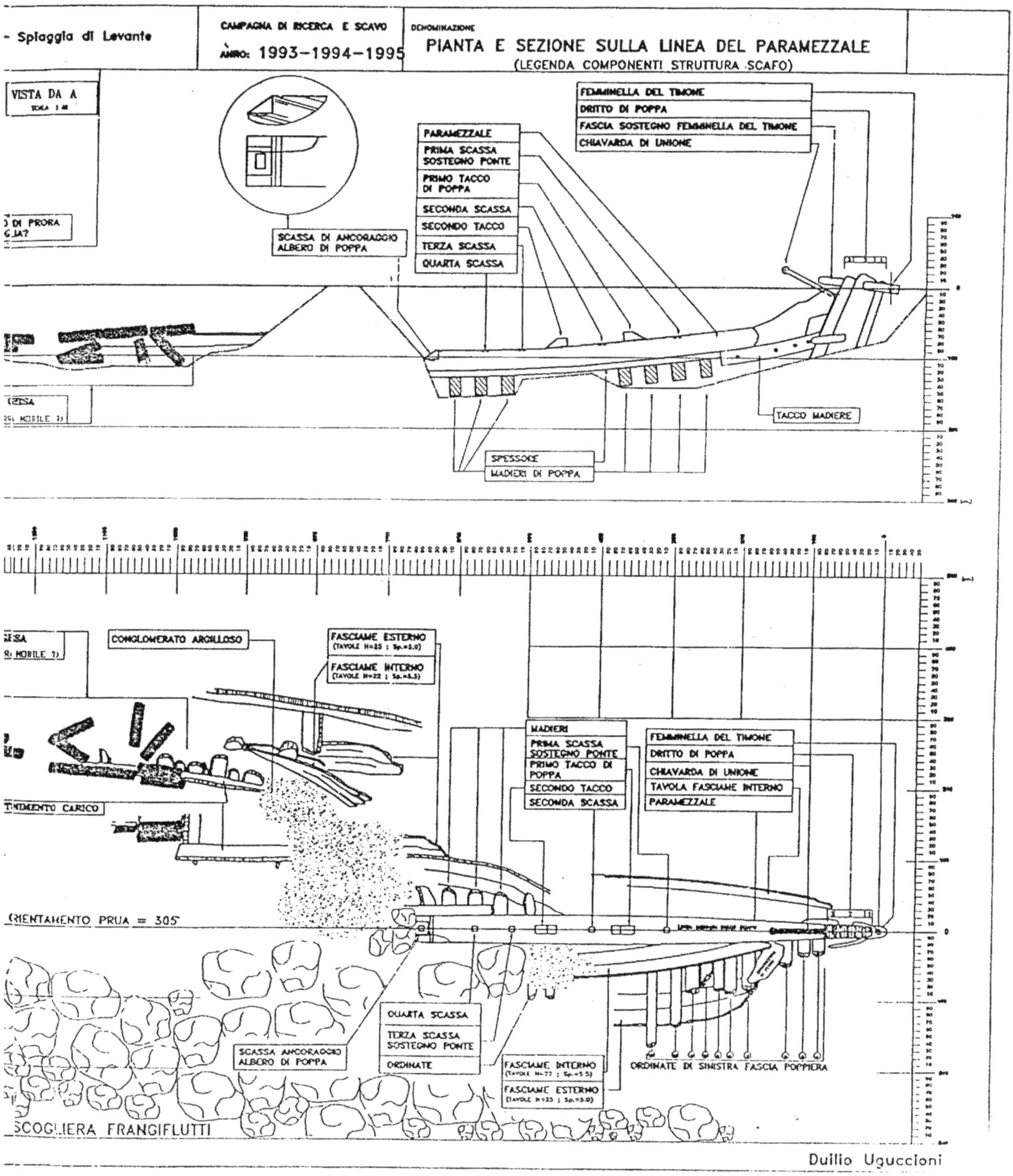
- Spiaggia di Levante
CAMPAGNA DI RICERCA E SCAVO
ANNO: 1993-1994-1995
DENOMINAZIONE
PIANTA E SEZIONE SULLA LINEA DEL PARAMEZZALE
(LEGENDA COMPONENTI STRUTTURA SCAFO)
VISTA DA A
FEMMINELLA DEL TIMONE
DRITTO DI POPPA
FASCIA SOSTEGNO FEMMINELLA DEL TIMONE
CHIAVARDA DI UNIONE
PARAMEZZALE
PRIMA SCASSA SOSTEGNO PONTE
PRIMO TACCO DI POPPA
SECONDA SCASSA
SECONDO TACCO
TERZA SCASSA
QUARTA SCASSA
SCASSA DI ANCORAGGIO ALBERO DI POPPA
TACCO MADIERE
SPESSORE
MADIERI DI POPPA
CONGLOMERATO ARGILLOSO
FASCIAME ESTERNO
FASCIAME INTERNO
MADIERI
PRIMA SCASSA SOSTEGNO PONTE
PRIMO TACCO DI POPPA
SECONDO TACCO
SECONDA SCASSA
FEMMINELLA DEL TIMONE
DRITTO DI POPPA
CHIAVARDA DI UNIONE
TAVOLA FASCIAME INTERNO
PARAMEZZALE
ORIENTAMENTO PRUA = 305°
QUARTA SCASSA
TERZA SCASSA SOSTEGNO PONTE
ORDINATE
SCASSA ANCORAGGIO ALBERO DI POPPA
FASCIAME INTERNO
FASCIAME ESTERNO
ORDINATE DI SINISTRA FASCIA POPPIERA
SCOGLIERA FRANGIFLUTTI
Duilio Uguccioni

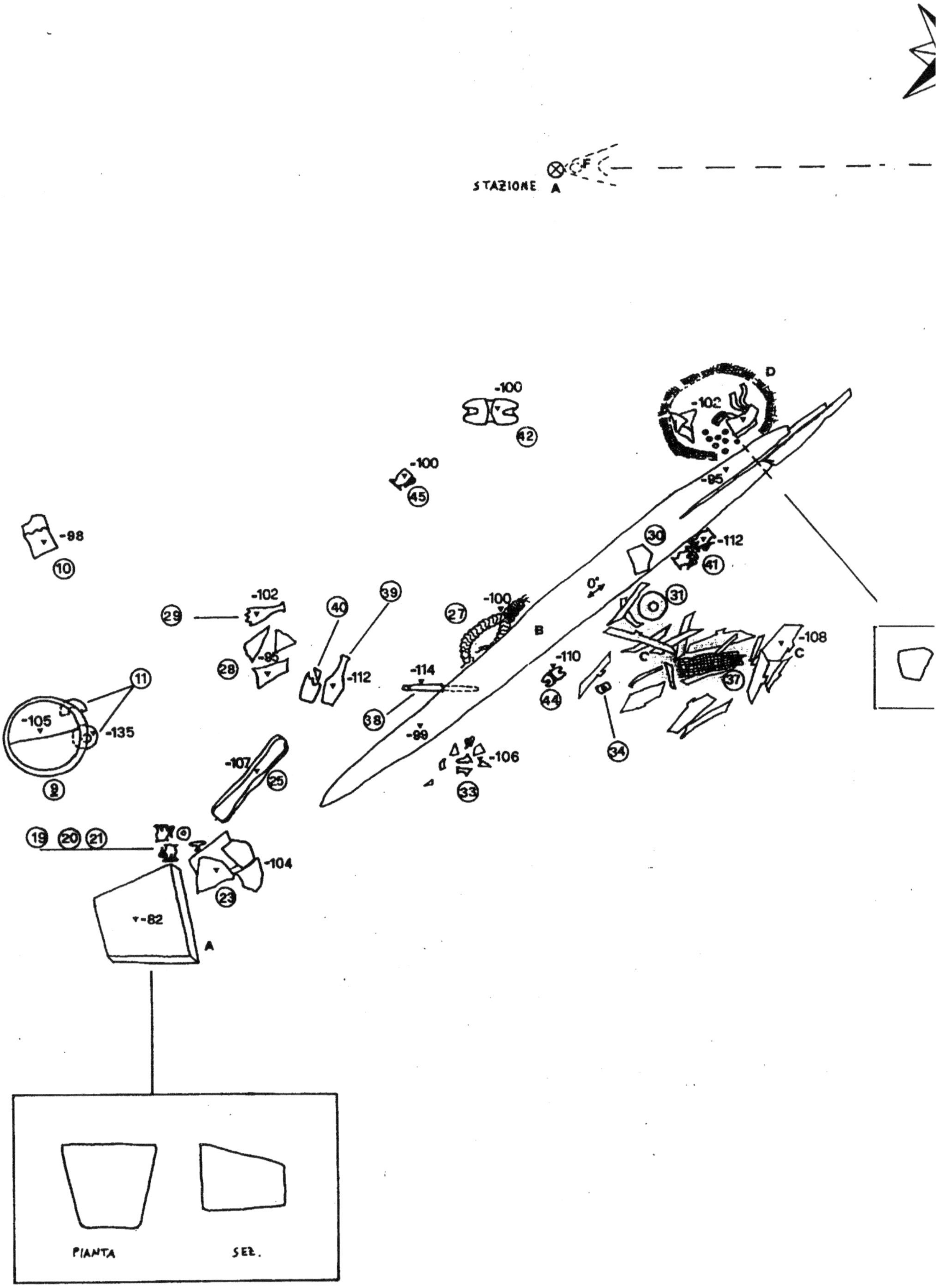

FIGURE 10. A LAYER OF MATERIAL (SHIP'S EQUIPMENT, GOODS AND FURNISHINGS) FALLEN OVERBOARD AFT AND AT

Soprintendenza Archeologica delle Marche
Ancona

Scavo archeologico subacqueo del relitto di fine XVIII-inizi XIX sec. cosiddetto "Galeone"

Pesaro, Spiaggia di Levante

settembre-novembre 1997

scala 1:20

TAV. 2

Legenda

A : parallelepipedo monossile
B : "trave" lignea affusolata alle estremità
C : ramaglie e pezzi di legno con corteccia, tagliati alle estremità
D : presunta cesta di fibre vegetali, con frammenti di pelle sottile e palle di piombo
F : estremità del dritto di poppa; concrezione con femminella del timone
S : scassa dell'albero di poppa
⊗ : stazione per il rilevamento archeologico 1997 (A e B)
↓ : direzione dell'inclinazione di giacitura dell'oggetto (orizzontale ↔)
▾ : punto dell'oggetto in cui è stata battuta la quota (rispetto al punto zero)
- 95 : profondità di giacitura dell'oggetto, nel punto in cui è stata battuta la quota, rispetto al punto zero
(10) : numero dell'oggetto rilevato, corrispondente a quello dell'elenco dei materiali

Stefano Medas

PRESENTLY UNDER EXCAVATION.

FIGURE 9.THE STERNPOST, WITH LARGE IRON PIN TO BOLT THE THREE PARTS TOGETHER, THE HEAD OF THE KEELSON AND THE FLOOR RUDDER STOP.

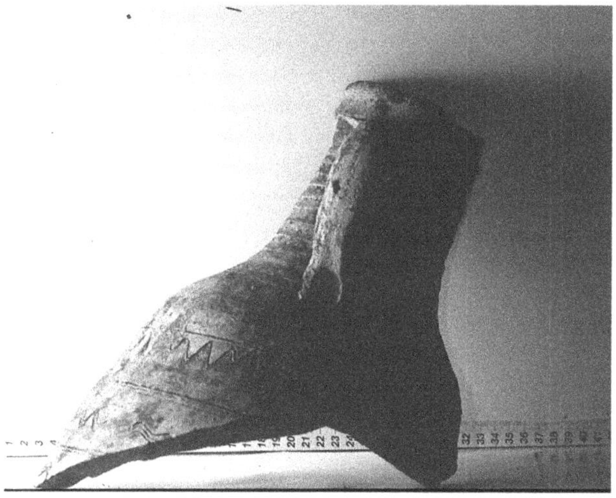

FIGURE 11. UPPER PART OF AN AMPHORA IN TERRACOTTA, PYRIFORM (OBCONIC) AND DECORATED WITH ENGRAVINGS.

Although to date we have no conclusive evidence as to the identity of the wreck, much of what is known about it coincides with what is written in the deeds consulted and reported in part above: the place where it sank; the date; the presence on board of arms (rifles and cannon); the presence on board of metal ingots (in the wreck, of cast iron) for ballast;[16] the presence on board of a mysterious passenger who seemed to have every interest in remaining such; the presence on board of horses (pieces of horseshoes and several bones of animals were found in 1978 and 1991); the presence on board (admittedly, obvious) of a master carpenter, testified by his tools in the wreck and expressly mentioned in documents; the link with Egypt, shown in the former case by the amphorae (Figure 11)[17] and in the latter by the port of destination of the final, fatal voyage: Alexandria in Egypt. Nonetheless, even if this identification should prove to be exact, we still have to explain the presence of numerous English artefacts on board.[18]

FIGURE 12. SMALL GLASS TANKARD WITH HEART-SHAPED FAMILY COAT OF ARMS.

A look into heraldry to identify the heart-shaped coat of arms painted or glazed with lozenges (Figure 12) on the

[16] Profumo, Riccardi, Uguccioni (eds.) (1996),34.

[17] Profumo, Riccardi, Uguccioni (eds.) (1996), 20.

[18] Profumo, Riccardi, Uguccioni (eds.) (1996), 20-30.

numerous clear glass tankards[19] found near the stern proved it to belong to the Fitzwilliams, an English family of medieval origins which died out in the first half of the 19th century. The last member of this family, one Lieutenant William Fitzwilliam Wentworth, was a strange individual who lived an adventurous, and to some extent mysterious, life in the Navy and the Merchant Navy. After being mentioned on board several ships in Europe, North America and North Africa (the Battle of Algiers, 1816) there is no news of him between 1816 and 1819.[20]

To hazard a guess - a wild one but with the exciting flavour of a mystery story - might not our Giuseppe Fabris, a passenger on board the Arduz unwilling to be held in the quarantine station of Ancona as required for shipwreck victims, be Lieutenant Fitzwilliam in disguise?

References

AA.VV. 1994, Il "galeone" di Pesaro, *Archeologia Viva*, 45, 70-74.

Anselmi S. 1991, *Adriatico. Studi di storia, secoli XIV-XX,* Ancona.

Anselmi S. (ed.) 1998, *Pirati e corsari in Adriatico*, Cinisello Balsamo.

De Nicolò M.L. 1989, La difesa del litorale marchigiano (secoli XV - inizi XIX), *Atti e memorie della Deputazione di Storia Patria per le Marche*, 94, 317-340.

De Nicolò M.L. 1999, *La costa difesa. Fortificazioni e disegno del litorale marchigiano in età moderna*, Ancona.

Godden G.A. 1986, *British Pottery and Porcelain Marks*, London, Barrie & Jenkins.

*Il Lazzaretto tra mare e città: dalla conoscenza al restauro verso il riuso della Mole di Luigi Vanvitelli,*1990, Atti del Convegno, Ancona, CLUA

Liburdi E. 1943, Sanbenedettesi schiavi in Barberia (Episodi di pirateria mediterranea del sec. XIX), *Atti e memorie della Deputazione di Storia Patria per le Marche*, ser. VI, vol. 1, 169-186.

Profumo M.C. 1982, Pesaro. Galeone del XVIII secolo, in *Archeologia Subacquea I. Bollettino d'arte*, suppl.4, 172.

Profumo M.C. 1986, Rinvenimenti sottomarini lungo la costa marchigiana, in *Archeologia subacquea* 3, *Bollettino d'arte*, suppl. 37-38, 39-48.

Profumo M.C., Riccardi E., Uguccioni D. (eds.) (1996), *Il relitto di Pesaro detto "il galeone". Rapporto preliminare*, Pesaro.

Profumo M.C. 2000, *Importuosa Italiae litora: Archeologia del mare nelle Marche*, Castelferretti, Sagraf s.r.l.

[19] Profumo, Riccardi, Uguccioni (eds.) (1996), 22, 26.

[20] Many thanks to my friend dott. Giacomo Pignata of Savona for his invaluable information.

www.ingramcontent.com/pod-product-compliance
Lightning Source LLC
LaVergne TN
LVHW071208210926
848482LV00015B/753